"A SUPERB ACCOUNT OF THE THREE-DAY BATTLE TO TAKE TARAWA."

—JOHN LEHMAN
Former Secretary of the Navy
Writing in the *Wall Street Journal*

"Without question, *Utmost Savagery* is the definitive history of this hellish battle."
—*Marine Corps Gazette*

"Harrowingly effective . . . A masterful report on a turning-point encounter in the context of a global conflict."

—*Kirkus Reviews*

"A gripping narrative of one of the bloodiest battles of WWII in the Pacific theater. But this account is more than battle history."
—*Publishers Weekly*

"His narrative is a brilliant example of colorful brevity. . . . Alexander writes with knowledge and experience. He put it all together to come up with a masterful overview. . . . This is one you won't put down."

—*Leatherneck*

D0551808

"A lot of books on frequently-written-about battles unfairly call themselves fresh accounts. Alexander has earned the title. . . . This is the first book to contain complete coverage of Japanese defensive preparations and accounts from the few Japanese troops that survived the fighting. Alexander's book is also a lesson in leadership, showing how frontline command became the difference between victory and defeat."

—*Arizona Republican*

"[An] outstanding account . . . The reader sweats throughout every hour of the battle as if the book were a novel. Alexander surpasses every other existing account of the battle by a considerable margin."

—*Booklist*

"Well written, well organized, thoroughly researched . . . It is highly recommended."
—*Naval Wargaming Review*

"Graphically conveys the violence and carnage of battle and illustrates the critical value of raw physical courage—men pushing forward in the face of almost certain death and taking objectives with no protection but their own initiative."
—*San Antonio Express-News*

"Books about battle smother this militant planet, but few are able to tell it as it was. Colonel Alexander, a Marine, has caught the truth: Marines and Japanese knew only how to win. No failure, no prisoners. I have never read a description of combat as honest and as frightful as this hand-to-hand explosion on Tarawa. Now we know how it was."

—EDDIE ALBERT, actor
Salvage boat officer
Red Beach, Tarawa

"A complex battle richly researched by a professional military historian and a brother Marine of another war . . . recognizes the landmark role of the 'Alligator (Amtrac) Marines' at Tarawa."

—THE HONORABLE J. T. RUTHERFORD
Former congressman, Marine PFC
Red Beach, Tarawa

"[An] excellent chronicle of the strategy, tactics, and operations of both sides is considerably enriched by inclusion of the . . . words of those on both sides who were there. . . . A particularly well written account of the assault on Tarawa, valuable to historians . . . and engaging to general readers."

—*Sea Power*

Tony Lyttle

UTMOST SAVAGERY

The Three Days of Tarawa

Col. Joseph H. Alexander, USMC (Ret.)

Foreword by Brig. Gen. Edwin H. Simmons USMC (Ret.)

IVY BOOKS • NEW YORK

Ivy Books
Published by Ballantine Books
Copyright © 1995 by Joseph H. Alexander

All rights reserved under International and Pan-American Copyright Conventions. Published in the United States by Ballantine Books, a division of Random House, Inc., New York, and distributed in Canada by Random House of Canada Limited, Toronto.

http://www.randomhouse.com

Library of Congress Catalog Card Number: 96-94776

ISBN 0-8041-1559-1

Maps by Mary Craddock Hoffman

This edition published by arrangement with Naval Institute Press.

Manufactured in the United States of America

First Ballantine Books Edition: January 1997

10 9 8 7 6 5 4 3

To Gale,
and to the men of the 2d Marine Division
and the Southern Attack Force
at Tarawa

It was a time of utmost savagery.
I still don't know how they took the place.
—Kerr Eby
Tarawa, November 1943

Contents

Foreword

AMONG THE LONG LIST OF U.S. MARINE CORPS battles, Tarawa has a special resonance. Even to those who know very little of Marine Corps history, it evokes images of a small sandy island in a coral atoll somewhere in the Central Pacific; amphibian tractors grinding their way across a barrier reef; dead Marines floating face down in the surf; an incredible maze of fortifications of concrete and coconut logs; a Japanese enemy absolutely determined to fight to the death; and three days of soul-searing, flesh-rending, unabated violence.

Col. Joseph Hammond Alexander, USMC (Ret.), has caught all of that and more in *Utmost Savagery: The Three Days of Tarawa*.

Fifty years after the battle, Tarawa needed to be reexamined. This is quite probably the most significant book—and there have been a good number of books, some fine, some not so fine—on Tarawa since Robert Sherrod wrote *Tarawa: The Story of a Battle*. Published in 1944 and kept in print ever since, Sherrod's classic gave an immediate and unsurpassed picture of the battle by a journalist-historian who was there.

Colonel Alexander was not there, but he has seen violent combat in a different sort of war, Vietnam, and eleven of his twenty-nine years of active service were spent in amphibian tractor battalions, in amphibian tractors that were direct descendants, improved but not greatly changed, of those tractors that crossed the reef at Tarawa.

Born in Charlotte, North Carolina, Joe Alexander has lived a peripatetic life. He has counted up thirty-eight moves: nineteen growing up (his father worked for AT&T) and nineteen during his Marine Corps service. Joe was commissioned by way of the Naval Reserve Officers Training Corps in 1960. His bachelor's degree from the University of North Carolina was in history; he has since earned a master of arts degree in history from Jacksonville University and a master's in national security studies from Georgetown University.

Joe had two tours in Vietnam. The first began in 1964, when he was the combat cargo officer in the assault transport USS *Lenawee* (APA 195). He took part in the initial landings at Hue, Danang, and Chu Lai. His second tour, in 1969, was spent as a company commander in the 3d Amphibian Tractor Battalion.

In 1980 and 1981 Joe attended the Naval War College, emerging as a distinguished graduate. Later, as a colonel, he served as chief of staff, 3d Marine Division, on Okinawa; director of the Marine Corps Development Center at Quantico; chief of the Strategic Mobility Branch at Headquarters, U.S. Marine Corps; and military secretary to Gen. Paul X. Kelley, 28th commandant of the Marine Corps.

Since his retirement from active service in 1988, Joe has made himself increasingly known as a military historian. Naval Institute Press published his *Sea Soldiers in the Cold War*, coauthored with Lt. Col. Merrill L. Bartlett, USMC (Ret.), in 1994. Joe's articles, which primarily concentrate on the various campaigns in the Pacific in World War II, have appeared in the U.S. Naval Institute *Proceedings*, *Naval History, Marine Corps Gazette, Leatherneck, World War II*, and like journals and magazines. Much in demand as a lecturer, he has served as a researcher, writer, and on-screen historian for six television documentaries on the Pacific War.

Utmost Savagery, superbly written and underlain with meticulous scholarship and research, establishes Colonel Alexander as the preeminent living authority on Tarawa. Significantly, the late Robert Sherrod is one of those who encouraged Joe to write this book. If Bob Sherrod had lived to see the finished product, he undoubtedly would have been well pleased.

—Brig. Gen. Edwin H. Simmons, USMC (Ret.)
Director of Marine Corps History and Museums

Preface

THREE THINGS COMPELLED ME TO PRESENT A fresh look at the amphibious seizure of Tarawa. Foremost of these was the availability of a wealth of new information about the battle, a surprising development in light of the extended coverage the subject has already received. This new evidence needs to be integrated, where appropriate, with the original primary sources.

Second, Tarawa endures as a significant benchmark in the development of doctrine for large-scale amphibious assaults against fortified positions. So much of what we Americans practice today in the name of "operational maneuver from the sea" stems from the critical lessons learned at Tarawa. Since in our passage from the Cold War era into the twenty-first century we are still defining an overarching national security policy, many readers may benefit from new perspectives on the costs and benefits of this distinctive operational art.

The third factor, equally compelling, difficult to quantify, relates to Tarawa's spiritual legacy. Few American battles of this century featured such savage fighting at sustained point-blank range within such a confined arena. These conditions placed unique demands on small-unit leaders and required uncommon courage on the part of individuals on both sides. To find a similar precedent of concentrated violence, we Americans would have to look back to our Civil War battle at "Bloody Angle" at Spotsylvania Court House. Tarawa continues to fascinate students of the battle, therefore, because of this same desperate fighting: two proud, seasoned, well-armed, ably-led, opposing forces locked in mortal combat on a tiny island from which there would be virtually no escape.

The "new evidence" on Tarawa comes from several sources. Most useful, and in some cases most startling, is the information available by translating the five volumes of *Senshi Sosho*, the Japanese war history series, which relate to the campaign in the Gilberts. The material contains accounts of two (of only eight) surviving *rikusentai*, the Japanese Special Naval Landing Forces; other accounts came from officers stationed on Betio and transferred elsewhere just before the American landing. Still other records show the Imperial Japanese Navy's plans for counterattacking in the Gilberts. Weighing these accounts against captured documents, other analyses from the Joint Intelligence Center, Pacific Ocean Area (JICPOA), and recently declassified ULTRA radio intercepts now available in the National Archives permits a welcomed view of the Japanese perspective of the battle.

The occasion of Tarawa's fiftieth anniversary commemoration prompted a number of surviving veterans to come forward with their accounts, many for the first time. These accounts, once validated, have proven invaluable. Col. David M. Shoup's personal papers, which include a cryptic but engrossing journal of his experiences in the Tarawa campaign, provide new insights into the personality of that enigmatic key figure. Additionally, we now benefit from computer-based "harmonic analyses" of Tarawa's tides during the period of the amphibious assault.

Such an abundance of new information affords several new outlooks on the battle. It enabled me, for one thing, to present a more balanced account between the American and Japanese forces, Marine and Navy units, and infantry and combat support outfits. More significantly, the net effect of the new material has given me a greater appreciation of just how precarious the American toeholds along Betio's shores were during those first thirty hours of the battle. The Marines were never more vulnerable than that first night. Why did not the

Japanese launch a counterattack in keeping with their doctrine and tactical plans? The reason may surprise you. The implications of what *might* have happened are sobering.

There is no such thing as a near miss in amphibious warfare. An assault launched from the sea is so complex, so inherently risky, that defeat—should it occur—becomes catastrophic. Most of the Marine officers on that beach were students of the disastrous Gallipoli campaign of World War I; more than one spoke of his fears of "another Gallipoli" that night.

Tarawa was the first major trial by fire of America's new doctrine of amphibious assault against a heavily-fortified beach. The "issue in doubt" reports from the landing force on D-Day were no exaggerations: the assault literally hung in the balance. A successful Japanese counterattack that first night along the four hundred yards of northern shoreline divided by the pier would likely have forced the landing to be aborted. Withdrawal of survivors under fire would have been twice as bloody as the forcible landing—worse than Dieppe. Tarawa would have become a national disaster. The consequences would have created a negative impact on both the Gilberts campaign and the larger Central Pacific drive itself. American confidence in our capability to launch any future assault from the sea against other fortified coastlines—Normandy, Iwo Jima, as examples—would have been crippled.

We can now see that the D-Day tides at Betio were hardly the only uncertainty for the Americans in this pivotal battle. So much was unknown, unproven, at risk.

In this book, then, I want to integrate new material with the original sources, to examine the critical operational, amphibious aspects of the assault, and to convey the human element, the great intangibles that motivated men of both sides to risk everything in such savage fighting in that obscure corner of the earth.

First, some administrative guidelines. I'll use west longitude dates and the "Yoke" time zone to harmonize the narrative with the original American accounts. I'll also use Japanese proper names in the Westernized style, that is, first name followed by surname, counter to Japanese custom.

U.S. Marine Corps units also bear a word of explanation. While the "2d Marine Division" is self-explanatory, the "2d Marines" refers to a regiment of that designation within the division. "Combat Team 2" identifies the 2d Marines as task-organized for an assault by the temporary addition of combat support elements (artillery, engineers, etc.). "1/2" refers to the 1st Battalion, 2d Marines. "LT 1/2" is the same unit, task-organized as a "landing team," with similar, though proportionate, combat support elements.

I use the 1943 phonetic alphabet (see Abbreviations and Code Names) in keeping with the times. Thus, "Able/1/2" refers to "A" Company, 1st Battalion, 2d Marines. Finally, you'll see frequent mention of tracked landing vehicles (LVTs), which are called equally either amphibian tractors or amtracs (actually, Shoup and Sherrod called them "amphtracs" in their initial accounts). The LVT made its tactical debut as an assault amphibian at Tarawa. And here was yet another great gamble . . .

Acknowledgments

MY INTEREST IN THE BETIO ASSAULT BEGAN IN 1948, when Uncle Keg Wheeler, a Marine who served in World War II, gave me Robert Sherrod's *Tarawa* to read. The combination of Sherrod's riveting narrative and my uncle's example of service influenced my later decision to devote nearly three decades as a Marine Corps assault amphibian officer—better described by Sherrod as "a wild-eyed amphtrac boss." Writing the fiftieth anniversary commemorative monograph on Tarawa in 1993 represented a singular honor.

The idea of undertaking a full-length book on the amphibious seizure of Tarawa emerged during the Nimitz Foundation seminar titled "1943 in the Pacific," held in San Antonio in May 1993. Three friends there offered their hard-nosed advice and encouragement: Paul Stillwell, director of history, the U.S. Naval Institute; Brig. Gen. Edwin H. Simmons, USMC (Ret.), director of the History and Museums Division, Headquarters, U.S. Marine Corps; and Helen Mac-Donald, curator of exhibits and programs at the Nimitz Museum.

Richard B. Frank, prizewinning author of *Guadalcanal*, educated me in the intricacies of the 104-volume *Senshi Sosho*, the Japanese war history series, and introduced me to Bunichi Ohtsuka of Austin, Texas, who superbly translated five volumes of that series relating to the Gilberts campaign for reference in this book.

Other professional and personal contributions to the book include Mary Craddock Hoffman's skillful maps and Tarawa veteran Larry E. Klatt's vivid sketches of the weapons, fortifications, and landscape of the battlefield.

Many people kindly shared their research with me, including William D. Bethard, a Tarawa historian in his own right and an expert on the records of D/2/18; Lt. Col. R. Clay Darling, USMC, who conducted a far-ranging examination of Lt. Deane Hawkins; Professor Donald W. Olson of Southwest Texas State University, who finally solved the mystery of the tides at Tarawa for us; Professor Howard Jablon, a biographer of David Shoup, who led me to the Shoup Papers at the Hoover Institution Archives; Col. Allan R. Millett, USMCR, who shared his knowledge of prewar Japanese amphibious warfare developments; the Honorable J. T. Rutherford, former U.S. Congressman from Texas, a Tarawa veteran and unofficial archivist of the 2d Amphibian Tractor Battalion Association; Col. Victor J. Croizat, USMC (Ret.), who has a superb grasp on the development and employment of LVTs in World War II; Col. Theodore L. Gatchel, USMC (Ret.), author of a forthcoming book on how military forces have tried to defend against amphibious assault; and John A. Lorelli, author of *To Foreign Shores*, an excellent rendering of amphibious assaults throughout World War II.

Maj. Jon T. Hoffman, USMCR, author of the definitive Edson biography *Once a Legend*, read most of the original manuscript and provided an invaluable critique. Benis Frank, the Marine Corps' chief historian, was a source of constant advice and guidance throughout the fifteen-month period of my research and writing.

In the process of research I conducted nearly fifty interviews with surviving Marine Corps and Navy veterans (as listed in the Bibliography). Five of those men, in particular, patiently provided the most extensive interviews: Maj. Gen. Michael P. Ryan, USMC (Ret.); Lt. Gen. William K. Jones, USMC (Ret.); Robert Sherrod; former Capt. Wallace E. Nygren, USMC; and former Navy Chief Pharmacist's Mate Robert E. Costello.

The following groups and individuals offered special advice

and assistance: the 2d Marine Division Association, especially President William Graham and past presidents Henry "Hank" Mast, Eddie Owen, and Col. Carroll D. Strider, USA (Ret.); the indomitable Mrs. Harriotte Byrd "Happy" Smith (General Julian's widow) and her assistant Mary Lou Driggers; Henry I. Shaw, Jr.; Col. Edward J. Driscoll, Jr., USMC (Ret.); Col. Leo B. Shinn, USMC (Ret.); Master Sgt. Edward J. Moore, USMC (Ret.); Lt. Col. Peter Lake, USMCR (Ret.); former Sgt. Melvin R. McBride, USMC; former Sgt. Harry Niehoff, USMC; Capt. Harry B. Stark, USN (Ret.); Col. Maxie R. Williams, USMC (Ret.); Eddie Albert; Sgt. Maj. Lewis J. Michelony, USMC (Ret.); Maj. Norman T. Hatch, USMC (Ret.); John Spencer; William J. Morgan, Jr.; Maj. Norman E. Ward, USMC (Ret.); Col. Elwin B. Hart, USMC (Ret.); Comdr. Robert Green, USN (Ret.) of the USS *Zeilin* Association; and all of the Tarawa veterans of the 2d Amphibian Tractor Battalion Association.

I also benefited immensely from personal notes and photographs shared with me by the families of two of the posthumous Medal of Honor recipients: Mr. Tom Bordelon, on behalf of his brother, Staff Sgt. William J. Bordelon, USMC, and Mrs. Alexandra Bonnyman Prejean, youngest daughter of 1st Lt. Alexander Bonnyman, USMC. Lt. Gen. Victor J. Krulak, USMC (Ret.), provided information about his reef test of LVTs in April 1943. Yohji Ono helped me find Akira Shibasaki, son of the resourceful commander of Japanese forces in the Gilberts.

I received invaluable research assistance from the following professionals: U.S. Naval Institute—Col. John G. Miller, USMC (Ret.), Mary Beth Straight, Charles L. Mussi, Ann Hassinger; Naval Institute Press—Dr. Paul W. Wilderson, Mary Lou Kenney, Susan Artigiani, Linda Cullen, and most especially my manuscript editor, Linda W. O'Doughda; Marine Corps Historical Center—the late Regina Helen Strother, Frederick J. Graboske, Danny A. Crawford, Robert V. Aquilina, Ann A. Ferrante, Lena M. Kaljot, Richard A. Long, Evelyn A. Englander, Capt. David A. Dawson, USMC, John T. Dyer, Jr., Amy J. Cantin, George McGillivray; Naval Historical Center—Kathy Lloyd, John Reilly; Marine Corps

Research Center, Quantico—A. Kerry Strong; Hoover Institution Archives—Linda Wheeler; Pacific Air Force Historian's Office—Gary D. Null; Pack Memorial Library, Reference Section, Asheville—Charles Cady, Jr.; National Archives—Dr. Timothy K. Nenninger.

Three gifted professors sequentially inspired my love of history: Dr. Peter F. Walker of North Carolina, Dr. G. Edward Buker of Jacksonville, and Dr. Roger W. Barnett of Georgetown.

Others, closer to the bone, lent a most welcome helping hand: Raymond F. Myers; Col. Richard T. Poore, USMC (Ret.); Stephen W. Woody; E. Gordon James; Lt. Col. James C. Hitz, USMC (Ret.); Mickie Booth; Cathy Booth; my brother and fellow historian, Capt. William T. Alexander, USNR (Ret.), and my son, Kenneth B. "Keg" Alexander, who handled the California research for me.

That's a multitude of mentors, editors, archivists, and contributors. I alone, however, am responsible for the opinions and conclusions herein.

Abbreviations and Code Names

Abbreviations

ADC	Assistant Division Commander
AKA	Amphibious Cargo Ship
Amtrac (or Amphtrac)	Landing Vehicle, Tracked (LVT)
APA	Amphibious Attack Transport Ship
BAR	Browning Automatic Rifle
CP	Command Post
CT	Combat Team
DP	Dual Purpose
IGHQ	Imperial General Headquarters
IJA	Imperial Japanese Army
IJN	Imperial Japanese Navy
IMAC	First Marine Amphibious Corps
JCS	Joint Chiefs of Staff
JPS	Joint Planning Staff
JICPOA	Joint Intelligence Center, Pacific Ocean Area
LCM	Landing Craft, Medium (a tank lighter)
LCVP	Landing Craft, Vehicle and Personnel ("Higgins Boat")
LSD	Landing Ship, Dock
LST	Landing Ship, Tank
LT	Landing Team

LVT	Landing Vehicle, Tracked (Amtrac)
SNCO	Staff Noncommissioned Officer
VAC	Fifth Amphibious Corps
3aBg	Japanese abbreviation for 3d Special Base Defense Force
S7Lg	Japanese abbreviation for Sasebo 7th Special Naval Landing Force

Code Names

Galvanic	Gilberts Operation
Longsuit	Tarawa atoll
Boxcloth	Apamama atoll
Kourbash	Makin atoll
Helen	Betio islet
Cora, Diana, Ella, Sarah	Other islands, Tarawa atoll
Joe, John, Otto, Orson, Steve	Islands, Apamama atoll

U.S. Phonetic Alphabet in 1943

Able	Jig	Sugar
Baker	King	Tare
Charlie	Love	Uncle
Dog	Mike	Victor
Easy	Nan	Whiskey
Fox	Oboe	X-Ray
George	Peter	Yoke
How	Queen	Zebra
Item	Roger	

Prologue: "Issue in Doubt!"

Betio Island, Tarawa Atoll, Gilbert Islands
D-Day, 20 November 1943

COL. DAVID M. SHOUP LEAPED OUT OF HIS DIS-
abled tracked landing vehicle (LVT) into the turbid green
waters of Betio's lagoon—and into unimaginable hell on earth.
It was 1000. In less than an hour the carefully designed
amphibious assault plan of the 2d Marine Division had degen-
erated into chaos. Shoup himself had already been wounded in
the leg, and as he waded painfully toward the long pier, he saw
knots of demoralized troops clinging to the pilings. Shoup was
the junior colonel in the Marine Corps, the brand-new commander of the 2d Marines, the original architect—and now the
executioner—of the assault plan for the Southern Attack Force
at Tarawa. The nearby Marines eyed him expectantly. Thirty-
eight years old, barrel-chested and bullnecked, he represented
their only hope.

Shoup reached the relative safety of the pier and reached for
the TBY handset from his radio operator, turning to survey the
wreckage along the north shore of Betio.[1] Radio communications between Shoup and his commander, Maj. Gen. Julian C.
Smith, had been fitful all morning. The flagship, the USS
Maryland (BB 46), steamed ten miles offshore, seemingly
oblivious. The command circuit seemed overloaded with a
bedlam of urgent messages, a reflection of the collective shock
experienced by the assault commanders. Both Shoup and Col.
Merritt A. "Red Mike" Edson, division chief of staff, had
warned their subordinates not to expect too much from the

preliminary naval bombardment, awesome as it may have appeared in its delivery. Japanese troops had somehow survived that awful pounding and were now resisting the invasion like a nest of angry hornets. The 2d Marine Division was a veteran outfit, prized by the Joint Chiefs of Staff for its amphibious expertise. The division had worked hard to prepare for this mission. Shoup was shaken by their sudden loss of momentum, the abject disarray.

Shoup could at least take comfort in the realization that the gamble to employ their tracked logistical haulers, the LVTs, as assault craft had paid off in spades. The leading elements of the three assault battalion landing teams made it to the beach with acceptable losses.

But the second part of the plan, equally critical, seemed to have failed. The LVTs were meant to retract from the beach and make shuttle runs to and from the reef with reinforcements. The Higgins boats, as half-expected, couldn't float over the coral. The small landing craft, loaded with troops, needed four feet; they got maybe three feet this morning, even with a supposedly rising tide. Shoup saw some LVTs conducting the transfer line operations, but not nearly enough. Many were shot to pieces, their thin skins readily penetrated by the entire array of Japanese weapons. Most Marines in the subsequent assault waves were forced to wade ashore hundreds of yards from the reef. Japanese gunners had a table-top shooting gallery. The huge American assault had bogged down.[2]

Shoup looked back at the lagoon, watching a Navy medium landing craft (LCM-3) bearing a Stuart M-3 light tank approaching the reef east of the long pier at full throttle. A large-caliber enemy gun on the eastern tail of Betio spoke once. Instantly, the large bow ramp of the Mike boat exploded. The tank slid forward and disappeared in deep water; the boat sank by the stern. A hell of a shot. Probably one of those large, twin-mounted 127-mm antiaircraft guns, firing horizontally.[3]

Turning back toward the island, Shoup scanned the shoreline. The beaches were numbered, from right to left, Red One, Red Two, Red Three. Shoup's position at the long pier marked the dividing line between Red Two and Red Three. Red One, farther to the west, reached to "the Bird's Beak" of Betio's northwest corner. Shoup commanded four battalion landing teams that day: three from his own regiment, plus the attached 2d Battalion, 8th Marines (2/8), under Maj. Henry P. "Jim" Crowe. Keeping Maj. Wood B. "Woody" Kyle's 1/2 in reserve, Shoup assigned Crowe's 2/8 to Red Three, Lt. Col. Herbert R. Amey's 2/2 to Red Two, and Maj. John F. Schoettel's 3/2 to Red One.

Shoup worried about Schoettel. An exchange of radio messages as Shoup reached the pier led the colonel to conclude that 3/2 was bad off and its commander demoralized.

0959 (Schoettel to Shoup): "Receiving heavy fire all along beach. Unable to land all. Issue in doubt."
1007 (Schoettel to Shoup): "Boats held up on reef of right flank Red One. Troops receiving heavy fire in water."
1015 (Shoup to Schoettel): "Land Beach Red Two and work west."
1018 (Schoettel to Shoup): "We have nothing left to land."[4]

At least Shoup had radio contact with Schoettel. He could not raise Amey, nor could he see much activity on Red Two. Shoup could see several disabled LVTs just offshore, burning fiercely.

Shoup had observed enough combat to know that things aren't always as bleak as they may seem. To his left, Crowe's 2/8 appeared to be making commendable progress. In the midst of Schoettel's gloomy reports, Crowe told Shoup in a clear radio communication, "Will cross airport to the beach; am past resistance." Good news. Shoup could also see several Sherman medium tanks trundling ashore from the reef on both flanks. They were the first Shermans he'd ever seen, borrowed for this operation from another command. There was hope. Shoup ordered Kyle to land 1/2 on Red Beach Two, then to attack west to relieve the pressure on Schoettel.[5]

At that moment David Shoup knew he represented the epicenter of the Americans' "storm landing" in the Gilberts. Success or failure would radiate outward in concentric circles from the tactical commander. Actually, as in any battle, two epicenters were at work during that hour at Betio. Five hundred yards south of Shoup, well protected by a concrete command bunker, stood his Japanese counterpart, Rear Adm. Keiji Shibasaki, Imperial Japanese Navy (IJN).

Shibasaki commanded the 3d Special Base Defense Force, the *tokubetsu konkyochitai*, which was responsible for defending the Gilberts and outlying Ocean and Nauru Islands. The Japanese commander, boyish looking despite his forty-nine years, had served the emperor since 1915, including combat tours in China as a field leader of the Special Naval Landing Forces.

Admiral Shibasaki had already suffered two unpleasant surprises that morning. First, the U.S. Marines had avoided his heavy defenses along the southern and western shores, where the Japanese themselves had landed. Instead, the invaders entered the lagoon and attacked from the north, the one sector where Japanese defenses were yet incomplete, the place Shibasaki intended to sow last with antiboat mines. Then, thinking himself still protected by the neap tide, he had been astounded to see the strange American landing vehicles—"the little boats on wheels"—cross the reef and waddle directly ashore. He sent two alarming reports to his superior officer, Vice Adm. Masashi Kobayashi, commanding the Fourth Fleet 540 miles away in Kwajalein. Then Shibasaki burned his classified papers.[6]

Now, as Colonel Shoup waded slowly shoreward parallel to the pier, Admiral Shibasaki struggled to feed reinforcements from the southern defenses into position along the northern coast. Communications were awful. Days of preliminary bombardment had knocked out much of his wire system, buried too shallow in the sand. He had to use runners to coordinate with his principal tactical subordinate, Comdr. Takeo Sugai, commanding the 7th Sasebo Special Naval Landing Force. Shibasaki had no idea whether his other forces in Makin, Nauru, and Ocean were also under attack. The sudden American assault had reduced his span of control to a half-dozen subordinates at his side.

Eight hundred yards west of Shibasaki's command post, in the heavily fortified curve of the reentrant soon to be known as "the Pocket," Commander Sugai coordinated the methodical firing of his gun crews. Earlier that morning Sugai had assembled his troops for a ceremonial burning of the unit colors. The rikusentai fully intended to die on Betio.[7]

Petty Officer Matsuo Chuma manned a Type 88 dual-purpose (anti-air/anti-boat) 75-mm gun in a five-sided parapet slightly west of Sugai's command post and just a few yards inland from the seawall. Chuma's platoon commander had positioned the four-gun battery perfectly to interdict landing craft approaching the pier or the reef, and the guns were having a field day against American LVTs and boats at ranges up to a thousand yards. Few weapons on either side would prove as well served on D-Day.[8]

In a Higgins boat offshore, John Schoettel's frustrations mounted as he watched more and more of his Marines fall in the water, or tumble afire out of burning LVTs. He had not exaggerated to Shoup. Landing Team 3/2 truly had "nothing left to land"—just the three boats slowly circling the reef with the battalion headquarters embarked. He had lost contact with Item Company, the first unit to reach Betio's shore, on the far right of Red Beach One.

At 1015, someone from King Company finally came up on the radio to report: "We are fifty yards inland and pinned down—casualties heavy—trying to make contact with Item Company on right—no contact with Easy Company/2/2 on left." Schoettel also feared the worst in the case of Love Company. Maj. Michael P. "Mike" Ryan and his troops had been embarked in Higgins boats. Their wade from the reef had been bloody, and Schoettel sensed they had died to the man trying to slog around the Bird's Beak.[9]

Mike Ryan's men were indeed in jeopardy. Their wade from reef to shore took the better part of an hour, and Japanese gunners in the Pocket shot down a third of their number. But unknown to Schoettel, Ryan and others were now ashore, and so were two of the Sherman tanks, operating with Ryan along Betio's west shore, by now out of sight from the northern reef.

First Lt. William Deane Hawkins, commanding the 2d Marines' elite scout-sniper platoon, had opened the bloody fight for Betio at 0855 by attacking the pierhead. The Marines needed to neutralize the pier immediately, or Japanese machine-gun crews would pour enfilade fire into the long waves of LVTs as they passed the pier on either side. Admiral Shibasaki knew this. As soon as he saw that the Americans meant to attack from the north, he rushed scores of troops from the southside to improvised firing positions along the pilings.

Hawkins's men, reinforced by a squad of combat engineers under Lt. A. Gordon Leslie, engaged these rikusentai—using flamethrowers, grenades, and K-Bar knives at very close range—with a ferocity that would mark the conduct of the ensuing battle. The going was tough, and Hawkins's men could not clear the entire seven-hundred-yard pier. Marines would die throughout the battle from sudden outbursts of fire from that structure.[10]

Now came the time for Woody Kyle's Landing Team 1/2, the regimental reserve, to enter the fray. The entire team—889 men—had debarked into Higgins boats from the USS *Harry Lee* (APA 10) two hours earlier. The first four waves crossed the line of departure in tight formation at ten-minute intervals. Then their boats slammed into the submerged reef. While Shoup tried to round up some LVTs, Kyle adjusted the landing plan in a "floating conference" with his company commanders. There were enough amtracs for two and a half rifle companies, barely half the landing team. Capt. Maxie R. Williams, commanding Baker Company, led his men in the hair-raising series of leaps from boats to LVTs while under fire. This done, the LVTs rumbled over the coral reef once again and headed for Red Beach Two. Fierce Japanese fire from the Pocket drove some vehicles far to the west, out of sight, where they eventually linked up with Major Ryan's "orphans." Only half of Williams's men would make it ashore.[11]

Eleven hundred feet in the air over the landing beaches, Lt. Cdr. Robert A. MacPherson flew his Vought-Sikorsky Type OS2U Kingfisher observation aircraft and watched the drama unfold below. In a day filled with massive communications failures, MacPherson and the other Kingfisher pilots would provide one reliable source of tactical information to Rear Adm. Harry W. Hill and General Smith on board the *Maryland*. Earlier, after MacPherson's plane had been catapulted from the battleship, Hill had queried MacPherson, "Is reef covered with water?" The grim response, "Negative." Now MacPherson circled over the reef, watching the desperate, nearly futile attempts of the Marines and sailors to make the transfer-line operation work. Later he would report: "The water never seemed clear of tiny men, their rifles held over their heads, slowly wading beachward. I wanted to cry."[12]

Far to the west, at the Japanese base in Ponape, Caroline Islands, Col. Manjiro Yamanaka, Imperial Japanese Army (IJA), hurriedly assembled his reinforced regiment near the pier, awaiting the arrival of two light cruisers. Yamanaka's soldiers had just commenced amphibious training when the colonel received an emergency message to prepare for embarkation and redeployment. The fifteen-hundred-man force, known to Japanese strategic planners as "the Ko Detachment," would constitute the ground element of the complicated counterattack plan. Yamanaka's orders: redeploy to Kwajalein in preparation for a counter-landing mission against the American invaders in the Gilberts.[13]

Within the huge lagoon at Kwajalein, radio operators on board the Japanese communications ship *Katori Maru* clutched their headsets tensely, listening for further word from Admiral Shibasaki at Tarawa. The ship had been the only station to receive Shibasaki's initial alarm messages that morning. Now the *Katori Maru* was the center of many questions from senior staff officers; Kwajalein was suddenly crowded. Vice Admiral Kobayashi and his Fourth Fleet staff had flown up from Truk two days prior amid the initial reports of a huge American fleet converging on the Gilberts. Advance elements of Adm. Mineichi Koga's Combined Fleet staff were starting to arrive. Butaritari Island in Makin atoll seemed under heavy attack. But Capt. Takemao Takeguchi, IJN, commanding the 67th Garrison Force at Nauru Island, reported no enemy in sight. Kobayashi began moving his limited surface and air units into the eastern Marshalls like pieces on a checker-board.[14]

Near Tarawa, on the *Maryland*'s flag bridge, Admiral Hill and Gen. Julian Smith likewise tried to piece together information about the situation ashore. Hill's Southern Attack Force may have silenced the Japanese coastal defense guns on Betio convincingly, but both commanders realized that, somehow, the antiboat guns had survived the preliminary bombardment and were slaughtering those Marines trying to get ashore from the reef. Smith had only two battalion landing teams of the 8th Marines in reserve. Maj. Gen. Holland M. "Howlin' Mad" Smith, commanding the V Amphibious Corps, and located ninety-five miles away near Makin (with his counterpart, Rear Adm. Richmond Kelly Turner), retained control over the 6th Marines, one-third of the division's assault troops.

Julian Smith ordered Maj. Robert H. Ruud, commanding LT 3/8, to report to Colonel Shoup and land where directed. He also ordered Maj. Lawrence C. "Larry" Hays to debark LT 1/8 into boats and stand by. Smith was playing his last card. Now he had to reconstitute a reserve force from the odds and ends of his division headquarters staff, "the cooks and bakers and candlestick makers."

Still uncertain of the situation ashore, Julian Smith transmitted a radio report to Holland Smith at 1028: "Successful landings Beaches Red Two and Three. Toehold on Beach Red One. Am committing one landing team from division reserve. Still encountering strong resistance throughout."[15]

The Americans had a great deal at risk. Tarawa was the centerpiece of the Gilberts invasion. Defeat there would scuttle Operation Galvanic, delay indefinitely the forthcoming assault on the Marshalls, and derail—perhaps fatally—the Central Pacific campaign.

As the fighting on Betio raged throughout this critical hour, two obscure events occurred that emitted small rays of hope. In the lagoon off Red Beach Three, the destroyer *Dashiell* (DD 659) finally established radio contact with Sgt. James B. Martin, TBX operator for Shore Fire Control Team #82, attached to Crowe's 2/8. Call fires on designated targets along the eastern flank commenced immediately.[16]

Slightly to the west, next to the pier and wading steadily past the floating bodies of scores of dead Marines, Colonel Shoup approached Red Beach Two. His odyssey was not yet over—he would be wounded again in the final few yards—but the fiercely stubborn assault commander from Battleground, Indiana, was coming in. His first order of business would be to send Lt. Col. Evans F. Carlson back to the flagship. The message from Shoup: "You tell the general and the admiral we're going to stick and fight it out!"[17]

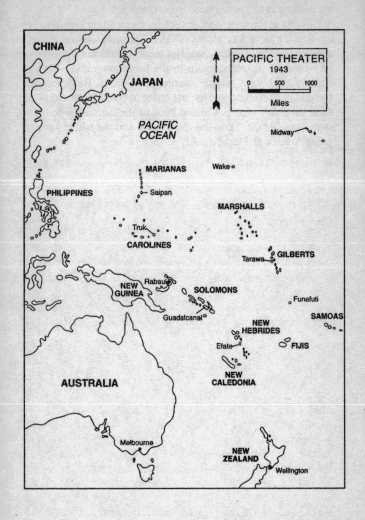

CHAPTER ONE

The Central Pacific Takes Center Stage

Our time has come to attack!
—Adm. Chester W. Nimitz
Pearl Harbor, 11 November 1943

BETIO WAS THE ISLAND; TARAWA WAS THE atoll; Galvanic was the code name for the operation to seize the Gilbert Islands.

The U.S. Central Pacific Force would forcibly capture the Gilberts in a campaign executed in exactly two weeks: one week of long-range bombardment followed by one of incredibly close combat. During seventy-six violent hours within this span occurred the bloody battle of Betio, which took the lives of six thousand human beings in a space of three hundred acres—the identical size occupied by the Pentagon building and its parking lots. Betio (which rhymes with ratio) has proven difficult to pronounce. So, we have come to identify the conflict as the Battle of Tarawa.

For the first thirty hours the amphibious assault of Tarawa hung in precarious balance. The Japanese garrison, fighting almost to the last man, sold their lives dearly, making the U.S. Marines pay for each square yard of sand and coral. "Tarawa was the only landing in the Pacific the Japs could have defeated," observed Maj. Rathvon McC. Tompkins, one of the key participants. Veteran combat correspondent Robert Sherrod agreed. "It was the only battle which I ever thought we were going to lose." Both the United States and Imperial Japan had a great deal at risk. The stakes were enormous.[1]

The extreme violence concentrated in the isolated Gilbert Islands throughout the last ten days of November 1943 was an

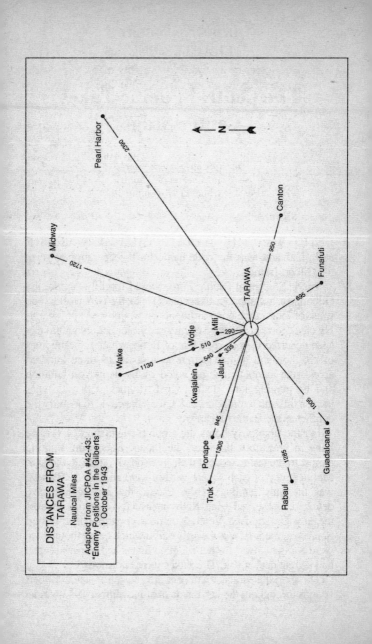

DISTANCES FROM TARAWA
Nautical Miles

Adapted from JICPOA #42-43:
"Enemy Positions in the Gilberts"
1 October 1943

aberration. The Gilberts were historically quiet and peaceful, a backwater corner of the world. With only a few exceptions, even the great swirls of the Pacific War had bypassed the Gilberts to that point.

The Gilberts comprise a vast area of eastern Micronesia in the Central Pacific and consist of sixteen atolls scattered along the equator. Three of these atolls—Tarawa, Makin, and Apamama—held military significance in the 1940s due to their potential use as airfield sites. Because military men tend to ignore existing political geography and lump areas together for convenience, strategic planners of both the United States and Japan included the unaffiliated and distinctly different islands of Nauru and Ocean in "the Gilberts" in World War II.

Military necessity also dictated that the Tarawa atoll would become the focal point of this chapter in the Pacific War. The Japanese built an airfield on Betio Island in that atoll. The crude strip itself was unremarkable, but whoever controlled that facility could influence the sea-lanes to the South Pacific and the approaches to the Marshall Islands to the northwest. The distances to other strategic points were daunting. Tarawa lay 2,400 miles from Pearl Harbor, 1,300 miles from Truk, 1,005 miles from Guadalcanal, and 540 miles from Kwajalein.

Betio is the principal island in the atoll. The island is barely two miles long, less than seven hundred yards wide at its center, flat, hot, and scruffy. It was an unlikely spot to become "the Gibraltar of the Pacific."

Navy Lt. Charles Wilkes was the first American official to visit the Gilberts, leading an exploring expedition through the islands in 1842. He found Tarawa (also known as Knox Island in those years) to be "thickly inhabited" by curious natives. One of Wilkes's ships went aground within the lagoon at Tarawa, a harbinger of events 101 years in the future. "She had taken the coral reef at high water, and the tide was rapidly falling, leaving her on her bilge and rendering her guns of no use."[2]

Great Britain administered the Gilberts as a crown colony throughout the decades before World War II. As war clouds gathered in the Pacific, the British took no defensive protective measures in the islands, despite their relative proximity to the Japanese-mandated territories in the neighboring Marshalls and Carolines. At best, British administrators equipped and positioned a few dozen New Zealand and native coast watchers. The Japanese quickly seized the Gilberts the day following Pearl Harbor, establishing a small outpost on Betio and a larger seaplane base on Butaritari Island, Makin atoll.

The long road back to the Gilberts for the Allies began in early October 1942 with the American occupation of Funafuti in the Ellice Islands, a valuable prize. The place had a decent harbor in which to assemble naval task forces. More important, Funafuti's newly built airfield soon accommodated B-24 Liberator bombers of the Seventh Air Force. Tarawa lay seven hundred miles to the northwest. For the first time Japanese positions in the Gilberts were in range of American land-based aircraft.

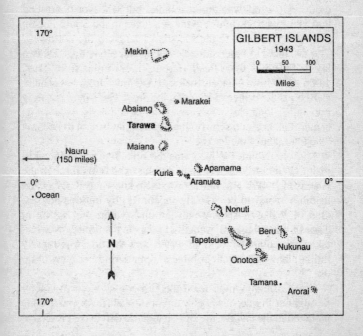

There was yet another dividend. American forces were beginning to master the art of operational security. The Japanese did not discover the existence of a fully functional bomber strip on Funafuti for another six months.[3]

By mid-1943 the Japanese had lost the strategic initiative in the Pacific: the Americans had recaptured the Central Solomons and the Aleutians; ahead lay offensive campaigns against the northern Solomons, New Britain, New Guinea, and Bougainville. The Combined Chiefs of Staff of Great Britain and the United States conferred in 1943 at Casablanca, Washington, and Quebec. Each occasion produced gradually increasing support to more offensive initiatives in the Pacific. The Allied decision to postpone the cross-Channel invasion of France until 1944 was the crucial factor bearing on the discussion. Delaying the massive amphibious assault of *Festung Europa* until 1944 meant that some of the limited amphibious ships and landing craft could be reassigned to the Pacific theater in 1943—for the time being.

America's leading advocate for greater offensive action in the Pacific in 1943 was Adm. Ernest J. King, wearing the dual hats of commander in chief, U.S. Fleet (COMINCH), and chief of naval operations (CNO). King thought the American Joint Chiefs of Staff ought to provide Adm. Chester W. Nimitz, commander in chief, Pacific Fleet (CinCPac), with sufficient ships, aircraft, and expeditionary forces to launch an entirely new campaign across the Central Pacific, using the old "War Plan Orange" route through the Marshalls and Carolines to either Formosa or the Bonins and the Japanese home islands.

King was bright, stubborn, outspoken. His counterparts on the Joint Chiefs and the Combined Chiefs grudgingly authorized a limited offensive in the Central Pacific within a constricted time frame in late 1943/early 1944. King could sense the unspoken imperatives in the nature of these top-level concessions: the limited new offensive must show an early return on investment. Any delays, postponements, or—God forbid—reversals could wreck the Central Pacific campaign for good. The critical shortage of amphibious troops, ships, and landing craft in all theaters of war in 1943 was the great limiting factor.

Both King and Nimitz sensed they would be using borrowed hardware on borrowed time.[4]

Given this provisional mandate from the Joint Chiefs of Staff, Admiral Nimitz and his CinCPac planners looked westward from Pearl Harbor to assess the new naval campaign. Their logical first objective seemed to be the Marshall Islands. Indeed, both the Orange Plan of the 1930s and the initial concept of the joint planning staff ignored the Gilberts and identified the Marshalls as the initial target in the Central Pacific. But in mid-1943 the Americans held scant intelligence information on the Marshalls: little more than submarine periscope photographs and a few refugee reports. The Japanese had eight operational airfields in the islands. They could readily reinforce the Marshalls from the nearby naval bastion at Truk or from airfields farther north and east. Planners knew next to nothing about defensive fortifications, hydrographic conditions, troop strengths.

Experience gained to date in limited amphibious operations in the Solomons and North Africa indicated that this kind of detailed information could be obtained only by sustained and accurate aerial photography. Therein lay the rub regarding the Marshalls. They were simply beyond reach at that point in the war. Rudimentary aerial photography required spending a long time over the target. Funafuti-based B-24 Liberators could reach the Marshalls at the extreme limit of their range, but they could not loiter, nor could land-based fighters protect them. Carrier aircraft did not yet possess this capability.

For all its advances in 1943, American technology had not quite solved the problems of sea-based aerial photography in vast oceanic areas. This was the "lack of a nail, lack of a horseshoe" factor that made CinCPac and the Joint Chiefs of Staff settle for the Gilberts as the first objective, instead of the more strategically valuable Marshalls.[5]

This was a pivotal modification to the fledgling Central Pacific campaign. The Marshalls would remain the strategic prize, but now the Gilberts must be seized first. And the clock was still ticking. Nimitz faced an early-1944 deadline for returning his borrowed amphibious ships and craft to the other theater commanders.

No one ever claimed that the Gilberts—especially Tarawa—would be an easy conquest. The argument was one of relative difficulties. The Marshalls—unknown, further distant, larger, protected by eight airfields—were considered much more of a risk than the closer, more familiar Gilberts, despite the forbidding Japanese citadel at Betio Island. Nimitz and his staff considered the Japanese fleet to be at least as strong as the U.S. Pacific Fleet and acceded the Japanese advantage of operating on interior lines to reinforce the perimeter. The Americans also maintained a healthy respect for Japanese land-based aircraft; they could readily see the ease with which air units could be rotated into the Marshalls. Moreover, Japanese positions in the Marshalls, combined with those in the Gilberts, represented a hydra-headed enemy. A Central Pacific task force risked defeat in detail by spreading itself too thin in going after these mutually supporting objectives.

There were still other risky factors. Any landing in eastern Micronesia would entail the first major American assault against a coral atoll. The tactical and hydrographic implications of this reality would severely test the nation's new amphibious doctrine. In addition, whatever force that could be assembled for this mission would be a hastily cobbled patchwork outfit without corporate identity or operational cohesion. The simpler the initial "shakedown" assignment, the better the chances for an early proof of success.[6]

Other compelling reasons for attacking the Gilberts first materialized. Military airfields represented a zero-sum factor. In American hands, the airstrip on Betio could support reconnaissance and bombing strikes in the Marshalls. While still in Japanese hands, however, the Betio site provided a serious threat to American sea lines of communication between Pearl Harbor and Samoa, Australia, and New Zealand. For example, the CinCPac Air Combat Intelligence Report for the week 25 April–1 May 1943 provided Japanese reconnaissance sectors flown by twin-engine Navy bombers from Tarawa to the south and east. The search fans covered Howland and Baker Islands to the east and the northern Ellice Islands, reaching nearly to Funafuti. Adjoining search patterns by patrol aircraft flown from Nauru, three hundred miles west-southwest of Tarawa, extended this daily coverage to include the Santa Cruz Islands and the northern edge of the Solomons.

The Gilberts thus threatened American merchant shipping and served as a well-armed outpost for the Marshalls. The Japanese airfields in the islands had to be seized or otherwise neutralized. The means for the former were coming to hand; the alternatives were not available.[7]

The vast oceanic expanses of Micronesia also dictated a change in naval tactics. Most of the previous amphibious assaults in the Solomons and New Guinea had been executed against large land masses, which offered penetration by surprise at undefended points. These scenarios featured relatively short distances between launch bases and target objectives, often short enough to enable a shore-to-shore landing without amphibious transports. After Guadalcanal, American commanders in the South and Southwest Pacific theaters conducted every amphibious landing fully within the protective umbrella of land-based air support.

These conditions were generally absent in the Central Pacific. Operation Galvanic, the campaign to seize the Gilberts, would feature unprecedented advances in long-range, fast carrier strike forces; large-scale, self-sustaining amphibious expeditionary units; and mobile logistic squadrons designed to sustain the momentum of those new forces. Admiral Nimitz was forming the elements of a "sea-going *blitzkrieg*" that would hold tremendous significance for the outcome of the Pacific War. But much would ride on the amphibious seizure of Tarawa.

Nimitz chose his chief of staff, Vice Adm. Raymond A. Spruance, to command the newly created Central Pacific Force. Spruance, the victor of Midway, was steady, centered, low-key (aptly described by his biographer, Thomas B. Buell, as "the quiet warrior"). Spruance would need all these attributes to prevail in the stormy days ahead.

Nimitz also took a hand in selecting Spruance's two principal subordinates, Rear Adm. Richmond Kelly Turner and Marine Maj. Gen. Holland M. "Howlin' Mad" Smith. Turner would command the Fifth Amphibious Force; Smith, the V Amphibious Corps (VAC). The similarity of titles is confusing. In a nutshell, Turner would command the amphibious task forces: the transports, landing craft, escorts, and naval gunfire support ships—and the assault troops in the initial phase of the landing. Smith would control all the expeditionary troops: a Marine division, an Army division, and base defense forces. Because Makin atoll was closer to the perceived enemy counterattack threat, Turner opted to position his flagship there and created the Southern Attack Force, commanded by Rear Adm. Harry W. Hill, to tackle Tarawa. Holland Smith assigned the 2d Marine Division, commanded by Maj. Gen. Julian C. Smith, as the Tarawa assault force.

The issue of command relations during the Gilberts campaign is an important key to studying the battle. Operation Galvanic would involve the largest joint-service amphibious operation of the Pacific War to date. The Americans had learned, with some difficulty, that unity of command in amphibious warfare is singularly critical. Under the precepts of amphibious doctrine (then and now), the naval strike force commander retains full responsibility for the assault until the landing force commander is securely established ashore. That's why Turner at Makin and Hill at Tarawa exercised full command authority throughout the critical phases of each battle. At Tarawa, Julian Smith did not assume full command ashore until 1458 on 24 November.[8]

Admiral Spruance, already racing the clock, began assembling the vast resources his Central Pacific Force would need for Galvanic. Meanwhile, the Japanese in the Central Pacific sensed the likelihood of an American initiative in that region and tried to make the most of their overextended situation. These were not the best of times for the Imperial Japanese Navy. Many senior officers still expressed chagrin over their inexplicable defeat at Midway the year before and shock over the recent death of Adm. Isoroku Yamamoto, their premier naval warrior.

As misfortunes mounted, interservice bickering within the Japanese armed forces increased. The Navy had long held the responsibility for providing land troops to garrison the Pacific islands. This worked fine as long as Japan maintained unchallenged air and naval supremacy. The equation changed after Midway, the Solomons, and the Aleutians. The Navy did not have the numbers to provide much more than the token reconnaissance and light security forces among the hundreds of conquered islands. The Imperial Japanese Army, preoccupied with the more strategic commitments in Manchuria, China, and Burma, had no incentive for dissipating resources to bail out the Navy.

An even larger issue was at work. The Army blamed the Navy for failing to resupply their beleaguered garrisons in Guadalcanal and Attu. Dying gloriously in battle was one thing; starving to death was another. Senior officers of both services confronted one another during a conference hosted by the Imperial General Headquarters (IGHQ) in Tokyo in May, shortly after the Attu disaster. As recorded by Army Col. Saburo Hayashi, "the Conference frankly acknowledged that island operations without command of the air and sea face no alternative but self-destruction."[9]

Col. Joichiro Sanada, operations chief, Army general staff, met with his naval counterparts following the conference as the heated debates continued. One of Sanada's staff assistants took the floor and spoke of his service's concern that defense of isolated islands would "repeat the tragedy of Attu." Then, apologizing for any impertinence, he asked: "Does the Imperial Navy after the sea battle of Midway have sufficient power to conduct the serious decisive battle throughout the front defense lines of New Guinea, Gilberts, Marshalls, Wake, and western Aleutians? You may be fighting in too large an arena."[10]

A long silence ensued. Then a naval officer from the combined fleet stood up in response. As Colonel Sanada recorded in his diary, the counterargument took these lines. "Our fleet has to repeat the way the Japanese Fleet fought in the Russo-Japanese War when they waited for the Russian Baltic Fleet to come to the Japan Sea. . . . And [regarding the Marshalls and

Gilberts] the garrison on land has to sustain enemy attacks for one week, and then we will use our counterattacking forces to destroy the enemy in pieces."[11]

Adm. Heihachiro Togo's smashing victory over the Russian fleet in the 1905 Battle of Tsushima was a highlight of Japanese naval history. The famous "Z Plan" of the Pacific War was simply the Imperial Japanese Navy's prolonged endeavor to lure the American fleet into similar favorable conditions for the "climactic decisive sea battle." This imperative dominated naval planning throughout the period 1942 to 1945. By 1943 Japanese naval strategists called the concept *Yogeki sakusen*, literally a "waylaying counterattack." In the view of the Navy Division, IGHQ, if reinforced garrisons on some of their perimeter islands (preferably in the Gilberts or Marshalls) could tie up an American invasion force, the combined fleet could then deploy large numbers of surface combatants and land-based naval aviation units to wreak decisive destruction on the enemy. The tactical mission of the garrison outposts was simply to hang on, endure the full fury of naval and air bombardment, and kill enough Americans to stymie the invasion until the great counterattack could arrive.[12]

The Japanese Army could sense the value of such a strategy, but senior Army officers after Midway had little faith that the fleet would ever find the right preconditions for victory. In fact, the Army throughout the operational planning conferences of mid-1943 favored a drastic constriction of the eastern perimeter in the Pacific. After the war, Lt. Gen. Tokusaburo Akiyama, one of the Army's best defensive planners, mourned the failure of IGHQ to reduce the perimeter to manageable proportions before the American invasions began in the Central Pacific. "The front lines almost everywhere were stretched too tightly, like overblown balloons. We should have retreated to regain reserve elasticity."[13]

The Army and Navy continued to argue about which service should reinforce the increasingly vulnerable island outposts. The Army was on again, off again. When the American submarine *Pollack* (SS 180) sank the transport *Bangkok Maru* carrying Army replacements for the Navy garrison at Tarawa, the chief of the General Staff cried, "Let the Navy defend the Gilberts!" As 1943 progressed, and the American threat to the Central Pacific became more obvious, the Army relented and agreed to send many battalions and plenty of heavy weapons to reinforce the Gilberts and Marshalls. It was then late November. The U.S. Central Pacific Force was converging on the Gilberts in unprecedented strength.[14]

CHAPTER TWO

The Japanese in the Gilberts

*21 January 1943: Bade farewell to mother, sister,
and beloved wife at Sasebo.*
—Petty Officer Chuma,
AA gunner, Sasebo 7th SNLF

THE FIFTEEN HUNDRED MARINES IN THE
assault waves of Colonel Shoup's Combat Team Two knew
they had a fight on their hands as soon as their LVTs
approached Betio's fringing reef. As the dust settled, Japanese
rikusentai began popping up everywhere. Automatic weapons
fire opened up on the advancing Marines from unseen positions along the pier on one flank and from a half-sunken
freighter on the other. Rifle fire crackled from a hundred
narrow openings in the seawall. Vicious antiboat guns lashed
out into the lagoon against the slow-moving Alligators.

From sheltered revetments inland, Japanese gunners rolled
out their Type 92 Howitzers and quickly began dropping 70-
mm high explosive shells among the assault waves, each disciplined crew firing another round every ten seconds. And
through it all sounded the methodical bursts of heavy machine-
gun fire, well sited and relentless—the heart of Admiral
Shibasaki's defense. As the LVTs lumbered closer, Japanese
officers leapt atop the seawall brandishing swords, challenging
the Marines to meet them hand-to-hand. The Americans were
storming directly into a hornet's nest.

This was not the first combat engagement between the U.S.
Marines and the Japanese rikusentai. Rivalry between the two
proud, seagoing forces began on Wake Island in December
1941 and was resumed at Tulagi and Gavutu. Some veterans in
the 2d Marines vividly recalled their bloody fight with the

23

Kure 3d Special Naval Landing Force in the Solomons. But the Tulagi and Gavutu assaults had occurred fifteen months earlier, a lifetime in the context of Pacific combat. Most Marines in the assault waves at Betio couldn't imagine a group of "damned sailors" putting up such a fierce resistance. *"Who are these guys?"*

Colonel Edson, division chief of staff, knew what to expect from the rikusentai. "Imperial Japanese Marines," he told the combat correspondents before D-Day, "[they're] the best Tojo's got." Edson's 1st Raider Battalion had sustained eighty-eight casualties in wrestling Tulagi from the Kure force the previous year.[1]

Whether the rikusentai were indeed "Marines" is a matter of interpretation, but the fact remains that the Imperial Japanese Navy employed designated landing forces for more than a century before World War II. The early version of the Navy's land combat force first appeared in 1830, organized somewhat along the lines of Great Britain's Royal Marines. Each man-of-war carried a complement of *kaiheitai*—sailors trained as infantry. Senior Japanese naval officers used such landing parties to quell domestic disorder in Saga Prefecture in 1874 and to conduct pacification missions in Formosa in 1875.

Gradually, however, naval officials concluded that such specialized forces were an inefficient use of shipboard assets. In 1886 the government enacted "General Rules for Naval Landing Forces," directing the establishment of land combat forces at naval bases in addition to traditional ships' detachments, thereby creating the *kaigun rikusentai*. The new organization drew an allotted proportion of naval recruits and graduates of the Japanese Naval Academy (although most junior officers were reservists). Commanders selected candidates with superior physical fitness and good judgment.[2]

Surprisingly, the world's premier amphibious force in terms of doctrine, tactics, men, and landing craft in the early 1940s was the Imperial Japanese Army. Where the rikusentai were useful in seizing isolated islands or spearheading a larger assault, the army troops were much more effective for amphibious landings in conjunction with sustained land campaigns. This was evident as early as World War I. The rikusentai seized the German-held islands of Saipan, Truk, and the Palaus, while the Army expeditionary forces landed on the Shantung Peninsula to seize Tsingtao.[3]

The rikusentai served for many years in the interwar period in China, but their tactical performance in the Chinese uprising of 1932 left much to be desired. Imperial Navy officials realized their landing forces needed more infantry training to retain their value, a goal they achieved slowly. Rikusentai in the 1937 Shanghai Incident fought with greater effectiveness. At the onset of World War II, naval landing forces served as mobile light infantry units, assaulting Guam, Wake (with stiff losses), the Gilberts, Java, Rabaul, and the Solomons. The Army, meanwhile, continued to conduct the larger landings against Hong Kong, Malaya, and the Philippines. Both services performed well in these early campaigns, contributing in their separate ways toward the overall success of Japanese arms in the first months of the war.

Sometimes the services cooperated smoothly. On 20 February 1942, for example, rikusentai paratroopers, special landing forces from the Kure, Sasebo, and Yokosuka naval stations, and Army troops from the 38th Infantry Division executed a model, joint-service landing to seize Koepang, Timor. In time, the Imperial Army chose to concentrate on inland warfare in China, along the Manchurian border with the Soviet Union or in certain large islands like New Guinea. The rikusentai took principal responsibility for the smaller islands scattered throughout the Pacific.[4]

By mid-1942, the peak of Japan's high tide in the Pacific, the Imperial Navy numbered four hundred thousand men. Fifty thousand of them were rikusentai, deployed throughout hundreds of islands and ships. Special naval landing force units commonly served as reinforced battalions of light infantry that would deploy for a campaign, then return to the home islands for reorganization. Navy officials frequently disbanded a returning rikusentai unit, its ranks depleted by casualties, sickness, or end-of-enlistment contracts, then used the surviving cadre to form a new force.

That neither the Yokosuka 6th nor the Sasebo 7th Special Naval Landing Forces defending Tarawa had any previous combat experience *as a unit* is therefore misleading. The units were new, but many of the troops were veterans, and most of the officers had served in coastal China. Warrant Officer Kiyoshi Ota, who would become the senior surviving Japanese officer in the Gilberts after the battle, had served as a member of the carrier *Hiryu*'s special landing party during the 1940 assault on Hainan Island. Petty Officer Chuma, the antiaircraft gunner on Red Beach One, was a veteran of Batavia, Saigon, Makassar, and the Celebes. Petty Officer First Class Tadao Onuki, a tank commander at Tarawa, had been a truck driver with the Rabaul expeditionary forces. On the other hand, Commander Sugai, who would fight so fiercely in command of the Sasebo 7th at Tarawa, was off the active rolls as recently as 1940, serving as professor and dean at the Kobe Higher Merchant Marine School.[5]

As Japanese strategy in the Pacific grudgingly shifted from offensive to defensive warfare, the configuration of rikusentai forces began to change. In the first year of the war the organization and equipment of the Special Naval Landing Forces reflected their role as mobile striking elements. Thus, the table of organization for the Maizuru 2d Special Naval Landing Force in 1941 described a unit of roughly one thousand sailors, mainly riflemen. The unit's crew-served weapons were modest: four Type 93 13-mm heavy machine guns, four Type 41 75-mm mountain (or "regimental") guns, and four Type 92 70-mm howitzers. Once assigned the primary role of island defense, however, these units sacrificed much of their mobility for heavier firepower, often in the form of pedestal-mounted naval guns and antiaircraft batteries. The Yokosuka 7th Special Naval Landing Force, which defended New Georgia in 1943, numbered eighteen hundred troops and fielded eight 120-mm guns and other heavy weapons.[6]

By late 1943 Special Naval Landing Force units actually resembled the reinforced base defense battalions of the U.S. Marines in terms of mission, troops, and certain weapons such as coast defense and antiaircraft artillery. The Japanese units, typically commanded by a Navy captain or commander, included antiboat and field artillery batteries, plus service and labor troops. The men wore Army-issue field clothing and equipment, distinguished by a small anchor on the front of the steel helmet instead of the Army star.

Rikusentai officers attended Army schools, then trained their troops in infantry tactics. Qualified enlisted men received additional specialist training in tanks or artillery, but the battalions performed much cross-training on their own. Most sailors in these units became proficient in handling a wide range of individual and crew-served weapons. Psychological conditioning accompanied military training: all recruits received instructions in "The Imperial Rescript to Soldiers," issued by Emperor Meiji in 1882, which demanded enduring loyalty and courage. The Shinto influence on recruit training was evident in the "War Song of Umi Yukaba," which included the prophetic words "Across the sea, corpses in the water. . . . I shall die only for the Emperor." Instructors reminded the recruits that, "Dai Nippon had not lost a war since 1598."[7]

In addition to the rikusentai, the Imperial Japanese Navy provided other kinds of land units in the Pacific War. The American's Southern Attack Force would encounter three of these at Tarawa: special base forces (*toku-betsu konkyochitai*), pioneers (*setsueitai*), and naval civil engineering and construction units (*kaigun kenchiku shesetsu butai*). Special base forces manned some of the tanks and all of the big guns at Betio. Many of the pioneers fought conspicuously. The labor forces and their civilian supervisors probably contributed little more than casualty handling and ammunition resupply.

Of all these naval land combat units, the rikusentai had the best training and the most élan. While combat effectiveness varied between units and regions, those men destined to defend Tarawa seemed exceptionally proficient. The rikusentai awaiting the 2d Marine Division along Betio's north shore were ably led, thoroughly trained, admirably proficient with their entire range of weaponry, skilled in camouflage and concealment, and imbued with a fierce fighting spirit. That they failed to recognize the identical combat qualities in the ranks of the amphibious force rumbling toward them was their one great mistake. Otherwise, the "damned sailors" were spoiling for the fight.

THE U.S. CENTRAL PACIFIC FORCE WOULD FACE an all-Navy force defending the Gilberts in Operation Galvanic. Although some small Imperial Japanese Army units were being assigned to the Carolines and Marshalls in late 1943, eastern Micronesia was still the preserve of the Imperial Japanese Navy. Admiral Koga, Yamamoto's replacement, flew the flag of his Combined Fleet headquarters aboard the battleship *Musashi* in the vast harbor of Truk, western Carolines.

The Combined Fleet was still a formidable force. Koga sought to husband his resources, awaiting any opportunity for the long-anticipated climactic fleet engagement. Meanwhile, he had three serious problems. One was logistical: Japan was running low on fuel. American submarines, having finally solved the problem of defective torpedo exploders, began to exert increasing pressure on Koga's fleet tankers. Koga could not afford to sortie his impressive fleet on a whim.

His second grave problem was the shortage of carrier-qualified naval aviators. Japan could not replace overnight the hundreds of pilots downed by the Allies in the Solomons. Regeneration of these precious assets was excruciatingly slow. But Koga knew the Combined Fleet would be helpless without its own carrier air to protect the battleships and cruisers.

Koga's third concern was combat intelligence. Where the Americans, through use of the decrypting machine ULTRA, could intercept radio messages of the Imperial Japanese Navy, Koga had nothing comparable. He sensed new American offensives in the wind. Rabaul was surely threatened, but where would the next blows fall? The Kuriles? Wake Island and Minami Torishima (Marcus Island)? Bougainville? The Marshalls and Gilberts? Koga could task-organize striking forces and dispatch them along interior lines to any threatened point along the perimeter, but he first had to distinguish between feints and the real thing. This worried him intensely.

Vice Admiral Kobayashi commanded the Fourth Fleet under Koga and operated his headquarters from the same lagoon. The comparison between the Combined Fleet and the Fourth Fleet was laughable. The Fourth Fleet was the smallest in the Imperial Navy. Established in 1939 as "The Mandates Fleet," it had attained little glory since seizing Rabaul on 23 January 1942. Kobayashi, however, had regional responsibilities that extended beyond the traditional high-seas focus of a fleet commander. He was also commander of the Inner South Seas Area Unit, and his resources reflected his duties.

By late 1943 Kobayashi's Fourth Fleet consisted of three light cruisers—*Isuzu, Naka, Nagara*—a destroyer division, several merchant ships ("*marus*"), and the 22nd Air Flotilla, a land-based naval aviation unit that included squadrons of twin-engine Betty bombers and four-engine Emily flying boats. Within the Inner South Seas chain of command, Kobayashi held authority over Rear Adm. Monzo Akiyama, commanding the 6th Base Force/Marshalls Area Defense Force at Kwajalein, and (as we will discuss) another flag officer who commanded the 3d Special Base Defense Force/Gilberts Area Defense Force at Tarawa. Finally, to resupply his far-flung garrisons, Kobayashi maintained an unimpressive armada of small craft, including twenty auxiliary-powered, wooden-hulled sailing vessels.[8]

Admiral Kobayashi was fifty-three years old and a veteran of thirty-two years' naval service at the time of the battle of Tarawa. A native of Yamagata Prefecture, he graduated from the Japanese Naval Academy in 1910. In addition to tours of duty at sea and in the Naval Division, IGHQ, Kobayashi spent almost four years in the United States. From 1925 to 1928 he attended Johns Hopkins University in Baltimore, then served as assistant naval attaché in the Japanese Embassy in Washington, D.C. Promoted to captain, he returned to the embassy as naval attaché during 1932–34. Kobayashi commanded two ships, the Hankou Area Special Base Unit (with young Captain Shibasaki as his chief staff officer), and the Shanghai Special Base Unit. As an admiral, he was chief of the Bureau of Hydrography and commander of Osaka Naval Port. Kobayashi assumed command of the Fourth Fleet/Inner South Seas Unit seven months before the Americans invaded the Gilberts.[9]

The convergence of the U.S. Central Pacific Force in the Gilberts in late November 1943 confirmed Admiral Koga's worst fears. The Combined Fleet commander worked frantically to shift surface, submarine, naval air, and combat troop reinforcements to the point of attack. Kobayashi deployed at once to Kwajalein and sought to funnel these reinforcements into action. As we shall see, the element of strategic surprise enabled the Americans to overwhelm their objectives in the Gilberts before the Japanese could mount an effective, coordinated attack.

After the war Rear Adm. Shunsaku Nabeshima, chief of staff to Admiral Kobayashi at the time of Tarawa, told his American interrogators that the Fourth Fleet was simply too small by itself to patrol and defend the vast oceanic areas of the Marshalls and Gilberts. "We had about two days' warning," he said. [10]

The duties of the Fourth Fleet/Inner South Seas Area Unit commander had been a lot easier during the opening months of the Pacific War. In the vernacular of the time, the British had not "militarized" the Gilberts. Japanese naval landing forces organized from the 51st Guard Force, 6th Base Force, seized the undefended islands with ease. They established a patrol seaplane base on Butaritari Island, Makin atoll, and seized the administrative center of the Gilberts at Betio. Japanese occupation forces, few in number, had the mission of reconnaissance and weather reporting. With the Combined Fleet supreme in most corners of the Pacific Ocean, the naval guard force saw little need for defensive measures.

Two events occurred in 1942 that changed the nature and extent of Japanese occupation significantly. Vice Adm. William F. "Bull" Halsey's carrier raid throughout the Gilberts and Marshalls in February caught the meager garrisons unprepared. The Japanese were irate. As Capt. Yoshitake Miwa, chief operations officer for Admiral Yamamoto's Combined Fleet, admitted later: "The attack was Heaven's admonition for our shortcomings. . . . Our staff could only grit their teeth and jump up and down in frustration."[11]

On 17 August 1942, in an attempt to divert Japanese attention from the American landings in Guadalcanal, the transport submarines *Nautilus* (SS 168) and *Argonaut* (SS 475) surfaced off Makin atoll and landed a force of the 2d Marine Raider Battalion. Colonel Carlson led his 220 men ashore in rubber rafts. The confused fighting that ensued on Butaritari Island brought military credit to neither side, but the Americans achieved another psychological victory. The diary of Adm. Matome Ugaki, Yamamoto's chief of staff, reflects the reaction of the Imperial Japanese Navy to Evans Carlson's raid. "Tuesday, 18 August 1942: *Makin*—enemy has withdrawn; eleven of the 70-man garrison remain. . . . The enemy tried to destroy the island, preceding us in attempting a submarine-borne landing. . . . The aim of this operation seemed to be to destroy our eyes at Makin, to defend Ocean and Nauru Islands. . . . They will make surprise attacks on other islands in this way, and we must never relax."[12]

The buildup of Japanese naval forces began the day after Carlson and most of his raiders departed the island. On 19 August a company-size counterlanding force arrived on Butaritari from Jaluit in the Marshalls. This force captured the nine U.S. Marines inadvertently abandoned by Carlson during the hasty evacuation. On 25 August landing forces from the destroyer *Ariake* seized undefended Nauru Island. The following day, the destroyer *Yugure* seized Ocean Island. Reports of these operations pleased Admiral Ugaki, but still he worried: "It is essential to send garrisons there promptly. We should never let Makin's case be repeated."[13]

One week after Carlson's raid, the Yokosuka 6th Special Naval Landing Force sailed from Japan with 1,509 men under the command of Comdr. Keisuke Matsuo. The rikusentai stopped to drop off one rifle company at Makin on 12 September; the balance arrived at Tarawa on the fifteenth. By December the detached company rejoined the battalion from Makin. This force, renamed and reorganized, became the nucleus of the defensive garrison that met the Marines at the

high-water mark on Betio's beach on 20 November the following year.[14]

The immediate task for Matsuo's men, however, was com-
pleting the forcible seizure of the Gilbert Islands. In short
order, Japanese naval landing forces occupied Apamama and
conducted thorough sweeps of the outlying atolls of Beru,
Abaiang, Maiana, Kuria, and Nonuti. By 6 October the Japanese had "sanitized" all sixteen atolls in the Gilberts. Swept up
in this process were five Europeans and seventeen unarmed
New Zealand coast watchers. One member of this group was
the Reverend Alfred D. Sadd, a retired missionary who had
been living on Beru. The Japanese assembled these men on
Betio Island and coerced them to build defensive fortifications.

Unlike the behavior they evidenced during their initial occupation of the Gilberts, the Japanese during this phase were
particularly vicious toward their captives. The garrison commander on Makin ordered the nine Marines on Butaritari
beheaded. Several months later, when one of the prisoners on
Betio cheered during an American air raid, Commander
Matsuo became furious. He immediately ordered all prisoners
brought before him, then drew his sword. Some of the native
Gilbertese witnessed the consequences. Alfred Sadd stepped
forward to offer himself as a sacrifice for the others, but he
simply became the first to die. All twenty-two men were
beheaded. The date was reportedly 25 October 1942.[15]

These events occurred as an unsavory chapter within the
much greater drama unfolding in the Solomons. As the battle
for Guadalcanal raged on and on, the Japanese IGHQ came to
the reluctant conclusion that things in the Pacific were not
going to be as easy as they originally believed. For one thing,
the requirements for reinforcing and resupplying embattled
garrisons on distant islands represented tremendous risks and
high costs. Army Colonel Hayashi blamed the "Naval High
Command" for failing to recognize the outer limits of their
offensive objectives. The Army, in Hayashi's view, "was
obliged to commit large forces to the Guadalcanal operations
and became involved in the local battles of the Japanese naval
landing forces."[16]

Both the Army and Navy Divisions of IGHQ began to look with concern at the undermanned garrisons elsewhere in the Pacific. Late in the Guadalcanal campaign Colonel Sanada, former member of the War Ministry and newly selected chief of operations, Army Division, IGHQ, recommended a major effort to build defenses in "rear strategic areas," meaning the isolated islands in Micronesia.[17]

Sanada's recommendations heightened tensions between the Army and Navy. The latter argued that even with fifty thousand rikusentai, it did not have enough men to protect all Imperial Japan's far-flung island conquests. The Navy demanded Army reinforcements, plus large quantities of Army anti-

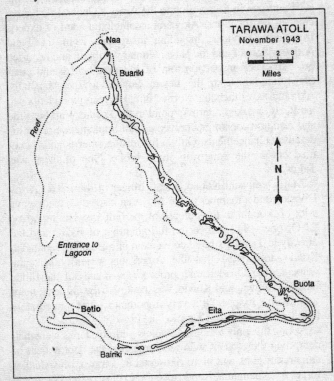

aircraft guns, tanks, field artillery pieces, heavy machine guns, and small arms. The Army rankled under these demands but reluctantly began to make plans for deploying up to sixty-four independent battalions to reinforce the long arc ranging from Burma to the Aleutians. The nature and extent of this commitment would vary widely for more than a year. As graphically demonstrated as late as the battle of Saipan, the services were rarely able to agree on command relationships in these joint ventures.[18]

Both services acknowledged the stark necessity for strengthening the strategic interior—quickly. But when no joint plan or priority allocation of resources appeared, the IGHQ turned in desperation to the Army's General Akiyama, chief of fortifications. Akiyama assembled a team of experts from both services, including instructors from the Field Artillery School and the Naval Gunnery School, and departed on a six-week inspection tour of Japanese-held island positions, ranging from the Lesser Sundas to the Marshalls. Akiyama saw much that worried him. His recommendations to the IGHQ marked a turning point in the Pacific War, but time and resource constraints prevented full implementation of his defense enhancements. Only a few of the outer islands benefited before the American storm broke. One of these was Tarawa.

Maj. Dempachi Kondo, a staff officer of the IGHQ Army Division and a member of the Akiyama inspection team, gave a lot of thought to the defense of the Gilberts. His report on 23 October 1942 gained the full attention of IGHQ and led directly to Tarawa's rapid conversion into a defensive citadel. Kondo anticipated that the Americans would attack the Gilberts after Guadalcanal, probably by means of the Ellice Islands. Tarawa, said Kondo, was the key to the Gilberts; there was no time to lose. "It is very important to start immediately to build the air base on Tarawa," he urged.[19]

Noting that only a thousand sailors with five tanks were then defending the atoll, Kondo recommended the deployment of antiaircraft guns and more rikusentai to Tarawa, plus smaller forces for Apamama. Kondo also found the existing command relationship unsuitable for quick reactions—troops defending the Gilberts were at the tail end of a long chain extending through the Marshalls to the Carolines. "The Navy needs to separate the Gilbert defense force from 6th Base Unit," he stated, adding, "they need to establish a new base defense force for the Gilbert Islands."[20]

The Japanese thus recognized Tarawa's strategic importance as a perimeter outpost as early as thirteen months before the American invasion. To the extent possible, IGHQ accorded Tarawa top priority and supplied the forces on Betio with generous amounts of troops, weapons, fortification materials, engineering expertise, and labor. American expeditionary forces would not encounter a more sophisticated series of defensive positions on any subsequent island until they reached Iwo Jima in 1945. Yard for yard, Betio was the toughest fortified position the Marines would ever face.

A Japanese construction force began building an airstrip on Betio Island less than a month after Major Kondo's report. The airfield took up much of the island's skinny interior, but within three months the runways were good enough for test flights of both fighters and bombers of the 201st Air Force. The construction force continued making improvements through March 1943, when the field became fully operational and aviation units moved on board.[21]

The task of building Betio's formidable defenses fell to the 111th Construction Battalion (sometimes called the 111th Pioneers). Lt. Isao Murakami formed this unit at the Kure Naval Station in late October 1942 for the express purpose of building Tarawa's defenses. The outfit was quite similar in organization and "can-do" spirit to the American naval construction ("Seabee") battalions. Murakami commanded nearly sixteen hundred men at Kure, divided into three main subordinate sections: armament (with ordnance and electrical sections), installations (civil engineering and construction), and transportation (boats and trucks). The force included nearly a thousand unskilled civilian laborers, but all hands received at least rudimentary military training.[22]

The 111th Construction Battalion left Japan on 10 December 1942 aboard two merchant marus. Ten days later they put into Kwajalein to take on two huge 20-cm (8-inch) naval cannons and turrets—eighty different components altogether. The force reached Betio on 26 December and unloaded hastily. Already, American bombers were conducting nuisance raids every few weeks.[23]

The rikusentai of the Yokosuka 6th Special Naval Landing Force, the original garrison on Betio, cheered at the sight of Murakami's big guns being unloaded. Commander Matsuo directed Murakami to address air defense requirements first. The pioneers had two twin-mounted, dual-purpose 127-mm antiaircraft guns ready for test-firing within two weeks. In another week they completed coastal emplacements for four 140-mm guns and the 8-inch guns. Photographs captured from the battlefield show the troops hard at work winching the big guns onto platforms. Other work details built command posts, ammunition magazines, range finders, searchlights, ready rooms, barracks, signal stations, and revetments for each major gun position. That was phase one. Next, the pioneers installed generator systems, built primary and secondary command posts, and constructed communications centers.[24]

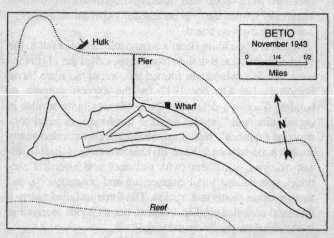

BETIO
November 1943

0   1/4   1/2

Miles

Hulk

Pier

Wharf

N

Reef

In mid-February 1943 an Army Field Fortifications Planning Team arrived on the island from Tokyo. While the team admired the quality of Murakami's work on the gun emplacements and command posts, they made urgent recommendations to improve the tactical defense of the island itself. Where the 111th Construction Battalion had been concentrating on reinforced cement structures, the Army team suggested maximum use of natural material like coral rock and coconut logs. Murakami left Betio's trees alone, but he sent his boat section to the outer islands daily to retrieve five thousand coconut logs. These became the principal component of a seawall built almost completely around Betio's perimeter. The pioneers also used the logs to build many of their firing positions. In addition, the Army team showed Murakami how to build improvised beach obstacles, tank traps, dugouts, observation posts, cisterns, and covered gun positions.[25]

Matsuo and Murakami were further encouraged in late February when the *Shim-Yubari Maru* docked at Betio's long pier to unload the first of four elements of Korean laborers of the Fourth Construction Unit and six thousand cubic meters of construction material, both resources critically needed.[26]

To this point, each of Major Kondo's recommendations had been implemented save one: Commander Matsuo was still subordinate to the 6th Base Force in the Marshalls. This changed on 15 February, when the Navy ordered the establishment of the 3d Special Base Force at Tarawa directly responsible to the Fourth Fleet Commander. Overnight, the Yokosuka 6th Special Naval Landing Force became *tokusetsu konkyochitai*, special base defense forces. A week later Tarawa received the first of its two flag officers. Rear Adm. Saichiro Tomonari arrived on Betio as Commander 3d Special Base Force/Gilberts Defense Unit. Commander Matsuo became his chief staff officer.

Admiral Tomonari was fifty-six years old in 1943. He had graduated from the Naval Academy in 1910 and served initially as a communications officer. As a captain he commanded four different ships, the last the *Kongo*-class battleship

Kirishima. His service as a rear admiral appeared unremarkable: a stint in the personnel department, a few months in command of the 5th Special Base Force in Saipan. But Tarawa was
nothing like Saipan. Here, on the outer edge of the empire,
everything was urgent.

Tomonari's command included forces on Makin, Apamama, Nauru, and Ocean, but the main concentration
remained at Tarawa. In addition to the newly designated 3d
Special Base Force, the 111th Construction Battalion, and the
expanding labor pool in the Tarawa Detachment, 4th Construction Unit, Tomonari also had a tiny "fleet": the subchaser
Takunan Maru, the auxiliary gunboat *Ikuta Maru*, two torpedo
boats, and a number of smaller craft suitable for waterborne
communications between the far-flung atolls of the Gilberts.
Elements of the 952d and 755th Air Groups represented naval
air forces on the island.[27]

The Japanese planned to defend Betio at the water's edge, a
static vice mobile tactical philosophy that would characterize
the defenses of some of the subsequent, larger islands in the
Central Pacific. This was not Tomonari's doing. Commander
Matsuo's "Battle Dispositions" of October 1942 contained the
directive, "Knock out the landing boats with mountain gun fire,
tank guns and infantry guns, then concentrate all fires on the
enemy's landing point and *destroy him at the water's edge*."
Employment of this water's-edge defense by Navy units was
so prevalent in 1943–44 that one can assume a central directive
of this nature emanating from the Navy Division, IGHQ.

Late-arriving Army units in the Marshalls and Marianas did
little to change the philosophy. Indeed, American forces did
not encounter interior-position defenses in depth until Biak,
Peleliu, Iwo Jima, and Okinawa, battles that exacted severe
casualties on the invaders. In any event, Tomonari accepted the
linear-defense philosophy without question. Betio was so
small that he may not have had any choice. Just as likely, he
retained the naval commander's traditional aversion to penetration at any point by an enemy "boarding party." His subsequent guidance to the 3d Special Base Unit in Secret Order #3,
"Combat Policies and Gist of Combat," urged destruction of

the enemy while still on the water. "Keep a strict lookout," he warned, "confirm the enemy's movements, and displaying all the characteristics of our military strength, waylay and annihilate him."[28]

Tomonari had plenty of construction workers; now he needed more fighters. On 1 February 1943, Comdr. Takeo Sugai formed the 7th Sasebo Special Naval Landing Force with 1,559 officers and men at Tateyama Naval Base, near Yokosuka. Sugai's orders changed rapidly. The chief of the Navy General Staff first assigned the new unit to the Southwestern Area Fleet for a reinforcement landing in Santa Isabela Island in the Solomons.

The unit left Yokosuka on 28 February aboard the *Saigon Maru* and the *Bangkok Maru*, arriving in Truk on 8 March. There the mission changed. Admiral Koga, the Combined Fleet commander, concerned with signal intelligence being generated from the Hawaiian Islands, issued operation order #499 assigning the Sasebo unit to the Gilberts. The marus delivered the force to Tarawa on 17 March. Commander Sugai reported to Admiral Tomonari for orders, although he fully expected the unit to be relieved by an Army force in short order.

Commander Sugai, a graduate of the fiftieth class of the Naval Academy, brought a well-rounded force to the Betio garrison. The Sasebo 7th had 27 officers, 38 warrant officers, and 1,542 enlisted men on the rolls to begin its deployment. The force included three rifle companies, a weapons battery, a mobile antiaircraft battery, a special duty unit with tanks and flamethrowers, and the usual communications, medical, supply, transportation, and maintenance units. Lt. Masahi Okada served as Sugai's adjutant; Lt. Hideo Taniura and Lts. (junior grade) Tamakichi Taniguchi and Goichi Minami commanded the rifle companies. Comdr. Gishiro Miura came later to serve as the gunnery officer. The Sasebo 7th brought these weapons to augment the plentiful amounts already on hand at Betio:

- four Type 41 75-mm mountain guns
- two Type 92 70-mm howitzers
- four Type 88 75-mm dual-purpose antiaircraft guns
- two Type 94 37-mm antitank guns

- eight Type 93 13-mm machine guns
- 12 heavy machine guns
- 27 light machine guns
- 36 "heavy grenade throwers" (50-mm "knee mortars")
- eight flamethrowers
- four Type 95 light tanks[29]

Pleased to have such a well-equipped fighting unit on the island, Admiral Tomonari assigned many of the former rikusentai in his base defense force as gunners for the heavier coastal guns and anitaircraft weapons. He also let them keep their original landing force weapons, adding considerably to the numbers of crew-served field pieces available on the island. Tomonari now had fourteen light tanks available, ten of which were manned by *konkyochitai* crews.[30]

Integration of the newcomers seemed to work well, with one exception. Whether from exhaustion or discouragement at no longer being the island commander, Commander Matsuo committed suicide two months after being superseded by Tomonari. The admiral picked Comdr. Watura Ezaka, a former gunnery instructor, to become the new chief staff officer.[31]

Tomonari had his hands full with operational problems. On 24 April 1943, Seventh Air Force B-24 bombers from Funafuti hit Tarawa and Nauru hard. Japanese bombers followed the attackers back to Funafuti, discovering the base for the first time, and bombed some of the parked planes. That a fully operational bomber base existed that near the Gilberts came as a shock to the Japanese.

The island commander reported the loss of eight men killed and sixteen wounded. The one-time communicator bemoaned the loss of his telephone lines, declaring his intention to bury all communications lines in the sand forthwith. In spite of his existing array of antiaircraft weaponry, Tomonari also asked for 25-mm machine cannons, evidently displeased with the 13-mm machine guns.[32]

Petty Officer Chuma, who spent a week at the Yokosuka School of Gunnery before embarking with the Sasebo 7th, was excited about the air raid. His 75-mm gun crew fired seventeen rounds and claimed credit for the one U.S. bomber shot down.[33]

Imperial Headquarters remained distracted during this time with incessant squabbling between the Army and Navy about the division of responsibilities in the Pacific. At length the Army agreed to provide a defensive garrison for Tarawa. Accordingly, the Army Division, IGHQ, directed the formation of an eight-hundred-man provisional battalion named the "South Seas First Garrison" under the command of Lt. Col. Magohei Fujino.

The unit sailed from Japan for Tarawa on 23 April aboard the *Bangkok Maru*. Since the ship would have approached the Gilberts during the night of a full moon, Japanese shipping authorities in Truk decided to play it safe and divert her to Jaluit Island in the Marshalls to await darker seas and thus greater safety from American submarines. Naval messages of this type, although encrypted, were easy marks for ULTRA intercepts. Sensing a rich prize, Navy intelligence staffers in Pearl Harbor contacted the submarine *Pollack*. As the *Bangkok Maru* approached Jaluit, the *Pollack* hit her with a spread of torpedoes. The maru sank in ninety seconds. More than half of the Army troops drowned, including the commanding officer. The survivors straggled ashore at Jaluit, where they spent the remainder of the war. Another submarine sank a second transport carrying the "South Seas Second Garrison" to Marcus Island. The Imperial Army was incensed.[34]

Without detracting from the achievement of the Joint Intelligence Center, Pacific Ocean Area (JICPOA) or the *Pollack*, we should nevertheless view this development in perspective. Fujino's mixed battalion had orders to replace, not reinforce, the Sasebo 7th Special Naval Landing Force. The soldiers may have been veteran fighters, but the fact remains that the unit was a patchwork of four rifle companies from as many disparate regiments, equipped with a few light field guns. Compared to the integrated combined arms force available in the Sasebo 7th, the South Seas Garrison would have brought less than half the fighters and still fewer guns to the table. American fortunes would have been better served if ULTRA and the *Pollack* had combined to sink the same maru two months earlier when it delivered the Sasebo rikusentai to Tarawa.

War is filled with irony. Three hundred men of the South Seas First Garrison survived the war; fewer than six Sasebo men lived through Tarawa.

In May 1943 Admiral Koga assembled the Pacific island garrison commanders for a conference on board his flagship, the *Musashi*. Despite the imposing presence of the super-battleship, the admiral could give them no good news; they would have to fend for themselves. Their only chance would be to immobilize the invasion force for a period of three to seven days. Then, and only then, the Combined Fleet might show up to engage the enemy in a decisive sea battle. The island commanders were sobered at this.

That night, Koga's chief of staff gathered the commanders for an informal dinner. "The situation is very bad for us," he admitted, "but please give our message to the men on the site. I hope you fight to the end." With tears in his eyes, Admiral Kuroshima drank a toast of sake to the doomed garrisons.[35]

Admiral Koga and his Fourth Fleet commander, Vice Admiral Kobayashi, continued to wrestle with the problem of defending the exposed island outposts throughout the summer. Koga issued a "Third Stage Operational Policy," which included counterattack guidelines. An American invasion of the Gilberts would prompt execution of *Hei* Operation #3, the movement of aircraft, submarines, ships, and reinforcements—as available—into the zone. Tarawa's mission remained the same: "The operational basis of each island will be secured by its own force until reinforcements arrive." Koga considered the Gilberts to be in the first line, "the most dangerous area." Both commanders conducted map exercises based on the assumption of an overwhelming American invasion of the Central Pacific. Regarding Tarawa, most staff officers concluded that the garrison had enough big guns and combat troops. What was most needed now was a ferocious fighting spirit, an esprit to justify the exorbitant resources invested in the small island, often at the expense of other threatened positions.[36]

In view of Tarawa's importance and exposed location, Koga and Kobayashi decided to assign a younger, more vigorous leader as commander 3d Base Defense Force. On 20 July, Rear Adm. Keiji Shibasaki reported to Tarawa to replace Admiral Tomonari. We have no record of Tomonari's reaction— whether surprise, disappointment, or relief. He left shortly thereafter for a staff assignment in Tokyo with the Navy Division, IGHQ. Tomonari would live through the war. Shibasaki would die at Tarawa.

Keiji Shibasaki was forty-nine years old, a native of Hyogo Prefecture, the third son of a farmer and fertilizer dealer. He graduated from the Naval Academy in 1915 and spent the next twenty-eight years in active service. He was a skilled navigator and instructor; as a lieutenant commander he had served as naval attaché to a member of the imperial family; and he had commanded a ship and a naval station. During the early years of war with China, Shibasaki spent nineteen months as a rikusentai officer, including a year under Admiral Kobayashi as chief staff officer of the Shanghai Special Landing Force. In May 1943, commanding the Kure Defense Squadron, he was promoted to rear admiral.[37]

From all accounts, Shibasaki performed wonders for the garrison. He was not an engineer—he had all the engineering expertise he would ever need in Lieutenant Murakami and the visiting staff instructors—he was simply a warrior. As much as any energetic commander could in the four months remaining before the invasion, Shibasaki was exceptionally good in improving defensive coordination and lifting troop spirits. He worked the troops hard, dividing the day into construction projects and military training, principally marksmanship and gunnery. According to Japanese Navy archives, the new admiral "immediately began to strengthen morale and carried out enhanced training, and as a result ... the garrison remarkably increased its fighting capability and they were full of confidence."[38]

Certainly, Commander Sugai and Commander Ezaka must have welcomed his fighting spirit. If they were expected to die defending their forlorn outpost, it might as well be under a fierce leader with combat experience. As the summer passed, field training assumed a new intensity; building pillboxes and strong points took on greater urgency.

AFTER THE BATTLE, NATIVE GILBERTESE TOLD the Marines about Admiral Shibasaki's boast that "one million Americans couldn't take Tarawa in a hundred years." Countless journalists have used those words ever since as a lead sentence in battle accounts, saying, in effect, "Aha! We took the island in seventy-six hours!" I personally doubt that Shibasaki intended those words to be his eternal epitaph. More likely, he used the expression to bolster the courage of his troops, a garrison of forty-five hundred men, far from home, sweltering on the equator, fearfully aware that an enormous American fleet was heading their way. As a professional naval officer, he probably knew his chances of prevailing against such a gathering storm were slim. His one hope may have been that the garrison could hold on, endure the inevitable shelling, and inflict such heavy casualties on the attackers that he could, in fact, give Koga his "three to seven days" to deploy the Combined Fleet.

While most Japanese naval officers did not like to admit it, there was the 1941 example of the American defense of Wake Island to consider, wherein the U.S. Marines, sailors, and civilians kept the invading force at bay for two weeks. Shibasaki had bigger guns, more men, and a coral reef. His garrison might hold on.

CHAPTER THREE

Amphibious Warriors

*The memory of Gallipoli, a heroic effort
with a tragic ending, was ever present.*
—Maj. Gen. Julian C. Smith, USMC

BY IRONIC COINCIDENCE, ADMIRAL SHIBASAKI
received orders to take command of the 3d Special Base Force
at Tarawa on 20 July 1943, the same date the U.S. Joint Chiefs
of Staff ordered Admiral Nimitz to prepare to assault the
Gilberts. From the start, Nimitz assigned the 2d Marine Division the mission of seizing the Japanese fortified outpost on
Betio Island, Tarawa atoll. The Joint Chiefs, looking ahead to
the Marshalls campaign, set D-Day in the Gilberts for late
November.

Fully five months before the battle, the Joint Planning Staff
recommended to the Joint Chiefs that the spearhead of the initial American campaign in the Central Pacific must be provided by *"battle tested shock troops with amphibious
training."* Few organizations in the Pacific fit that description
in mid-1943; of these, the Joint Chiefs of Staff selected the 2d
Marine Division.[1]

Admiral Spruance, suddenly a fleet commander with a
critical operational mission and no fleet, began building the
forces needed for the job. Significantly, less than two weeks
after the Joint Chiefs' tasking directive, Spruance flew to New
Zealand to confer with the senior leadership of the 2d Marine
Division.

That division had spent the previous several months recovering from the rigors of Guadalcanal in idyllic New Zealand.
Spruance's "shock troops" were still assigned to the First

Marine Amphibious Corps (IMAC); they were not yet under the operational control of his Central Pacific Force. Until Spruance arrived, the division fully expected its next objective to be Rabaul. Spruance's sudden visit to Wellington the first week of August came as a surprise.

Gen. Julian Smith maintained division headquarters in the Windsor Hotel on Willis Street in downtown Wellington. Since Spruance indicated he wanted to discuss top secret operational matters, Smith convened a handful of his senior assistants in a guarded hotel room to hear the message. The participants included the two chiefs of staff—Capt. Charles J. Moore for Spruance and newly joined Colonel Edson for Smith—as well as Lieutenant Colonel Shoup, division operations officer. Shoup is the only principal known to have kept any kind of record. His cryptic chronology scrupulously avoids the mission assigned, simply mentioning two means of traversing coral reefs: "plastic boats" and "amphtracs."[2]

At this meeting Julian Smith and his staff learned for the first time that the division would be reassigned to the Central Pacific Force for the forthcoming campaign in the Gilberts. They would soon come under the administrative command of Gen. Howlin' Mad Smith of the V Amphibious Corps and the operational control of Admiral Turner of the Fifth Amphibious Force; each command had yet to be established. They also learned that their target would be Tarawa.

Few of the officers had ever heard of Tarawa, but they did know about Makin from Evans Carlson's spectacular and costly raid the previous year. Most realized the unique tactical difficulties presented by fringing coral reefs that characterized the atolls in the Central Pacific. Crossing these barriers under fire would place a premium on accurate tidal predictions, a resource sorely lacking in the Gilberts. Shoup had heard of Navy experiments with shallow-draft plastic landing boats. "Not available," replied Spruance, already knowledgeable of the resources reasonably procurable in the Pacific. Then, according to Shoup's subsequent memoirs, he added, "You'll have to use conventional wooden landing craft."[3]

Latter-day journalists have concluded that Spruance thereby

tried to squelch the use of Marine Corps LVTs, but Spruance was talking about wooden Higgins boats in lieu of the plastic craft; he likely did not even know what an LVT was at that early stage. Smith, Edson, and Shoup knew, of course, and good evidence corroborates that they immediately began to investigate how to convert their logistic support LVTs into assault vehicles for Tarawa. That was a key product of the top secret conference. More importantly, the 2d Marine Division now had a clear mission, the first operational assignment for the entire organization in its brief history.[4]

Gen. Julian Smith took command of the 2d Marine Division on 1 May 1943. The division consisted of three infantry regiments (the 2d, 6th, and 8th Marines), an artillery regiment (the 10th Marines), a composite engineer regiment (the 18th Marines, which included engineers, pioneers, and Navy Seabees), and assorted special and service battalions.

Established in February 1941, the 2d Marine Division underwent piecemeal fragmentation of its major components during its first two years of existence. The Joint Chiefs, increasingly desperate for combat-ready troops, deployed the 6th Marines to Iceland in 1941 and the 8th Marines to Samoa in early 1942. The 2d Marines became attached to the 1st Marine Division and participated in America's first opposed landing in the seizure of Gavutu and Tanambogo on D-Day of the Guadalcanal offensive. Eventually, the 8th, 6th, 10th, and 18th Marines—essentially all elements except the division commander and his staff—joined the fighting on Guadalcanal. The division did not coalesce as an integral whole until the 18th Naval Construction Battalion reached New Zealand from Guadalcanal in mid-April 1943, two weeks before Julian Smith assumed command.

Smith's immediate concern became the physical condition of his troops. The division had suffered 293 killed, 15 missing, and 932 wounded in the Guadalcanal campaign. Worse, fully 95 percent of the surviving troops returned with incapacitating tropical diseases, principally malaria. The disease varied in virulence, but with thirteen thousand confirmed cases of malaria, the division would have to replace half its strength before the next campaign. The cool air and benevolent atmosphere of New Zealand would accelerate the healing, but Smith knew he needed plenty of time to get the veterans back in shape and to absorb new replacements before serious, progressive training could take effect. A consummate military trainer, Smith would find this to be his biggest challenge.[5]

The epic battle of Tarawa would represent the pinnacle of Julian Smith's life and career. He was fifty-eight and had been a Marine Corps officer for thirty-four years at the time of Operation Galvanic. He was born in Elkton, Maryland, and graduated from the University of Delaware. Smith often served abroad or afloat with naval expeditionary forces during America's interminable "small wars" in Panama, Mexico, Haiti, Santo Domingo, Cuba, and Nicaragua. Like many other frustrated Marine officers, Smith spent the duration of World War I in Quantico, hoping in vain for orders to France. Until World War II, however, his combat specialty would remain in the realm of counterguerrilla warfare: he received the Navy Cross for conspicuous gallantry fighting Nicaraguan guerrillas.

Meanwhile, he attended the Naval War College and the Army Command and General Staff School. Similar to shipmates Red Mike Edson and Jim Crowe, Smith was a distinguished marksman and former rifle team coach. At his best as a teacher, he instructed at Quantico and Newport and served as commanding officer of the FMF Training School at New River until the spring of 1943, when Maj. Gen. Commandant Thomas Holcomb ordered him to command the 2d Marine Division. Smith was overjoyed at the assignment. For years he suffered from sprue—a form of pernicious anemia resultant from his extended field duty in the tropics—and he worried that he would never have the chance to contribute materially to the war effort in the Pacific.

Smith's contemporaries respected him highly. Although unassuming and self-effacing, "there was nothing wrong with his fighting heart." Lt. Col. Raymond L. Murray, one of his battalion commanders, described Smith as "a fine old gentleman of high moral fiber; you'd fight for him." Others described him as "soft-spoken but steel-nerved." The frequent presence of the elderly officer in a gray raincoat at division training exercises throughout New Zealand became commonplace. Smith's troops perceived that their commanding general had a genuine love for them. They called him—then and now—"General Julian."

The unpredictable neap tides of Betio came as no surprise to Julian Smith. "I'm an old railbird shooter up on the marshes of the Chesapeake Bay," he said. "You push over the marshes at high tide, and when you have a neap tide, you can't get over the marshes." He was equally realistic about the chances of landing boats that would face the reef on D-Day.[6]

Notwithstanding his decades of service, Smith had never commanded a Fleet Marine Force unit larger than the barebones 5th Marines in 1938. By comparison, the standard Marine Corps division in the early war years was enormous. The Corps had revised the table of organization for a division just as Smith took command. At the full authorized strength of 19,965 officers and men, Marines and Navy, it would be the largest division in the military world.

As Smith tried to get his hands around this sprawling mass, he saw some things that reassured him and many others that did not. The division's greatest asset would be its collective combat experience gleaned in the Solomons. Even with 45 percent new men in the ranks, the organization would hardly be surprised by anything the Japanese might throw at them. This was good. But Smith also saw that two years of fragmentation had created semiautonomous baronies along regimental lines. There was little sense of the division as central authority. Moreover, not all of the regimental and battalion commanders exhibited the vigor and professionalism Smith expected. Some, including several officers with distinguished records in World War I, would have to be replaced before the next campaign.

Smith's own staff looked competent, but they alone in the division lacked combat experience as a functioning entity under fire. And in spite of the high regard bestowed on the division for its amphibious expertise by the Joint Chiefs of Staff, Smith saw wide gaps in the body of knowledge needed to prepare and execute a major amphibious assault. Indeed, only a few units of the 2d Marines had ever landed against opposition, and subsequent losses to combat and malaria had dissipated the ranks of those veterans.

Smith did not hesitate to ask for help in whipping the division into shape for the campaign to come. At his request, the commandant assigned Colonel Edson to be Smith's chief of staff. Edson was already a legend in the Pacific War, receiving his second Navy Cross as commander of the 1st Raider Battalion at Tulagi and the Medal of Honor for stark heroism as commander of a composite force of raiders and paratroopers at "Edson's Ridge" on Guadalcanal. Tough, competent, visionary, thoroughly professional (he single-handedly wrote the USMC "Small Wars Manual" in 1940), and combat savvy, Edson did not suffer fools; he was thus the perfect counterpoint to Julian Smith's easygoing, paternalistic leadership style.

Edson had priceless experience to share with Smith and the senior commanders in the division: he knew the Japanese, especially the rikusentai; he was familiar with the role and limitations of naval gunfire in amphibious assaults; he was a past master of infantry weapons; and he knew men. Although equally enigmatic and ambitious, he gave Julian Smith every ounce of his loyalty throughout the Gilberts campaign.[7]

Veteran combat correspondent Richard W. Johnston survived Tarawa and knew both officers. His appraisal has withstood the test of time. "Edson was in many ways the antithesis of Julian Smith, and in consequence they made a good team. When Smith smiled, his whole face seemed to glow. Edson's smile was accomplished wholly with his mouth, and above it his pale blue eyes gleamed with the impersonal menace of pointed pistol muzzles. Smith was the brilliant planner and inspirational leader; Edson would function as hard-boiled administrator, in bivouac or in battle."[8]

Both Smith and Edson served the 2d Marine Division well, but there emerged a third member of the top leadership—a junior partner, as events proved—whose performance both in planning and executing the assault eclipsed that of all others. Like the division as an entity, David Monroe Shoup commenced Operation Galvanic untested in sustained combat. At the time Admiral Spruance visited Wellington in August 1943, Shoup was a lieutenant colonel, the division operations and training officer. Indeed, he sailed from New Zealand in November in that rank and capacity. By the time he landed on Red Beach Two on Betio, however, Shoup wore the fresh eagles of a colonel and commanded the reinforced 2d Marines. He would be the only living Marine to receive the Medal of Honor for Tarawa.

A possibility for strained relations definitely existed between Shoup and Edson; both men were strong willed and ambitious. But each man possessed an abiding loyalty to Julian Smith and a fierce desire to mold the 2d Marine Division into a formidable fighting force. Shoup respected Edson's combat experience and sense of realism. Edson appreciated Shoup's careful staff workmanship and willingness to challenge the accepted ways of doing business. Both men worked tirelessly, in direct contrast to other senior officers who made no bones about their enjoyment of liberty in New Zealand.

An excerpt from the field notebook David Shoup carried during the battle of Tarawa reveals a few aspects about its inscrutable author. "If you are qualified, fate has a way of getting you to the right place at the right time—tho' sometimes it appears to be a long, long wait." For Shoup, the combination of time and place worked to his benefit on two momentous occasions: at Tarawa in 1943, and as President Dwight D. Eisenhower's deep selection to become the twenty-second commandant of the Marine Corps in 1959.

David Shoup was thirty-eight at the time of Tarawa, and he had been a Marine officer since 1926. He served twice in China, spent a year of temporary duty with the Civilian Conservation Corps during the Great Depression, and briefly toured Japan in early 1936. Various commanders, appreciative of Shoup's keen mind, had assigned him as operations officer on the regimental, brigade, and division levels.

Unlike such colorful contemporaries as Edson and Evans Carlson, Shoup had limited prior experience as a commander and only fleeting exposure to combat. He had served briefly as an observer with the 1st Marine Division in Guadalcanal and the 43d Army Division in Rendova during the summer of 1943, receiving a Purple Heart in the latter action. Based solely on his record to date, Shoup was an unlikely candidate to assume command of eight battalion landing teams in some of the most savage fighting of the war. Obviously, there was more to the man than his early record reflected.

Time correspondent Robert Sherrod noted his first impression of Shoup en route to Betio. "He was an interesting character, this Colonel Shoup. A squat, red-faced man with a bull neck, a hard-boiled, profane shouter of orders, he would carry the biggest burden on Tarawa." Another contemporary described Shoup as "a Marine's Marine," a leader the troops "could go to the well with." First Sgt. Edward G. Doughman, who served with Shoup in China and in the Division Operations section, described him as "the brainiest, nerviest, best soldiering Marine I ever met." It is no coincidence that Shoup was also considered the most formidable poker player in the division, a man with eyes "like two burn holes in a blanket."[9]

Smith, Edson, and Shoup would dominate the battle of Tarawa. Other senior officers, for reasons of fate, chemistry, or different levels of competence, would play lesser roles. Brig. Gen. Leo D. Hermle served as assistant division commander (ADC), a difficult post under any conditions. The ADC must be prepared to take charge at the sudden loss of the division commander, but he is not normally in the division's chain of command. In this case, Julian Smith gave orders directly to his regimental commanders and instructions to his general and special staffs through Edson. Hermle had a small staff with which to form an alternate command post, but he never earned the confidence of his commander that Edson and Shoup enjoyed. This is as much a reflection of the "appendage role" of the ADC as anything else, although Smith on several occasions during the campaign believed Hermle had let him down. Hermle did his best, was courageous under fire (later becoming the first general officer ashore at Iwo Jima), and helped reduce some of the slaughter of the 8th Marines on D+1 at Tarawa, but this was not to be his shining moment.[10]

Six field-grade officers, from as many commands, would contribute significantly to ultimate victory at Betio. Major Crowe, the salty commander of LT 2/8, would lead the sustained battles on Red Beach Three by his fierce personality. Crowe possessed impressive combat skills: jungle-fighting experience in Guadalcanal backed by stateside credentials as distinguished marksman, distinguished pistol shot, national record holder for the Browning Automatic Rifle, and coach of the Marine Corps Rifle Team.

Crowe's executive officer, Maj. William C. Chamberlin, a former college professor and an unlikely counterpoint to Crowe, would equal his commander in combat presence, providing unflagging senior leadership along the edge of the dangerously exposed eastern flank of Betio for three days and nights. Maj. William K. "Willie K." Jones, the competent commander of LT 1/6, would play a pivotal reinforcing role and sustain the brunt of the Japanese counterattack on D+2.

Newly promoted Maj. Mike Ryan, still commanding "Love" Company in LT 3/2, would become the pivotal figure on which the fate of the battle would hinge during the first thirty hours. Lt. Col. Presley M. Rixey, commanding the 1st Battalion, 10th Marines, a pack howitzer outfit assigned to Shoup's Landing Team Two, would add new definition to the concept of close fire support. Maj. Henry C. Drewes, commanding the unique 2d Amphibian Tractor Battalion, would provide the imagination, energy, and driving combat leadership needed to make the initial ship-to-shore assault so relatively successful.

Between them, these six officers would receive four Navy Crosses and two Silver Stars. One would die; another would be grievously wounded. The battle of Tarawa would have been lost without them.

Julian Smith likewise inherited an exceptional general staff. While still untested in combat, each staff section contained men of considerable energy and talent. The primary staff officers—Lt. Col. Cornelius P. Van Ness as D-1 (personnel), Lt. Col. Thomas J. Colley as D-2 (intelligence), Shoup as D-3 (Operations and Training), and Lt. Col. Jessie S. Cook, Jr., as

D-4 (logistics)—served as effectively in their roles as any general staff officers in the Pacific at that time.

The intelligence section was particularly noteworthy: a mixture of veteran regulars and irrepressible reservists who together rendered invaluable service to Julian Smith and indeed to the V Amphibious Corps and CinCPac. Quality ran deep in each staff section. Shoup had a highly competent assistant in Lt. Col. Dixon Goen. So rich was the division in trained staff officers, however, that Smith could afford to transfer Shoup and Goen to the 2d Marines en route to Tarawa and replace them with Lt. Col. James R. Riseley and Maj. Rathvon McC. Tompkins without missing a beat.

And throughout the workup for Tarawa shone the rigorous guiding light of Red Mike Edson, the relentless chief of staff. In a letter to General Holcomb, Julian Smith wrote, "Edson is a tower of strength."[11]

Several other strong personalities in the ranks of the division had emerged from the crucible of Guadalcanal. Former noncommissioned officers Alexander "Sandy" Bonnyman and William Deane Hawkins received combat commissions as first lieutenants. William J. Bordelon's strong leadership and coolness under fire resulted in a meritorious promotion to staff sergeant. Bonnyman's unbridled exuberance as a student pilot caused the Army Air Corps to terminate his flight training in the 1930s. Hawkins had tried earlier to enlist in the Army and the Navy, but both services rejected him because they found his bodily scars from a childhood burn accident "disfiguring." The Navy had earlier rejected Bordelon's application for enlistment. The examining physician found webbing between his toes—good for amphibians, not good according to peacetime standards.

All three of these "rejects" would achieve the nation's highest combat honors at Tarawa. Bonnyman and Bordelon became combat engineers; Hawkins led a scout-sniper platoon. Tarawa would place a special value—and exact a cruel price— on the division's engineers and scout-snipers.[12]

Survivors of the Guadalcanal campaign referred to it as "Operation Shoestring." The Marines had landed there in

August 1942 armed and equipped essentially as their forebears had been in World War I. They wore leggings and shallow "tinpot" helmets and carried M1903 Springfield bolt-action rifles. Initial combat supplies were critically short: some assault troops were issued only a grenade apiece the night before the landing.[13]

The Tarawa assault came fifteen months later and reflected the incremental gearing up of America's manufacturing and distribution systems. The 2d Marine Division troops carried M-1 semiautomatic rifles, M-1 carbines, Browning Automatic Rifles, or 12-gauge shotguns. The division rated nearly twelve hundred machine guns, including both light and heavy .30 caliber and the ageless M2 .50 caliber. Each regiment carried a mix of 60-mm and 81-mm mortars. Other indirect fire support at Tarawa would come from four battalions of field artillery, three equipped with the versatile M1923-E2 75-mm pack howitzers, one with 105-mm howitzers. On paper, the division also rated fifty-four Stuart M3 light tanks, one hundred LVT-1 Alligators, twelve 75-mm self-propelled antitank guns ("half-tracks"), and fifty-four M3-A1 37-mm antitank guns.

Under the division's table of equipment the Marines belatedly received backpack flamethrowers, a highly welcome weapon. There were problems associated with flamethrowers, however. The weapons weighed seventy pounds, seriously impeding the mobility of men scrambling for firing positions in soft sand. Operators had to be carefully trained to lean into the force of the spray; without good footing and a solid brace, a Marine could be bowled over and burn himself to death. More critically, the division rated only twenty-four weapons. This number would leap to 243 (one per rifle squad) by the time of the Saipan invasion—too late for Tarawa.[14]

Another weapons deficiency worried the senior officers. The division rated 243 of the new M-1 antitank rocket launchers, but these "bazookas" arrived in the South Pacific too late for Tarawa. Shoup's dispatch journal indicates that the Supply Service in Nouméa was preparing to ship sixty-six rockets and launchers during the final hectic week before the division's embarkation. Even if they had reached New Zealand in time, however, there would have been no opportunity for familiarization and training with the new weapons. "We say send Wellington—hope someday get them," wrote Shoup. Ironically, the 27th Infantry Division, based in Hawaii and much closer to stateside supply depots, received their bazookas in plenty of time for the Makin landing. This was a lost opportunity for the Marines. Bazookas would have been valuable against Admiral Shibasaki's light tanks and coral bunkers on Betio.[15]

The most critical problem in the E-100 list of "major weapons and transportation" for a Marine division existed in an unseemly reliance on motor transport equipment. This provision burdened the division with 59 ambulances, 441 trailers, 73 miscellaneous tractors (not LVTs), and 1,147 "assorted other vehicles." It was almost as if the Marine Corps, limited to light pack-mule expeditionary missions for so many years, had suddenly decided to equip itself to fight on the plains of central Europe. This abundance of non-tactical vehicles placed an impossible requirement for square footage in the cargo holds of the amphibious ships available for Operation Galvanic. Smith and Edson decreed that some of these vehicles go directly to Hawaii, the division's next stop after Tarawa. This number should have been quadrupled. The division embarked more than 650 vehicles and 200 trailers on board ships of the Southern Attack Force and used barely a fraction of this amount ashore on tiny Betio. Such a heavy logistics tail was unbecoming "an amphibiously trained division."[16]

New field uniforms for Marines appeared in limited quantities in the Pacific prior to Tarawa. The troops quickly downgraded the official name—"Uniform, utility, herringbone twill, camouflage, P1942"—to "cammies." These were made of reversible ("green side out/brown side out") Army twill, a nonporous material that tended to double in weight when wet, another dubious attribute for amphibious forces. Theater logisticians originally limited distribution to the Marine raider battalions or the scout-sniper platoons in infantry regiments. The elite connotation made the utilities more attractive to the balance of the Fleet Marine Force. Many—but certainly not all—

assault troops in the 2d Marine Division wore "green-side" cammies into combat at Tarawa, the troops doubling the number of pockets by cutting slits with their K-Bar knives for access to the reverse side. The elite attraction of the cammies soon faded with the noonday heat of the equatorial sun. More useful uniform accessories appeared simultaneously with the first camouflage helmet cover, a reversible design of the same material that fit over the M-1 steel helmet shell. The covers had six "ears"; troops at Tarawa soon learned to drape the rear two ears as a neck shield.[17]

The scout-sniper platoons in each infantry regiment became the first units in the division to receive the new camouflage utilities. The division created these units in April 1943 based on lessons learned from jungle fighting in Guadalcanal. The handpicked troops received training in advanced marksmanship, scouting and patrolling, map reading, camouflage, and demolitions. The snipers carried Springfield "03" rifles with Lyman telescopic sights.

As events turned out, the scout-sniper platoon of the 2d Marines was bound for glory at Tarawa. This would be attributable to the influence of their newly assigned platoon commander, Lieutenant Hawkins, who had spent months in a New Zealand hospital recovering from malaria and jaundice incurred in Guadalcanal. The Marine Corps had accepted Hawkins, "burns and all," and sent him through the scout-sniper school at Camp Elliott founded by then-Marine Gunner Jim Crowe in 1940. Hawkins was a small man, standing five foot ten and weighing 147 pounds at enlistment, but he seemed increasingly a giant to the high-spirited marksmen and outdoorsmen who comprised the scout-snipers. Hawkins led by example, took care of his troops, and displayed an indomitable spirit. "I'm fine and fit as a fiddle," he wrote his mother as he recovered from his jungle illnesses. To his old friend Ballard McClesky he wrote his personal philosophy after Guadalcanal: "I looked death in the face and found it was pretty liberal. I am confident nothing will ever get me now. I'll live a long life and die of old age."[18]

The scout-snipers provided observation, raiding, and long-

range rifle fire capabilities to infantry regiments. Higher level
scouting and patrolling came from the division scout company,
the forerunner of the modern reconnaissance battalion. At
Tarawa, as dictated by the E-100 table of organization, the
scouts operated as "Dog" Company, 2d Tank Battalion. They
were not tankers, but trained scouts, responsive to the division
commander. The "odd-couple" relationship with the tank battalion resulted from an earlier coexistence by both units at
Camp Elliott and Jacques Farm, California, but the scouts were
also tied to the tankers for maintenance support.

Here again, the Marine Corps was fighting an island-
hopping amphibious war with an organization better suited for
the deserts of North Africa. Thus, the division's table of equipment saddled the scout company with mechanized equipment,
including Marmon-Herrington light tanks (two-man crews,
machine guns only) and armored scout cars. Red Mike Edson
took time during the final training preparations for Tarawa to
write an angry letter to the commanding general of Marine
Corps Schools who had released a training manual for division
scout companies that institutionalized the reliance on vehicular
reconnaissance. Meanwhile, the company swapped their
wheeled scout cars with the New Zealand Army for tracked
Bren gun carriers. This provided a marginal improvement in
tactical mobility at the expense of much greater maintenance
requirements. In disgust, the scouts took a hard look at their
real operational environment and began to focus on surrepti-
tious landing by rubber boats. This small unit became the first
in the division to take the forthcoming amphibious mission
seriously.[19]

The scouts used two different kinds of rubber boats: one carried seven men, the other ten. Propulsion generally came from
paddles because the outboard motors available were not
designed for frequent submerging in salt water during high
seas or plunging surf.

Most Marines were familiar with rubber boats. The Marine
Corps Equipment Board developed the LCPR ("Landing
Craft, Personnel, Rubber") as early as 1938 from a version of
the Navy's standard, inflatable life raft. Carlson's raiders used

LCPRs to strike Makin in 1942. Marine Capt. James L. Jones would lead the Force Reconnaissance Company against Apamama using the same craft. And his older brother, Willie K., would lead LT 1/6 ashore over Betio's Green Beach in rubber boats during a nail-biting gamble that worked to great tactical advantage on the second evening of the battle to come.[20]

Tarawa would represent the zenith of large-scale use of rubber boats in amphibious operations in the Pacific War. Post-battle analysis would reveal that the uncontested, daylight landing of the eight hundred men of Major Jones's LT 1/6 during the height of the fighting succeeded only as a result of desperate protection by Ryan's "orphans" on the beach and immense good fortune. Subsequent reports of serious losses of Army troops during a rubber boat landing in Arawe further discredited the technique. But the 2d Marine Division prepared for Tarawa with rubber boats as a legitimate option to crossing the reef.

Traditionally—at least for the preceding five years—the first battalion of each regiment was known as "The Rubber Boat Battalion," designated to maintain proficiency in this means of the ship-to-shore movement. Fortunately for the 2d Marine Division, Major Jones took this tasking seriously. Landing Team 1/6 was well qualified to land on Betio by those means on D+1. Likewise, the Marines of Major Hays's LT 1/8 fully expected the call to land by rubber boats in their role at Tarawa as division reserve. Jones, however, was the acknowledged master of this skill. The troops called him "Admiral of the Condom Fleet."[21]

Of all the varied components in his huge new command, Julian Smith had the most difficulty comprehending the role and mission of the composite engineer regiment known as the 18th Marines (Engineers). The first battalion, the combat engineers of Maj. August L. Vogt, seemed straightforward enough. While all Marines in the division were arguably riflemen, these troops had technical training of immediate tactical value: demolitions, obstacle breaching, mine clearance, temporary bridging, flamethrowers. Smith already knew he would rely heavily on these Marines to help clear the obstacles and strong points along Betio's fortified perimeter. As he watched them train, Smith was impressed by the quality of the battalion's junior officers and staff noncommissioned officers, men like Bonnyman, Bordelon, and a hardworking lieutenant named Gordon Leslie.

The regiment's second battalion initially confused Julian Smith, new as he was to large-scale amphibious warfare. These Marines were the "pioneers" under Lt. Col. Chester J. Salazar, many of whom were earmarked to serve as shore party troops, that is, working parties responsible for unloading combat cargo on the beach, stashing the supplies in protected dumps, delivering the goods on request to frontline units. But other members of 2/18 were combat engineers, similar to their counterparts in the first battalion. Some of them would serve as machine gunners to provide immediate protection to their teammates as they cleared obstacles for the infantry. Smith admired their esprit.

The third battalion in the 18th Marines were the Seabees, the resourceful, irreverent, irrepressible sailors of the 18th Naval Construction Battalion under Comdr. Lawrence E. Tull. The Seabees were always in demand in the Pacific; this unit was late joining the 2d Marine Division because they were building yet another airfield in the Solomons. Although they suffered a brief identity crisis in joining the division, having to change their designation to 3/18 and convert their naval rates to Marine Corps ranks, they adapted quickly. These were strong, good-humored professionals, mainly former oil-field workers from Texas and Oklahoma.

Because they had so many rated technicians, the unit became known in New Zealand as "The Battalion of Sergeants." Carpenter's Mate First Class Larry E. Klatt, for example, simply exchanged his rank insignia for that of a staff sergeant. Klatt had worked as an apprentice in a Denver architectural firm before the war and had become a gifted draftsman. His talents would pay valuable dividends immediately after the battle when the commander in chief, Pacific, demanded immediate scale drawings of the Japanese fortifications. Overall, the Seabees' job at Tarawa would be to repair and upgrade the airstrip on Betio. Julian Smith knew it would be done rapidly and well.[22]

Smith was also pleased with his artillery regiment, the 10th Marines, commanded by newly promoted Brig. Gen. Thomas E. Bourke. Marine Corps artillery support for amphibious operations in 1943 was generally light, the premium being placed on tactical mobility. That was the reason three of the four battalions were armed with 75-mm pack howitzers and why 155-mm howitzers were left to the less mobile defense battalions, external to the division. Theoretically, the limited firepower available in light howitzers would be offset by naval gunfire and close air support, although Edson, a former aviator, worried about the sufficiency of the latter, given the lack of airground training opportunities.

No Marine Corps air support would be available to support the division at Tarawa. This disappointed the Guadalcanal veterans who had benefited from the personal service provided by pilots (of all services) of the Cactus Air Force flying from Henderson Field. The vast distances of the Central Pacific worked against a repeat of this kind of intraservice support. The nearest Marine Corps squadrons to Tarawa were based in Samoa and the Ellice Islands, single-engine fighters and dive-bombers lacking the "legs" to reach the Gilberts. Holland Smith had earlier requested the use of escort carriers to bring Marine aviation units directly to the operating area. That was still a luxury as far as the Navy was concerned.

Air support of Galvanic would, therefore, be in the hands of the Army Air Forces (long-range bombing and photo-reconnaissance) and Navy (direct support). Admiral Spruance would deploy nearly nine hundred carrier aircraft to the Gilberts. Direct support for the Marines of the Southern Attack Force would come from five escort carriers of Rear Adm. Van H. Ragsdale's Task Group 53.6. The Navy fliers had plenty of guts and enthusiasm but not a great deal of experience in flying close air support of ground operations on a tiny island.[23]

Julian Smith met with Lt. Col. Alexander B. Swenceski, commanding the 2d Tank Battalion. The tankers were full of fight but frustrated. Their Stuart light tanks were fragile, relatively thin skinned, and, with 37-mm cannons, definitely under gunned. The U.S. Army had already fielded the new Sherman M4 medium tanks; some were earmarked for the Marine Corps. Swenceski understandably wanted the transition to begin before the next battle, but the thirty-four-ton Shermans required special handling capabilities for amphibious assaults: not only the new medium landing craft (LCM-3) but also an entirely new ship.

Few amphibious transports or cargo ships could safely convey a thirty-four-ton load by swinging boom from a cargo hold into the pitching confines of a landing craft alongside. Nor could the big tanks safely negotiate a ramp-to-ramp transfer from a tank landing ship (LST) to an LCM in the open seas. The answer appeared to lie in the revolutionary new dock landing ships (LSDs), which could transport LCMs preloaded with Shermans in a floodable stern well directly to the objective area, but the very first ship of this type had only been commissioned that August. Hoping that the USS *Ashland* (LSD 1) could indeed arrive in time for Galvanic, Julian Smith wrote the commandant asking for medium tanks for the 2d Marine Division. Meanwhile, Swenceski's tankers provided the division with fresh venison by hunting wild deer in the New Zealand mountains.[24]

When Smith commanded the 5th Marines five years earlier, there had been no such thing in the Fleet Marine Force as an amphibian tractor battalion, or even a militarized LVT. In view of the sudden press to consider his LVTs as a possible means of beating Betio's fringing reef, the new commanding general spent considerable time with the 2d Amphibian Tractor Battalion. Here was another outfit undergoing an identity crisis, in this case the metamorphosis from "seagoing motor transport drivers" to new leaders of the tactical assault.

The Marines originally used LVTs as logistics vehicles; the light armor and token armament of the LVT-1 Alligators proved suitable for such a role. Being true amphibians, the vehicles provided the opportunity for seamless delivery of supplies from ship direct to inland dumps. Reflecting the original design of their civilian inventor, Donald Roebling of Clearwater, Florida, the military versions of the "Swamp Gator" could swim, surf, traverse beach obstacles, and maneuver through marginal terrain beyond the beachhead. But these primitive early amphibians, the LVT-1 Alligators, were prone to throw a track in soft mud or to lose the main engine when salt water splashed over electrical solenoids or into exhaust ports. In addition, the vehicle's bilge pumps ran only when the engine operated. A dead engine in the open seas or surf zone often resulted in a sunken LVT.

Moreover, elements of the battalion served in Guadalcanal throughout the campaign and their vehicles showed it. According to Major Drewes, the battalion commander, the division should not count on using more than seventy-five of its one hundred Alligators for the Tarawa assault.

Smith, Edson, and Shoup conferred with Drewes at length immediately after Spruance left New Zealand. Could his remaining operational Alligators, they asked, transport the assault elements of the division over the reef against Japanese fire? Drewes's answer was the mix of optimism tempered by realism that the three senior officers had come to appreciate. Yes, he said, it could be done, but only with some superhuman efforts on the part of all hands, including the general. First, the battalion needed to modify the best seventy-five of its beat-up vehicles to minimize the possibilities of throwing a track or losing the engine while waterborne.

Then, somewhere, somehow, they had to locate a supply of armor plate and get some good-hearted local factory to install sheets along the exposed cabs. Drewes also said they would need many more machine guns, up to four per vehicle, including a pair of forward-firing Browning M2 .50-caliber guns. Next, the battalion would need to run seagoing and surfing tests to see if the added weight of armor and machine guns adversely affected the vehicles' metacentric height, possibly making them dangerously top-heavy, subject to capsizing. These tests would be critical, Drewes said, and New Zealand did not offer the combination of reef and surf conditions needed for validation.

Finally, even if all this worked out, the division would still not have the tactical lift to land all assault elements. Seventy-five LVTs would simply not do the job. Drewes suggested that the commanding general make a special appeal to obtain new LVT-2 Water Buffaloes. At least a hundred of these new craft were said to be sitting on the piers of San Diego, awaiting transportation to the Pacific.

Julian Smith did not flinch. Converting LVTs from a logistical to a tactical role made imminent sense. It was the only way he could be assured of traversing the reef at any tide. He directed Edson and Shoup to give Drewes everything he needed: machine guns, mechanics, contacts with the American auto plants around Wellington, an available island somewhere in the theater for proof testing, shipping to and from the test site. Smith would go after the LVT-2s.[25]

Technically, Holland Smith was not yet Julian Smith's superior officer. The V Amphibious Corps would not assume administrative responsibility for the 2d Marine Division until 15 September 1943. But Julian Smith chose to go to the one man who could truly rattle cages on the division's behalf. The subsequent confrontation between Howlin' Mad Smith and "Terrible" Turner was one for the ages. Some historians have concluded that Admiral Turner did not want additional LVTs for the Marines because he was confident his wooden Higgins boats could cross the reef with ease. But both his biographer, George C. Dyer, who served with Turner, and his flag secretary, Harry B. Stark, provide more realistic accounts.

Stark recalls that Turner was as apprehensive about the tides at Tarawa as anyone on the operation. Dyer reported that Turner's principal concern was purely the war at sea. The new LVTs could reach the amphibious objective area only aboard slow-moving LSTs, which would require additional escorts and would risk being detected by Japanese maritime patrol aircraft. Or perhaps Turner simply enjoyed watching Holland Smith's face turn purple with rage. At the height of the shouting match, Smith stated his own bottom line: "No LVTs, no operation." Turner acquiesced. But someone else, probably Spruance, divided the LVT-2s, fifty for the 2d Marine Division at Tarawa, fifty for the 27th Infantry Division attacking Makin. This in turn rankled Shoup, who already knew the Japanese at Makin numbered less than five percent of those defending Tarawa, but Julian Smith had the coveted LVT-2s to offer Henry Drewes—if the LST convoy could reach Tarawa in time.[26]

Having overcome this particular operational hurdle, Julian Smith returned to his immediate challenge of getting the sprawling division prepared for Tarawa. He faced significant problems in manpower, supply, planning, and—initially— morale. He opted to focus on training.

Spruance's warning order in the Windsor Hotel occurred during the first week of August. Julian Smith knew then that he had less than three months before embarkation to prepare the division for a major amphibious assault against a strongly fortified coral atoll. Amphibious training typically involves embarkation aboard dedicated ships, underway drills, debarkation into LVTs or Higgins boats, and hitting the correct beach at the right time. Astonishingly, the division was unable to conduct valid amphibious training on even a regimental scale until mid-October, two weeks before sailing for Tarawa.

Moreover, while the division staff conducted several command post exercises, Julian Smith was never able to conduct a division-level practice landing until the unit arrived in Efate for rehearsals en route to Tarawa. And even at Efate the division lacked many key players: their designated close air support carriers, the medium tanks, the LVT-2s. Nor was there any way at Efate to coordinate and evaluate supporting arms: the gunfire ships fired on a different beach from the landing site, the planes were gone, the artillery never got ashore.

To be fair, the division had conducted legitimate amphibious training on New Zealand's west coast in June on both a battalion and a regimental level. That was in the days before Spruance's alarming visit and the arrival of Red Mike Edson. The training was ragged. Nine men drowned when heavy surf swamped a stranded landing craft at dusk. Worse, Tokyo Rose crowed about the accident over the radio. In September, an unexpected sandbar off South Island claimed several vehicles

and caused personal injuries during unhappy training between
the 18th Marines and the USS *Ormsby* (APA 49). Again,
Tokyo Rose knew the facts early.[27]

Actually, the most satisfactory amphibious training conducted in New Zealand during the final workup for Tarawa
involved the use of LCPRs, the rubber boats. The distinction
of being the first unit in the division to get wet after Spruance's
visit went to the scout company. The first battalions of the 2d,
6th, and 8th Marines did the same in September, working with
the USS *Feland* (APA 11). The division scouts also conducted
the last amphibious training in New Zealand, a night landing
by rubber boats in Hawkes Bay, again from the *Feland*. The
ship had an uncommonly low freeboard, ideal for launching
these small craft. She would carry Willie K. Jones's LT 1/6 to
Tarawa, loading the troops first into Higgins boats and towing
the rubber boats to just seaward of the reef. The USS *Doyen*
(APA 1) would provide the same service for the scouts at
Tarawa atoll.

Amphibious training is by nature intended for larger units,
starting at the battalion level and working progressively
through more complex training of regiments and divisions. All
of this required a generous number of amphibious ships,
which, as we have seen, were in high demand worldwide in the
early fall of 1943. Rounding up uncommitted ships for non-
combat practice landings in New Zealand was a tough propo-
sition. The nearby 3d Marine Division had equal demands
while preparing for its assault landings on Bougainville, scheduled ahead of Tarawa.

Nimitz, Spruance, and Halsey did what they could. In rough
terms, every man in the 2d Marine Division—even the
Seabees—likely had opportunity for one quick embarkation,
debarkation, and landing. Some amphibious ships simply
could not get to New Zealand in time. The *Doyen*, *Sheridan*
(APA 51), and *LaSalle* (AP 102) did not reach Wellington
until the week of embarkation for Galvanic. The *Ashland*, the
brand-new LSD, had to bypass New Zealand altogether and
join the task force at Efate. And the three LSTs bearing LVT-
2s from San Diego via Samoa did not join the Southern Attack

Force until the early morning hours of D-Day in the transport area off Betio Island.[28]

The essence of amphibious warfare is an assault launched from the sea against a hostile shore, an operational scenario typified by the mandate to build combat power immediately from ground zero to full striking strength to attain landing force objectives and avoid defeat in detail. The Joint Chiefs might have characterized the 2d Marine Division as "amphibiously trained," but that was a stretch. As we have seen, two of the three infantry regiments landed administratively—that is, without opposition—at Guadalcanal. Of the field-grade officers of the 2d Marines who could be counted as veterans of Gavutu-Tanambogo, only Major Ryan, Maj. Stoddard G. Cortelyou, and a handful of others were still on the rolls. Add to this, by providence, Red Mike Edson, veteran of the assault landing on Tulagi and the Tasimboko Raid.

Amphibious expertise involves more than simply hitting the right beach on time in the prescribed tactical formation. Amphibious assaults are as much logistical as they are tactical in nature; indeed, there is a closer match of these two warfighting components than in most other military operations. In many cases, whether an assault from the sea succeeds or fails will depend on how carefully the ships are loaded to support the scheme of maneuver ashore. Amphibious expertise requires other arcane skills: parallel and concurrent planning with a Navy staff usually far away; intricate combined arms coordination; the choreography involved in moving large numbers of heavily laden men from crowded troopships, down cargo nets into one craft, across heaving gunwales into yet another, and on to the distant shore. And all of this seemingly amid great chaos and confusion.

An amphibiously trained Marine should know such nautical lore as marlinespike seamanship, cargo handling, waterproofing, basic semaphore, the use of tag lines to lower crew-served weapons into landing craft, and how to find one's way from the troop compartment to the debark station, say, starboard side aft, when the combat cargo officer announces, "Boat Team Three Dash Sixteen, lay to Green Nine—NOW!"

Julian Smith regretted the lost opportunities to refine amphibious proficiency at sequentially higher levels, but he did not lose sleep over it. He knew the division would finally have two weeks on board amphibious shipping en route to the Gilberts, plenty of time to catch up on the requirements of shipboard functions. Like a good athletic coach, he chose to emphasize the fundamentals, taking advantage of New Zealand's many training areas and firing ranges.

The daily personnel reports prepared by Colonel Van Ness sobered him. Malaria still claimed huge numbers of his veterans. In July he wrote Lt. Gen. Alexander Archer Vandegrift, commanding IMAC, suggesting the establishment of a malaria treatment and convalescent camp in the theater. Smith told Vandegrift he thought it was a crime that current medical policy required sending many of these men back to the States. "The loss of these battle experienced personnel has hurt the Division very much." Vandegrift was unable to help. As late as 1 September Smith reported to the commandant that his sick list averaged eighteen hundred Marines each day, "85% of whom are malarial patients."[29]

Smith made Red Mike Edson his training ramrod, a task relished by the chief of staff. Edson wrote his wife that there were "so many things I see to be done that I scarcely know where to begin." But, in truth, Edson had been down this road before. If Smith desired training in fundamentals, Edson was exactly the right man to see it through. Eighteen months earlier he had built the fledgling 1st Raider Battalion into a formidable fighting force by applying the same approach. According to historian Jon T. Hoffman, "Red Mike concentrated his efforts [with the Raiders] on four areas: physical fitness, marksmanship, individual skills, and small-unit tactics." To the discomfiture of several older, less driven regimental commanders in New Zealand, Edson relentlessly pursed these same four objectives. In retrospect, one cannot fail to see Edson's "fingerprint" on these basic military capabilities throughout the rank and file of the division in the successful seizure of Tarawa.[30]

If the division lacked amphibious ships for training, they always had an abundance of hiking trails available. All battalions conducted forced marches of extended distances with full arms and equipment. The Seabees covered sixty miles in three days. Colonel Murray's 2d Battalion, 6th Marines, already renowned for prodigious hikes, continued to build its reputation, gaining a level of fitness that would provide the edge when chasing the last of the rikusentai throughout Tarawa atoll.

But no one would surpass the achievement of Major Crowe's 2d Battalion, 8th Marines: 140 miles round-trip. This gave LT 2/8 bragging rights, but no one said much around the corpsmen of any unit. As Pharmacist's Mate First Class Robert E. "Bob" Costello recalled, "Not only did we accompany the Marines throughout each hike, we also spent every minute of the rest breaks treating blisters—we never sat down and took off our packs."[31]

First Sgt. Lewis J. Michelony of the 1st Battalion, 6th Marines, credited the workup training for the unit's sustained performance in combat on Betio. "The training in New Zealand placed us in the best physical condition any unit ever had been. We were fed delightfully and worked like Trojans. By the time we boarded ship we were as fit as the Chicago Bears football team."[32]

Captain Williams commanded Baker Company, 1st Battalion, 2d Marines. "They really turned us loose; it was the best training on earth," he recalled. "We could be in the boondocks within fifteen minutes from leaving Camp Paekakariki. We had lots of leeway. It was a great opportunity for small unit leaders, especially squad leaders, to practice fire and maneuver, to gain confidence and initiative." Maxie Williams, who would be the first officer to cross to Betio's south shore on D+1, remembered the frequent presence of the commanding general. "General Julian was always out in his raincoat, checking his troops."[33]

Maj. Thomas A. Culhane, Shoup's operations officer in the 2d Marines at Tarawa, reflected ten years after the battle on the value of small unit training before the assault. The key to victory, in his view, was "the high state of training and discipline of the individual Marine, his morale, and his confidence and determination to continue the attack."[34]

Intensified training took a toll. Fifty-one Marines died from varied causes during the workup for Tarawa. Another was lost overboard from the *Feland* while under way for the objective. But Julian Smith, Red Mike Edson, and David Shoup could sense they had done their level best to prepare the division for the assault.

Squad leaders were the principal beneficiaries of the fundamental training in New Zealand. Many veteran sergeants, including Bonnyman, Hawkins, and Bordelon, had been commissioned or promoted after Guadalcanal, but a good percentage of the infantry squad leaders were new. Those new "buck" sergeants faced an enormous challenge. The twelve-man rifle squad was still the smallest tactical unit—the Marine Corps would not establish the four-man fire team until Operation Forager in the Marianas in 1944—and squad leaders had a difficult span of control. The chaos to come at Tarawa would place a premium on young NCOs who could step up and take charge of an improvised unit. Few ranks would be more vulnerable. Two hundred and seventeen sergeants would become casualties at Betio. Some of the survivors would command platoons before the fighting ended.[35]

THE JOINT PLANNING STAFF CONVINCED THE Joint Chiefs of Staff that a naval campaign through the Central Pacific would be feasible, in part, if spearheaded by "battle-tested shock troops with amphibious training," further identified as either the 1st or 2d Marine Divisions. The staff report, JPS #205, also described the Marine units as "atoll specialists." The latter characterization was erroneous. The only atoll specialists in the Pacific in mid-1943 wore the uniforms of the Japanese rikusentai. Nor did the 2d Marine Division truly qualify as "amphibious experts." Ironically, the same military organization that would forever after be remembered as the pioneers of forcible amphibious assault came to Tarawa with hardly any more recent hands-on amphibious training than did the green 27th Infantry Division of the U.S. Army, scheduled for Makin. As we have seen, the reasons for the success of the 2d Marine Division against withering Japanese fire at Betio lay elsewhere, closer to the bone.

The untiring efforts of Smith, Edson, and Shoup produced a cohesive division with high morale and esprit, well armed and equipped, a unit in top physical condition despite lingering malaria effects. Assault troops knew well the basic tools of their trade: weapons proficiency and field firing, close combat techniques, fire and maneuver, tactical leadership, fire discipline.

Combat proficiency was not evenly distributed across the spectrum, however. The division's amphibious expertise was adequate, not outstanding. Division-level command and control capabilities lacked sufficient testing. The division also had the wrong mix of vehicles: too many Jeeps and trucks, not enough medium tanks, half-tracks, or LVTs. Combined arms training suffered from the absence of Sherman tanks and lost opportunities for learning how to integrate teams of tanks, infantry, and engineers for assaulting fortified positions.

The division would suffer a thousand casualties a day at Betio, the highest casualty rate sustained by any division in the war. After the battle, interrogators asked one captured rikusentai when he thought the tide of battle had turned in favor of the invaders. "When the dying Americans kept coming, one after another," was the alleged reply. The best weapon the Marines brought to Tarawa proved to be their inherent aggressiveness, ingrained from boot camp, enhanced by their combat leaders. In this respect, the Joint Chiefs—and America—got exactly what they sought: "battle-tested shock troops." Sherrod found a better phrase. "These were *shock-proof* Marines."[36]

CHAPTER FOUR

Movement to Contact

*War is a tough business, and we sometimes
gain more than we lose by pressing forward
against the enemy before we are entirely ready.*
—Vice Adm. Raymond A. Spruance, USN

AUGUST 1943 MARKED THE INTENSIFICATION OF
both American and Japanese efforts concerning Tarawa and
the Gilberts. Shortly after Admiral Spruance concluded his
meeting in Wellington with the 2d Marine Division, U.S.
forces seized four islands in or near the Ellice group—Nuku-
fetau, Nanomea, Canton, and Baker—to provide enhanced
bomber support in time for Operation Galvanic's kickoff.
Added to the earlier base at Funafuti, the new operating sites
brought the entire string of the Gilberts and Nauru and Ocean
Islands within bomber range. The eight heavy bomber squadrons of the Seventh Air Force would play a key role in
Galvanic.[1]

At Tarawa, Admiral Shibasaki worked steadily to improve
his defensive capabilities. During the same time Julian Smith
hosted Spruance in Wellington, Shibasaki received the report
of a team of twelve touring instructors, experts in land combat,
antiaircraft gunnery, and underwater defenses, headed by the
distinguished Namizo Sato, principal of the Naval Mine
School. The team inspected Japanese garrison positions in the
Marshalls and Gilberts throughout July and August; Tarawa
received detailed inspection because of its position as the first
outpost on the external perimeter.[2]

On 8 August Shibasaki convened a meeting of Tarawa's
"Defense Planning Section" in his command post. His senior
staff and commanders discussed antiaircraft defenses, naval

gunnery, and ground combat operations in response to the recommendations of the Sato inspection team. Commander Sugai
of the Sasebo Seventh Special Naval Landing Force insisted
that the garrison's 13-mm machine guns "must form the basis
of the defense," becoming thereby the principal ground
weapons used by the rikusentai. Commander Ezaka, Shibasaki's senior staff officer, argued against removing the 13-mm
weapons from their dual antiaircraft role "until after the 25-
mm machine-cannons arrive," in reference to the special
request made by their former base commander after the April
air raids. No doubt influenced by Sato and his staff, Shibasaki
stated the need to lay antiboat mines "300–500 meters out from
the beach" in conjunction with tetrahedrons and other offshore obstacles.[3]

Namizo Sato and his experts would have served Shibasaki
better by staying on Betio longer. Shibasaki wound up with
plenty of mines—nearly three thousand on the island,
according to Japanese and American sources—and he planted
them with his usual tactical sense, enhancing the southern,
western, and northeastern beaches by priority, where he
expected the Americans to land. By attacking through the
lagoon against the northern shore, however, the Americans
missed many of these weapons. Nor did mines seriously
hamper their reinforcement landings against the western beach
on the second and third day. Two LVTs blew up spectacularly
near Green Beach, but two entire battalion landing teams, a
tank platoon, and the commanding general made it ashore in
the west without incident.

The Japanese garrison often set the mines inexpertly. After
the battle the Americans found many antiboat mines whose
horns had been installed without benefit of watertight gaskets.
Shibasaki made few mistakes at Betio, but this error made a
huge difference. Betio's formidable defenses may have proven
unassailable if those three thousand mines had been sown as
deftly as, for example, the 56th Naval Guard Force would do at
Tinian the following year.[4]

Shibasaki pressed on, always balancing the need for
working parties against the requirement for advanced tactical

training. By mid-August he learned of Admiral Koga's *Hei* Plan #3, the sequential counterattack against an American invasion of the Gilberts. He knew his own mandated role to withstand an enemy assault for three to seven days. Shibasaki felt confident of achieving that objective at Betio and probably had growing assurance that Nauru could stand on its own as well. Makin, Ocean, and Apamama were a different story, particularly the latter, where only an observation party of twenty-five men stood watch. But Apamama could be converted into the best airfield in the Gilberts, according to a team of engineers from Truk and Tokyo who inspected the atoll in late May.[5]

Shibasaki then turned to his first line of defense, the imposing coastal defense guns. Many of his men were graduates of the Tateyama Gunnery School, a training facility in Chiba Prefecture east of Tokyo that opened in June 1941 to teach land and antiaircraft gunnery to the naval landing forces. Petty Officer Chuma, for example, spent two weeks at Tateyama and a week at the nearby Yokosuka Naval Gunnery School to learn advanced antiaircraft gunnery before embarking with the Sasebo Seventh on board the *Bangkok Maru* for Tarawa.

Some sources indicate that a sizeable detachment of the Tateyama school staff came to Tarawa for intensified training of the Betio garrison. This would account, in part, for the remarkable proficiency displayed by the rikusentai with such Army weapons as the 70-mm howitzer, 75-mm mountain gun, 37-mm antitank gun, and—at least in the antiboat mode—Chuma's, "7cm mobile AA gun."[6]

By contrast, gunners assigned to the larger coastal defense weapons, principally former rikusentai of the Yokosuka 6th, were much less skillful. Those with previous experience on capital ships may have been familiar with heavy ordnance up to 8 inch/45 caliber, but the naval landing forces had generally been mobile light infantry to this point, and many found the huge, static guns daunting. Shibasaki would have surely seen this, and there is evidence that he conducted frequent firing exercises, even encouraging the initiation of fires at extended ranges out to twenty thousand meters in the case of the 8-inch guns. Shibasaki always sought to build confidence in the Betio garrison.[7]

IN NEW ZEALAND JULIAN SMITH WAS IN THE confidence-building business too. He knew from the start Betio would be tough, but neither he nor his staff knew much about the target. Spruance promised to make the resources of his JICPOA available to the division's intelligence section immediately. This would help. This first map of Betio Island that Lt. Col. Jack Colley could produce was nothing more than a slightly modified version of the crude sketch made by the 1842 Wilkes Expedition. From such humble beginnings, however, came a remarkably thorough, interagency intelligence collection and analysis effort, which may surprise those who still regard Tarawa as a "somebody goofed" campaign.

Intelligence information on Tarawa came from four sources: ULTRA intercepts, aerial photographs, submarine photographs, and briefings from former residents or traders, principally New Zealanders. ULTRA's value stemmed from the fact that Shibasaki and his entire chain of command represented the Imperial Japanese Navy, whose codes had been deciphered for many months. Although the cryptologists uncovered nothing spectacular in these intercepts, their drudging work produced valuable insights about the identity, size, and status of the Japanese garrisons. This useful information came from routine monthly strength reports, logistics requests, and aviation operational status reports. As historian Ronald Lewin has admitted, however, "What signals intelligence could not do was to provide topographical knowledge, nor could it penetrate the camouflage of those defensive positions."[8]

Nor could the former residents provide information about the Tarawa defenses because the Japanese buildup did not begin until after Carlson's raid in August 1942. The transport submarine *Nautilus* took hundreds of periscope photographs of Betio's shoreline in a dangerous patrol throughout the Gilberts in September. The photos were useful to ship-to-shore coxswains but less so to intelligence analysts. The island was simply too flat, the strong points too artfully concealed.

As it turned out, the Seventh Air Force best served the intelligence team with its series of vertical and high oblique aerial photographs taken by crew members of B-24 Liberators flying over Tarawa from their new bases in the Ellice Islands. These were superb. David Shoup later described the advance aerial photographs of Tarawa as the best of the Pacific War. Colley's photo interpreters outdid themselves. The 2d Marine Division's enemy situation map (SITMAP) distributed on 22 October 1943 became a collector's item before the war ended. Events proved the identification of enemy strong points and weapons positions to be 90 percent accurate.

And Colley kept the SITMAP current, even when Shibasaki's frenetic work added new dimensions to the defenses. As late as D-Day-minus-2, with the Southern Attack Force steaming for Tarawa, a Seventh Air Force Liberator took yet another roll of aerial photographs, intercepted the U.S. flagship, and dropped the film squarely onto the battleship's moving deck. Colley's staff quickly developed and analyzed the film, which showed the late addition of "tetrahedron-shaped horned scullies on the reef half the width of Red Beach Three." That was to be Major Crowe's beach. Crowe got the word on his troop transport thirty hours before the landing.[9]

Good intelligence saved lives at Tarawa, no doubt, but the disturbing fact remained that Betio Island appeared about as accessible as a porcupine. Julian Smith, Edson, and Shoup received the intelligence analyses without blanching, but each could see the grave difficulties ahead. Just about every hydrographic and topographic feature on Betio favored the defender, from the unpredictable tides and fringing coral reef to the flat nature of the terrain, which would permit near universal machine-gun coverage by simple traverse. The senior officers could see some of the mines Shibasaki had sown in the waters; each fresh batch of aerial photographs reflected even more of the weapons. They could also see the abundance of horned scullies, steel-tipped tetrahedrons, and coral rock cairns dotting the offshore approaches, along with double-apron barbed wire and steel cable. Moreover, what seemed to be hundreds of machine guns and antiboat gun positions covered each cluster of obstacles.

With one or two exceptions, the intelligence staff identified the caliber, number, and location of every crew-served weapon on the island. Understandably, the 8-inch coastal defense guns drew the most attention. Postwar historians for the ensuing quarter century called them the "Singapore Guns," captured from the British with the fall of Malaya and brought to Tarawa as ultimate, fully operational war trophies. In 1977, however, British writer William H. Bartsch submitted proof that the legendary guns were not at all the spoils of war. Bartsch reported that the Brits had no 8-inch guns at Singapore. Serial numbers from the Tarawa guns proved that they had been sold by Vickers to the Japanese in 1905, a legitimate transaction during the Russo-Japanese War.[10]

Admiral Shibasaki's big guns on Betio were scary, but they would kill few Marines. Japanese gunners were much more deadly with their smaller caliber, direct-fire weapons—the 75-mm mountain guns and AA guns (firing horizontally), plus the rapid-firing 37-mm antitank pieces. Their indirect fire weapons proved to be equally lethal. Many Marines reported the accu-

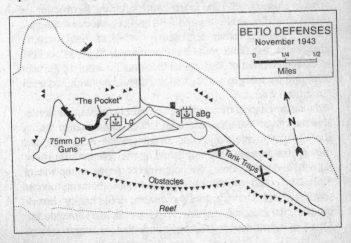

racy of Japanese "mortar fire" that rained over the exposed reef and along the seawall the first hours of the battle.

Technically, the Japanese had no "mortars" at Tarawa. The rikusentai forces did not include mortar platoons, and the American Marines would not face the dangerous trench mortars of the Imperial Japanese Army until the Central Pacific drive moved farther west. Indirect fire at Tarawa came from the half-dozen Type 92 70-mm howitzers and the ubiquitous M89 50-mm heavy grenade dischargers, the infantry weapon the Americans mistakenly called "knee mortars" because the curved monopod appeared to fit the gunner's knee (the M89's recoil would break bones if fired in this fashion, actually). Some U.S. Marines reported finding Japanese range markers and aiming stakes positioned inside the reef.[11]

Japanese field gunners blew up American LVTs, landing craft, and tanks with spectacular results, but the real slaughter came from Commander Sugai's well-sited machine guns. Sugai used the big 13-mm guns on the flanks and directed their fields of fire along wire entanglements and other obstacles. He ensured flanking fire discipline by sealing off the front embrasures of the reinforced emplacements. At heart the rikusentai were transplanted naval infantrymen, at their best with small arms at close range. Late in the battle, after the destruction of their vaunted coastal guns and field artillery weapons, the surviving Japanese fought tenaciously with just their machine guns, rifles, and hand grenades. Commander Sugai's "pocket" at the intersection of Red Beach One and Two fought the surrounding Marines to a standstill for three days with just such basic firepower.

Not every aspect of scrubby, baking Betio served the defensive needs of Admiral Shibasaki. The coral island had a shallow water table, which prevented the kind of underground digging the Japanese accomplished on the volcanic islands of Saipan and Iwo Jima. The paucity of fresh water meant Shibasaki could not afford additional reinforcements on his small island; his evaporators and cisterns could barely accommodate the existing garrison. And try as they might, the Japanese could never effectively bury their communications wire deep enough in the powder-soft sand. Their field telephone systems would be vulnerable to the first high explosives to hit the island.

All things considered, however, Shibasaki could hardly have asked for a better place to make an extended stand against an American invasion. The crown jewel of his defensive system remained the protective reef itself. At low tide the reef surrounded the island with a perfectly flat, cleared field of fire. Surviving Americans would characterize it as "a billiard table without any pockets." Fifty years after the assault, journalist Tom Infield evaluated the combination of hydrography, firepower, and strong points protecting Betio and concluded, "In the fall of 1943, it could have been the most heavily fortified place on earth."[12]

THE STORY OF THE BATTLE OF TARAWA IS INEX-tricably linked to the tides that remained so unpredictably low for the first forty-eight hours of the amphibious assault. Julian Smith and Harry Hill, given no alternative to the landing date of 20 November, hoped that morning for a rising neap tide high enough to provide unobstructed passage of boats as well as amphibian tractors. It was not to be. In essence, while the first three waves of assault troops in LVTs crossed the reef without incident, the Marines never got the necessary four feet of water over the reef to permit passage of landing boats bearing the balance of the assault forces, supporting arms, and reinforcements.

What they got, instead, was a sullen tide that never rose more than a foot above mean level. This has been called "The Tide That Failed." As a fatal consequence, no landing boats could cross the reef, thousands of Marines had to wade the six- to eight-hundred yards to shore, and hundreds fell to Japanese gunners. The scene was graphic. No American who ever saw it can deny the feelings of rage and helplessness he experienced. Worse, for years after the battle the "laggard tide" remained inexplicable—fate, bad luck, the fortunes of war.

America's senior political and military leaders did little to counter the bad luck theme. "A sudden shifting of the wind"

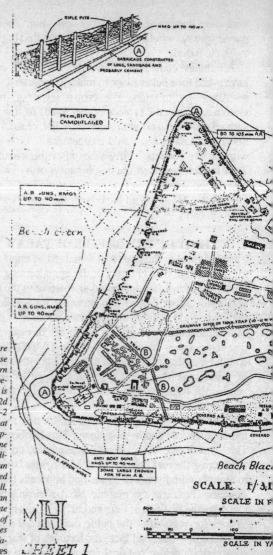

The detailed picture of estimated Japanese defenses on western Betio one month before the assault is taken from the 2d Marine Division D-2 intelligence map that accompanied the operations order. Some estimates of the caliber of individual gun emplacements proved inexact, but, overall, the map provided an extremely accurate composite picture of what the Marines could expect at Tarawa. MARINE CORPS HISTORICAL CENTER

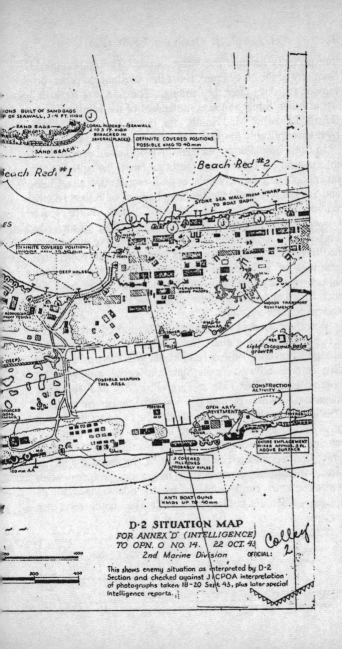

D·2 SITUATION MAP
FOR ANNEX "D" (INTELLIGENCE)
TO OPN. O NO. 14. 22 OCT. 43
2nd Marine Division   OFFICIAL:

This shows enemy situation as interpreted by D-2
Section and checked against JICPOA interpretation
of photographs taken 18-20 Sept 43, plus later special
intelligence reports.

unexpectedly lowered the waters around Tarawa, explained Secretary of the Navy Frank Knox in a Washington press conference ten days after the landing. "The tide was freakish," wrote Julian Smith to the commandant of the Marine Corps. Recalled Howlin' Mad Smith, "the Japanese . . . were helped by the inexplicably low tide which held for two days."[13]

In truth, amphibious planners in 1943 lacked precise tidal information on Tarawa and therefore based their predictions on extrapolated data from places as distant as Australia, Chile, and Samoa. Nor could the "Foreign Legion" of Gilbert Islands sailors accompanying the Southern Attack Force reach consensus among themselves about the tide. Some, like Maj. Frank L.G. Holland, a New Zealand reserve officer who had lived next to Betio for years before the war, issued dire warnings of a "dodging" low tide on D-Day, but many others—equally qualified—predicted ample water over the reef. Smith and Hill had little choice but to hope for the best and prepare for the worst.

Was the persistent low tide on D-Day indeed fate or "bum scoop" or something else? The controversy lacked scientific interpretation until 1987, when Donald W. Olson, professor of physics at Southwest Texas State University, published his seminal essay "The Tide at Tarawa" in *Sky and Telescope* magazine. Olson explained that low tidal ranges are not only affected by quadrative factors, that is, the twice-monthly neap tides caused by the moon being in its first or last quarter, a relationship understood by mariners for thousands of years. Much less appreciated is the effect of the moon's monthly orbit, which creates increased tidal ranges at its perigee—when it's closest to earth—and *decreased* tidal ranges at its apogee—when it's farthest from earth. The combination of a

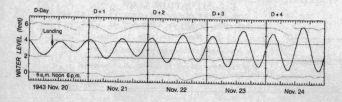

perigean and spring tide is often enough to cause coastal flooding. Conversely, when an apogean tide coincides with a neap tide, the range will be uncommonly low.

Professor Olson's research included calculations based on "harmonic analysis." He found only two dates in 1943 when apogee occurred within twenty-four hours of quadrature, 12 April and 19 November. The impact of this phenomenon can be visualized by consulting the chart on page 82 (courtesy of Dr. Olson and *Sky and Telescope*), which displays the tidal range at Betio during the battle. As Dr. Olson concluded: "Thus the landing at Tarawa was scheduled for one of only two occasions in 1943 when apogean neap tides could occur. . . . In fact, from 9 A.M. until 10 P.M. on D-Day the water hovered within six inches of its mean level, 3.3 feet. It was an apogean tide of reduced range, but technically neither a dodging tide nor a vanishing tide."[14]

None of the meteorologists on the staffs of Spruance, Turner, Hill, Holland Smith, or Julian Smith knew anything about harmonic analysis or apogean neap tides in the fall of 1943. Advance knowledge of the pending phenomenon might have curbed staff optimism about Operation Galvanic, but it probably would not have been sufficient cause for delaying the landing. The Joint Chiefs of Staff had already postponed D-Day in the Gilberts five days; any further delay of the new date of 20 November would compromise the more strategically important Marshalls campaign to follow. Admiral King was in no mood for foot-dragging. "Spare no effort to speed up training," he wired Nimitz, "and . . . get on with the war."[15]

Did the uncooperative tide at Tarawa contribute to inordinate U.S. casualties? Consider the alternatives. A rising spring tide may have caused other problems for the assault force. Laden landing boats would still have grounded on the sloping coral shelf fifty to one hundred yards off shore. Some would surely have been ruptured by submerged horned scullies no longer visible to coxswains. Open wooden boats filled with troops may have proven real "crowd-killers" against direct-fire antiboat guns at point-blank range. Marines reaching the beach in a high tide would have lost the defilade shelter provided by the seawall; all hands would have faced the unrelenting fire that grazed the top of the coconut logs; and the wounded would have drowned on the spot.

Moreover, the apogean neap tide actually saved the lives of assault troops riding the LVTs by reducing the time the vehicles required to close the final distance from reef to beach. Floating LVTs were agonizingly slow—three to four knots at best—but once their tracks touched the solid coral shelf, the vehicles could move the final six hundred yards at three times their waterborne speed.

That most combat correspondents rode landing boats (not LVTs) shoreward and thereby experienced firsthand the horror of the long wade from the reef under fire is one reason Tarawa's fickle tides attained such lasting notoriety. These men saw little of the subsequent fighting inland, where three-fourths of the American casualties occurred, but their graphic reports of the slaughter of the boated troops captured the imagination of the American public.

To the Marines who fought at Tarawa, the real shocker was not low water over the reef but the tactical survival of the Japanese garrison despite the unprecedented preliminary bombardment. Seven months later, at Saipan, many of the same Marines and sailors would face another fringing reef, one made more hazardous by the absence of a lagoon and the resultingly vicious surf. But neither the reef nor the tides at Saipan became a factor in the battle. Assault forces used 732 LVTs to land eight thousand Marines in the first twenty minutes. Here, as at Tarawa, inadequate preliminary bombardment did little to destroy Japanese gun positions, leading to the preponderance of American casualties ashore, inland, well past the reef.

AS DAUNTING AND DANGEROUS AS BETIO would be to his landing force, Admiral Spruance had broader concerns and more unknowns as campaign planning developed for Galvanic. No one could be sure about the timing and intensity of the Japanese long-range naval counterattacks sure to come. As Spruance recalled: "[A]t this time, the Japanese fleet was about as strong as ours . . . [and] it was free to operate against us on interior lines. . . . The Japanese air was still strong and aggressive. It had developed a dusk torpedo attack, using flares for illumination, which had proved effective against ships and difficult for us to counter. We had no carrier night fighters then."[16]

Spruance and his admirals had confidence that the Central Pacific Force would prevail against the Imperial Japanese Navy on the open seas, especially with the arrival of the new *Essex*-class fleet carriers. But Spruance, Turner, and Hill worried about the vulnerability of the amphibious task force once it concentrated in the Gilberts. They fully expected the Japanese to strike the cluster of transports and cargo ships at anchor off the contested beachheads. At sea the ships could move and disperse. Once the landing began, however, the task force became like a wild animal pausing to give birth in a forest of predators. Turner had lost his own flagship to a Japanese torpedo bomber attack at Rendova just a few months earlier. Nimitz, for both strategic and operational reasons, gave Spruance explicit orders, "Get the hell in, then get the hell out."[17]

The need for haste, the uncertainty of the tides, the known strengths of the Japanese garrison at Betio, the unknown factors of Japanese counterattack capabilities—all these would place a heavy strain on the Navy's fledgling amphibious doctrine. Few commanders would have imagined that the tentative—indeed radical—doctrine for opposed amphibious landings first proposed by a small group of Marine Corps and Navy officers in Quantico in the 1930s would have survived the first two years of the war. While the doctrine had proved sufficient in the Solomons, New Guinea, Aleutians, North Africa, and Sicily landings, it had never been fully tested under heavy fire.

As operational doctrines go, the concept for forcible amphibious assault was still brand-new and unproven. Fleet Training Publication #167, "Landing Operations Doctrine," was barely five years old in 1943 and had already sustained three major changes. The ultimate amphibious disaster at Gallipoli had occurred only twenty-eight years earlier. The U.S.

Marines were increasingly identifying their own role as amphibious shock troops. Another Gallipoli could easily knock them back into their former "colonial infantry" mission.

Interestingly, the senior leadership at Tarawa lacked combat experience in amphibious warfare. Kelly Turner and Holland Smith were among the best in the amphibious business, but both would spend Galvanic in the vicinity of Makin, protecting the entire force from Japanese excursions based in the Marshalls. Spruance would be near Tarawa in the USS *Indianapolis* (CA 35), but the victor of Midway, destined to prevail in some of the greatest amphibious assaults in history, began Galvanic with little practical experience in the complex art. In the Southern Attack Force, Harry Hill had previously commanded a battleship division; Julian Smith, a training command. David Shoup would become both the architect and the executor of the assault plan, but he had never conducted a landing under fire.

Only Capt. Herbert R. Knowles, commanding Transport Division Eighteen, and Red Mike Edson could draw on actual combat experience in amphibious assaults against the Japanese. Knowles commanded the USS *Heywood* (APA 6) at Tulagi and the Aleutians, while Edson commanded the 1st Raider Battalion during the Tulagi landing. Admiral Hill, as Commander of the Southern Attack Force, would have been well-advised to listen more often and more closely to these two veterans during the abbreviated planning phase.[18]

The Joint Chiefs originally assigned the Central Pacific Force the mission of seizing Nauru Island in addition to the Tarawa and Apamama atolls. Nauru, not at all a spit of coral and sand like Betio, was large and rugged, its narrow beaches surmounted by steep cliffs. This was to have been the objective of the unproven 27th Infantry Division, an Army National Guard outfit based in Hawaii. Kelly Turner and Holland Smith rendered valuable service to both Spruance and the Army by recommending the substitution of Makin for Nauru. Spruance concurred and went to King and Nimitz with the proposal. It made good sense. The Army would seize Makin, the Marines Tarawa and Apamama. Nauru would rot on the vine.

Julian Smith's general staff began planning for their portion of the Galvanic as soon as Spruance left Wellington, gaining a running start over their supporting and senior organizations. Except for joint intelligence gathering, however, the Marines did their initial planning in a vacuum. The senior staffs were still being created out of whole cloth by Spruance, Turner, and Holland Smith, and the operational components were scattered over much of the Pacific Ocean. In fact, the 2d Marine Division never had the chance to work and rehearse with Admiral Hill and his staff until 22 October, barely a week prior to final embarkation.

As a veteran operations officer, David Shoup was in his element throughout the planning process, but the guiding hand of Red Mike Edson allowed the entire staff to focus and flourish. Edson's masterful role as chief of staff surprised Julian Smith. "He was a revelation to me," he wrote the commandant of the Marine Corps after the battle. "I knew he was a fine field commander but was not aware of his ability as a staff officer."[19]

Edson's "Estimate of the Situation—Gilberts," dated 5 October 1943, remains one of the finest examples of completed staff work produced by either side in the Pacific War. The detailed estimate, "compiled and submitted by Merrit A. Edson," made the most of solid intelligence reporting and critical military analysis to provide a recommended decision by the division commander.

Edson gave the Japanese garrison full credit. The Special Naval Landing Forces, he said, are "among the best fighting forces available to the enemy. Prior experience has indicated that these troops will fight tenaciously. . . .[the enemy] undoubtedly has a well-considered scheme of defensive maneuver, and he will have predetermined ranges to the critical points." Where some of his contemporaries would speak of Tarawa as potentially a cakewalk, Edson had no illusions. "The enemy must endeavor to hold it and to make its capture as costly to us as possible. This will be his first attempt to defend an atoll . . . as it is our first endeavor at seizing one."[20]

Looking back at the early history of the Pacific War, Edson warned, "From his experience in the capture of Wake

Island, which was weakly defended as compared to Betio, the enemy may feel confident of his ability to hold it without much naval support, especially in view of air support available in the Marshalls."[21]

Edson already knew that VAC intended to withhold the 6th Marines as corps reserve and that Betio must therefore be seized with only the assault elements of two regimental combat teams. (A combat team was essentially an infantry regiment reinforced by a pack-howitzer artillery battalion, a company of tanks, a company of engineers, and a platoon of scout-snipers.) To the table of organization figures for these combat teams Edson applied an administrative loss figure of up to 30 percent to reflect understaffing, D-Day requirements for shore party units and ship's platoons (hatch crews), and ineffectives. His estimated total for CT-2 and 8, combined, came to 6,268 combat troops. Experience would validate his speculation: fewer artillerymen ashore would be offset by dismounted crews from disabled LVTs who fought as infantry. The number is significantly low for an opposed landing of this magnitude. Conventional wisdom required a troop superiority of three to one over the defenders. The Marines would barely muster a 1.66:1 advantage over Shibasaki's garrison on D-Day.

Edson examined each of Betio's potential landing beaches, concluding that the north shore, facing the lagoon, offered fewer mines and obstacles and a gentler surf than the more directly accessible southern or western beaches. The study concluded with a single recommended decision for the commanding general: "To land on the north coast of Betio between the north-west corner of the island and the eastern end of the airstrip, with three [battalion] landing teams abreast, at H-Hour, D-Day, in order to seize the island and to destroy the hostile garrison thereon."[22]

Julian Smith valued the professional staff work involved in this study, but he worried that seizing Betio would shatter his fine division unless they could devise ways to offset the defender's advantages. The innovative idea of using LVTs as assault craft would help. So would entering the lagoon to hit the island from the north. There had to be other ways of skinning this difficult cat.

Shoup and Edson proposed a landing plan that featured a sustained preliminary bombardment of several days' duration, advance seizure of neighboring Bairiki Island as an artillery fire base, and a decoy landing. General Smith took these proposals to the planning conference held in Pearl Harbor in early October for the principal officers involved in Operation Galvanic: Nimitz, Spruance, Turner, Hill, and Holland Smith. The conference jolted the officers of the 2d Marine Division. While the Marines had realized from the start that their operation plan must reflect the themes of operational security, conservative use of limited assets, and maximum speed of execution (stressed by Spruance), they were not prepared for

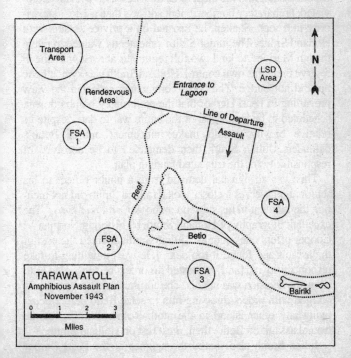

the cumulative impact these factors would have on the landing force.

The Marines were stunned to hear the restrictions imposed on their assault by CinCPac. Nimitz declared that the requirement for strategic surprise limited preliminary bombardment of Betio to about three hours on the morning of D-Day. Time constraints and the imperative to concentrate naval forces to defend against a Japanese fleet sortie also ruled out advance seizure of Bairiki and any decoy landings. Holland Smith upheld his earlier decision to withhold the entire 6th Marines as corps reserve.

All of Julian Smith's tactical options had been stripped away. The 2d Marine Division was compelled to make a frontal assault into the teeth of Betio's defenses with an abbreviated, preparatory bombardment and less than a 2-to-1 superiority in troops. Shaken, he insisted on a private session with Holland Smith. The junior Smith vehemently wanted to retain the 6th Marines, to land two full regiments abreast with one in reserve under his own control. Holland Smith was sympathetic but did not budge. The corps commander reflected the view prevailing in Pearl Harbor that the preliminary bombardment, scheduled to be the largest of the entire war to date despite its relative brevity, would make mincemeat out of Betio's defenders. Julian Smith then demanded to be absolved of responsibility for the truncated landing plan.

This was an unusual demand from a junior officer to his senior and deserves a closer look. Holland Smith did not mention the incident in his subsequent book *Coral and Brass*. The excellent biography of Holland Smith by historian Norman V. Cooper offers one account. "Julian Smith counted the cost of the assault and found it too dear. [He was] unwilling to take responsibility . . . [and] requested his orders be so worded as to show the decision was not his. The corps commander promptly obliged with orders directing him to seize Betio before occupying any other island in the atoll. Responsibilities for the frontal assault on Betio, then, must rest on Holland Smith."[23]

Julian Smith also shared the agonies of the Pearl Harbor

conference with his wife, Happy. As she recalled the events of the time:

> Julian told me several times that he hoped history would bring out the truth regarding the tactical plans for Tarawa. His battle plans had been discarded and he received verbal orders to engage in a full, frontal assault, even though there were some who had doubts that the island could be taken under those conditions, for it violated all good doctrine. That is precisely why Julian asked Holland Smith to put his orders in writing. For if the assault proved unsuccessful he didn't want to wind up the scapegoat and become known as the General most responsible for the slaughter of his own troops.[24]

Holland Smith's VAC OpPlan #1-43 for Galvanic was correspondingly explicit in its tasking for Julian Smith's command. The primary mission for the 2d Marine Division ("less 6th Marines reinforced") would be to land on Helen Island [the code name for Betio], "seize and occupy that island, *then* conduct further operations to reduce the remainder of Longsuit [Tarawa] Atoll." In short, take Betio first, and do it without the 6th Marines.[25]

Julian Smith and his staff returned to New Zealand with only a few weeks to adjust their plans before embarkation. Now, more than ever, they needed reassurance that their LVTs could climb a coral reef and remain seaworthy enough to run transfer line operations between reef and beach if the boats got hung up in marginal water. The enterprising Major Drewes soon had encouraging news to report.

The 2d Amphibian Tractor Battalion had indeed improved the basic mechanical condition of the seventy-five LVT-1 Alligators salvaged from Guadalcanal. The battalion maintenance officer, 1st Lt. John A. Speed, led a team of mechanics and New Zealanders who developed field expedients to tackle the problems of thrown tracks and drowned engines. The "field fixes" were not regulation, but few Alligators would falter for mechanical problems on D-Day, despite the long-range ship-to-shore movement in choppy seas.

Providing improvised armor protection for the otherwise exposed LVT crews was a harder nut to crack. Drewes, Speed, and Lt. Mike Sisul spent weeks searching for steel plate tough enough to repel machine-gun bullets but light enough not to interfere with the vehicle's sea-handling capabilities. Once the team found the right plate, they had to go to Wellington to find a factory to make the seventy-five installations. An obliging auto plant put on extra shifts to accomplish this project just before the load out. The improvised armor was a limited asset—the thin plates covered only the cab directly in front of the driver and two forward gunners—but it created confidence and saved lives as well. "I know it worked," recalled Speed, "because coming into the beach [at Tarawa] when the enemy fire hit the plates it sounded like bells ringing."[26]

Drewes further modified his vehicles with three machine-gun mounts apiece and stern grapnels for ripping up barbed wire. In field training he made his drivers approach the beach while machine guns carefully fired live rounds close overhead. In October Capt. Fenlon A. Durand and 1st Lt. Bonnie Little took a detachment of tankers and "Tractor Rats" on board the USS *Harris* (APA 2) for reef-crossing tests in the Fiji Islands. The ships carried a half-dozen modified Alligators and two brand-new Sherman medium tanks, the first to arrive in the South Pacific. The tests involved running Alligators over the reef near the entrance to Suva harbor and unloading medium tanks from LCM-3s at the reef's edge. Durand sent a favorable message to the division on 16 October, reporting that it was "determined entirely feasible to land both light and medium tanks under these conditions," that "tanks operate normally on reef as on rocky ground," and that "amphibian tractors climbed on and off reef with entire ease." This came as welcome news to the Marines in New Zealand.[27]

The Marines' decision to employ thin-skinned, slow-speed logistical LVTs as assault craft was one gamble at Tarawa that worked and, in fact, represented a landmark in the conduct of ship-to-shore movements. Assault amphibian vehicles remain the centerpiece of the surface assault half a century after Galvanic. The innovation had several "fathers." The anonymous author of "Change 2" to *Landing Operations Doctrine*, released just before the Guadalcanal landings in 1942, suggested that LVTs should be employed for "crossing coral reefs and negotiating underwater obstacles."[28] The following May, the Joint Chiefs of Staff directed IMAC in Nouméa to expend two vehicles for an "exhaustive test of loaded LVT crossing coral reef under heavy surf conditions."

Lt. Col. Victor H. Krulak got the call to conduct testing, based on his recent service with the prototype LVTs at Dunedin, Florida. Krulak was apprehensive. "As far as I knew," he recalled, "no one had yet tried to ride an LVT through both coral and heavy surf, and the picture of what might happen to a fifteen-thousand-pound unsprung iron box when a wave brought it crashing down on a coral ledge was not encouraging to any of us." Surprisingly, the LVTs performed well under exactly those conditions. Krulak could report with confidence that a loaded LVT could indeed negotiate a plunging surf of up to six feet on a coral reef.[29]

The Joint Chiefs' query resulted from the initiative taken by Col. David R. Nimmer, USMC, a Guadalcanal veteran serving in the Pacific War Plans section of the Joint Planning Staff. Armed with Krulak's favorable report, Nimmer could address the problem of assaulting the Central Pacific atolls known to be protected by fringing coral reefs. Joint Planning Staff #205 of 10 June 1943 therefore contained the statement that the amphibian tractor would be the most suitable craft to assault coral atolls, citing recent tests in the South Pacific in which amtracs "negotiated fringing reefs in all conditions up to a 10-foot surf."[30]

But there is a curious aspect to this story. Whereas the 2d Marine Division was also a member of IMAC and knew from early August that their LVTs would have to be the key to unlocking Tarawa's natural obstacles, it appears that IMAC did not share the results of Krulak's reef-surf tests with Julian Smith. As we have seen, the 2d Marine Division did not know for sure that the Alligators could operate in that environment until after the Fiji tests in mid-October. Julian Smith later credited David Shoup with the idea of using LVTs to spearhead the assault.[31]

At this time, the Marines in New Zealand learned that a shipload of new LVT-2 Water Buffaloes would reach Samoa in late October, too late for advanced training but just possibly with time enough for redeployment to Tarawa. Major Drewes went to Red Mike Edson for help in forming a provisional amtrac company to receive, inspect, and operate the fifty new vehicles. No one had men to spare, but Edson made it happen. Drewes provided LVT drivers and crew chiefs, the tankers gave up some mechanics, the special weapons battalion sent machine gunners. At one moment, for example, PFC Mirle W. Yancey was a loader on a 75-mm half-track in the special weapons battalion; a day later he joined "A-1" Company as an LVT machine gunner.

The provisional company soon numbered 111 men under the command of Capt. Ray "Hootie" Horner. The detachment boarded the merchant ship *Robin Wentley* and arrived in Samoa on 21 October. A week later a strange new ship with a chopped-off stern appeared offshore. It was the *Ashland*, the nation's first dock landing ship. As the men watched, the *Ashland* ballasted down by the stern and launched fifty Water Buffaloes. The new amtracs looked more streamlined and seaworthy than the box-like Alligators. The LVT-2s were longer, wider, more powerful, faster (albeit a relative term with LVTs), and carried a greater payload than their predecessors. Engineers had also designed an improved track and suspension system for the Water Buffalo. Obviously, someone had listened to the complaints from the field.[32]

Lt. Manuel Schneidmiller headed a detachment of thirty-nine LVT mechanics who escorted the Water Buffaloes from San Diego to Samoa. Headquarters had ordered Schneidmiller to deliver the new vehicles, then proceed with his detachment to Nouméa for duty with another Fleet Marine Force command. But to Hootie Horner, these mechanics represented the only available expertise with the new vehicles in the Pacific. Tarawa's daunting beaches loomed. In bald-faced piracy,

Horner "appropriated" Schneidmiller and his mechanics into the 2d Marine Division "for the duration."[33]

Horner's men had much to do in very little time. The LVT-2s, while new and improved, were still designed as logistic support vehicles, still unarmored. Moreover, the vehicles had large "windows" along the front and sides of the cab, good for observation but bad for hostile fire. Samoa was not New Zealand, and Horner did not have the time for a large-scale armor-plating job. Lt. Sidney S. Key recalled that the officers installed some scrounged steel plating to narrow the front openings, but when they tested the improvised shields, they discovered that even a rifle bullet would penetrate them. There was nothing else they could do.[34]

Three LSTs arrived in Samoa on 5 November for final training and embarkation for Tarawa. Horner's mixed force of tankers, gunners, and tractor rats found the flat-bottomed, rough-riding tank landing ships about as foreign as the *Ashland*. LVTs and LSTs were made for each other, a marriage of military utility because the amtracs could be loaded and launched at sea without the necessity of a port facility. Debarkation down the bow ramp at sea with LVTs was easy; the trick was backing the vehicles aboard, especially in rough seas. Doing so took practice and teamwork.

As the LVT floated past the ship's lowered ramp at an angle, a crewman poised topside caught the "monkey fist" tossed by the boatswain's mate on the ramp, who then passed heavy hemp lines to be cross-attached to stern mooring bits. The LVT crew chief, perched precariously in front of the driver, relayed the signals of the boatswain. Timing the waves and watching the alignment, the boatswain shouted profane orders to both the LVT and the dozens of sailors heaving the tow lines down the tank deck. A good team could snatch an LVT on board in two minutes, regardless of the seas. Inexperience and impatience would damage the vehicle or the bow ramp—and often injure the participants. Horner's men learned fast.[35]

Major Drewes flew to Samoa directly from the division's rehearsal landings in the New Hebrides with the final draft of the assault plans. On 10 November, the 168th birthday of the

Marine Corps, the small force of three LSTs and a lone escort destroyer sailed from Samoa. On the fifteenth they stopped in the Ellice Islands to rehearse the landing plans, albeit without troops. The new vehicles worked well; their unprotected radios failed almost immediately, an exact forecast of Tarawa.

In New Zealand Shoup could only assume that the new LVTs would reach Tarawa intact and in time. Knowing that assumptions are the hallmark of failed operations, he then prepared alternate ship-to-shore plans: one with the full complement of seventy-five Alligators and fifty Water Buffaloes, the other without the newcomers. Edson approved.

The two officers also looked for other means to reduce the vulnerability of their troops to Shibasaki's bristling defenses. They agreed to hit the six-hundred-yard pier just before H-Hour, with Hawkins's scout-sniper platoon to eliminate defilade fire against the oncoming LVTs. Encouraged by the Fiji tests, they similarly planned to bring the Sherman medium tanks ashore early, putting them in the fifth assault wave. And both Edson and Shoup placed high hopes on the intra-theater request submitted during the Honolulu conference for the Seventh Air Force to drop "daisy-cutters" on Betio early on D-Day. The standard Liberator bomb was a five-hundred pounder. Each daisy-cutter contained a ton of high explosives, fused to detonate just above the ground. The Marines figured such bombs would wipe out many of the exposed Japanese antiaircraft crews as well as any troops being moved from the stronger southern shore to reinforce against the Marine landing on the north.[36]

It was time for the Marines to leave New Zealand. They did so with universal regret. For the 2d Marine Division, New Zealand represented an interlude of felicity between the green hell of Guadalcanal's jungles and the white hell of Tarawa's blazing beaches. Nearly six hundred Marines took New Zealand wives; almost everyone in the division counted lasting friendships among the population. The troops tried to make light of their pending departure, saying "Bye, bye, Mama, we're off to Yokohama!"

The 2d Marine Division left New Zealand with difficulty for

other reasons too. Embarkation, the arcane science of combat loading to support the scheme of maneuver ashore, is a skill that cannot be finessed, and a labor strike by New Zealand dockworkers in the middle of the load out did not help. Many fresh lieutenants learned about embarkation the hard way—on the job. Recalled Lt. Peter Lake of the 6th Marines: "We had a rather short time to meet the schedule—the orders were to load the damn stuff or else. The docks were jammed with supplies and gear. The old first in, last out rule was forgotten. It was really chaos and we barely made the deadline—I'm sure some of the ships were listing when they left port."[37]

The division took elaborate measures to enhance operational security at the end. Julian Smith and Harry Hill scheduled a long-anticipated, division-level landing exercise in Hawkes Bay and even arranged host nation support in terms of aircraft, trucks, and a big dance at the end. The ruse may have worked for a day or two. The Southern Attack Force sailed on 1 November 1943, the same day the 3d Marine Division landed on Bougainville. The veterans quickly realized they were steaming away from Hawkes Bay. Seabee Petty Officer William J. Morgan wrote in his diary, "Here we go at last. . . . Nobody knows where."[38]

Even Tokyo Rose was quiet at first. Two days later she was as impudent as ever, announcing over the radio, "There are a hundred ships under way from New Zealand, and Japanese submarines have a torpedo waiting for every one of them." The convoy indeed encountered a Japanese submarine leaving New Zealand. Extended depth-charge attacks by the convoy's escorts ended the threat but not the general uneasiness. "All I can think of is war, and I can't write you about it," Julian Smith said in a departure letter to his wife.[39]

AT TARAWA SOME OF ADMIRAL SHIBASAKI'S defensive readiness had begun to unravel. The command reached a peak of combat preparedness around the middle of September. Betio's airfield hosted eighteen naval aircraft, principally Type 96 twin-engined, mid-winged, medium-range bombers (which the Americans called "Nell-23s"). Then, on

18–19 September, the Americans struck the Gilberts with a fury. Seventh Air Force bombers and Navy carrier planes conducted the first large-scale air attacks of the campaign, bom-

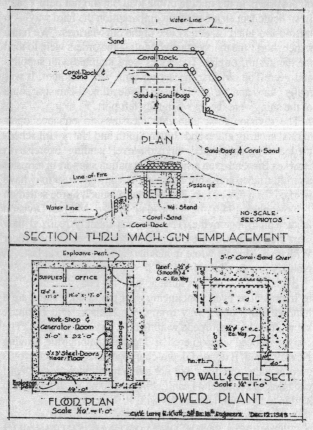

Schematic drawings of Japanese fortifications drawn on the scene by Carpenter's Mate Klatt of the 3d Battalion (Seabees), 18th Marines. The top drawing portrays one of many small machine-gun emplacements built on Betio. The bottom drawing reflects how the shortage of reinforcing steel hindered Japanese construction efforts just before the battle. In this case, although the ceiling of the power plant exceeded five feet in thickness, the lower three feet were totally unsupported.

LARRY E. KLATT; MARINE CORPS COMBAT ART COLLECTION

barding Betio, Makin, and Nauru.[40] The air raids damaged Betio heavily. As recorded by an artilleryman in Shibasaki's command: "The island is a sea of flames. . . . Seven of our medium attack bombers were destroyed and a great number of our guns were damaged. . . . A great number of men were killed and wounded." A survivor of the 755th Naval Air Group on Betio reported extensive damage to communications facilities, mentioning plans to build a bomb-proof, concrete transmitting station by October. The *Ikuta Maru* was expected to deliver building supplies, he said.[41]

The September air strikes against the Gilberts produced four benefits for the Americans. They marked the last regular use of Tarawa as a Japanese airbase; they caused Admiral Koga to sortie the Combined Fleet from Truk in anticipation of an American invasion; they produced yet another outstanding series of aerial photographs of Tarawa; and they revealed the general weakness of Betio's antiaircraft fire. As JICPOA reported on 1 October, "There is no central control over the batteries, no attempt is made to establish a standing barrage, and fire is of moderate intensity and inaccurate."[42]

Shibasaki had more problems. The bombers blew up the island hospital, and he could no longer effectively treat the many members of the garrison who fell ill to the combination of hard labor and canned food. With great reluctance, he allowed his gifted engineer, Lieutenant Murikami, to return to Japan with several hundred acutely sick troops and laborers.

But what Shibasaki most needed was a massive resupply of construction material. For months he had looked in vain for a cargo ship like the *Ikuta Maru* to bring cement and steel reinforcing bars and steel rails for tetrahedrons. His "Gilberts Area Defense Force Operations Order #19" of 20 October 1943 contains frequent references to "when the cement arrives" or "until the materials are sent." Shibasaki had ambitious projects to complete, from "shellproofing the commanding officer's combat command post" to fabricating forty-five hundred obstacles to cover Betio's "8,000 meters coastline."[43]

After the battle, Warrant Officer Kiyoshi Ota told his interrogators that "the weak point in the defensive installations was that all the pillboxes were not yet converted to concrete." Indeed, American forces found no concrete whatsoever among Betio's otherwise ample stores. Still other construction material seemed in critically short supply. Some Marines reported that the Japanese had used lengths of chain in the absence of reinforcing bars. In another example of makeshift construction, the Japanese covered Betio's power plant with a concrete slab roof *five* feet thick. But when Larry Klatt and the 3/18 Seabees examined the structure, they found the garrison had rationed their remaining steel reinforcing bars almost to the point of disaster. According to Klatt, the Japanese builders put the re-bar "in the compression face, or top, of the slab instead of in the tension face, or bottom, which was the reverse of good engineering practice. There were thirty-seven inches of free-hanging concrete without a bar in it."[44]

Few Marines or Seabees at Tarawa at the time were yet aware of the tightening ring being applied by U.S. submarines against Japanese merchant ships in the Central Pacific. Shibasaki's supply ship would never arrive.

Admiral King's "whipsaw strategy" also came into effect at this time. The Japanese knew a major American invasion loomed, but they could not tell whether the main thrust would be in the South Pacific or the Central Pacific, hardly imagining that two main efforts would be launched in both theaters within three weeks of each other.

Admiral Koga had difficulty covering all approaches. Another flurry of intelligence signals in mid-October prompted him to sortie a significant task force of three carriers, six battleships, and eleven cruisers to Eniwetok and beyond toward Wake Island. The force found no sign of an American fleet. Fatefully, Koga then concluded that American activity in the Central Pacific was likely a ruse, an attempt to distract the Combined Fleet while the enemy struck a major blow toward Rabaul. Koga dispatched 173 planes from Carrier Division I to Rabaul, followed by a large number of heavy cruisers.

These forces stepped into a buzz saw. U.S. Navy carrier aircraft from Rear Adm. Frederick C. "Ted" Sherman's Task Force 38 struck Rabaul on 5 November and again on the eleventh (assisted by Rear Adm. Alfred E. Montgomery's Task Group 50.3, loaned by Nimitz). The two strikes severely damaged most of the cruisers and shot down well over a hundred of Koga's skilled carrier pilots. Admiral Fukudome stated the devastating strategic impact of these losses. "Fleet air strength was almost completely lost, and although the Gilberts fight appeared to be the last chance for a decisive battle, the fact that the fleet's air strength had been so badly depleted enabled us to send only very small air support to Tarawa."[45]

THE SENIOR COMMANDERS INVOLVED IN GAL-vanic did not realize the significance of the Rabaul action until after the campaign. There would be plenty of Japanese submarine threats and a few air raids each night, but the mighty Combined Fleet would not sortie in the absence of its protecting carrier aviation units. Not knowing any of this, the Marines and sailors of the Southern Attack Force generally cussed Admiral Montgomery's task group for missing the rehearsal landings at Efate. It would have been helpful to have the aviators participate, because the rehearsal was generally a sterile affair. The troops landed on one beach, the gunfire ships shelled another; there was no air support; neither the tanks nor the LVTs were allowed ashore; the new LVT-2 Water Buffaloes were still far away. Major Jones did take the opportunity to exercise his condom fleet, putting LT 1/6 afloat in the rubber boats amid the catcalls of the bystanders. The division scouts also practiced going ashore in rubber boats, time well spent. The main ship-to-shore landing went smoothly, under the circumstances.

Edson criticized the LVT crews for hitting the beach five minutes early, saying "early arrival of waves [is] inexcusable; late arrival [is] preferable." The follow-on landing boats grounded seventy-five yards from the beach, an easy wade for the troops jumping over the sides. Rear Adm. Howard F. Kingman, commanding the fire support group, made his forgettable boast that he would "obliterate" Betio by naval gunfire. A dozen combat correspondents joined the force. Some, like Sherrod, had already seen more combat than half the officers and troops assembled in Efate.[46]

One event at Efate had a great impact on the bloody battle to come. Gen. Julian Smith summarily relieved Col. William M. Marshall of command of the 2d Marines—the combat team with the most pivotal role to fill in the Tarawa assault—and replaced him with David Shoup. Such measures are never done lightly. Shoup was still a lieutenant colonel, twenty years younger than Marshall, a novice in combat command. Initial reports indicated that Marshall took sick, or suffered a heart attack. Edson's letter to Col. Gerald C. Thomas at Marine Corps headquarters implied other reasons. "We relieved Bill Marshall of command of the 2d Marines at the rehearsal area," Edson wrote, "and gave that Regiment to Shoup. It had become increasingly evident that Bill could not carry the ball. . . ." Julian Smith used blander words in a post-battle letter to the commandant, reporting that "Marshall broke down completely, which we were prepared for and replaced him by Shoup."[47]

Captain Williams, a company commander in LT 1/2, recalled that the troops regarded Colonel Marshall fondly, calling him "Uncle Bill" as a term of endearment. Williams understood that Marshall's problems with Julian Smith and Edson came to a head when Marshall fell asleep during the critique of the first rehearsal landing, then failed to answer specific questions about the regiment's role in the forthcoming assault satisfactorily. In an interview late in his life with Clay Barrow, Julian Smith repeated the claim that Marshall suffered a nervous breakdown. The 2d Marines muster roll for November supports a medical basis for Marshall's relief. The colonel left the regiment on 8 November for a field hospital in Efate, then rode a ship back to the regional hospital in New Zealand, a regrettably short exit from the campaign.[48]

Julian Smith promoted Shoup to colonel on the spot, gave him Colonel Goen as executive officer, and sent him off to find his regimental headquarters on board the USS *Zeilin* (APA 3). Assuming command of a regiment is not an easy undertaking, even in garrison. Shoup found it particularly demanding to exert the power of his personality over the sprawling Combat Team Two embarked on several ships and distracted by their own concerns for the immediate future. Julian Smith did not worry. Shoup had shown he was tough and resourceful.

Once the Southern Attack Force left Efate, Admiral Hill ordered the various ships to break out the landing plans and tell the troops where they were heading. The announcement of Tarawa as the next objective surprised most of the men. Many had wagered the task force was on its way to Wake Island, a place where the Marines had a score to settle with the Special Naval Landing Forces. Unit commanders quickly pointed out the plentiful opportunities available with the rikusentai waiting at Betio. Petty Officer Morgan was older than most others in the landing force and expressed concern in his diary about their orders. "This is to be a hell of a mess," he wrote, "and we will no doubt have our asses shot off."[49]

Julian Smith had experienced the "half-life" of a warrior's prolonged movement to contact nearly thirty years earlier in Mexican waters. "It does not seem real to me at all," he wrote Happy after leaving Efate, "but that was the same way at Vera Cruz [1914], just like any other day until we got ashore and were in the fight. The next time we land we will go in shooting."[50]

Sherrod rode the *Zeilin* to Tarawa with Shoup. After hearing much heady talk about "obliteration" and "another Kiska," Sherrod sought a dose of reality from the new regimental commander. "Shoup says we may have to wade ashore," Sherrod jotted in his field notebook. Shoup told Sherrod he hoped to use the first empty amtracs as a shuttle service between the beach and the reef if the boats could not cross. Sherrod also found some veteran NCOs who had a healthy respect for the task ahead. "The Japs are the damnedest diggers in the world," a sergeant said, adding, "It's like pulling a tick out of a rug to get one out of his hole."[51]

As the Southern Attack Force drew closer to the Gilberts, Seventh Air Force bombers from the new bases in the Ellice Islands joined with carrier air groups to pound Betio, Makin, and Nauru for a solid week. Kelly Turner sent a force of heavy cruisers ahead to Tarawa on 19 November, D-Day-minus-1, to battle the coastal defense guns. By this time Shibasaki,

Kobayashi, and Koga all knew a major invasion force was storming into the Gilberts. The previous day Lt. Kichi Yoshuyo, IJN, had radioed a breathless contact report after his maritime air patrol. "Enemy fleet sighted . . . several carriers and others too numerous to mention."[52]

Shibasaki already had his hands full with the swarms of enemy air strikes. The heavy expenditure of 13-mm ammunition by his AA gunners during the week (51,160 rounds, nearly three-fourths of his total stock at Tarawa) alarmed him greatly. He needed these weapons fully armed for their central role in the ground defensive fire plan. Shibasaki sent an urgent message back through his chain of command. "We must quickly replenish ammo for the 13-mm machine guns on Tarawa and Makin." It was already too late.[53]

Shibasaki nevertheless still dealt from a position of strength. According to the *3d Special Base Defense Force Wartime Diary*, the admiral commanded the following forces on Tarawa before the battle:[54]

Unit	Officers	Men	Total
3d Special Base Defense Force	41	861	902
Sasebo 7th SNLF	61	1608	1669
755th Air Group Detachment	0	30	30
111th Construction Unit	?	2000	2000
Total	102	4499	4601

Historians Philip A. Crowl and Edmund G. Love examined the Japanese preparations for the American invasion and concluded that "Tarawa was the most heavily defended atoll that would ever be invaded by Allied forces in the Pacific. With the possible exception of Iwo Jima, its beaches were better protected against a landing force than any encountered in any theater of war throughout World War II."[55]

Petty Officer Morgan's final diary entry before the battle

seemed to sense the forbidding task ahead. "We are going against the Jap Marines, the Imperial Guard."[56]

On the night before D-Day, Gen. Julian Smith sent a message to the officers and men of the division, asking that it be read over the public address systems of the various ships. The troops stirred in their crowded compartments to hear his words coming over the loudspeakers. "A great offensive to destroy the enemy in the Central Pacific has begun. Our Navy screens our operation and will support our attack tomorrow with the greatest concentration of aerial bombardment and naval gunfire in the history of warfare. It will remain with us until our objective is secured. . . . Garrison troops are already en route to relieve us as soon as we have completed the job. . . . Good luck and God bless you all."[57]

Smith then penned a final note to Happy, saying, "It is now in the hands of Providence and the fighting hearts of the Marines." It was about to become a squad-leader's battle.[58]

CHAPTER FIVE

Into the Gates of Hell

*The Marines have a way of making you afraid
—not of dying, but of not doing your job.*
—First Lt. Bonnie Little, USMCR (killed on D-Day),
last letter to his wife

THE THREE LSTS BEARING THEIR VALUABLE
cargo of new LVT-2 Water Buffaloes approached Tarawa atoll
in the early morning darkness of D-Day. On board the *LST
243*, 1st Lt. Wallace E. "Wally" Nygren mounted his lead
amtrac and circled his arm over his head. At this signal, each
Marine driver started his Continental air-cooled radial engine.
As Nygren recalled the scene: "Then the ship's anchor chain
rattled. We were at our station. Slowly the bow doors swung
open and I could smell the tropic air. The upraised ramp in
front of me fell forward into the water and there lay the dark
and heaving ocean. Every crew chief stood tensed on his gun
platform watching me. I gave the arm signal 'forward.' We
rushed down the ramp into the water. Correct timing was
important. If you hit the ramp on the upward roll, it could break
under the weight of the tractor."[1]

The *LST 243* launched all seventeen LVTs in fifteen minutes, reflecting good teamwork between the ship and the LVT
crews. Now came the hard part. The complex landing plan
required Nygren's reinforced platoon to find certain Higgins
boats carrying assault troops of LT 2/2 from the *Zeilin* in the
darkness, conduct a cross-deck (gunwale-to-gunwale) transfer,
and land them on Red Beach Two. Simplicity is the essence of
good amphibious planning. At Tarawa, the combination of
last-minute arrival of the LSTs, physical separation of assault
troops from their amtracs, choppy seas, and Japanese preemp-

106

tive shelling created enough "friction of war" to disrupt David Shoup's overly complicated plan.[2]

Lieutenant Nygren knew the general direction in which the *Zeilin* lay from the LSTs, but the third-quarter moon provided little visibility from his low-riding LVT, already rolling uncomfortably in the westerly swells. Unknown to the amtrackers, Admiral Hill had ordered the transports to shift anchorages to preclude masking the fire of his gun support ships. Many Marines were still struggling down the cargo nets into the Higgins boats tied up alongside when the transports abruptly weighed anchor. The small craft bobbed along behind the underway ships like abandoned ducklings in a farm pond.

To this point Operation Galvanic had progressed smoothly. By paying strict attention to operational security and communications discipline, the Americans had covertly assembled the entire Central Pacific Force in the Gilberts from many directions, thus attaining strategic surprise. And while the Japanese knew from D-Day-minus-2 that a huge invasion fleet had entered the Central Pacific, they were still unsure of its objectives.

The American preliminary air strikes hit islands throughout the Gilberts and eastern Marshalls. Admiral Kobayashi launched every possible long-range aircraft at his command to search for the American task force, including eleven Navy bombers of the 755th Air Group that landed briefly on Betio's airstrip—leaving just before the aerial and surface bombardment of November nineteenth. But these intense patrols were of little value to Kobayashi. In the end, it was Admiral Shibasaki's worried sentries on Betio who discovered the location and objective of the American fleet. The Southern Attack Force was at hand.[3]

The Japanese initiated the battle of Tarawa, opening up with their big coastal defense guns at 0507. Admiral Hill reacted with counterbattery fire from the battleships *Maryland* (BB 46) and *Colorado* (BB 45), impressive shooting at considerable range. Fourteen-inch shells from the battleships hit the magazine for one of the 8-inch batteries, producing a spectacular fireball and a series of secondary explosions.

This initial exchange of fire provided a memorable experience for the men in the transports and the hundreds of small craft well within range of the Japanese guns. Once again, the transports retreated, leaving the boats and LVTs behind. As Lieutenant Nygren recalled: "A large waterspout shot up into the air immediately ahead of us. I could see other huge splashes to the sides. [We heard] the unmistakable sounds of large shells screaming over our heads. We were being shelled from the island!"[4]

The small craft found themselves as much in jeopardy from the fleeing ships as from the Japanese shells. "Dark shapes loomed up out of the night and crossed our bows," said Nygren. "We were in danger of being run down by our own ships." In the confusion that ensued, several Marine and Navy officers would blame the "A-1" Company for having their LVT-2s out of position, but the point is academic. The situation might have been eased had the LVT-2s been available at Efate for the rehearsal landings. On the other hand, given the restrictive circumstances and the Japanese fire, it is a wonder the Southern Attack Force ever launched the ship-to-shore movement at Betio.[5]

Navy control officers finally marshaled the loaded Higgins boats into some semblance of order and led them back toward the LST rendezvous spot. Nygren saw the craft materialize out of the darkness, "a hodge-podge mess, looking for amtracs. . . . I looked for boat signs indicating Red Beach Two-Second Wave. I could see none. It was going to be catch-as-catch can."[6]

Cross-decking heavily laden infantrymen between boats and tractors in the choppy seas took time, but it went well. Then the LVTs seemed to circle endlessly, waiting for the signal to move toward the line of departure. The Marines found this to be an ordeal in itself. The LVTs barely maintained steerageway, a rough ride for nervous troops trying to digest a heavy, prebattle breakfast of steak and eggs. The amtrackers and troop leaders had it better, riding up front, braced against the swells, breathing fresh air instead of exhaust fumes. They also had a front row seat to watch "the heaviest bombardment of the war." Battleships, cruisers, and destroyers pounded the island, sending huge columns of smoke skyward. Amid all this, the sun rose, red and ominous.

Finally, Navy control officers led the LVTs in long columns from the "revised" transport area toward the line of departure: the LVT-1 Alligators—the first wave—on the right, the LVT-2s guiding to their left. Rough seas punished the vehicles and sprayed their vulnerable radio sets; few LVTs retained operational communications beyond this point. The LVTs, crowded with troops and burdened by the weight of their improvised armor plating, could not achieve the planned 4.5-knot speed of advance. Their route, nearly ten miles through the lagoon to the northern beaches of Betio, would demand the utmost of primitive assault vehicles. Never again would the Navy-Marine Corps team undertake such a prodigious ship-to-shore odyssey with LVTs. At Tarawa they had no choice. Betio had to be assaulted first; only the lagoon beaches offered a fighting chance, and Japanese coastal defense guns prevented a closer transport area.[7]

While the columns of amtracs battled the westerly headwinds, Admiral Hill ordered his minesweeper task unit to sweep and mark the entrance to the atoll lagoon. These four ships—the destroyers *Ringgold* (DD 500) and *Dashiell* and the minesweepers *Pursuit* (AM 108) and *Requisite* (AM 109)— had the most hazardous mission of the task force. Underwater demolition teams would have helped, but these stealthy reconnaissance units were not operational in the Pacific in time for Galvanic. While the Americans possessed fair intelligence about Japanese mines around Betio, no one knew what to expect at the mouth of the lagoon. Here the foreign legion of accompanying sea captains really paid dividends.

Lieutenants James Forbes, Gordon Webster, and Stanley Page of the Royal New Zealand Naval Reserve served as pilots on board the endangered flotilla, guiding them safely into the shallow waters under heavy fire. The *Pursuit* led the way, entering the lagoon at 0620 at ten knots, followed by the *Requisite*. The two craft swept a channel three hundred yards wide and twenty feet deep. Surprisingly, they found no mines. The craft then steamed to a point six thousand yards north of Betio to mark the line of departure. Two accompanying landing craft from the USS *Monrovia* (APA 31) provided smoke-screen protection during this approach, but Japanese gun crews had opened a steady fire, including one of the twin 5.5-inch batteries on the eastern tip. Thirty to forty rounds landed within two hundred yards of the *Pursuit*; one clipped off her jackstaff. The minesweepers bravely returned fire with their 3-inch mounts, but they clearly needed help.[8]

The *Ringgold* and *Dashiell* rushed into the channel at this time like two well-armed lawmen entering a tough saloon. The former hoisted her battle colors and led the way at fifteen knots, immediately drawing fire. The Japanese 5.5-inch battery nailed the *Ringgold* with two quick hits in succession. One struck her after engine room at the waterline, starboard side; the other hit the forward torpedo mount and sliced through the deckhouse and sick bay. Neither round exploded. The *Ringgold* closed to within two thousand yards of the beach, guns blazing. Within the first hour, in spite of touching bottom in shoal water, she fired 325 rounds from her 5-inch/38 gun mounts.[9]

The *Dashiell* entered the lagoon a minute behind the *Ringgold*. Her crew could clearly count twelve Japanese batteries on Betio firing at them. The *Dashiell* dodged frequent near misses and suffered one casualty to shrapnel while shooting 264 rounds of counterbattery fire. Japanese major-caliber fire diminished, although it would continue intermittently throughout the remainder of the long day.[10]

The small ships had done their work. The lagoon was as safe as it would ever be. The minesweeper *Pursuit*, now serving as primary control ship for the ship-to-shore movement, pointed her searchlight back toward the swept channel to provide a beacon through the heavy smoke and dust for the assault waves.

While this portion of the assault plan worked well, Admiral Hill had his hands full trying to coordinate the preliminary bombardment. The flagship *Maryland* paid a price for her role in the initial counterbattery fire. The shock of her main batteries firing knocked out the fragile communications circuitry installed at the last moment to convert the resurrected Pearl Harbor victim into an amphibious force flagship. For a critical period on D-Day morning Hill could not communicate with either his aviators or the ship-to-shore control officers. By that time, the *Maryland* was ten miles offshore. Neither Hill nor Julian Smith could directly influence the battle.

The D-Day plan established H-Hour at 0830. Aircraft from the carriers would kick off the action with a half-hour bombing raid at 0545. Then the fire support ships would bombard the island for the ensuing 130 minutes. The planes would return for a final strafing run at H-Hour-minus-5 minutes, then shift to inland targets as the Marines stormed ashore. None of this worked according to plan. Admiral Shibasaki's preemptive fire demanded immediate counterbattery missions and necessitated the second shift of the transport area. With the Japanese fire seemingly suppressed, Hill ordered a cease-fire over the TBS (Talk Between Ships) circuit at 0542 in anticipation of the air strike. A long silence followed.

The carrier air group had changed their plans, postponing their strike by thirty minutes to allow sunlight to illuminate the

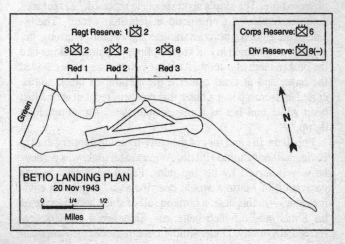

tiny island. Admiral Turner approved the change, but no one told Admiral Hill, the amphibious task force commander. Hill, baffled by the no-show and perplexed by his sudden inability to communicate with the carriers, held the cease-fire in effect for twenty-three minutes, waiting anxiously for the planes to appear. This lapse gave Admiral Shibasaki an unexpected grace period to redeploy forces and organize damage control teams against the raging fires. Hill, in a great rage, ordered his ships to resume fire at 0605. Murphy's Law applied: the planes appeared five minutes later, made several noisy passes over the island, then disappeared. Hill and Smith realized the ships would have to deliver the brunt of the preparatory pounding.

The subsequent bombardment was a sight to behold. To the Marines in the amtracs or still aboard ship it appeared that perhaps Admiral Kingman had been right: the Southern Attack Force would indeed obliterate Betio. Sherrod thought, "Surely, no mortal men could live through such destroying power . . . any Japs on the island would all be dead by now." Master Sgt. Roger M. Emmons, serving with the Marine detachment on board the USS *Tennessee* (BB 43), watched as the island became completely obscured by smoke and dust, limiting observed fire. The ship's spotting plane reported, "Target area completely black." Correspondent Johnston wrote: "The inside of the lagoon was like a smoldering volcano. The long, flat island was canopied in smoke, its splintered palms looking like the broken teeth of a comb. At many points orange fire studded the haze, and at dead center a great spiral of black smoke curled up from a pulsing blaze that now was red, but at first had been white and hot as a magnesium flare. An ammunition dump."[11]

For all the fire and fury of the early-morning gunnery duel at Betio, neither Admiral Hill nor Admiral Shibasaki was particularly well served by his big guns. Faced with what a later generation of Marines would describe as a "target-rich environment"—in this case, a horizon full of ships within range of his 8-inch and 5.5-inch batteries—Shibasaki's gunners performed abysmally. Under similar circumstances the American defenders of Wake Island in the recent past and the Japanese defenders of Tinian in the near future would inflict grievous hits on the invasion fleet.

Discounting the near misses, the coastal defense guns on Betio hit only one ship, the *Ringgold*, with two rounds—both duds. The battleship *Colorado* closed to within two thousand yards of the southern reef to deliver near point-black fire in the initial duel with the shore batteries. The USS *Anderson* (DD 411), escorting the battleship, reported that "*Colorado* maintained little more than steerageway during this period, and it is almost uncanny in that she was not hit."[12]

Japanese gunners also shot poorly at extended ranges, according to the commanding officer of the USS *Salt Lake City* (CA 25). "The Japanese fired hopelessly outranged 5-inch guns . . . nullifying their excellent camouflage." Admiral Hill concurred. "Given his assets and our nearly dead-in-the-water targets, the rate and volume of his fire was remarkably low and the accuracy poor."[13]

With the notable exception of the sharpshooting counter-battery fire by his battleships in the opening salvos, Admiral Hill could not have been pleased with the accuracy and effectiveness of his own heavy guns. Indeed, the failure of the preliminary bombardment on D-Day to reduce substantially the Japanese strong points along the northern beaches became the most critical shortcoming of the battle. Two overestimations came into effect here. Hardly a soul in the bombardment force had any experience whatsoever trying to destroy fortified positions, yet all hands expected the sheer weight of powder and steel to prevail, regardless. The second factor concerned an exaggerated fear of counterattack by Japanese surface and submarine forces.

These were valid concerns. The Southern Attack Force knew of the recent swarming Japanese counterattacks against the American landings at Empress Augusta Bay three weeks earlier. They did not know (or failed to appreciate) the significance of the American spoiling attacks that destroyed so many Imperial Navy aircraft at Rabaul, thereby immobilizing the most dangerous ships of the Combined Fleet. Speed of execution remained the overriding principle; vigilance against counterattack remained the corollary. This is why the battleships and cruisers of the Central Pacific Force maintained at least a third of their magazines in reserve for surface action. And this explains Admiral Turner's decision to assign four battleships to pound lightly defended Makin and only three to Tarawa. Turner figured any Japanese surface attack would hit Makin first.

The bombardment force at Betio made errors in range, deflection, trajectory, ammunition selection, and fuse settings. Many salvos missed the island entirely. Noted one after-action analyst, "A very large number of shells were falling into the water close to shore." Other miscalculations produced countless ricochets, visible to observers far removed from the atoll. Lt. Raymond F. Myers, USNR, the fighter director officer on the USS *Bunker Hill* (CV 17), recalled his amazement at seeing large-caliber naval shells impact far at sea—ricochets from the battleships, not Japanese fire. Lt. Bob Hanger of Fox Battery, 2/10, remembered watching "half the projectiles ricochet out to sea and explode in the ocean." For those closer to the island, ricochets were downright scary. As the *Anderson* reported: "The splashes of the 'overs' plus the ricochets, of which there were one or two in each salvo, were plainly visible in the lagoon. . . . That no damage resulted to own forces is considered wholly a matter of good luck. . . . At times there were four ricochets from a five-gun salvo."[14]

The Japanese garrison found the bombardment terrifying but endurable. Warrant Officer Ota rode out the storm in a concrete, log, and sand bunker. "The bombardment was violent beyond expression," he later wrote, "a frightening and horrifying experience! It went on and on, without ceasing; the shriek and rumble of heavy shells and the terrific explosions. . . . My position received a direct hit but none of us were wounded; we were only buried by sand."[15]

The Marines in the wallowing LVTs—wet, scared, seasick—were oblivious to any deficiencies in the bombardment.

Clouds of black smoke and brown dust marked the location of Betio off the starboard side. Maybe, many thought, this was going to be a cakewalk after all. But the LVTs could not maintain the schedule, the long columns beating against the westerly current and headwind, guiding on the older, slower LVT-1 Alligators of the first wave. Hill and Julian Smith reluctantly postponed H-Hour from 0830 to 0845. A few minutes later they postponed it again to 0900. Sorry communications prevented all players from getting the word. The columns of LVTs finally executed a flanking movement and turned toward the distant beaches.

At 0824 the first line of amtracs swept past the *Pursuit* across the line of departure, still six thousand yards from touchdown. A minute later, precisely on schedule for the original H-Hour,

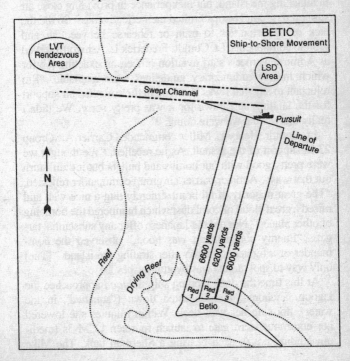

the second group of carrier aircraft roared over Betio. Kelly Turner had tried to instill flexibility in his component commanders in the Fifth Amphibious Force with this guidance: "Times of strafing beaches with reference to H-hour are approximate; the distance of the boats from the beach is the governing factor." The instructions did not stick. Hill had to abort the air strike for another half hour. The planes remained on station, but with depleted levels of fuel and ordnance.[16]

The much ballyhooed "obliteration" proved a bust. Although air and naval bombardment improved sharply as the battle progressed, neither supporting arm contributed significantly during the preliminary stage. Air support was particularly disappointing on D-Day morning. The pilots flying SBDs, SB2Cs, and TBFs displayed valor and aggressiveness in attacking the island, but inexperience in providing close air support to ground troops limited their effectiveness. So did the lack of opportunities to train or rehearse between air and ground components. Lt. Comdr. Frederick L. Ashworth served as Admiral Turner's staff aviation officer, an exacting job for which merely rudimentary guidelines were available. "I'm reluctant to say that I was involved in the so-called air support for the landing at Tarawa for it was pretty sorry. We didn't really know what we were doing."[17]

Lt. Comdr. Henry L. Miller commanded Carrier Air Group 23 in support of the assault. As he recalled, "We thought we were pretty good with our bombs and bullets but it didn't turn out that way." Another carrier air group commander reflected, "The great majority of all bombs merely dug a nice well and raised a great cloud of coral dust which hampered the bombing of other planes." Nor did the Japanese offer any substantial targets. "Enemy concealment was good," observed the commander of a fighter squadron after strafing the island. "[The] only way to spot targets was by gun-flashes."[18]

At this time the dock landing ship *Ashland* approached the lagoon, anchored, and ballasted down ("squatted" in the water), flooding her well deck. Within minutes she lowered her enormous stern gate to launch fourteen LCM-3s (medium landing craft), each bearing a Sherman tank. The Mike boats followed their guide toward the *Pursuit* on the line of departure.

Colonel Shoup had no intention of commanding his reinforced combat team from a safe distance. The first page in the field notebook Shoup carried contained two entries, probably written during the Pearl Harbor conference the month before. One comment was vintage Shoup: "Go ashore." Well before 0800 Shoup led his regimental headquarters group down the slippery cargo nets from the *Zeilin* into an LCVP secured to the sea painter alongside. "We get in LCVP," he wrote in his journal, "strain to see, to get messages. Rough, wet, overfull." His journey from the *Zeilin* to Red Beach Two would take nearly five hours that morning.[19]

Interestingly, the other first-page comment in Shoup's field notebook concerned the two-thousand-pound daisy-cutter bombs he expected the Seventh Air Force to drop on Betio. "Request Daisy Cutters all along Red Beach Center between airfield and north edge of island." Shoup may very well have been "straining to see" if the B-24s were, in fact, delivering this heavy ordnance, valued for its above-ground wallop. But no Liberators arrived over Betio on D-Day, and no such bombs ever hit the island.

Moreover, Seventh Air Force records contain no evidence of such a request from either the 2d Marine Division or the V Amphibious Corps. The often-told story that the bombers took off from the Ellice Islands loaded with daisy cutters for Betio—only to abort the mission when the flight leader crashed—cannot be substantiated by Air Force archives. The Seventh Air Force, which "flew the longest missions against the smallest targets in the war in support of the Central Pacific campaign," would not have dodged this mission. The probable explanation: the tasking request, having to zigzag across the Pacific through the convoluted chain of command, never got in the right hands. The landing force, already handicapped by inexpert naval and air bombardment, would have benefited immensely from even a few such bombs—anything to take out the uncovered firing positions of the dual-purpose 75-mm and 13-mm gun crews.[20]

The assault troops, unaware of this additional setback, now had the smoking island in sight. The amtracs chugged forward in three ragged lines. Forty-two LVT-1s comprised the first wave; twenty-four LVT-2s, the second; and twenty-one LVT-2s, the third. Shoup had a lot of eggs in one basket, risking fifteen hundred Marines on the assumption that his amtracs would negotiate the fringing reef as they had at Fiji.

Japanese antiaircraft guns on Betio began firing airbursts over the advancing waves of LVTs. These were scary but harmless. The rikusentai gunners had overcharged the shells with explosives, nearly vaporizing the shrapnel. This represented a break for the Marines, for none of the LVTs had overhead covers. Proper airbursts by high explosive shells fired by Japanese 75-mm mountain guns would have killed many Marines. As it was, the troops were simply "doused with hot sand."[21]

On Betio Admiral Shibasaki tried to rally his troops to withstand the coming onslaught. Earlier, at 0559 (Tarawa time), he wired Admiral Kobayashi that he was under attack and that the Americans had launched landing craft. Admiral Koga, advised of this flash report, ordered the activation of *Hei* operation #3, the counterattack plan for the Gilberts. Two days earlier, with the first reports of the approaching invasion force, Koga had ordered nine *I*-class, long-range fleet submarines to the Gilberts from bases in the Carolines. These were already under way, the most effective counterforce Koga would produce. Meanwhile, Kobayashi began moving land-based air units into the Marshalls.

At 0930 on 20 November Shibasaki sent a second report:

Enemy is approaching all over the shore north of the pier, inside atoll, with more than one hundred amphibious tanks within visible sight. Later, 200 or more landing craft observed. Inside the atoll three [?] special type cruisers and four or more destroyers and minesweepers have entered and are making bombardment to cover the landing force. Other parts of the fleet are outside atoll. Visibility not very good and their movements are not very well known. Several tens of carrier planes and float planes are used by enemy for air superiority. All of our forces are in high morale, having decided to fight until death.[22]

On the *Maryland* Harry Hill knew the LVTs were still running late, but he had already postponed H-Hour twice, and he was afraid the smoke and dust would cause his gunfire to fall among the assault waves. At 0855 he ordered a cease-fire. Julian Smith and Red Mike Edson protested the decision vehemently; Hill would not budge. Shoup's assault waves would have to traverse the final fifteen hundred yards, the most vulnerable segment of their long approach, without benefit of naval gunfire support. And Shibasaki would receive a second grace period to move reinforcements across the island to meet the attack coming from the north.

Many military historians have softened their critique of Hill on this point, saying that at least the destroyers *Ringgold* and *Dashiell* maintained a hot fire throughout the landing, despite Hill's order. They did not. The action reports and deck logs of both ships reflect a rigid adherence to the cease-fire, with one brief exception. The *Dashiell* fired one three-minute mission on Betio's eastern tip from 0912 to 0915. The *Dashiell* otherwise cooled her heels in great frustration from 0855 until 0934, a period of thirty-nine minutes. The *Ringgold*'s guns remained silent for exactly an hour.[23]

The *Dashiell*'s officers were incensed. Why, they asked, could not the commanding officer of a fire support ship fifteen hundred yards off the beach give a better assessment of the naval gunfire needed to support the assault than the officer-in-tactical-command "who was over the horizon"? The two destroyers in the lagoon had already done more to soften the immediate landing beaches than the rest of the entire task force. Another half hour of direct fire against all three Red Beaches would have saved many American lives. It was not to be.[24]

The Americans in the lagoon had momentary hopes that the naval aviators would fill the gap. The orbiting strike group returned promptly at 0855, once again heeding their wristwatches instead of the progress of the landing waves. The planes no doubt caught some of Shibasaki's troops in the open, crossing the runway from south to north, but low fuel and ordnance limited their time on target to a few minutes at best. The beach approaches grew quiet.

"Because the naval bombardment had ceased," recalled Warrant Officer Ota, "we took advantage of the opportunity to position ourselves carefully, to emplace our machine gunners and riflemen in the best spots, and to rearrange our ammunition supplies to the best advantage. The enemy landing craft were fast approaching."[25]

The long pier dividing Red Beach Three and Two jutted out six hundred yards to the reef's edge and provided a landing site for all boats at any tidal stage. One Higgins boat detached itself from the approaching formation and sped directly for the end of the pier. With a fierce yell, Lieutenants Hawkins and Leslie led their scout-snipers and engineers onto the landing and swarmed up the ramp. Marines and rikusentai met hand-to-hand. The real battle of Tarawa had begun.

As the first wave of Alligators neared the reef, the Marines could watch the drama unfolding on the pierhead and see the rest of the smoking island waiting for them. Their first view of Betio proved unremarkable. The stubby Burns-Philp cargo pier, really only a high-tide wharf, appeared on the far left, marking the eastern edge of Red Beach Three. The main pier seemed to stretch forever, its walkway clearly swept by fire. To the right, just seaward of the reef and roughly marking the boundary between Red Two and Red One, sat the rusted hulk of the scuttled interisland steamer *Nimonea*. The lead wave broke perceptibly into its three components: the left, bearing Crowe's LT 2/8, swinging slightly southeast to clear the pier en route to Red Three; the center, bearing Amey's LT 2/2, bending slightly southwest toward Red Two; the right, bearing Schoettel's LT 3/2, bypassing the *Nimonea* to aim more directly for Red One. Japanese fire intensified. "Forget about a cakewalk!" someone said.

Suddenly the reef appeared, dead ahead. The Navy control

boats stopped, their job done. For a moment every man in the arena, Japanese and American, seemed to pause. The Alligators hit the coral hard, hesitated, then ground over it to waddle into the shallows beyond. The faster Water Buffaloes, no longer honoring the prescribed three-minute interval between waves, came right behind, slithering over the reef like so many ungainly otters. The assault plan, envisioned by Shoup and implemented by Major Drewes, worked like a charm. The sight of these metal monsters so easily crossing the reef unnerved the rikusentai. "We could see the American landing craft coming towards us like dozens of spiders scattering over the surface of the water," wrote Warrant Officer Ota. "One of my men exclaimed, 'THE GOD OF DEATH HAS COME!' "[26]

Lashed by their officers, the Japanese turned to their guns. The Americans, after all, were now in their preregistered killing zones. Every working weapon along the north and west shorelines (many of these completely untouched by the bombardment) blazed forth in fierce, interlocking bands of fire. The well-served 70-mm howitzers and 50-mm grenade throwers added a hail of plunging fire along the beach approaches.

Petty Officer Chuma's Type 88 dual-purpose 75-mm gun crew, ineffective against the fast-flying strike aircraft, now saw the opportunity for redemption. Firing from the deadly Pocket, the crew lowered the gun's long barrel to its minimum angle, minus ten degrees. The weapon could fire 15,200 yards at this angle; at 300 to 1,000 yards the crew could hardly miss. The Type 88 fired high explosive shells with a muzzle velocity of 2,450 feet per second. Chuma's crew sought to maintain a firing rate of fifteen rounds per minute, or one shot every four seconds. Four guns made up this battery.[27]

Warrant Officer Ota made his troops hold their fire until the Americans came within 150 yards of the beach. Then, "All our positions opened on the enemy landing craft with a tremendous volume of machine gun and rifle fire."[28]

Petty Officer Tadao Onuki, crew chief of a Type 95 light tank assigned to the 3d Special Base Defense Force, opened up with his 37-mm main gun. "There we broke our silence," he later related. "Under roaring fires, enemy craft wrecked, American soldiers went down one after another, went falling into the sea."[29]

The amtrackers were not exactly defenseless in those final minutes. Gunners in the first wave fired ten thousand rounds from their bow-mounted .50-caliber machine guns, hosing down the pier pilings and the beachfront, the only real suppression against the beach defenses of the morning. Some of the LVT-2s in the quickly intermingling second and third waves opened up with their heavy machine guns too. This was risky. The first wave LVT crews had their hands full with Japanese fire from the front and flanks; close overhead fire from their immediate rear was not welcome. At least one crewman in the lead wave fell with a .50-caliber round in his back.[30]

The final hundred yards to the beach seemed a kaleidoscope of violence to the amtrackers. Enemy troops suddenly appeared in plain sight. Captain Durand saw a Japanese officer standing defiantly on the seawall dead ahead, waving a pistol, "just daring us to come ashore." Lt. Norman E. Ward, leading six LVT-1s toward Red One, saw "Japs come out into the water, shooting and throwing grenades." These the Marines quickly dispatched. The real problem came from those more disciplined rikusentai who maintained their camouflaged and protected positions, firing point-blank at the thin-skinned LVTs.[31]

The Marines had the momentum. Touchdown times reflected the irregular shoreline and the intensity of enemy fire: 0910 on Red One, 0917 on Red Three, 0922 on Red Two. While Hawkins and Leslie held the distinction of the first Marines to engage the enemy at Betio, the crew of LVT-1 #49 ("My Deloris") would later claim to be the first to touch the island. PFC Edward J. Moore drove "My Deloris" that stormy morning. The Alligator served as right guide vehicle in Wave One on Red Beach One, hitting the beach squarely on "the Bird's Beak." Moore tried to force his LVT over the five-foot seawall, but the vehicle stalled in a near vertical position while machine guns riddled the cab. Moore reached for his rifle only to find it shot in half. He escaped the stricken vehicle but became a casualty within minutes.[32]

Very few of the LVTs could negotiate the vertical seawall. Stalled on the beach, the vehicles were immediately vulnerable to preregistered howitzer fire, as well as hand grenades lobbed into the open troop compartments by Japanese troops on the other side of the barrier. Cpl. John J. Spillane, a former short-stop prospect for the St. Louis Cardinals, served as crew chief for one Alligator jammed against the seawall on Red Two. Accounts vary, but Spillane caught at least two (and probably four) Japanese grenades barehanded in midair, tossing them hurriedly back over the wall. Nobody's luck lasted that long on Betio. The final grenade exploded in his hand, grievously wounding him, but he gave his embarked troops a few critical moments to scramble to relative safety along the seawall.

The second and third waves of LVT-2s, wearing their lighter armor plating and exposed to an increasing crescendo of fire, took a heavier pounding coming in. The 75-mm dual-purpose guns in the Pocket destroyed several in the shallows just offshore.

"The Americans appeared to be surprised and confused [by the intense fire]," recalled Warrant Officer Ota. "Many of the landing boats collided with each other." This happened to Private First Class Yancey, the former half-track gunner suddenly retrained as an LVT-2 machine gunner. His Water Buffalo collided with another in the wild dash toward Red Three; Yancey had to leave his gun and begin emergency bailing.[33]

Lieutenant Nygren's LVT-2 ran into Shibasaki's freshly planted obstacles during the approach sprint toward Red Two. As he remembered the scene:

> Ahead of us in the water loomed a barrier of concrete tetrahedron blocks with iron rails projecting outward. . . . The gaps [between obstacles] were closed by rows of barbed wire strung on posts. . . . the tractors had been forced together as we were funneled into the wire by the

concrete blocks. Major Drewes' tractor was only three feet to my right. I pointed to the water ahead, churned up by the enemy fire. He shook his head pessimistically. . . . We hit the wire head-on and tore it to shreds. We rolled towards the beach, dragging fifty feet of wire and posts behind us.[34]

PFC James A. Thompson got his first taste of combat that morning as an Alligator crewman in the first wave approaching Red Two. An infantryman stuck his head up between the two forward machine-gun stations to see the beach. "A single bullet struck him in the middle of the forehead and he collapsed in a heap at our feet." The Alligator made it to the beach. After a moment's hesitation, the embarked troops rolled over the sides and struggled for cover. The driver began backing off the beach, "wisely keeping the armored bow towards the fire."[35]

Other LVTs survived the gauntlet of Japanese fire to reach the beach intact. Lieutenant Key had no problem guiding his LVT-2 to Red Three on the initial run. Cpl. James C. Walker, crew chief on a Water Buffalo, lost two of his four crewmen but delivered his assault troops over Red Two. And Lieutenant Schneidmiller, the officer "shanghaied" in Samoa, made it safely through the maelstrom of Red One. Sgt. Floyd North's Alligator had a real head of steam by the time it hit Red Two and became one of only a few vehicles to traverse the seawall. As his LVT crunched inland, the .50-caliber machine gun snagged a thick enemy communications line and parted it. North stopped the vehicle at the edge of the taxiway and looked for other Marines. They were alone. "We were receiving gun fire from all directions. I told the driver to back down, and as we neared the seawall we hit a palm tree. We began receiving Japanese mortar fire, at which time we abandoned the amtrac." Whizzing shrapnel wounded North in three places.[36]

Lieutenant Nygren found being ashore on Red Two a dubious distinction. The Water Buffalo out of the water now represented a large, immobile target. Nearby rikusentai hosed it down with machine-gun fire. "Something hit me a tremendous blow and knocked me down. I sat sprawled on the gun platform, dazed. My right hand was a bloody mess. Tommy Kane [the driver] was also down, his leg spurting blood." Technical Sgt. Morris Wimer rushed forward to help. "The next minute he was down beside me, a bloody hole in his chest. . . . I was sure he was going to die."[37]

Nearby, Private First Class Thompson's Alligator caught the attention of Japanese machine gunners as the vehicle backed off Red Two and turned toward the reef. "Our engine stalled because bullets had ripped holes in the radiator. [Sgt. Vincent] Schondel and I crawled back into the engine room and took turns trying to start it with a hand crank. In the midst of this a shell burst over us, and I was splattered with shrapnel on my left side and abdomen. . . . Seconds later our gasoline tank ignited and the three of us went over the side."[38]

As grim a picture of loss and destruction that these accounts convey, the fact remains that the great tactical gamble of the 2d Marine Division succeeded beyond anyone's expectations. Logistical LVTs could indeed be converted into assault vehicles. Surprisingly, the Japanese knocked out only eight of the eighty-seven LVTs in the initial assault waves, most of these near the Pocket. Within a span of fifteen minutes, the 2d Amphibian Tractor Battalion succeeded in landing fifteen hundred Marines of Regimental Combat Team Two. Smith and Shoup could not have asked for better results.

Now came the hard part—maintaining the momentum of the assault. The tide would be no help. No boats would penetrate the reef for the first thirty hours of the battle. Shoup critically needed the off-loaded LVTs to return to the reef and conduct transfer line operations, cross-decking more troops and combat cargo from the Higgins and Mike boats. Here is where "the wheels came off" the landing plan. Japanese fire exacted an increasing toll among the LVTs. The 13-mm machine guns of the rikusentai easily penetrated the thin skins of the LVTs. Some of the hulls already resembled slabs of Swiss cheese. Fifteen LVTs, similarly peppered by this fire, recrossed the reef only to sink in deep water from the punctures. Others, like the vehicles crewed by Thompson and North, achieved the first leg of the mission only to be abandoned under intense fire. Many other vehicles, under way at full throttle for five hours by now, simply ran out of gas after touchdown, drifting into the killing zones.[39]

Heavy casualties among the assault troops once ashore made it necessary for other vehicles to serve as evacuation craft, further slowing the transfer line process. Cpl. Norman S. Moise's LVT made it safely to Red One, then tried to convey a load of wounded Marines back to the reef. An antiboat gun on Betio's west coast found the range. "A terrific blast splattered me onto the cargo deck." Moise, severely wounded, retained enough presence of mind to evacuate his wounded passengers and crew, then leapt from the burning vehicle. Japanese machine gunners from the reef stalked the survivors in the water. Moise made the unpleasant discovery that rikusentai gunners had somehow occupied the scuttled *Nimonea*.[40]

The few surviving LVTs that could execute the transfer line procedure played hell getting back ashore. Lieutenant Key's second trip became his last. His LVT-2 suffered a direct hit by plunging fire—probably from a 70-mm howitzer shell—as it nosed onto Red Two. The blast severely wounded Key and killed his crew chief and driver.[41]

Somewhere in the desperate fighting along Red Two, Lt. Bonnie Little, 2d Amphibian Tractor Battalion, rode to his death, firing the LVT's heavy machine gun as the vehicle charged a particularly deadly pillbox. He would never know that the Marine Corps had recently announced his selection to captain.[42]

Cpl. Harold D. Ellis served as crew chief and driver of Major Drewes's LVT-2. PFCs Walter F. Buczak and George Joseph manned the machine guns. Under Drewes's energetic leadership the Water Buffalo retracted from Red Two and made two transfer line operations, delivering reinforcements from the reef to the beach. Their luck ran out while retracting for a fourth run. One of the Japanese 75-mm dual-purpose guns near the Bird's Beak, then to their rear, hit the vehicle squarely: a bull's-eye shot right through the open door to the crew cab. The explosion killed Drewes and Ellis instantly.

Visibly shaken, Buczak took over the gory controls and

drove the vehicle clear of the impact zone. Buczak and Joseph
spent several wretched hours trying to get one of the ships to
salvage their slowly sinking vehicle and provide a burial for
their slain commander. Finally, the *Sheridan* agreed to help.
Sailors aided the two Marines in bringing Drewes's shattered
body on board, just as the LVT sank alongside.[43]

THE FOURTH WAVE OF ASSAULT TROOPS IN
landing boats contained all three battalion landing team commanders. How each dealt with the problem of getting ashore
reflects the nature of the man and his concept of the battle
raging to his front.

On the left, Major Crowe's losses among the LVT waves on
Red Beach Three had been minimal: no more than twenty-five
casualties. The pier sheltered Crowe's men from fire from the
Pocket; earlier shelling by the destroyers in the lagoon suppressed some of the fire from the east. But the Japanese could
reinforce their positions from the entire eastern end of the
island. Japanese weapons along the immediate left flank,
roughly from the Burns-Philp wharf inland, had not been suppressed and proved heavy from the start, forcing the LVTs to
bear sharply toward the right, toward the pier. "I'm losing my
goddamned front!" Crowe exclaimed to photographer Staff
Sgt. Norman T. Hatch from their vantage point on the engine
cover of a Higgins boat. "Coxswain, put this damned boat in."

The sailor gunned the LCVP full-bore toward Red Three,
hitting the reef so hard the impact knocked staff and commander into a heap. Crowe jumped up and vaulted over the
gunwale into the water. Hatch, striving to protect his fragile
film containers from the water, straggled behind. Crowe covered the five-hundred-yard wade so fast he reached dry ground
only four minutes after the last LVT. Equally important, the
LT 2/8 comm section arrived literally on Crowe's heels. It
would take Sgt. Elwin B. "Al" Hart several frantic minutes to
locate and assemble the major components of his TBX radio
set—one of his men was down—but soon he would become
the most valuable radio operator on the beach.

Many combat photographs of Tarawa show one man

standing tall amid scores of troops huddled against the seawall on Red Beach Three. A closer examination would reveal a man with a bristling red mustache, unlit cigar clenched in his teeth, a shotgun cradled in his arm. This was Maj. Jim Crowe, a tower of strength throughout the battle. The Marines on Red Three needed his indomitable spirit; they had landed adjacent to some of the most formidable defenses on the island.

Crowe had explained the tactical objectives to each officer and NCO in advance, anticipating chaos and losses. He also ordered the LVT drivers to cross the seawall without stopping. Most failed in the attempt, but a handful penetrated inland with elements of Easy Company (see chapter six) embarked. Crowe was already close to achieving his D-Day objectives, but he worried about his exposed right flank. He could not see LT 2/2.[44]

Landing Team 2/2 was in dire straits from the beginning. Seaward of Red Two, Colonel Amey flagged down a pair of LVTs to accept the transfer of his boated command group. He could see the slaughter just beyond the seawall and along the open beaches to his right; he knew he must get ashore. Relentless Japanese fire from the Pocket forced one of the LVTs, bearing Amey's executive officer, westward toward the Bird's Beak. Amey's LVT became ensnared in the same obstacles encountered earlier by Nygren and Drewes. Dead stop.

Amey led his staff over the sides and into the shallow water. The beach appeared only the length of a football field away. "Come on!" he yelled, waving his pistol, "those bastards can't stop us." A disciplined Japanese machine gunner, still firing short bursts along his assigned sector of the barriers, hit Amey in the throat, killing him instantly. Landing Team 2/2 had already been badly shot up; now their commander was down. Lt. Col. Walter I. "Walt" Jordan, an observer from the 4th Marine Division, found himself senior officer on the beach and assumed command. The battalion remained scattered, gone to earth inland or still clinging to the meager protection of the seawall.

The seawall on Red Two was incomplete, yet instead of being an avenue of direct approach for a mechanized amphibious column, it became a killing ground devoid of any cover or concealment. Many Marines from LT 2/2 died here trying to carry the fight inland. Five of Easy Company's six officers were dead. Fox Company penetrated inland several dozen yards but lost half its number. Golf Company barely had a toehold.

Marines of Major Schoettel's LT 3/2 fell by the scores trying to get ashore over Red One on the right flank. Both King Company on the left and Item Company on the right lost half their men in the first two hours. King Company tried to land squarely against the Pocket, entering the only concave stretch of the northern shore. Schoettel would lose seventeen of his thirty-seven officers this day.

Item Company made progress over the seawall along the Bird's Throat and Beak, but it paid a high price, including the loss of the company commander, Capt. William E. Tatom, killed before he could even debark from his LVT. Capt. J. Wendall Crain, a widely respected Guadalcanal veteran, took command and worked his survivors inland toward those heartless Type 88 dual-purpose guns.

Inland from the beach the battlefield took the form of a deadly barroom brawl. Japanese sailors sallied forth from their gun positions and magazines to meet the Marines hand to hand. Rikusentai bayonets inflicted several casualties among the Americans, but the Marines were adept close-combat fighters themselves. The sands became littered with the fallen from both sides: stabbed, hacked, choked to death.[45]

Maj. Mike Ryan's Love Company and the battalion weapons company comprised the fourth wave in Higgins boats for LT 3/2. Ryan found the barrier reef no surprise. "We had been warned that the reef might prove an obstacle to boats. We were prepared to wade in." The reef is farther from the beach at that point; Love Company probably had to traverse seven hundred yards under increasing fire. The Japanese seemed at first preoccupied with shooting at the last of the LVTs heading for Red One. Then the gunners spotted the clots of wading men coming behind. Machine-gun fire stitched the water, and many Marines dropped.[46]

Amid the confusion, Ryan spotted "one lone trooper

through the fire and smoke scrambling over a parapet on the beach to the right," marking a new landing point. Ryan vectored his men toward the Bird's Beak and beyond, westward, wrapping onto Green Beach. Japanese fire was unremitting, cutting down fully a third of Love Company in the water, but the troops surged forward, many remembering the "duck-walk" from high school football days. Ryan reached the beach and looked back over his shoulder. "They looked like turtles. All I could see were helmets with rifles held over them," as his men scrunched ashore.[47]

Schoettel maintained good communications with Shoup but lost contact with his line companies during the critical first hour. He remained in his Higgins boat, convinced the landing team had been shattered beyond relief and totally unaware of the relative success attained by Crain against the battery of 75-mm guns and by Ryan on the far right. Schoettel did provide one valuable, often-overlooked service that chaotic morning. Heavy Japanese fire turned away the flotilla of six Mike boats bearing Sherman tanks destined for Red One. Schoettel quickly intercepted the withdrawing column and reversed their course. The tanks would have as difficult a time getting ashore over Red One as anyone else, but Schoettel's forceful action at this point ensured that Mike Ryan would have the combat edge to survive the night on the beach.[48]

An early radio report, unidentified by call sign and probably representing an infantryman picking up the handset from a fallen radio operator, sent shivers down the spines of those in higher echelons listening intently for news from the beach. "Have landed," the messenger reported. "Unusually heavy opposition. Casualties 70 percent. Can't hold."[49]

EARLIER WE DISCUSSED THE EVENTS OF THE critical period between 1000 and 1100 on D-Day, when the situation hung in the balance. As that hour ended, Shoup, working his way slowly shoreward, intercepted a file of demoralized, weaponless troops wading back to the reef. "We can't get in, we're going back to the ship," one said. "Pick up weapons from the dead and go in," Shoup ordered.[50]

CHAPTER SIX

Gaining Toeholds on D-Day

*I in my tank kept shooting until the gun barrel became red
hot . . . [yet] under our fires they came in large numbers,
one after another, floating the shallows, stepping over their
friends' bodies.*
—Petty Officer Second Class Tadao Onuki,
Imperial Japanese Navy,
3d Special Base Defense Force, Betio

ELEMENTS OF EASY COMPANY, LT 2/8, MADE THE
deepest penetration of Betio's defenses on D-Day morning.
Major Crowe picked 1st Lt. Aubrey Edmonds, a Guadalcanal
veteran promoted from the ranks, to lead the assault elements
of Easy Company ashore on the right flank of Red Three.
Shibasaki's coconut-log seawall remained incomplete in that
sector, and the torrent of fire from the LVT machine guns
knocked out the three Japanese gun positions dug into the berm
nearby. "We hit the soft spot," said Edmonds. Several LVTs
lurched inland, crossed the northern edge of the taxiway, and
disgorged the troops near the main runway.

Edmonds organized firing positions exactly where Crowe
wanted. He had ninety men, a few machine guns, and a slight
rise from which to shoot down groups of rikusentai still
crossing the island to reinforce the northern beaches.
Edmonds's small force would hold that position for five hours,
but they became increasingly vulnerable. Edmonds expected
Fox Company to come up on his left, but the unit ran into a
buzz saw on that flank and could hardly progress beyond the
beach. His own first platoon, thwarted by the seawall, would
drift inland to the west, essentially out of contact. Edmonds
could find no sign of the 2d Marines farther west. He had no
working radio. Navy planes strafed his positions every few
minutes, unable to distinguish one group of brown-clad
infantrymen from another on the embattled island.[1]

131

Easy Company's first platoon attained a major penetration of the Japanese defenses on their own, but they did so without benefit of the mobility and shock action of tracked vehicles. The platoon landed in two LVTs on the extreme right of Red Three, just east of the long pier. Here the seawall was intact; rikusentai lay waiting just beyond. The LVTs lunged fruitlessly against the vertical coconut logs as machine-gun bullets sliced through the exposed bottom plates. Warrant Officer Leonard A. Booker led his platoon out of the stalled vehicles and onto the beach. A Japanese rifleman rose up and shot Booker right between the eyes. The platoon sergeant went down. The troops hesitated. Sgt. Melvin McBride, another Guadalcanal veteran, took command. The platoon was terribly exposed. McBride, crouching low, went down the line of Marines, looking each one in the eye, yelling, "When I say go, we go!"[2]

Sergeant McBride stood 6′4″, weighed 225 pounds, and did not suffer fools. PFC Bill Fratt watched McBride closely. "When he said 'go,' we *went!*" The Marines made good progress, surprising several groups of Japanese who boiled out of their temporary shelters in trenches and wrecked buildings. The troops dashed forward—gasping in the heat—crossed the taxiway, and took up positions behind log revetments parallel to the main runway. "We could see the south coast through the palm trees, maybe a hundred yards beyond," recalled Fratt. The revetment and several adjoining bomb craters offered good protection, but McBride worried about their isolation. Somewhere to their left, out of sight, was Edmonds. The platoon had drifted westward in their dash, into the 2d Marines' zone, but McBride could see no sign of Colonel Amey's landing team.[3]

McBride's men shot down a number of Japanese trying to infiltrate north across the island, but, if anything, they were more exposed than Edmonds's larger force off to their east. Navy attack aircraft, under orders not to damage the precious runway, had no compunction about going after the small cluster of troops hiding in the revetments they took to be

Japanese. "They'd bomb us on the way in, then strafe us on the way out," said Fratt. Japanese troops opened up accurate, searching rifle fire. A well-aimed bullet killed Fratt's assistant squad leader. The next round struck Fratt's rifle on the gas port. "Felt like I'd stuck my fingers in an electric socket." Fratt rolled over, grabbed the Springfield '03 from his fallen leader (assistant squad leaders sometimes carried the older rifle for its use as a grenade launcher), and began stripping rounds out of his M-1 clips to feed into the bolt action rifle.[4]

"Here comes one of our tanks," yelled a Marine manning the revetment. But it was a *Japanese* tank, and it came around the revetment out of nowhere. From far away, Lieutenant Edmonds spotted the tank, fired a rifle grenade at it, but missed. By then the tank had moved right in the middle of McBride's men. McBride and one of his Browning Automatic Riflemen leaped on top of the moving vehicle, trying to stuff a grenade through the hatch. Nearby Japanese troops blew them off with a burst of fire, killing the Browning Automatic Rifleman, seriously wounding McBride. Fratt had no rifle grenades to go with his newly acquired Springfield. The tank rolled toward him and a group of Marines desperately hugging the near edge of their bomb crater. But the tank crew could not depress

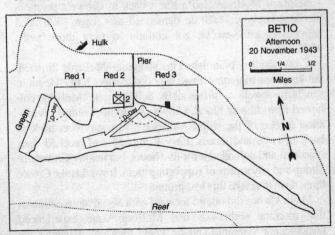

the barrel low enough to shoot. Then the vehicle stalled. The Marines, badly scared, screwed up their courage to tackle the armored vehicle with their bare hands.[5]

This may well have been Petty Officer Onuki's tank. He had been operating in the general vicinity of the inner taxiway and the beach. "I realized I was deep in American forces and wanted to come back. Suddenly the engine of my tank halted. . . . Enemy soldiers swarmed around my tank." Onuki somehow restarted the engine and clanked away, toward the beach.[6]

Edmonds had seen enough. He went back to report to Crowe, who told him to pull back his men to clear the way for a series of naval and air strikes in those target areas. Edmonds also found out what had happened to Fox Company. Capt. Orlando A. Palopoli told him, "I've lost all my officers and half my NCOs." Palopoli himself died of wounds shortly thereafter. Edmonds returned to his exposed position and directed the retrograde of his men. He insisted on being the last man back across the island; a howitzer or knee mortar explosion behind him filled his lungs with shrapnel. Edmonds would barely survive, but his fight had ended.[7]

Sergeant McBride also made it back to Crowe's position, bleeding heavily. McBride demanded of Crowe, "We need heavy weapons—we've got nothing to fight those tanks with!"

Crowe angrily brandished his shotgun—McBride flinched, thinking for a moment Crowe intended to shoot him. "Dammit, son," Crowe yelled, "*this* is all the hell I've got!" McBride collapsed from loss of blood. Crowe saw to his eventual evacuation to one of the ships. McBride's few survivors trickled back in twos and threes. Easy Company had reached their objective and defended it for five hours, but neither Crowe nor Shoup had any means of supporting them. It would take Crowe three days to retake this lost ground.[8]

Major Crowe did not go forward with his advance elements that morning. Edmonds and McBride were experienced Guadalcanal veterans, and he knew they could handle the situation without his presence. Crowe probably chose the right course by staying on the beach, greeting the exhausted and terrified waders as they came ashore, directing them to specific units and tasks. The other beaches, lacking such a legendary "welcoming committee," suffered extended periods of disorganization and confusion.

PFC Carroll D. Strider, a demolition man from C/1/18 attached to LT 2/8, recalled the stabilizing presence of Crowe and his executive officer, Major Chamberlin, on Red Three that hectic morning. Strider landed with the second wave, feet dry, carrying "demolitions pack, blasting caps in my front pocket, two five-gallon cans of diesel fuel, combat pack, carbine, 90 rounds of ammo." Strider hugged the seawall under heavy fire. Then he heard the loud voice of Major Chamberlin behind him. "Get the hell over that seawall!" Recalls Strider, "Over we went." Once Easy Company's remnants returned, Crowe and Chamberlin staked out defensive positions within 150 yards of the beach, nothing more. Red Three would still be the largest beachhead on the island by nightfall.[9]

Good tactical communications, a rarity throughout the island, facilitated Crowe's relative success. Both his TBX sets were working, one linking Shore Fire Control Party #82 with the destroyers in the lagoon, the other in contact by lucky accident with the division command post on the *Maryland*. Eighteen-year-old Sergeant Hart manned the telegraph key and earphones on this rig. Hart could not raise Shoup (still making his own way ashore) on the regimental command net, but he discovered that the persistent "unknown station" on that frequency was actually the division headquarters trying to contact *anyone* on the beach. Later, when Shoup established his command post (CP) ashore, Hart and LT 2/8 continued to serve as a relay station between the regimental commander and General Smith. Time and again throughout the battle, Sergeant Hart's Morse code signals would represent "the Voice of Tarawa" to the division commander and his staff.[10]

Colonel Shoup's radios worked, but only intermittently. Receiving at best merely fragmentary reports of the early fighting, Shoup hoped the fourteen Sherman medium tanks would provide the tactical momentum needed to break the stalemate along the beaches. The combat debut of the Shermans proved inauspicious on D-Day, however. Shoup's landing plan assigned the medium tanks to the fifth wave. Eight Shermans, under 1st Lt. Lou Largey, would land over Red Three; the other six, under 1st Lt. Edward Bale, were destined for Red One. After some hesitation the Mike boat coxswains dropped the ramps of the LCM-3s directly on the coral reef, and the fourteen tanks trundled across without incident.

Marine Corps Shermans at that point in the war did not come equipped with fording kits; the vehicles could not operate in water deeper than three feet. While the tankers hoped their "field expedient" sheet-metal stack extensions would protect the crews operating at low tide within the reef, they worried about unseen shell craters or potholes. Indeed, one of Largey's tanks sank offshore in such a hole en route to the beach. Most of the crew, riding low in tight quarters, drowned.

Bale's tankers on the right flank had a longer run from the reef to the beach. Knowing this, the 2d Tank Battalion assigned a reconnaissance platoon whose dismounted members would precede the vehicles with markers to identify dangerous holes in the turbid waters. "Each of us would carry three orange metal floats about the size of a soccer ball," recalled PFC M. F. Swango. Each float had a five-foot rope attached to a small metal anchor. But the ropes became tangled, the anchors would not hold; the process took too long. The scouts then spread out in a line, trying to show the column of tanks the best route to the embattled beach. Japanese sharpshooters shot down scout after scout; each time, another tanker volunteered to take the lead. The bravest of these brave men was Sgt. James R. Atkins, who offered himself as a "human channel marker" during the final, most dangerous approach to the beach. Atkins led the column ashore, but paid for it with his life.[11]

Lieutenant Bale's orders were to pass through a gap blasted by engineers in the seawall and proceed inland. But as he approached the beach, Bale had to make an agonizing decision. The gap in the seawall was now littered with dead and wounded Marines. Rather than grind over the bodies of his own breed, Bale ordered his six tanks back into the lagoon to proceed around the Bird's Beak to land at another gap farther west. Bale's decision saved several lives but proved costly. The column of tanks, now operating blindly without Sergeant Atkins, lost four vehicles in deep shell holes, a significant setback. The bottom line on the ship-to-shore movement was this: no Shermans lost to enemy fire; five lost because of the absence of fording kits.

As tough as it was for the tankers to get ashore, the real problem facing them was how to fight effectively once they arrived. Few Marines had any concept of practical, combined arms tactics in the fall of 1943. "Conventional wisdom," based on fragmentary reports of Army experiences with tank warfare in North Africa, called for forward deployment of the vehicles for independent missions against enemy bunkers and tanks. In this regard, the Marines were guilty of ignoring the tactical lessons learned from their own recent history. During the sharp fighting to secure Tanambogo in August 1942, a Marine M-3 light tank had deployed far ahead of the infantry. Japanese rikusentai appeared out of the jungle, swarmed over the vehicle, set it ablaze, killed two crewmen, and pulled the driver out of his hatch by his legs and nearly hacked him to death before rescuers arrived. The obvious imperative for coordinated tank-infantry tactics still had not made it into doctrine in time for Tarawa.

This helps explain why Largey's tanks were simply waved forward by the infantry battalion commander with vague orders to "knock out all enemy positions encountered." The tank crews, buttoned up under fire, were virtually blind. Without accompanying infantry they became fair game for every weapon on the island, including the Japanese Type 41 75-mm mountain gun. Small wonder that Largey's "Colorado," sizzling and smoking in the lagoon after its headlong dash for safety, was the only survivor on Red Beach Three. Nor did the last two Shermans on Red Beach One fare much better. One was soon lost to enemy shell fire. The second,

Lieutenant Bale's "China Girl," was the victim of a bizarre encounter with a Japanese light tank. The heavier Marine tank demolished its smaller opponent, but not before the doomed Japanese crew released one final 37-mm round, a phenomenal shot, right down the barrel of "China Girl." For the remainder of D-Day, Bale's tank served only as an armored machine gun.

It was a long day for the entire 2d Tank Battalion. Colonel Swenceski, commanding the battalion, was blown out of his LVT and severely wounded in the assault. Swenceski survived by clinging to a pile of dead bodies for the next twenty-four hours to keep from drowning. When his successor tried to land a platoon of light tanks to reinforce Lieutenant Largey on Red Beach Three, the maneuver served only to provide handsome targets for Japanese gunners. In a display of naval gunnery not seen since the Marines defended Wake Island two years earlier, the rikusentai sank four Mike boats with embarked M-3 light tanks even before the craft could reach the reef.[12]

WARRANT OFFICER OTA AND HIS MEN CON-tinued to occupy positions just inland from the seawall on the western edge of what the Americans called Red Beach Two. The two groups of antagonists were barely ten feet apart and had been exchanging grenades and taunts for an hour. Ota was a master mechanic, hardly a *samurai*, but he had seen enough combat to know he had to lead his men over that seawall. "Follow me," he shouted to his men, waving his sword as he leapt over the barricade. "My men did not follow ... and I found myself alone on the beach. For some reason, perhaps because they were startled, the Americans did not shoot at me." Ota swung his sword at the astonished Marines, then jumped quickly back over the seawall before they could come to their senses. A flurry of grenades followed from the beach, killing some of his men and wounding Ota in the head and knee.[13]

Red Beach Two was a killing ground for both sides D-Day morning. As LT 2/2 paid a stiff price getting ashore, so in particular did their attached engineers. These Marines were a breed apart: competent infantrymen, blessed with the skill and nerve to be demolitions experts, flamethrower operators, or obstacle broachers. Staff Sergeant Bordelon was among the best and brightest of the gifted group. This Texan who was rejected by the Navy for the webbing between his toes had found a home in the 2d Marine Division. His men loved him, his officers respected his attitude. "Lots of hard work," he wrote home earlier, "but it's all part of the job." When Japanese shell fire disabled his LVT and killed most of his platoon at H-Hour, Bordelon led the handful of survivors toward the shelter of the seawall. Sgt. Eldon Beers and PFC Jack Ashworth stuck close to Bordelon. They had two packs of dynamite between them.

Bordelon quickly fused the dynamite into four explosive charges. Japanese machine-gun positions fired from every hand at the Marines still in the water. Bordelon stood up and faced the machine gunners, lobbing one charge, then another, directly into the emplacements. "That eliminated those Japs," said Beers later, but Bordelon sustained a wound in his left arm and shrapnel wounds to his face. The most dangerous strong point sat with impunity some distance inland, firing steadily at the wading Marines. Bordelon crawled forward and managed to stuff one of the charges through the firing slits, destroying the gun and crew, but he took another bullet through the same arm, and the fourth charge blew up in his hand just as he threw it.[14]

By now seriously wounded, Bordelon refused treatment and ran out into the exposed shallows to rescue one of his engineers calling for help. Sergeant Beers then joined Bordelon in attempting to silence a fourth Japanese position shooting at the Marines. The rikusentai knocked Beers down with a grenade blast, wounding him severely in the stomach. Bordelon pulled him to relative safety, then disappeared, looking for a corpsman for his friend. There were no corpsmen to be found on that contested beach, but Bordelon returned with a grenade launcher. He and another Marine went after the Japanese position. Again the rikusentai cut loose, hitting Bordelon in the shoulder and wounding his partner. Bordelon pulled the other man out of danger, took an upright position to fire the grenade launcher, and was shot dead in the exchange.[15]

In a battle highlighted by individual and small unit bravery on both sides, Sergeant Bordelon provided an awesome example of personal courage. "Bill was the bravest Marine I ever saw," said Eldon Beers. "He was also the finest leader of men in and out of combat," Private First Class Ashworth wrote to the family, "Without him, troops would not have been able to land." Capt. Paul R. Zidek, Bordelon's company commander, wrote, "He died a real fighting man . . . and he was killed doing a job he would ask no one else to do."[16]

It is impossible to calculate the impact Bordelon's heroics had on the critical situation on Red Two that morning. Not only did he knock out four deadly Japanese gun positions, more importantly, he also galvanized the survivors into assuming the offensive and taking the fight to the Japanese beyond the beach. Bordelon became one of four Marines to receive the Medal of Honor for Tarawa (three posthumously), and he was the only enlisted man to be so recognized. No one ever disputed the appropriateness of the award in his case. His conduct in those few minutes had indeed been "valorous and gallant above and beyond the call of duty."

The Marines struggling against Japanese pillboxes quickly realized the value of combat engineers. Ryan and Crain desperately needed teams of flamethrower operators and demolition men to help clear the labyrinth of bunkers west of the Pocket on Red Beach One. Knowing this, one assault squad of engineers from Dog Company, 2/18, tried to fight their way ashore near this point from their disabled LVT. The squad included PFC Russell L. Jarrett, age twenty, the youngest of eight children, who had recently left his Illinois farm to learn how to work with decorative cast iron. When he joined the Marines after Pearl Harbor, his unit promptly classified him as a blacksmith. But this morning Jarrett was a machine gunner. The squad splashed ashore into the teeth of a Japanese defensive complex. The Marines overran the first position, then were shot down in the cross fire from the supporting strong points.

The entire squad, including Jarrett, died within the first thirty yards of the water's edge.[17]

Easy Company, 2/2, suffered heavy losses while grabbing a toehold on Red Two. Five of the company's six officers fell within a matter of minutes. PFC David "Red" Spencer's LVT took a direct hit approaching the left flank of the beach, near the pier. The survivors hit the seawall, hesitated, then crossed inland. "There were only four or five of us left. . . . we didn't have any officers at all by noon," said Spencer. Navy planes buzzed overhead, trying to knock out a Japanese tank. "They were closer to killing us than the Japs. We were pissed off at them."[18]

On Red Beach One, Marines from LT 3/2 continued to work their way ashore from the reef. PFC Howard Frost of Item Company recalled their vulnerability. "You would hear a thud and someone would fall." Frost was awestruck by the accuracy of the Japanese 75-mm dual-purpose guns firing from just inland along the Bird's Throat, even though he wasn't the target. One shell streaked overhead and seemed to "vaporize" a landing craft. "I saw the boat, heard a tremendous thud, then saw nothing."[19]

PFC Perry F. Grisdale's duty as assistant machine gunner in Love Company was to carry the M1919A4 light machine gun ashore from the reef. The gunner had the privilege of carrying the tripod; two other Marines "humped" ammo. Grisdale could see the dead Marines dotting the exposed sand spit off the Bird's Beak, so he and the gunner swung to their left to stay clear. A bullet then struck the gunner; Grisdale shifted the machine gun to the opposite shoulder, grabbed his buddy with the other arm, and dragged him the last hundred yards ashore. He was dead. Grisdale's machine gun was useless without the tripod and ammo. He picked up a carbine and offered to serve his lieutenant as a runner. Once over the protective seawall, Grisdale ran like a scared rat. As he dashed by an enemy bunker, someone grabbed him by the collar. Terrified, he turned to see the friendly face of Major Ryan. "Where are you going? There's nothing up ahead but Japs!" Ryan sent Grisdale back to the beach to bring more men forward.[20]

Several Coast Guardsmen, assigned to the Red Three beach party from the USS *Arthur Middleton* (APA 25), waded ashore from the reef as part of the seventh wave. Fireman Apprentice Karl Albrecht provides a vivid account of his experiences getting ashore.

> We beach party members were armed with old Springfield rifles. . . . Word was passed to load weapons. I didn't know how. A Marine showed me how it was done. . . . In the distance I could see the beach. It was lined with amtracs, all of which appeared to be burning and smoking. . . . The attack appeared to have dissolved in confusion. I was terror stricken and amazed at the same time. We were Americans and invincible. We had a huge armada of warships and a division of Marines. How could this be happening? I kept as low as possible in the water and tried to pull my body up inside my helmet. . . . I discovered the rows of Marines along the beach weren't lying there waiting for orders to move. They were dead. There were dead all over. They appeared to outnumber the living.[21]

Getting ashore from the reef took Lt. George D. Lillibridge of Able Company, 1/2, the better part of seven hours. Japanese machine gunners raked his LVT, killing the crew chief and both gunners. The surviving crewman got the vehicle started again, but only in reverse. The stricken LVT then backed wildly through the entire impact zone until it broke down again, drifting with the current.[22]

Although Sherrod was no stranger to combat, the landing on D-Day at Betio was one of the most unnerving experiences in his life. The correspondent accompanied Marines from the fourth wave of LT 2/2 attempting to wade ashore on Red Two. In his memorable words: "No sooner had we hit the water than the Japanese machine guns really opened up on us. . . . It was painfully slow, wading in such deep water. And we had seven hundred yards to walk slowly into that machine-gun fire, looming into larger targets as we rose onto higher ground. I was scared, as I had never been scared before. . . . Those who were not hit would always remember how the machine-gun bullets hissed into the water, inches to the right, inches to the left."[23]

Getting ashore on Betio on D-Day grew more hazardous as the day progressed. The supply of LVTs dropped precipitously: a mere sixteen of the original eighty-seven vehicles remained operational by sunset. The thirty-eight remaining LVTs, which had not been employed in the initial assault, were mainly Alligators preloaded with critical combat supplies that had to be off-loaded—or dumped—before troops could be carried.

Meanwhile, Admiral Shibasaki's reinforcements from the southern and eastern sectors had successfully dragged their crew-served weapons through the soft sand to reinforce the north shore. Shoup assessed the fire patterns and concluded that Bob Ruud's LT 3/8, freshly assigned to the 2d Marines by Julian Smith, would have a better chance getting ashore on Red Three, landing behind Jim Crowe. At 1103 Shoup radioed Ruud: "LT 3/8 land Beach Red 3 proceed protect left flank 2/8. Go as far as possible on reefs with boats." This became the last communication between the two officers on D-Day. For the next six hours Shoup and Ruud were never more than a mile apart, yet neither could communicate with the other.[24]

Ruud divided his landing team into seven waves, but the distinctions blurred once the boats approached the reef. Japanese antiboat guns zeroed in on the landing craft with frightful accuracy, often hitting just as the bow ramp dropped. Survivors reported the distinctive "clang" as a shell impacted, a split second before the explosion. "It happened a dozen times," recalled Sergeant Hatch, watching from the beach. "[T]he boat blown completely out of the water and smashed and bodies all over the place." Sherrod reported from a different vantage point. "I watched a Jap shell hit directly on a [landing craft] that was bringing many Marines ashore. The explosion was terrific and parts of the boat flew in all directions."[25]

Some Navy coxswains, seeing the slaughter just ahead, stopped their boats seaward of the reef and ordered the troops off. The Marines, many loaded with radios or mortars or extra

ammunition, sank immediately in deep water; most drowned.
The reward for those troops whose boats made it intact to the
reef was hardly less sanguinary: a six-hundred-yard wade
through withering cross fire, heavier by far than that endured
by the first assault waves at H-Hour. The slaughter among the
first wave of King and Love Companies was terrible. Seventy
percent fell attempting to reach the beach.

Seeing this, Shoup and his party waved frantically to groups
of Marines in the following waves to seek the protection of the
pier. A great number did this, but so many officers and noncommissioned officers had been hit that the stragglers were
shattered and disorganized. The pier itself was a dubious
shelter, receiving intermittent machine-gun and sniper fire
from both flanks. Shoup himself was struck in nine places,
including a spent bullet that bruised his bull neck. His runner
crouching beside him was drilled between the eyes by a
Japanese marksman.[26]

Capt. Carl W. Hoffman, commanding 3/8's weapons company, had no better luck getting ashore than the infantry companies ahead. "My landing craft had a direct hit from a
Japanese mortar. We lost six or eight people right there."
Hoffman's Marines veered toward the pier, then worked their
way ashore.[27]

Frustrated at being unable to contact Shoup, Major Ruud
radioed his original regimental commander, Col. Elmer Hall.
"Third wave landed on Beach Red 3 were practically wiped
out. Fourth wave landed . . . but only a few men got ashore."
Hall, himself in a small boat near the line of departure, was
unable to respond. General Hermle, assistant division commander, interceded with the message, "Stay where you are or
retreat out of gun range." This added to the confusion. As a
result, Ruud himself did not reach the pier until mid-afternoon.
It was 1730 before he could lead the remnants of his men
ashore; some did not straggle in until the following day. Shoup
dispatched what was left of LT 3/8 in support of Crowe's
embattled 2/8; others were used to help plug the gap between
2/8 and the combined troops of 2/2 and 1/2.[28]

Julian Smith had by now committed five battalion landing

teams to the assault. The fact that four of these were badly shot up and barely clinging to toeholds on Betio's north shore slowly dawned on those officers waiting for news offshore. Colonel Murray, commanding LT 2/6 and disgusted at being part of the VAC reserve, sat on the forecastle of the USS *J. Franklin Bell* (APA 16) listening to fragmentary reports over the division command net. Murray at first shared a common conclusion of those who observed the massive preliminary bombardment of the small island. "I thought, 'My God, there isn't going to be anybody left to fight when we get on that island—we're just going to be able to walk [right] over it.' "[29]

Earlier, during the rehearsal landing, Murray jokingly asked his friend Jim Crowe to "save him some Japanese to shoot." Now, as he tried to make sense of the urgent, disjointed radio messages, Murray became aware that the Japanese had not only survived the bombardment, they were also fighting fiercely. "I suddenly realized that things were not going as well as everybody thought. . . . that this was a very, very serious situation."[30]

The destroyers *Ringgold* and *Dashiell*, no longer fettered by the cease-fire order, made a significant difference on the left flank in support of Jim Crowe's LT 2/8. Crowe's disciplined protection of his radio assets made this possible. Shore Fire Control Party #82, attached to Crowe, established communications with the ships at 1030.

The *Dashiell* commenced call fire missions immediately; the *Ringgold* took over at 1043, maneuvering all the while to avoid fire from shore batteries that refused to be silenced for long. The *Ringgold* fired one hundred rounds of call fire in the following twenty minutes, often moving in dangerously close to the reef. From the Japanese lines, Warrant Ota marveled at this bold approach. "With the naked eye we could clearly see the American sailors on the destroyers' decks." From the exposed left flank of Red Three, Major Chamberlin noted: "At one time Commander John B. McLean had his *Dashiell* so close to the beach her crew could've hit the Japs with rocks. . . . Once she beamed over the radio, 'How are we shooting?' I reported, 'Fine, but don't get any closer.' Their last shell had landed just 25 yards in front of our line. That's what I call close fire support."[31]

Colonel Shoup and his small party continued wading shoreward along the pier, trying to roust scattered groups of Marines seeking protection among the pilings. A Japanese tank lighter, grounded in the low tide, provided the last shelter en route to the beach, and Shoup found dozens of Marines cringing behind it. Here Shoup lost his temper.

> Mortar shells getting closer as number of men grows larger. I say "Is there an officer?" No one says. I turn up captain's bars. I unbutton my holster—Marine with fear and trembling and only head out of water pulls at my leg. I look into his face. He says "For God's sake, no, Colonel!" I button the holster . . . point to my eagles. "Are there any of you cowardly sons of bitches got the guts to follow a Colonel of the Marines?" I start through . . . turn later [and] see about ten following—my heart beats big thumps. The Marines are coming in and will be okay![32]

For Shoup it was out of the frying pan, into the fire. The final hundred yards proved toughest of all. As he recorded: "Shell bursts. Man behind screams, flops forward on face, hands smack water at my side. Piece of something gets in my leg. Concussion puts me down in the water. . . . Carlson comes out when he hears I'm down. . . . I crawl closer, gather all I have and to my feet and to the beach."[33]

This concluded Shoup's five-hour odyssey from the *Zeilin* to Red Beach Two. It was high noon. Shoup sent Major Culhane and Capt. John Bradshaw east to look for Major Crowe, then led his bedraggled group of radio operators, observers, and assistants toward a forward command post. This was a dubious vantage point, the seaward side of a battered but still occupied Japanese blockhouse some fifty yards inland from the beach.

En route Shoup encountered Colonel Jordan, the observer who had suddenly found himself in command of LT 2/2 with the death of Colonel Amey. "Find Jordan," Shoup jotted in his journal, "get bad news of Amey. I direct Jordan take command 2/2. . . . note his peculiar position: unknown, no staff or exec." Shoup's encouragement probably meant the world to Jordan, who moments earlier had transmitted a message bordering on panic: "We need help; situation bad."[34]

Major Crowe followed with a peevish message to Shoup about his dangling right flank. "Can you tell me where 2/2 is?" Stabilized by Shoup, Jordan began to exercise full command. Thirty minutes later he provided the grim but dispassionate details. "All communications except runners out of commission. Amey killed. I assume command pending arrival of Major Rice [XO]. Fox Company is about 100 yards in from Beach Red Two. George Company is behind Fox Company and intermingles if snipers are still in the woods. No word from Easy Company."[35]

Walt Jordan may have been a stranger to the scattered Marines of LT 2/2, but he was no stranger to disaster. Assigned to command the Marine Barracks in besieged London during 1941, Jordan had taken passage on board a Norwegian ship that German U-Boats torpedoed in the English Channel. Jordan survived the explosions, helped passengers and crew clear the sinking vessel in life rafts, then maintained morale and discipline among the survivors until rescued by the Royal Navy several days later. Jordan may have regarded the chaos along Red Two at noon on D-Day as the ultimate shipwreck.[36]

Jordan was one of a half dozen observers assigned from the newly formed 4th Marine Division, an outfit that would soon have the responsibility of storming across other Japanese-held coral atolls in the Marshalls. Later, both the 2d and 4th Divisions would team for the assaults on Saipan and Tinian. The 4th Marine Division observers at Tarawa experienced the operation at extremely close quarters. Japanese machine gunners killed one observer, Lt. Col. David K. Claude, as he accompanied the 2d Marines' scout-sniper platoon in operations against inland strong points. Colonel Carlson, famous for his exploits with his 2d Raider Battalion at Makin and Guadalcanal, accompanied Shoup throughout the tortuous trip ashore, then made two dangerous journeys for Shoup back to the *Maryland*, delivering invaluable firsthand reports to Admiral Hill and General Smith.

Shoup's initial problems seemed manifold: reenergizing attack momentum, rebuilding tactical integrity, restoring communications, getting fuel for the surviving LVTs, bringing ammunition ashore. Yet he was staggered by the great number of casualties that required medical attention and evacuation. Navy surgeons and hospital corpsmen, organic to the assault elements, served the 2d Marine Division heroically at Tarawa, suffering nearly ninety casualties themselves. At first, wounded men were bundled into rafts or LVTs and dispatched back out to the transport area, miles at sea. This took forever, wasted precious LVT assets, and proved sometimes fatal, as evidenced by Norman Moise's experiences trying to evacuate wounded aboard his LVT.

Shore party troops from the 2d Battalion, 18th Marines and the various troop transports, frustrated in not having a secure beach with which to work, turned their talents toward this problem. After a certain point, no LVT left the beach without a full load of wounded. The vehicles proceeded just to the reef, where Higgins boats waited to receive the stretchers. These hasty cross-decking operations scared the wounded Marines, helplessly strapped to their litters while bullets and shrapnel whickered close by. The boats began taking wounded to the closest ships, the ones in the lagoon.

Less than an hour after touchdown, Higgins boats crammed with wounded Marines began approaching the *Ringgold, Dashiell, Pursuit,* and *Requisite.* The small ships were ill equipped to treat large numbers of critically wounded men, but they did their best, even the *Ringgold,* her sick bay gutted by the Japanese shell. As the commander reported in his action report: "1010: Wounded Marines from first wave commenced arriving alongside. About 40 wounded Marines were treated on board during following 24 hours. . . . two Marines died and were buried at sea."[37]

Pharmacist's Mate First Class Stanley Bowen landed with Fox Company, LT 2/8, on Red Three on D-Day morning. Bowen handled his first combat casualty almost immedi-

ately, a Marine with his leg blown off. Overcoming his initial
shock, Bowen treated scores of Fox Company's injured, men
wounded in the sharp fighting around the Burns-Philp pier and
the inland strong points. "I never got hurt, even though I had
guys hit while I was patching them up," he recalled. Members
of the 2d Marine Division Band served as stretcher bearers,
dangerous work on that flat island. Twelve of these musicians
became casualties themselves.[38]

Pharmacist's Mate First Class Costello served with a regi-
mental aid station in the 2d Marines at Tarawa. By noon on
D-Day Shoup began calling for medical reinforcements.
Costello grabbed his gear—"carbine, pistol, medical pack
weighing forty-five pounds"—and followed Lt. Herman R.
Brukhardt and fellow corpsmen Herbert B. Estes and James
Whitehead over the side and into a Higgins boat.

Costello's experiences getting ashore replicated many
others that violent day. Before it even neared the reef, his boat
received heavy fire from Japanese gunners hidden on the
Nimonea. Twice the coxswain turned back. At length the
medical team transferred to a stray LVT that rumbled ashore
on Red Two. As Costello and his team hit the sand, an officer
ran up gasping, "Are you a corpsman?"

"Yes."

"Thank God!"

The human carnage along the beach appalled Costello.
"You could not move without stepping on a body." Dr.
Brukhardt moved the team into a freshly captured Japanese
bunker, some of whose slain former occupants "came back to
life" with rifles blazing more than once. In the subsequent
thirty-six hours, Brukhardt, Costello, Estes, and Whitehead
treated 126 casualties under unimaginable conditions, yet only
four died.[39]

AT SEA ON THE *MARYLAND* JULIAN SMITH AND
Red Mike Edson struggled to understand the situation ashore.
Both had seen enough of war not to be unduly influenced by
initial combat reports. Direct contact with Shoup, however,
varied between intermittent to nonexistent. They knew he was

finally ashore—no small reassurance—but they wondered whether any one man could bring order out of the chaos that seemed to persist hour after hour. Good communications with Crowe on the left flank helped, but soon it seemed that Crowe had withdrawn his early penetrations to deal with the cat fight under way directly to the east. Jordan's grim report at least lifted the shroud of mystery on Red Two. But Schoettel's pessimistic reports led the landing force commander to believe that LT 3/2 had been wiped out.

For all Julian Smith knew, Mike Ryan and all other company commanders on Red One had died going ashore. Nor were Smith and Edson encouraged by the fragmentary reports of the earlier landings of 1/2 and 3/8. Julian Smith was down to his last battalion: Major Hays's LT 1/8, boated from the *Sheridan* since 1300. Any other reinforcements must come from the miscellaneous units attached to the division headquarters. The Southern Attack Force sorely needed the 6th Marines, the corps reserve.

Julian Smith did not hesitate. Overall command of the amphibious operation still belonged to Admiral Hill. Smith quickly got his concurrence. At 1331 Hill released this message to Admiral Turner near Makin: "CG 2d Marine Division requests release of CT 6 to 2d Mar Div. Issue in doubt. I concur." Whether Hill or Smith selected the words "issue in doubt" is immaterial. The message created an instant chill among the various naval staffs listening to the command circuit. Naval officers exchanged worried glances. The last time the Marines had used that phrase occurred when the Japanese landed for the final time on Wake Island in 1941.[40]

Kelly Turner conferred at length with Holland Smith. Two hours later Turner authorized Hill and Julian Smith to employ the entire 6th Marines. Smith now had four battalion landing teams (including 1/8) available. The question then became where to feed them into the fight without getting them chewed to pieces like Ruud's experience earlier that afternoon. This would preoccupy Smith for the next twenty-four hours.[41]

Julian Smith, meanwhile, continued to influence the action ashore. In the absence of reliable communications with Shoup,

(*left*) An aerial view of Betio Island, from the west, which shows the coral reef. Bairiki Island lies due east. (U.S. NAVAL INSTITUTE)

(*below*) Japanese construction troops winch the barrel of an eight-inch Vickers naval cannon into its turret on Betio. The photograph came from a Japanese camera found on the battlefield. (STANLEY C. JERSEY)

(*above*) Japanese sailors man one of the four Type 89 127-mm/.40-caliber, twin-mounted, dual-purpose antiaircraft guns found on Betio. The Type 89 was the heaviest AA gun in the Japanese arsenal. This mount was positioned along Betio's southern shore, near the western end of the airstrip. In the battle, the crews fired them horizontally at ships and landing craft. This film was retrieved from a captured camera.
(BOARDMAN COLLECTION, MARINE CORPS HISTORICAL CENTER)

(*left*) Maj. Gen. Julian C. Smith, USMC (right), commanding general, 2d Marine Division, confers with his chief of staff, Col. Merritt A. "Red Mike" Edson, USMC. (U.S. MARINE CORPS)

(*above*) Col. David M. Shoup, USMC, who commanded the reinforced
2d Marines at Tarawa.
(U.S. MARINE CORPS)

(*below*) An aerial view of the assault waves as they crossed the line of
departure at 0832 on D-Day from a Kingfisher observation plane. The
LVTs still have a forty-minute run to the beach.
(MARINE CORPS HISTORICAL CENTER)

(*above*) The first wave approaches the beach. LVT-1 ("Whiskey Sour") features two Browning .50-caliber heavy machine guns mounted forward and a .30-caliber light machine gun mounted on each gunwale.
(NATIONAL ARCHIVES)

(*below*) Into the gates of hell. Somewhere ahead, underneath all that smoke, is Betio. Somewhere ahead, closer, is the reef.
(U.S. MARINE CORPS)

(*left*) Staff Sgt. William J. Bordelon, USMC, of San Antonio, Texas, killed at Betio on D-Day. Bordelon, a combat engineer with the 18th Marines attached to LT 2/2, was the only enlisted Marine to receive the Congressional Medal of Honor at Tarawa.
(THE C. D. BORDELON FAMILY)

(*below*) This aerial view looks north across the island at Red Beach One from the Kingfisher aircraft on D-Day afternoon. The "Pocket" begins on the upper right of the re-entrant; the battery of Type 88 75-mm dual-purpose guns is located at the upper left. At least ten disabled LVTs can be seen in the shallows off the beach.
(MARINE CORPS HISTORICAL CENTER)

(*above*) A Navy Higgins boat approaches the USS *Harry Lee* (APA 10) with casualties from the assault waves. The Marine on the engine hatch cover died before he could be brought on board; the other Marine, huddled forward, survived.
(NORMAN S. MOISE)

(*below*) Yard by yard. Much of the fighting ashore occurred at close range, where grenades and M-1 carbines often did the job.
(U.S. MARINE CORPS)

(*above*) Attack of Bonnyman's "Forlorn Hope": the improvised squad of assault engineers reach the moment of truth near the top of the Japanese bombproof on D 2.
(U.S. MARINE CORPS)

(*below*) Death and devastation at the end of the battle.
(U.S. MARINE CORPS)

(*above*) Carnage along Betio's north shore after the battle. Scenes like this, published broadly in newspapers and magazines, shocked the American public.
(U.S. NAVAL INSTITUTE)

(*below*) The remains of a Marine Corps Sherman medium tank still mark Red Beach Two, fifty years after the battle.
(PETER L. COOPER)

he radioed his assistant division commander, General Hermle, at 1343 to proceed to the end of the pier, assess the situation, and report back. Hermle and his small staff promptly debarked from the *Monrovia* and headed toward the smoking island. Like everyone else trying to get ashore that day, Hermle found his passage hotly disputed. The ADC spent four hours getting to the pierhead.

General Smith could also overhear Major Schoettel's plaintive messages transmitted from his Higgins boat outside the reef. At 1310 Schoettel's air liaison officer, embarked with the battalion commander, radioed "cannot land because of heavy fire." Later, Schoettel himself sent the doleful message: "CP located on back of Red Beach One. Situation as before. Have lost contact with assault elements."[42]

Julian Smith had heard enough. Taking the microphone, he ordered: "Direct you land at any cost, regain control your battalion and continue the attack!" Two hours later Schoettel and his small party waded ashore and reported to Shoup. Moving six hundred yards to the west to join Ryan was out of the question at that time. Shoup put Schoettel's headquarters party to work guarding the exposed regimental command post.[43]

On Red Beach Two Shoup consulted with his artillery officer, Lieutenant Colonel Rixey, commanding the 1st Battalion, 10th Marines, attached to Combat Team Two for the assault. Rixey had accompanied Shoup throughout the long odyssey ashore that morning, and Shoup held him in high regard. Rixey commanded a battalion of 75-mm pack howitzers, semi-portable weapons originally designed for mule-borne expeditionary forces but ideal for amphibious assaults. Gun crews could readily disassemble the weapons into six major components. The largest element weighed 225 pounds, not an easy burden in the water, but the weapon certainly offered flexibility to the landing force.

Shoup and Rixey quickly scrapped the original plan to land the guns on Red One. Both men had also seen firsthand the advantage of using LVTs in traversing the final six hundred yards ashore. They decided the safest means of getting the guns into the battle ("safety" being a relative term on Betio) would be to assemble enough LVTs to land the battalion in column on the extreme left flank of Red Two, the so-called boat channel along the pier.[44]

Getting even a few operational LVTs together for this movement took hours; at that, Rixey had only enough to embark two sections of Able and Baker Batteries. Switching the bulky howitzer components from boats to tractors while under a hot fire proved to be a hair-raising experience for the cannoneers and amtrackers. Somehow, the transfer succeeded. In the confusion, three sections of Charlie Battery followed the LVTs shoreward in Higgins boats, immediately running afoul of the reef. The battery's senior NCOs somehow found enough strong-armed volunteers in the water to help unload the components from the boats and hump them ashore. The 1st Battalion, 10th Marines, thus struggled ashore literally piece by piece, the process taking the remainder of the day and much of the night.

This was a heroic and significant achievement. Shoup's artillery support would be open for business at the beginning of morning nautical twilight the next day—just in the nick of time.

Julian Smith and Red Mike Edson knew nothing of these endeavors. The two officers had just ordered Hays's LT 1/8 to land on a new beach on the northeast coast of Betio (the Bird's Tail) and work west toward Crowe's ragged lines—a tremendous risk. Smith's overriding concern focused on the likelihood of a Japanese counterattack from the east against Crowe and Ruud. Once he had the 6th Marines, Smith admitted he was "willing to sacrifice a battalion landing team" if it meant saving the landing force from being overrun in the darkness to come.

To the great benefit of his troops, Hays never received these orders. When the Kingfisher pilot later reported a column of troops being landed on Red Beach Two (Rixey's artillery sections, as it turned out), the commander and his chief of staff assumed Major Hays had unilaterally decided to take LT 1/8 ashore there—not at all what the boss intended. "We cursed and tore our hair," reported Edson, "then plotted 1/8 ashore on our maps." Seven hours later, Smith and Edson would be astounded to discover LT 1/8 still circling in boats north of the line of departure.[45]

On Betio at 1415 Shoup received a welcome surprise when Major Ryan came up on the net to report that he had several hundred Marines and a pair of tanks in a thin line five hundred yards beyond Red Beach One on the western end of the island. This represented by far the most successful progress of the day and the sole good news to come over the air. Shoup, fearing the worst, had assumed Schoettel's companies and the other strays who had veered in that direction had been wiped out. Shoup's erratic communications, however, kept him from sharing the news with Julian Smith.

Ryan's composite troops had indeed been successful on the western end. Learning quickly how best to operate with the medium tanks, the Marines carved out a substantial beachhead, overrunning many Japanese gun turrets and pillboxes. But aside from the tanks, Ryan's men had nothing but infantry weapons. Critically, they had no flamethrowers or demolitions. Ryan had learned from earlier experience in the Solomons that "positions reduced only with grenades could come alive again." By late afternoon he decided to pull back his thin lines and consolidate. "I was convinced that without flamethrowers or explosives to clean them out we had to pull back . . . to a perimeter that could be defended against counterattack by Japanese troops still hidden in the bunkers."[46]

Most other Marines on Betio that afternoon faced the fundamental choice whether to stay put along the beach or to crawl over the seawall and carry the fight inland. For much of the day the fire coming across the top of those coconut logs was so intense it seemed that "a man could lift his hand and get it shot off." Late on D-Day, many were too demoralized to advance. When Major Tompkins, bearing messages from General Hermle to Colonel Shoup, first arrived on Red Beach Two at the foot of the pier, he was appalled at the sight of so many stragglers. Tompkins wondered why the Japanese "didn't use mortars on the first night. People were lying on the beach so thick you couldn't walk."[47]

Conditions were congested on Red Beach Three as well, but there was a difference. Major Crowe was everywhere, "as cool as ice box lettuce." No man was a straggler. Crowe constantly fed small groups of Marines into the lines to reinforce his precarious hold on the left flank. Captain Hoffman of 3/8 was not displeased to find his unit suddenly integrated within Crowe's 2/8. "There we were," Hoffman recalled, "toes in the water, casualties everywhere, dead and wounded all around us. But finally a few Marines started inching forward, a yard here, a yard there." It was enough. Hoffman was soon able to see well enough to call in naval gunfire support fifty yards ahead.[48]

Marines and hospital corpsmen were not the only Americans in harm's way in the vicinity of Betio on D-Day. Several Navy control officers rode the LVTs of the initial assault waves to the beach at H-Hour. U.S. Coast Guardsmen provided captain and crew for the *Arthur Middleton*. Coast Guard Ens. Friend W. Gleaton rode Private First Class Moore's LVT-1 ashore on the Bird's Beak and lived to tell about it. Japanese riflemen shot Lt. (jg) Robert R. Stehle in the nose as he commanded Wave One toward Red Beach One. Other Japanese gunners blew up a *Middleton* Higgins boat. The ship also picked up a stray amtrac, abandoned and drifting through the transport area just before H-Hour.[49]

Legend also places another drifting LVT in the transport area that morning, this one allegedly steaming close aboard the *Zeilin*, ten thousand yards from the maelstrom ashore. The bridge watch leveled a dozen binoculars to starboard. No one was at the LVT's helm! Bluejackets manning a ship's boat overtook the macabre craft, boarded her, and cut the throttle. A signalman sent the *Zeilin* the semaphore message: "Three men aboard—two Marines, one Navy surgeon—all dead." The *Zeilin* made ready for the burial-at-sea service, the first of many among the transports.[50]

The *Zeilin* was already an amphibious workhorse, having earned her spurs at Tulagi, Guadalcanal, Attu, and Kiska. Several members of her crew served with distinction at Tarawa, including Lt. (jg) Robert J. Kiechlin, USNR, awarded the Navy Cross for extraordinary heroism as wave commander of the first wave, Red Beach Two, and his subsequent action rescuing wounded Marines from the water along the reef while under heavy fire. Motor Machinist Mate Third Class Robert H. Vinson, a Higgins boat engineer, spotted an LVT with engine trouble on the reef, swam over to it, helped restart the engine, then stayed fully exposed to Japanese fire helping Marines transfer from a boat to the vehicle.[51]

The USS *Biddle* (APA 8) lost a Higgins boat to Japanese shellfire on D-Day. Her shore party somehow got ashore on Red Two, likely the first to reach the beach intact, but Red Two was no place for shore party operations. The sailors grabbed rifles and entrenching tools and helped defend the thin perimeter. The unit's medical section went to work treating the rows of wounded lined up behind the seawall. The *Harry Lee* sent two boatloads of shore party sailors to the pier. Japanese gunners sank one boat; the other off-loaded, but enemy fire forced the team to withdraw for the night a half hour later.

The *LaSalle* lost a boat in a collision with an LVT. Her medical department already had its hands full with the grim work that would preoccupy all the ships in the amphibious objective area for days to come, namely, receiving boatloads of wounded Marines. The small ships in the lagoon could no longer handle the flow.[52]

In the meantime, Lt. (jg) Eddie Albert, already a star of stage, screen, and radio, but now serving dutifully as salvage officer from the *Sheridan*, rode herd north of the line of departure on the slowly circling boats containing Major Hays's LT 1/8. They were still waiting for the word to land.[53]

Lieutenant Hawkins also had to wait to get ashore on D-Day. Hawkins and one section of his scout-sniper platoon, augmented by Lieutenant Leslie's engineers, had initiated the battle for the pier just prior to touchdown. Now they were stranded, trying for hours to flag down any passing LVT for passage to the beach. Gunnery Sgt. Jared Hooper, leading the other two sections, came ashore around 1400. To his chagrin, Hawkins did not reach Red Beach Two until 1615, thirteen hours after debarking from the *Zeilin*. His day would come with the dawn.[54]

Meanwhile, Leslie and one other engineer succeeded in hitching a ride on a shoreward-bound LVT, but Japanese gunners hit the vehicle hard as it reached the tetrahedrons, killing the crew. The two engineers then swam for hours toward the line of departure. There a small craft picked them up, half-drowned, totally exhausted. They would return ashore the next day.[55]

Lieutenant Lillibridge of Able Company, LT 1/2, continued to languish on board his disabled LVT, hours after Major Kyle's forces had struggled ashore on Red Two. The sole surviving amtrac crewman tried again and again to restart the engine, but the vehicle drifted farther away from Betio. "I had the horrible feeling we were simply going to drift out to sea and be lost forever," Lillibridge recalled. Finally, late in the afternoon, "the driver got the engine working, although badly, and we gasped and choked and snorted our way back towards the island." Because the Japanese still ruled the approaches to Red Two, Lillibridge and his men had to transfer to another LVT, then dash under fire from the beach to an inland trench line. But they were finally ashore.[56]

Robert Sherrod crawled up to Shoup's exposed command post. Shoup appeared grim, admitting, "We're in a tight spot—we've got to have more men." Sherrod looked out at the exposed waters on both sides of the pier. Already he could count fifty disabled LVTs, tanks, and boats. The prospects did not look good.[57]

Ragged communications did not help the situation. At 1740 Julian Smith received a faint message that General Hermle had reached the end of the pier and was under fire. Ten minutes later Smith ordered Hermle to go ashore and take command of all forces. To his everlasting chagrin, Hermle never received this word. Nor did Smith know his message failed to get through. Absent any word from his boss, Hermle stayed at the end of the pier, sending runners to Shoup and trying with partial success to unsnarl the evacuation of casualties and the delivery of critical supplies ashore. Hermle did valuable work in this capacity, but he had unknowingly missed a great personal opportunity. Smith would not give him a second shot.[58]

CHAPTER SEVEN

Dark-Eyed Night

*The night of D-Day was the greatest danger
to our landing forces . . . this was the crisis of the battle.*
—Maj. Gen. Julian C. Smith, USMC

THE JAPANESE DEFENDERS HAD THEIR OWN command and control problems. They had killed Americans by the hundreds; wreckage littered the northern beaches and dotted the lagoon; but the enemy kept coming. Naval ships and planes pounded them ceaselessly. The transmitter station would not last much longer. At 1630 the communications ship *Katori Maru*, stationed in Kwajalein, intercepted her last message from the Tarawa garrison: "Enemy under support of fleet bombardment and aerial bombing have entered . . . the harbor and are continuously landing men and materials. We are fighting them near the north-south line leading to the pier."[1]

Military historians for the ensuing half century have surmised that Admiral Shibasaki died in the heavy fighting waged by the 8th Marines around his command post on the third day of the battle. Translations of the newer Japanese war histories, however, provide an altogether different scenario. According to both the Navy and Army accounts of the battle, Admiral Shibasaki died on the afternoon of the *first day* while shifting his command post from the two-story concrete blockhouse inland from the Burns-Philp pier to an alternate site along the south coast. In the Navy account Kiyoshi Ota states that Shibasaki abandoned his original position voluntarily in order to make the blockhouse available to the hundreds of wounded rikusentai being brought to that vicinity.

This is plausible. Shibasaki faced no compelling military necessity to evacuate the blockhouse. The position was hardly untenable (indeed, it still stands intact fifty years later), and Shibasaki could not have influenced the battle any more effectively from a site along the southern shoreline. He had no other bomb-proof shelter to offer his many wounded men.

While we are unlikely to know Shibasaki's exact motives for trying to move himself and his staff to a different location, we now know from the *Senshi Sosho* accounts that a high-caliber shell caught the party in the open and killed them all. The Army version states this occurred at 1500 on D-Day; the Navy account says 1700. The Army record may be more exact in this case.[2]

Fittingly (if unknowingly), the embattled destroyers in the lagoon may well have been responsible for dispatching the Japanese commander and his staff. Shibasaki's blockhouse sat in the border between Shoup's designated target areas 216 and 214. Both the *Ringgold* and *Dashiell* were firing call missions into those target areas between 1430 and 1530, trying to knock out a persistent field gun. Sometime after 1458 the *Dashiell* fired several salvos into this vicinity, reporting that "the fire also unearthed a lot of Japs just east of the gun position, so we opened up on them." When the *Dashiell* ran low on ammunition, the *Ringgold* assumed the fire mission at 1516 and reported, "Commenced call fire on eastern edge of area 214 . . . area [stated to be] full of Japanese."[3]

The *Ringgold* used area fire in two- and three-gun salvos. The 5-inch/38 mounts of the destroyers could neutralize an area two hundred yards by two hundred yards in two minutes of rapid firing. According to naval gunfire specialist Maj. Donald Weller, the weapon was ideal for shore bombardment because it fired "a projectile with thin walls and a relatively heavy bursting charge and had a combination time and quick-acting percussion fuse. Its explosion in the air or on the surface released a large number of lethal fragments." A single 5-inch/38 airburst would have made quick work of any troops in the open.[4]

Petty Officer Onuki's most reliable account of the fighting on D-Day, published in Japan in 1970, brings us tantalizingly close to the true facts in Admiral Shibasaki's death. According to Onuki:

> The situation of our battle was worse and worse for us. The headquarters for Rear Admiral Shibasaki and others had to move from the first command post to the second post, and our tank was ordered to cover their move. Around that time our tank unit was hardly able to move because of shortage of fuel. . . . I was getting out of my tank. At that instance, one shell from an enemy ship came and exploded with a tremendous sound, and two of my friends who got out of the tank before me disappeared, blown up by the shell. I could not find their remains.[5]

HAD THEY KNOWN OF THE DEATH OF SHIBA-saki and his entire 3d Special Base Defense Force staff, the Marines on and near Betio might have been a shade less apprehensive as darkness thickened. "That first night," stated Lt. Norman Ward, "was a bitch." Sherrod, veteran that he was, faced the night with foreboding. "I was quite certain that this was my last night on earth. We had twenty feet along perhaps one-sixteenth of one-half of our side of the island, plus a few men on either side of the airstrip. The Japanese had nearly all the rest. . . . if the Japs counterattacked, what could we do except shoot at them from behind our seawall until they finally overwhelmed us."[6]

Crowe and Ruud had been preparing for the night for the previous few daylight hours, fully aware of the likelihood of a major attack from the east. Crowe's presence, in particular, served the morale of his battered troops almost as effectively as having another company of riflemen suddenly on hand.

West of Crowe's lines, and just inland from Shoup's CP, Capt. William T. Bray's Able Company, LT 1/2, settled in for the expected counterattacks. The company had been scattered in Kyle's bloody landing at midday. Bray, sorely wounded, reported to Kyle that he had men from a dozen different units in his company, including several sailors who swam ashore from sinking boats. The men were well armed and no longer strangers to each other, and Kyle was reassured.

Altogether, some five thousand Marines had stormed the beaches of Betio on D-Day. Fifteen hundred of these were dead, wounded, or missing by nightfall. The survivors held less than a quarter of a square mile of sand and coral. Shoup later described the location of his beachhead lines the night of D-Day as "a stock market graph." His Marines went to ground in the best fighting positions they could secure, whether in shell holes inland or along the splintered seawall. Despite the crazy-quilt defensive positions and scrambled units, the Marines' fire discipline was superb. Here the leavening of combat veterans throughout the ranks served to calm jittery nerves. The troops seemed to share a certain grim confidence; they had faced the worst in getting ashore against murderous fire; they sure as hell were not going back across that reef.

Offshore, the level of confidence diminished. On the *Maryland*, Gen. Julian Smith was gravely concerned. "This was the crisis of the battle," he recalled. "Three-fourths of the island was in [the] enemy's hands, and even allowing for his losses he should have had as many troops left as we had ashore." A concerted Japanese counterattack, Smith believed, would have driven most of his forces into the sea. As Edson later confided to his friend, Col. Gerald C. Thomas, "A strong Japanese counterattack that night would probably have been disastrous. . . . there were certainly 500 or 600 Japs under good control immediately east of our left flank."[7]

The counterattack never materialized. The battlefield was spooky enough: land crabs scuttling through fallen palm fronds, wounded men crying for help, things crashing about in the shadows. Red Mike Edson and Julian Smith had trained their men well. No Marine opened fire on phantoms. Some Japanese infiltrated through to the beach with machine guns and proceeded to swim out to the half-sunken LVTs and landing craft dotting the near lagoon. They would be there in the morning. That was it.

Historians have universally pointed to the destruction of Japanese land-line communications during the preliminary bombardment as the factor that disrupted any organized counterattack the first night of the battle. We may now conclude that the death that afternoon of Admiral Shibasaki and his staff was the greater contributing factor. Otherwise, an intelligent counterattack—not a *banzai* charge—would most certainly have ensued.

An immediate counterattack against any enemy beachhead was a prime tactic of Japanese island defenders in the Pacific in the middle years of the war. Admiral Kobayashi's "Gist of Battle" instructions directed garrison commanders to maintain reserve forces—augmented by tanks, where available—to launch decisive counterattacks, throwing the invaders back into the sea. The Japanese were good night fighters. Soldiers and naval landing forces alike knew how to probe enemy lines to locate unit boundaries and automatic-weapons positions as a prelude to an all-out attack. Tank-infantry counterattacks against the Marine beachheads at Saipan and Tinian, for

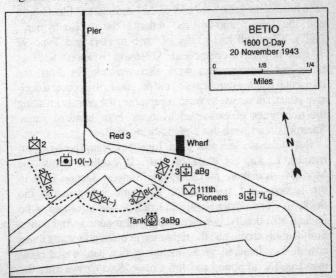

BETIO
1800 D-Day
20 November 1943

0   1/8   1/4

Miles

example, were well planned, violently executed. Shibasaki's survivors on Betio, even without their inspirational leader, would display similar prowess two nights later in a series of stinging attacks against the 1st Battalion, 6th Marines.

Red Mike Edson and Julian Smith were right: the Marines on Betio that first night were indeed vulnerable. A gap of six hundred yards, dominated by the Pocket, existed between the forces of Major Ryan, Captain Crain, and Lt. Sam Turner on the west and the thin lines of Colonel Jordan and Major Kyle in the center. But the critical danger for the Marines lay in the east. Shibasaki, alive and alert, would have ignored the western enclave to concentrate instead on the narrow stretch of perhaps four hundred yards between the Burns-Philp wharf and Shoup's CP. Four hundred yards. Shibasaki's only substantial reserves lay waiting in the east (whence they would strike the night of D+2).

The Americans were painfully tethered to the long pier, their only lifeline to the Southern Attack Force. The Japanese had the capability that night of assembling upwards of a thousand men behind the joint bulwarks of the headquarters blockhouse and the large, sand-covered redoubt (later "Bonnyman's Hill"). They still had plenty of knee mortars and Type 92 70-mm howitzers operational. Offensive weapons such as tanks and flamethrowers were also available. In short, the rikusentai had the numbers and the firepower to execute a decisive penetration, east to west, recapturing the pier and routing the thin ranks of exhausted Marines. Four hundred yards. Sherrod's fears were that close to being realized.

But Shibasaki was now dead. Likely enough, so was Commander Ezaka, his chief of staff. In biblical terms, the Marines—and more precisely, Fire Support Section Four in the lagoon—had "smitten the shepherd and scattered the flock." If Commander Sugai still lived, he was boxed up in the Pocket: still deadly, but increasingly surrounded. And Julian Smith, to his credit, had the right men in place protecting those critical four hundred yards, including two hard-nosed commanders, David Shoup and Jim Crowe. Said Crowe after the battle, "I never did think that the situation was in doubt. *I* never had any doubt." The 2d Marine Division was on Betio to stay.[8]

THE SENIOR LEADERS OF THE CENTRAL PACIFIC Force and the 2d Marine Division worked all night trying to determine the status of the battle and to prepare plans for the second day. Historian Fletcher Pratt, writing soon after the battle of Tarawa, reported that Admiral Spruance's staff became so concerned about Julian Smith's "Issue in Doubt" message on D-Day that they spent the night preparing emergency evacuation plans. This seems unlikely. Spruance, on board the flag-configured heavy cruiser *Indianapolis*, steamed in formation off Tarawa atoll with Admiral Hill and the Southern Attack Force that night. The fleet commander made no mention in his official report or subsequent correspondence about preparing "withdrawal plans" that evening, nor did Captain Moore, his chief of staff. Had Spruance been truly concerned, he would have summoned Hill and Julian Smith to his flagship for a heart-to-heart discussion about the conduct of the battle. He did not. Spruance was a consummate delegator. He maintained confidence in his subordinates and gave them plenty of leeway to fight the battle.[9]

Nor is there any evidence in Shoup's assorted and cryptic notes and journals about making withdrawal plans that first night. Shoup did discuss the possibility in general terms the night before the landing with his executive officer and operations officer, but this represented normal contingency planning, covering all the bases in advance. Like the other Marines ashore on Betio the night of D-Day/D+1, Shoup seemed to accept the grim fact that dying on the island would be a better fate than fleeing back over the reef under that murderous fire.[10]

Much farther to the east, in Pearl Harbor, Admiral Nimitz reviewed the somber reports from Tarawa with concern, but there was little he could do. "I've sent in there everything we had, and it's plenty," he reasoned. "I don't know why we shouldn't succeed."[11]

* * *

LANDING TEAM 1/8'S ENDLESS WAIT IN THE boats stretched through the night. Colonel Hall, commanding the 8th Marines, joined his remaining battalion bobbing up and down in the choppy swells, waiting for the word. "Cramped, wet, hungry, tired and a large number . . . seasick." At one point, Chaplain W. Wyeth Willard passed Hall's boat and yelled, "What are they saving us for, the Junior Prom?" The minesweeper *Pursuit* tried to ease the discomfort of the men in the crowded boats along the line of departure, distributing eight hundred meals from her tiny galley. Lieutenant Hanger of Fox Battery, 2/10, while not with the 8th Marines that night, nevertheless spent thirty hours in another Higgins boat, an unforgettable experience.

> Seasickness became a major problem. Coxswains stopped engines and dropped sea anchors to keep us more or less in the same place. We were left bobbing around like a wood chip in a whirlpool. Stomachs began to churn. . . . This was the kind of sea you'd hardly feel aboard ship, but it was a major force to a small boat without power. Action of the sea is perpetual motion, inescapable. Up by the bow, roll to port, down by the stern, roll to starboard, up, down, starboard, port, forever and ever. No wonder stomachs turn inside out.[12]

The 850 Marines of Major Hays's LT 1/8 rode Higgins boats supplied by their transport, the *Sheridan*. Lt. John Fletcher, USN, served as Boat Group Commander for the twenty-six small craft, assisted by Eddie Albert. As the former actor recalled, "My job was to assist Fletcher in controlling those twenty-six boats, plus support any boats needing repairs, refueling, or rescue at sea. My boat—Number 13—was not a landing craft. It didn't have a bow ramp or a high, protective freeboard. It was agile and speedy, meant to assist any boat in the column should an emergency develop. We had a three-man crew on Number 13: a coxswain, a gunner with a .30-caliber air-cooled machine gun, and myself."[13]

Generally, good relations existed between the *Sheridan* and

LT 1/8 during the crowded journey from Wellington to Tarawa. The crew made room for the troops to conduct calisthenics or rifle-firing exercises en route. The captain gave Chaplain Willard permission to seal the holes in a rear observation turret for a provisional baptismal font (Willard baptized sixty-two Marines and sailors therein). Said Eddie Albert of the Marines, "They were a good outfit. We felt terrible that so many were lost that second morning." Marine Lt. Frank Plant recalled how the crew came up on deck to wish the troops well when they debarked over the side to begin their long trip to Betio.[14]

Conditions ashore during the remaining hours of darkness were hardly reassuring. General Hermle roused stragglers from underneath the pier to help carry supplies to the crowded beach, a tortuous process. Hermle's radios failed altogether at midnight. Now he could not even talk to Shoup. The ADC dispatched Major Tompkins and Capt. Thomas C. Dutton from his small staff to wade in and find Shoup. The round-trip took three hours.

Other shadowy figures, rikusentai in twos and threes, slipped into the lagoon and waded out to the wrecked landing craft. A number reinforced the original detachment of snipers and machine gunners on the *Nimonea*. Shoup thought the scuttled merchantman had been cleared by Marines who "crawled up the anchor chain during morning of D-Day." The *Ringgold*'s log for 1219 on D-Day reflects a specific fire mission against the *Nimonea*: "At request of Marine officer in landing boat, opened fire on a grounded hulk near the beach, western end of Betio Island, in the lagoon. Was informed hulk contained snipers. Hit on first salvo; hulk began to smoke. Fired 20 rounds."[15]

Whether the *Nimonea* had been sanitized or not on D-Day became immaterial. The hulk now contained several machine-gun crews with plenty of ammunition. Other rikusentai took advantage of the general confusion in the waters along the pier to assume new firing positions among the pilings. Come daylight, Major Hays's survivors would accurately claim they were "shot at from four directions at once" as they struggled ashore.

Shortly after 0400 a flight of four Japanese *Rikko* naval bombers from the 22d Air Squadron in the Marshalls raided the burning island. Bombs fell indiscriminately on friend and foe but did little damage to either. Yet even the Guadalcanal veterans found the experience unnerving.

Several miles offshore on the *Maryland*, Julian Smith and Red Mike Edson tried to make sense of the jumbled tactical situation within a near-total communications vacuum. In the darkest hours of the night the naval TBS net constituted the sole reliable circuit available to the flagship. By this means, shortly after midnight, Smith and Edson learned to their amazement that Hays's LT 1/8 and Hall's regimental command group were *not* ashore but languishing along the line of departure.[16]

Four hours later the commanding general radioed Colonel Hall via the *Pursuit*: "Land CT 8 less LT 2/8 and LT 3/8 eastern tip of Betio . . . seize eastern tip, change direction northwest. Establish contact 2/8. . . . H-Hour 0900 Yoke . . . Naval Fire Support has been arranged by Division. Am attempting to get LVTs. If not successful, landing must be made with LCVPs." Hall sent his boat hurriedly into the darkness, seeking Major Hays to relay this strange new mission.[17]

The division scouts on board the *Doyen* suffered similar "yo-yo orders" during the post-midnight hours. Slated to conduct armed reconnaissance missions on the neighboring islands within Tarawa atoll, the scouts waited impatiently for word to launch their rubber boats. Finally, this message came at 0348: "Proceed to beach." Muted cheers. Ten minutes later came an "as-you-were" message: "Do not put boats in the water." Not-so-muted curses. General Smith put the matter to rest with a direct message at 0420 over TBS to the *Doyen*: "Do not land [scouts]. Execute same mission tonight."[18]

Julian Smith could thus talk to some of his units afloat using the TBS circuit but still had no contact with any leader ashore. He assumed General Hermle had landed and taken command of the five battalions by now, but he could not get confirmation.

In the remaining hours of darkness Smith sent these messages to both Hermle and Shoup, hoping that, between them, one would get the word:

> 0003: Will dawn end run to Green Beach or East end of Betio relieve pressure? Which is best for you?
>
> 0028: Hostile machine-gun located wrecked hull on reef off Red 2. Will bomb daylight.
>
> 0103: Can you send 30 LVTs control vessel immediately for tactical purposes?
>
> 0337: Collect 30 LVTs and send to control boat for boating CT 8. Report expected time of arrival.
>
> 0500: CT 8 less LTs 2/8 and 3/8 will land target areas 201 to 205 [northeast tail of Betio] at 0900.[19]

Shoup and Hermle spent much of this time about six hundred yards apart: one ashore, the other at the pierhead, both attended by radio operators. Neither officer received any of these messages from the commanding general, but Hermle had a vital message for Julian Smith. When Major Tompkins and Captain Dutton finally returned to Hermle's position at 0345, they brought word that Shoup wanted Hays's LT 1/8 to come ashore at daybreak on Red Beach Two, close to the pier. Hermle looked for an empty Higgins boat in the darkness, found one, rode it at high speed into the lagoon, and went aboard the *Ringgold*. This took an hour. The Division D-3 Journal records receipt of the first message from the assistant division commander since his arrival at the pierhead nine hours earlier. "0513: From ADC (on RINGGOLD): Shoup desires 1/8 to land on Beach Red Two."

This caused consternation on board the *Maryland*. The division staff had been working for hours with their counterparts on Admiral Hill's staff to coordinate Hays's landing on the eastern tip of Betio. They had arranged air strikes and naval gunfire support, established a new line of departure, designated control officers, and fully expected Hermle or Shoup to have the thirty LVTs fueled and on hand for the assault landing, as requested long before. Hermle's surprising 0513 transmission knocked the whole thing into a cocked hat. More than one officer muttered, "What the hell is Hermle doing on *Ringgold* when he was ordered to take command ashore?"

Julian Smith suppressed his frustration and calmed the staff. At 0522 he radioed Colonel Hall in his flotilla of Higgins boats, canceling the eastern operation and ordering "Land immediately Beach Red Two." At 0535 Hermle rephrased his original message this way: "Recommend Larry [Hays] land Amey's Beach [Red 2] at once." Julian Smith coldly ordered Hermle to report to him on board the *Maryland*. Although this took hours, Smith was still furious. The two men finally realized the extent of the collapse of communications between them throughout the night, but Hermle was now out of the fight. Colonel Hall, meanwhile, took off once again to find Hays with this latest change in orders.[20]

THE FRICTION OF WAR FRUSTRATED ADMIRAL Kobayashi in the Marshalls as well. Although Japanese submarines reached the western Gilberts by the afternoon of the twenty-first, the other elements of the *Hei #3* counterattack plan appeared to move glacially. Redeployment of the "Ko Detachment" seemed particularly sluggish.

Colonel Yamanaka commanded the Ko Detachment, a mixed force recently detached from the 52d Army Division and assigned to 4th Fleet in the Central Pacific. Yamanaka commanded the headquarters element and one infantry battalion of his former 107th Regiment, but the remainder of the force consisted of communications, engineering, and supporting arms units. He had plenty of light fire power—75-mm mountain guns, 37-mm field pieces, a number of heavy machine guns—but he lacked mobility.

The Ko Detachment had just commenced initial amphibious training in Ponape, Caroline Islands, on 17 November when the commander received sudden orders to deploy to the southeastern region, doubtlessly in response to the American invasion of Bougainville. Just as abruptly, higher headquarters canceled those orders and directed Colonel Yamanaka to prepare for a counterlanding in the Gilberts. The light cruisers

Naka and *Isuzu* arrived in Ponape the morning of the twenty-first to take the Ko Detachment to the Marshalls for staging, but embarkation took thirty hours and the ships had insufficient room for Yamanaka's many field pieces.

The cruiser *Nagara* and a destroyer steamed to Ponape to embark the remaining components. The entire Ko Detachment did not reach Kwajalein until the twenty-fourth. Yamanaka then tried to train his men in amphibious assault techniques, but the force had only a couple of operational landing craft available. Training suffered.

By the twenty-fifth, Admiral Kobayashi had assembled four light cruisers and seven destroyers as the reinforcing support unit for the Gilberts counterattack. Too little, too late. Admiral Koga, stung by his earlier air and surface losses near Rabaul, refused to deploy his battleships from Truk without the protection of trained replacement carrier pilots. Spruance's carriers and battleships would have destroyed Kobayashi's light surface force in a matter of minutes in the Gilberts. The ill-prepared Ko Detachment would find it extremely difficult to execute an opposed counterlanding. Besides, time seemed to have run out for the garrisons at Tarawa and Makin. The communications ship *Katori Maru* had heard nothing over the airwaves for several days.[21]

The great counterattack plan was a bust. Only two years earlier the Japanese maintained the premier amphibious forces in the world. A year prior the Imperial Japanese Navy dominated the Pacific. Now the Combined Fleet could not muster the forces to execute a counterlanding with fifteen hundred troops against a precarious American beachhead. Tarawa would reflect this shifting of the tides of war.[22]

IN THE STRUGGLE TO GET ASHORE, ITEM COMpany, 3/8, lost a ceremonial silver chalice, its good-luck symbol from the Guadalcanal campaign. Survivors mourned this almost as much as their other losses in men and material that day. That night a Marine found the chalice tumbling in near-shore waves along Red Three, amid the surge of bodies. It was a welcome sign.[23]

CHAPTER EIGHT

"We Are Winning!"

Tarawa was one of those rare battles in which every partici-
pant became a hero in spite of himself. Just getting ashore,
or trying to, was a major act of courage.
—Lt. George D. Lillibridge
(*American Heritage*, 34 [October–November 1983])

DAWN OF THE SECOND DAY FOUND MAJ. MIKE
Ryan lying flat on his back in a pool of blood at the entrance to
a captured Japanese bunker on Green Beach. Ryan was asleep,
not dead; the blood came from one of the bunker's defenders.
At midnight, exhausted from making yet another round of his
patchwork perimeter, Ryan simply dragged the corpse out of
the way and collapsed in sleep, unaware of the residue. Two
days later Julian Smith would come ashore at Green Beach,
stare at Ryan, and exclaim, "My God, are you hurt?" Only then
would Ryan notice the blood stains covering the back of his
utility jacket. Meanwhile, there was a job to do.

The ultimate American victory at Betio evolved from the
attack executed during one intense hour the second morning by
the hodgepodge assortment of Marines and sailors fighting
under the leadership of Major Ryan on Green Beach. Ryan's
"orphans," the most unlikely of units, became the first on Betio
to integrate tanks, tactical aircraft, and self-directed naval gunfire in support of an inland assault. Ryan's seizure of the entire
western end of the island made possible the event Shoup and
Julian Smith had sought since the first chaotic moments of the
D-Day assault: the opportunity to land reinforcements across a
secure beachhead with full unit integrity and supporting arms.
Sounds simple, given the small island and the preponderance
of American firepower, but intense Japanese resistance and lin-

gering communications failures delayed the maneuver until the second day's end.

The onset of morning nautical twilight revealed the extent of the previous day's slaughter. The reef and beaches of Tarawa already looked like a charnel house. Lieutenant Lillibridge surveyed what he could see of the beach at first light and was appalled. "[A] dreadful sight, bodies drifting slowly in the water just off the beach, junked amtracs." The stench of dead bodies covered the embattled island like a cloud. The smell drifted out to the line of departure, a bad omen for Hays's troops, disoriented and lethargic, getting ready to start their run to the beach.[1]

Shoup's predawn request to General Smith, as relayed sequentially through Major Tompkins and General Hermle, specified the landing of Hays's LT 1/8 on Red Beach Two "*close to the pier*." Shoup wanted no repeat of the disasters that befell Kyle's LT 1/2 and Ruud's LT 3/8 trying to land in traditional waves on line the previous day. By contrast, Rixey had landed his pack-howitzer sections in column formation, hugging the pier all the way in to the beach, and hardly lost a man. Shoup himself had slogged ashore along that route; he now saw it as the only safe approach.

As we have seen, however, the key component of Shoup's request did not survive the tenuous communications route to Smith. Hermle's messages simply specified "Red 2" or "Amey's Beach." The commanding general thus ordered Colonel Hall and Major Hays to land on Red Two at 0615. Hall and Hays, lacking communications with Shoup and totally oblivious of the situation ashore, assumed LT 1/8 would be making a covered landing. The *Pursuit* signaled Lieutenants Fletcher and Albert to form their boats into waves and guide them to Red Two. The exhausted Marines cheered as they finally got under way for Betio. Colonel Hall paused to ask the *Pursuit* to radio the flagship: "LT 1/8 leaves Line of Departure at 0615."[2]

Things quickly went awry. The apogean neap tide lapsed even lower than D-Day, barely attaining two feet. The coral barrier would prove totally impassable; indeed, parts of the flat apron inshore of the reef would be drying in the morning sun. Japanese gunners along the entire northern coast—especially those in the Pocket—could hardly believe their luck: daylight, low tide, no LVTs. The rikusentai moved up spare ammunition and charged their weapons.[3]

Shoup saw the neat waves of Higgins boats approaching the reef opposite Red Beach Two and roared in frustration. Marines all along the seawall stared in helpless fascination.

Hays's men, surprised at the reef obstacle and the increasing enemy fire, slowly climbed out of their snagged boats to begin the five-hundred-yard trek to shore. Many of them drifted dangerously far to the right flank, fully within the beaten zone of the multiple guns firing from the Pocket. "It was the worst possible place they could have picked," said Red Mike Edson later. Now all Japanese gunners opened an unrelenting fire. Enfilade fire came from the snipers and machine gunners who had infiltrated to the disabled LVTs offshore and the *Nimonea* at the reef's edge. Hays's men began to fall at every hand.[4]

The horror had just begun. The big dual-purpose antiaircraft guns along the eastern tail leveled their long barrels and began zeroing in on the Higgins boats themselves, waiting for the

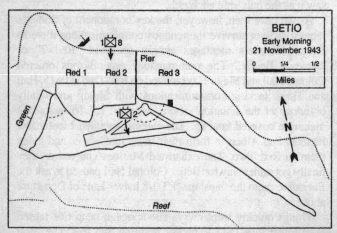

moment the craft slammed into the reef and began lowering the bow ramp. Observing this from the shore, Sergeant Hatch's dismay was such that he could not bring himself to use his movie camera. "It was uncanny to watch a ramp go down and a bunch of guys make a surge to come out and a shell explode right in their face, like the guy had dead aim and was looking right down into that boat and fired right into it. . . . the boat blown completely out of the water."[5]

The Marines on the beach did everything they could to stop the slaughter. Shoup called for naval gunfire support. Two of Colonel Rixey's 75-mm pack howitzers (protected by a sand berm erected during the night by a Seabee bulldozer) began firing at the blockhouses at the Red 1/Red 2 border, 125 yards away, with delayed fuses and high explosive shells. A flight of F4F Wildcats attacked the hulk of the *Nimonea* with bombs and machine guns. Crowe and Jordan spurred their troops to get over the seawall and provide covering fire for the exposed men in the water. Lieutenant Hawkins, enraged at the heavy losses occurring among the 8th Marines, launched a virtually single-handed offensive inland from Red Two. All these measures helped, but for the large part, the Japanese continued to rip the struggling Marines with a withering cross fire.

The bloodbath sickened correspondent Sherrod. "One boat blows up, then another. The survivors start swimming for shore, but machine-gun bullets dot the water all around them. . . . This is worse, far worse than it was yesterday." Within an hour, he could count "at least two hundred bodies which do not move at all on the dry flats."[6]

"Troops landed too far west of pier," reported General Hermle from the *Ringgold*. "Receiving machine-gun fire from the right."[7]

Japanese gunners shot Lt. Dean Ladd before he could wade the first hundred yards inside the reef. "A sickening splat, like an inner tube snapped across my abdomen, shocking me. I realized a bullet had hit me nearly dead center below the naval. I quickly removed my pack, small radio, helmet and web belt. I was too weak to maintain my balance, forgetting about everything but trying to keep my head above water. . . . The closest man to me, PFC Thomas F. Sullivan, came to my rescue."[8]

First Lt. Frank Plant, the battalion air liaison officer, accompanied Major Hays in the command boat. As the craft slammed into the reef, Hays shouted, "Men, debark!" and jumped into the water. A murderous fire greeted the troops that followed. Plant helped pull the wounded back into the boat, noting that, "the water all around was colored purple with blood." As Plant hurried to catch up with Major Hays, he was terrified at the sudden appearance of what he took to be Japanese fighters roaring right toward him. These, however, were the Navy Wildcats aiming for the nearby *Nimonea*. The pilots were exuberant but inconsistent: one bomb hit the hulk squarely; others missed by two hundred yards. An angry David Shoup came up on the radio at 0755: "Stop strafing! Bombing ship hitting own troops!"[9]

As PFC Bill Crumpacker recalled: "All hell broke loose. There was firing from the pier, left flank, from the grounded ship, right flank, and from dead ahead, the island." Lt. Albert Tidwell, told by Major Hays to expect an unopposed landing, lost exactly half his platoon "before we even touched the beach." Chaplain Willard agonized at the loss of so many of "his boys." "Fire from enemy positions mowed them down as a scythe cuts through grass."[10]

The Higgins boat carrying Sgt. John White and his squad from Charlie Company, 1/8, never reached the reef. A Japanese dual-purpose gun crew sank the boat in deep water, north of the coral barrier. Many of the Marines had just unbuckled their life jackets, anticipating a quick debarkation into shallow water. The boat went down swiftly. Some troops, heavily laden, drowned. The survivors flailed the water, struggling toward the reef. Sergeant White's life belt caught under his armpit, momentarily saving him. Then someone underwater grabbed his leg in desperation, dragging him below the surface. White shook loose, came up for air, sank again, the turbid waters surreal with men in their death throes.[11]

White reached the reef, exhausted, but helped other survivors to safety. Relative safety. Ahead lay the long wade under fire to the beach. This took two hours. Sergeant White lost half his squad; he was the only one to reach the beach in possession of a weapon.[12]

PFC William Murphy figured he owed his life to two different individuals that endless morning. At first it was the *Sheridan*'s coxswain, braced fully upright and dangerously exposed at the throttle, who kept nosing his Higgins boat along the reef, searching for a closer approach. The line of the reef varied. The coxswain found one small indentation that saved the embarked Marines a hundred yards of wading. Then, close to the shore, the 5'2" Murphy stepped into a shell hole and sank out of sight. "My lieutenant, Bill Lundigan, who was 6'3" or more, grabbed me by the back of my jacket and pulled me out of the hole, saying 'Take it easy, Murph.' I never saw him again."[13]

Pharmacist's Mate Costello and his team paused in their treatment of wounded men in the damaged pillbox to watch the drama unfold in the shallows directly to their front. Costello saw something he would never forget.

> It was terrible watching the Marines being shot down. By that time I felt our cause was hopeless and the Marines would never get on the island. . . . [Then] I watched one Marine coming in carrying a heavy load and saw him get hit. He continued coming in and I saw him get hit again, and still he kept coming, and then he was hit a third time. When he reached the shore I grabbed him, saying, "You stupid S.O.B., why in hell didn't you drop that load and crouch in the water so you wouldn't make such a target?" As I dressed the wounds in his arm, jaw, and shoulder, I heard him mutter, "They said we had to get this ammo to the Marines on the beach—that they were running short—I had to bring it in."[14]

At the end, only such primeval courage enabled the survivors to struggle ashore against the hellish cross fire. Hays reported to Shoup at 0800 with about half his landing team. He had suffered well over three hundred casualties; others were scattered all along the beach and the pier. Worse, the unit had lost all its flamethrowers, demolitions, and heavy weapons. Shoup directed Hays to attack westward toward the Pocket, but both men knew that small arms and courage alone would not prevail against fortified positions.

By now Shoup had reestablished communications with General Smith on the *Maryland*. He tried not to let his discouragement show, but Shoup admitted, "The situation does not look good ashore." A minute later, with a sense of desperation evidently clouding his judgment, he radioed: "Request rubber boat battalion 6th Marines [LT 1/6] be landed at once on Beach Red Two. Turn left and attack through 2/8. Old ship off Beach Red Two should be bombed prior to landing the units. ADC was not consulted. Situation still uncertain."[15]

The drama of Hays's landing had yet to play out. Scores of wounded Marines clung to the reef or lay in the shallows; other men huddled in forlorn groups, weaponless and demoralized. Japanese snipers in the hulks nearby began to pick them off methodically, one by one. Navy Lieutenants Fletcher and Albert, trying to herd their empty and shot-up boats back to the *Sheridan*, noticed the crisis and returned to the reef. Both officers began pulling wounded Marines on board, then transferring them to a Higgins boat for delivery to the transports. This was a slow process.

Meanwhile, the sluggish tide finally began to rise, just enough to endanger the more critically wounded men along the reef. Japanese machine gunners on the *Nimonea* began dueling with the sailors manning the guns on the small craft. Albert's salvage boat broke its propeller on the coral, and the crew transferred to a Higgins boat. The new coxswain, Boatswain's Mate Third Class Larry Wade, was fearless, but the craft carried several large drums of gasoline, and the Japanese gunners used incendiary rounds. "I'll never know how we lived through it," Albert recalled. "I remember our crew stamping out small fires all around the fuel drums. But we kept shooting back, and we kept pulling more wounded aboard."[16]

Pulling wounded men from the water onto the low-riding salvage boat had been fairly easy, but the Higgins boat had a high freeboard. Albert had to hang onto the gunwale with one hand while leaning far over the side and pulling mightily with the other. "It was awful. Sometimes I think we hurt the men more by pulling them up by their broken arms or legs than if we'd left them in the water. I still don't like to think about it."[17]

Other Navy boat crews pitched in, bravely rescuing most of the stranded men under steady fire. At length, Albert's boat approached a group of about thirty-five Marines whose boat had been sunk beneath them. They were unhurt but also unarmed. "I offered to take them back to the ship. They refused. They asked me to bring them rifles so they could fight their way ashore and join their outfit."[18]

Many acts of unit and individual bravery on both sides of the reef gave the men in the water a slightly better chance of survival. Clearly, the most spectacular of these was performed by Lieutenant Hawkins of the 2d Marines scout-sniper platoon. The world will probably never know what prompted his burst of conspicuous gallantry. No doubt he chafed at having missed so much of the first day's action by being stranded on top of the pier and separated from the bulk of his platoon. Likewise, his initial sense of helplessness in watching the Japanese shoot down so many of Hays's men must have motivated him intensely. Maybe Hawkins, like Shoup and Crowe, simply burned with an indomitable fire that would not even consider defeat. Whatever the cause, Hawkins resolved to take matters along Red Beach Two into his own scarred hands.

According to the report of the scout-sniper platoon, (subsequently verified and expanded by research conducted by then-Maj. Clay Darling for the Marine Corps Command and Staff College), Hawkins organized and led two assaults that morning. The first kicked off at 0630, just as Hays's lead waves began tumbling out of their boats along the reef. Hawkins led two sections of his scout-snipers westward along Red Two and just inland from the seawall. The team advanced about seventy-five yards, Hawkins insisting on leading the attack on each fortified position. At one point, as he crouched directly beside one position, tossing grenades through the firing slits, a Japanese tossed one of the grenades back. The explosion wounded Hawkins severely, shredding his chest with shrapnel. He held his ground, nonetheless, and continued throwing grenades inside the pillbox until the firing and screaming stopped.[19]

The unit returned to Shoup's CP, but Hawkins refused medical treatment, reorganizing his men and once more leading them westward, toward a series of strong points that still fired on Hays's men in the shallows. Again he led each assault—absolutely fearless—crawling or dashing up to the pillbox, tossing in grenades, leaping up to shoot through the slits. His bravery was superhuman, but it could not last in the maelstrom. About 1030 a Japanese marksman shot him in the right shoulder. The wound would prove mortal. "Boys," he told Gunnery Sergeant Hooper, "I sure hate to leave you like this." Ironically—perhaps fittingly—Hawkins fell within fifty yards of the spot where Sergeant Bordelon had died the day before.[20]

The scout-snipers took their fallen leader to the regimental aid station, the improvised operating room in the bomb-damaged Japanese pillbox where Doctor Brukardt and his corpsmen labored. Buck Estes tried to reassure Hawkins, "We're going to get you patched up, Hawkeye." But Doctor Brukardt could see the wound was fatal. The bullet had severed the axillary artery (in Costello's words, "his armpit had been destroyed"), and Hawkins had lost a lot of blood. According to Brukardt, "Successful treatment would have consisted of immediate surgery to locate and clamp the artery to prevent further bleeding, as well as the transfusion of large amounts of blood."[21]

This was patently out of the question. Brukardt and his crew had available only sulfur powder, morphine syrettes, standard bandages, and a few units of plasma. Brukardt performed on the dirt floor what surgery he could with a scalpel and a flashlight. None of this could save Hawkins. He lived only ten minutes after his men brought him to the aid station. Now they wept, unashamedly.[22]

Reports of Hawkins's death saddened the Marines ashore. Said Colonel Shoup, "It's not often that you can credit a first lieutenant with winning a battle, but Hawkins came as near to it as any man could." Hawkins, among other contributions, helped break the logjam along Red Beach Two.[23]

Inshore from that beach, spread along a revetment, Captain Williams's Baker Company, 1/2, continued to wait for further orders. Williams had forty to fifty men, including a machine-gun section. His radio had failed. Williams arranged for a land-line connection back to Shoup's CP, but as soon as he picked up the field telephone he wished he had kept out of contact. "Major Culhane [regimental operations officer] was a screamer," said Williams. "We feared him more than the Japanese." Culhane ordered Williams to attack south across the island. "Go get your feet wet, boy," yelled Culhane to Williams. "We got 'em on the run."[24]

Great, thought Williams. "It was a suicide order: no cover, wide open, flat as a pancake." They could only hope to catch the Japanese off guard. They did. Screaming like banshees, Williams's men dashed across the airfield and tumbled into a long trench that ran parallel to Black Beach, the south shore. Other Marines, surprised by the charge, leapt up and raced after them, including Private First Class Fratt, the survivor from Easy, 2/8, still firing his Springfield.[25]

The Marines had cut the island in two, but the position was tenuous. The Japanese counterattacked viciously, then spent the remainder of the day working around Williams's thin line with snipers and grenadiers. Woody Kyle, commanding LT 1/2, joined Williams in this exposed position. Major Kyle was fit, only twenty-eight, and had been decorated for bravery in Guadalcanal. He and Williams helped steady some raw nerves. The Marines were in for a hair-raising twenty-four hours. Japanese troops set up machine guns to sweep the long runway and taxiway; additional reinforcements paid hell crossing. Surviving Marines from How Company, 2/2, the weapons company, countered the Japanese fire with their .30-caliber water-cooled Browning heavy machine guns. The Marines mounted these weapons on the much lower light machine-gun tripods, reducing their vulnerability. The duel continued for hours. "You could not see the Japanese," recalled Lieutenant Lillibridge, "but fire seemed to come from every direction."[26]

By this time Colonel Jordan lost contact with the forward elements of LT 2/2. Shoup ordered him across the island to reestablish command. Jordan did so at great hazard, but he found precious little left to command. His decimated rifle companies could account for only fifty men between them. With Kyle on the scene with his beleaguered but larger force, Jordan realized his own presence was superfluous. He organized and resupplied these survivors to the best of his abilities, then—at Shoup's direction—merged them with Kyle's force and returned to the regimental command post in his original role as an observer. The division (especially LT 2/2), owed Jordan a great deal for his initiative and competence. The landing team had suffered a casualty rate exceeding 50 percent and lost Herb Amey, their popular leader, but Jordan had stepped in to pick up the pieces and maintain their fighting spirit.

In contrast to LT 2/2, the combined forces of Majors Crowe and Ruud on Red Beach Three had plenty of troops and weapons. But their left flank still rubbed raw against three large Japanese bunkers, each mutually supporting and seemingly unassailable. The stubby Burns-Philp commercial pier remained a bloody no-man's-land as the forces fought for its possession. Learning from the mistakes of D-Day, Crowe ensured that infantry teams always accompanied "Colorado," his one surviving Sherman tank. Communications between the 8th Marines and the supporting destroyers in the lagoon remained in effect; fire support flourished accordingly. While the outspoken Crowe continued to disparage the accuracy and effectiveness of the air support ("Our aircraft never did us much good."), he became enthusiastic about the naval guns. "I had the *Ringgold*, the *Dashiell*, and the *Anderson* in support of me. . . . Anything I asked for I got from them. They were great!"[27]

Naval gunfire could do just so much. The destroyers themselves had a rough second day in the lagoon. Two ships ran aground. The *Anderson*'s "overs" from the ocean side of the island landed dangerously close aboard the lagoon destroyers. And from time to time the Japanese would bring a damaged coastal defense piece back in action. Nor could Crowe, Ruud, or Chamberlin do much to break the deadlock on the eastern flank. The three Japanese strong points were formidable enough.[28]

Then, evidently during the first night, Lieutenant Minami, commanding the third company of the Sasebo 7th Special Naval Landing Force, redeployed most of his combined-arms force from the eastern sector to reinforce the base defense troops arrayed in and about the strong points. Vicious fighting characterized this portion of the battlefield all day. By nightfall, the Marines had little to show for their heavy losses.[29]

With Crowe and Ruud stonewalled on the east, Kyle across the island but hanging on for dear life, and Schoettel and Hays lacking heavy weapons and stalled in attacking the Pocket, it was now all up to Major Ryan and his makeshift battalion on the western end. Ryan truly had a bunch of orphans under his loose command. He had elements of all four companies of Schoettel's LT 3/2; the equivalent of a platoon from George Company, LT 2/2; and more than a hundred members from Kyle's LT 1/2. Others straggled in from some unspeakable odyssey getting ashore, some from the 8th Marines, others "dismounted" amtrackers, tankers, or Navy boat crewmen. A wounded staff noncommissioned officer, one of the newcomers, limped up to Ryan, saluted, and asked what he could do to help. Ryan put him to work organizing the stragglers into rifle squads. "Through the years I have treasured that salute," said Ryan.[30]

Tall, sandy-haired Mike Ryan was twenty-seven years old at Tarawa, a native of Osage City, Kansas. Ten years earlier he had enlisted in the Marine Corps Reserve. The Corps called him to active duty in November 1940 with the 15th Reserve Battalion in Galveston and commissioned him a second lieutenant. During the initial war years some stiff-necked officers in the regular establishment viewed reservists as inferior beings, less qualified and unprofessional. One of these die-hard regulars who also served at Tarawa would pay Ryan a back-handed compliment after the battle, saying gracelessly, "I never imagined a *reserve* officer could achieve such battle-field distinction!" As in each of America's declared wars, reservists in World War II would earn their spurs quickly, often prominently.[31]

Ryan's fortunes on D+1 were greatly enhanced by three developments during the preceding night: the absence of a Japanese spoiling attack against his thin lines; the repair of the medium tank "Cecilia"; and the arrival of Lt. Thomas Greene, a naval gunfire spotter with a fully functional radio. Ryan took his time organizing a coordinated attack against the nest of gun emplacements, pillboxes, and rifle pits concentrated on the southwest corner of the island. He planned the attack carefully with his executive officer, Capt. Robert O'Brian, and the other company commanders (including Captain Crain, Lieutenant Turner, and Lieutenant Bale, the tanker).

Poor communications continued to hamper the Marines ashore. In this case, Ryan could talk to the fire support ships but not to Shoup. It seemed to Ryan that it took hours for his runners to negotiate the gauntlet of fire back to the beach, radio Shoup's CP, and return with answers. Ryan's first message to Shoup announcing his attack plans received the eventual response, "Hold up—we are calling an air strike." It took two more runners to get the air strike canceled. Ryan then ordered Lieutenant Greene to call in naval gunfire on the southwest targets. Two destroyers responded quickly and accurately.[32]

At 1120 Ryan launched a coordinated tank-infantry assault. "Lieutenant Greene played his radio like a master organist to walk that naval gunfire just ahead of us," Ryan said. But the ships balked when Greene asked for fire as close as fifty yards. The commanding officers called up Julian Smith of the TBS circuit and asked his permission to fire that close to his Marines. "Go ahead," replied Smith, glad to know of offensive action under way in that presumably quiet corner.[33]

Within an hour Ryan's patchwork force seized all of Green Beach and were ready to attack eastward toward the airfield. At

1225 the *Anderson* radioed the flagship: "Am in semaphore communications with Marines on southwest corner of island. Message: Marines have secured Japanese from point. Need water badly." It was Captain Crain. Green Beach and the far shore were fully in American hands.[34]

Ryan's achievement was remarkable, not the least because he did it with such an improvised force and by using still untested fire support procedures. His assault killed or scattered much of the 2d Company, Sasebo 7th Special Naval Landing Force, charged with defending the western sector. Moreover, the Marines overran and destroyed a formidable series of defensive positions, including two 140-mm coastal defense guns, two tandem-mounted 8-inch guns, three Type 41

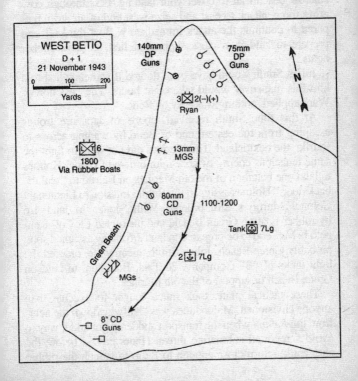

pedestal-mounted 80-mm coastal guns, a pair of Type 94 rapid-firing 37-mm guns, and dozens of 7.7-mm heavy machine-gun positions. Here, at last, was a protected beachhead.[35]

Nevertheless, Ryan still faced terrible communications problems. Twice he reported heavy mines inshore of the reef along the southern end of Green Beach, but that message never reached any higher headquarters. But General Smith knew of Ryan's success and was overjoyed. For the first time Smith had the opportunity to land reinforcements on a covered beach with full unit integrity. Three minutes after receiving word of Captain Crain's appearance on the southwest tip, Smith radioed the 6th Marines: "Land one LT immediately south half Beach Green. Suggest column of companies. Our troops now hold shallow beachhead to cover your landing. Pass through covering force, attack to east and seize west end of air strip, prepared to continue the attack immediately. Boat third LT and prepare to land it in close support of first. . . . Tow rubber boats."[36]

Julian Smith would have been floored if someone had told him this maneuver would take eight hours. The "Friction of War" applied: nothing was easy on Betio.

At this time Smith received reports of Japanese troops escaping from the eastern end of Betio by wading across to Bairiki, the next island. The Marines did not want to fight the same tenacious enemy twice. Smith ordered Colonel Holmes to land one battalion of the 6th Marines on Bairiki to "seal the back door." Holmes assigned the Bairiki mission to Lieutenant Colonel Murray's 2/6, ordered Willie Jones to land 1/6 by rubber boat on Green Beach, and instructed Lt. Col. Kenneth F. McLeod to be prepared to land 3/6 at any assigned spot, probably Green Beach. Julian Smith, meanwhile, ordered the light tanks of "B" Company, 2d Tank Battalion, to land on Green Beach in support of the 6th Marines.

These tactical plans took much longer to execute than anyone envisioned. Major Jones was "halfway down the nets" from the *Feland* when the transport suddenly got under way to avoid a reported submarine threat. Hours passed before the ship could return close enough to Betio to launch the rubber boats and their LCVP tow craft. The light tanks were among the critical items not truly combat loaded, being carried in the very bottom of the cargo holds. Indiscriminate unloading during the first thirty hours of the landing had further scrambled supplies and equipment in intervening decks. It took hours to get the tanks clear and loaded aboard lighters.

Shoup was bewildered by the long delays. At 1345 he sent Jones a message: "Bring in flamethrowers if possible. . . . Doing our best." At 1525 he queried division about the estimated landing time of LT 1/6. He wanted Jones ashore and on the attack before dark.[37]

Admiral Hill ordered the *Requisite* out of the lagoon to sweep the seaward side of the reef off Green Beach. The minesweeper spent an hour searching for moored mines, found none (and did not have the angle to see the mines in the shallows), and returned to the lagoon to serve as primary control ship for Murray's forthcoming landing on Bairiki.[38]

IN THE MEANTIME COLONEL SHOUP AND HIS small staff faced daunting logistical support problems. Shoup organized teams to strip the dead of their ammunition, canteens, and first aid pouches. Heroic logistic delivery resulted from the combined efforts of Colonel Salazar, commanding the shore party; Capt. J. B. McGovern, USN, acting as primary control officer on board the *Pursuit*; Maj. Ben Weatherwax, assistant D-4 (logistics officer for the 2d Marine Division); and Maj. George L. H. Cooper, operations officer for 2d Battalion, 18th Marines. Between them, these officers gradually brought some order out of chaos. They assumed strict control of resupplies and used the surviving LVTs judiciously to keep the shuttle of casualties moving seaward and critical items flowing from the pierhead to the beach.

All of this was performed by sleepless men under constant fire. The pierhead remained a dangerous place. Laden small boats seemed to cover the surface of the lagoon. Few officers knew which supplies were carried in which boats. Admiral Hill's determined race to off-load his transports came to a sudden halt in late afternoon. No more empty boats were available. The composite shore party could unload at best three or four boats an hour at the pierhead. Upwards of two hundred loaded boats circled out of gun range in the lagoon. Here the relative newness of amphibious doctrine and the paucity of training time put a severe crimp in the assault.

Navy chaplains were also hard at work wherever Marines were fighting ashore. Theirs was particularly heartbreaking work, consoling the wounded, administering last rites to the dying, praying for the souls of the dead before the bulldozer came to cover the bodies from the unforgiving tropical sun. Many Marines had been cut down at point-blank range by high-caliber Japanese guns. Merely identifying the dead under these conditions proved daunting. The chaplains at Tarawa surpassed themselves. Three of them—Wyeth Willard, F. W. Kelly, and J.V.E. Loughlin—would receive combat awards for exceptionally meritorious conduct under fire.[39]

Late in the afternoon the first two Jeeps reached the pierhead, each towing a 37-mm gun. Intersecting Japanese fire had minimized movement along the top of the pier. The drivers decided to risk it, gunning their vehicles and driving wildly down the length under a fusillade of shots. Sherrod grinned at the sight. "If a sign of certain victory were needed, this is it. The jeeps have arrived."[40]

Sherrod was right. The tide of battle began to shift perceptibly toward the Americans as the afternoon progressed. The fighting was still intense, the Japanese fire still murderous, but the surviving Marines were on the move, no longer gridlocked in precarious toeholds on the beach. Rixey's pack howitzers were adding a new definition for close fire support. The shore party efforts had greatly improved the resupply of ammunition and fresh water. Morale seemed uplifted too. The troops knew the 6th Marines were coming in soon. "I thought up until 1300 today it was touch and go," said Rixey. "Then I knew we would win."[41]

By contrast, a sense of despair seemed to spread among the defenders. They had shot down the Marines at every turn, but with every fallen Marine, another would appear, rifle blazing, well supported by artillery and naval guns. The great *Yogeki* counterattack plan failed to materialize. Increasingly, Japanese troops began committing suicide rather than risk capture. The *Bushido* code actually saved American lives. If the Japanese had chosen to fight to the last man instead of killing themselves, the Marines would have experienced a sizeable increase in their own casualties. Sherrod encountered the bodies of two Japanese suicide victims under a gun turret, "hands off, guts out," he noted factually in his journal.[42]

Shoup sensed this shift in momentum. Despite his frustration over the day's delays and miscommunications, he was buoyed enough to send a situation report at 1600 to Julian Smith that closed with these terse words, which have become classic: "Casualties: many. Percentage dead: unknown. Combat efficiency: *'We are winning.'* "[43]

His aside to Sherrod at roughly the same time was more revealing. "I think we're winning but the bastards have got a lot of bullets left."[44]

At 1655 Ray Murray's LT 2/6 landed against light opposition on Bairiki Island. One Japanese machine-gun crew opened a hot fire on Murray's boats, but carrier air support redeemed itself with a single strafing run. The rikusentai had chosen their firing position unwisely. Strafing bullets ignited nearby drums of gasoline and vaporized the entire crew. During the night and early morning hours, Lt. Col. George R. E. Shell's 2d Battalion, 10th Marines, landed on the same island and began registering their pack howitzers. Rixey's fire direction center on Betio helped this process, while the artillery forward observer attached to Crowe's LT 2/8 on Red Beach Three had the unusual experience of adjusting the fire of the Bairiki guns "while looking into their muzzles." The Marines had practiced this earlier on New Zealand. Smith finally had artillery in place on Bairiki.

Elsewhere, Major Jones and LT 1/6 were on the move. It had been a day of many false starts. At one point, Willie K. and his men had been debarking over the sides in preparation for an assault on the eastern end of Betio when "The Word" changed their mission to Green Beach. When the *Feland* finally returned to within reasonable distance from the island, the

Marines of LT 1/6 disembarked for real. Using tactics practiced with the Navy during the Efate rehearsal, they used LCVPs to tow their rubber rafts to the reef. There the Marines embarked aboard their rafts, six to ten troops per craft, and began the thousand-yard paddle toward Green Beach.

Major Jones remarked that he did not feel like the "Admiral of the Condom Fleet" as he helped paddle his raft shoreward. "Control was nebulous at best. . . . the battalion was spread out over the ocean from horizon to horizon. We must have had 150 boats." His Marines were apprehensive, knowing they were sitting ducks. "The whole island seemed to be on fire," said 1st Lt. Baine Kerr, expecting to be riddled by Japanese gunners any second. Traversing that thousand yards from reef to beach took the better part of an hour, and the Marines, backlit throughout by the setting sun, were perfect targets. But Ryan's men had performed masterful work clearing the beach. No Japanese had a clear shot at this slow-moving armada throughout the hour.

There were other concerns. The frequent appearance of anti-boat mines moored to coral heads beneath the surface alarmed Jones intensely. The rubber rafts passed over the mines without incident, but the landing team also had two LVTs accompanying the ship-to-shore movement, each preloaded with ammo, rations, water, medical supplies, and spare radio equipment. Guided by the rafts, one of the LVTs made it ashore, but the second drifted into a mine that blew the heavy vehicle ten feet in the air, killing most of the crew and destroying the supplies. It was a serious loss, but not critical.

Well covered by Ryan's men, the landing force suffered no other casualties coming ashore. Jones's battalion became the first to land on Betio essentially intact.[45] It was after dark by the time his troops assumed defensive positions behind Ryan's lines. The light tanks of Baker Company continued their attempt to come ashore on Green Beach, but the high surf and great distance between the reef and the beach greatly hindered landing efforts. Eventually, a platoon of six tanks managed to reach the beach; the remainder of the company moved their boats toward the pier and worked all night to get ashore on Red

Beach Two. McLeod's LT 3/6 remained afloat in Higgins boats beyond the reef, facing an uncomfortable night.

Within the Japanese positions in the interior of the island, Warrant Officer Ota assembled the survivors of his platoon and nursed his painful wounds. "Later that night," he recalled, "there were rumors that the Americans had also occupied the western end of Betio Island. We did not know what to believe or what to do because we had no communications."[46]

By dusk Lieutenant Colonel Rixey had his entire artillery battalion ashore, the process having consumed the previous twenty-eight hours. Yet despite this protracted exposure and the forward placement of his pack howitzers, Rixey's casualties had been miraculously light: seven dead, eighteen wounded. Capt. Kenneth L. Brown, a battery commander, died while leading an attack against a Japanese pillbox that threatened his cannoneers as they reassembled the pack howitzers for the initial fire missions.[47]

On the second evening Rixey positioned his guns in a tight circle. Two of them pointed out into the lagoon; one aimed directly at the *Nimonea*.[48]

Ninety-five miles northwest of Tarawa, on board the battleship *Pennsylvania*, Admiral Turner and Gen. Holland Smith strained to hear any useful reports from the battle under way at Tarawa. Fleet communications suffered some of the same failings as the tactical radios ashore. The VAC G-3 (operations officer) told Smith that he had monitored orders issued to the commanding officer, 8th Marines, to conduct landings during the night by rubber boats on the outer islands within Tarawa atoll. Lacking other information, Holland Smith assumed the 2d Marine Division planned to deploy Hays's LT 1/8—the only boat-trained battalion in the 8th Marines—for this mission. The senior Smith wondered why Julian Smith had made such a strong case for the corps reserve the day before if he still had the division reserve available for this ancillary mission. More war friction. Hays's battalion, of course, had already entered the breach and fought itself ashore. The intercepted message was simply Julian Smith telling the *Doyen* to launch the division scouts by rubber boats within the lagoon that night.[49]

Capt. John R. Nelson's scouts had two principal missions as they debarked from the *Doyen* in the tropical darkness. First, they had to determine the extent and location of Japanese forces and installations within the outer islands of Tarawa atoll. Second, they had to find "Sergeant Joseph," an English-speaking Gilbertese native trained earlier by the British. Doing so took all night, but the scouts accomplished both missions without being discovered.

This stealthy operation reflected the benefits of the scouts' concentrated training in the new field of amphibious recon-naissance. All that shipboard and surf-zone training in New Zealand paid dividends. The scouts debarked swiftly from the ship, boarding LCVPs that towed their rubber boats toward the designated islands. Each island had its own fringing reef; many stood a thousand yards off the beach. The scouts silently trans-ferred into their rubber boats and began the long paddle ashore. Each platoon had its own islet to reconnoiter. The second pla-toon somehow tracked down Sergeant Joseph and delivered him safely to the flagship at daybreak. Another platoon assumed covert observation positions along the main footpath on Buota Island (the "bend of the elbow"). A large force of rikusentai passed "within spitting distance," heading north. The scouts continued to shadow this force, greatly facilitating the eventual assault by Murray's LT 2/6 at the end of the battle.[50]

Julian Smith sensed that Shoup, having run the show ashore for the first critical thirty-six hours, was now in over his head. By late D+1, however, eight infantry and two artillery battal-ions were deployed either on Betio or nearby Bairiki. With LT 3/6 scheduled to land early on D+2, virtually all the combat and combat support elements of the 2d Marine Divi-sion would be deployed. It was time to send in the chief of staff.

Red Mike Edson reached Shoup's CP by 2030 and found the barrel-chested junior colonel still on his feet, grimy and haggard but full of fight. Edson assumed command, allowing

Shoup to concentrate on his own reinforced combat team, and began making plans for the morrow.

Shoup had no grounds to object to Edson's assumption of command and willingly shared his knowledge of the battlefield with the chief of staff. In Shoup's eyes it probably helped that Edson was a proven combat warrior. Earlier, however, Shoup had resisted being relieved by senior officers. The first occurred during the night of D-Day, when General Hermle reached the pierhead. Shoup bluntly told Hermle not to come ashore, that "there was no place to land." This was a stretch. Rixey's artillerymen were filing ashore along the pier through-out the night—unscathed. Later, Shoup instructed Major Tompkins to tell Hermle to "get out from under that pier" and "go out and get in communications with the division."[51]

Then, at 1400 on the second day, Colonel Hall reached Shoup's CP, accompanied by his full regimental communications suite. Hall was twenty years senior to Shoup. He had, in fact, been division chief of staff before Edson. Hall was a veteran and hardly gun-shy, but he did not burn with the same intensity as Shoup. He wisely allowed him to retain overall command ashore. Shoup, recalled Hall, "was doing very well and was the division's selected commander, [and] was in a position to know more about what was going on ashore." Hall would render valuable service in command of the embattled 8th Marines.[52]

Explaining the fluid tactical situation ashore to Edson took Shoup several hours. As Edson formulated his attack plans for the third day, the division again went to ground in anticipation of Japanese bombing raids or counterattacks. The former occurred early in the morning—a pair of *rikko* bombers dropped their payload on the 6th Marines lines—but once again no concerted counterattack erupted. With Admiral Shibasaki and his staff dead, and Commander Sugai still bottled up in the Pocket, tactical command of any reserve forces would have devolved to Lieutenant Minami. It may have been Minami who finally orchestrated the series of counterattacks the third night, but no surviving Japanese had that capability this night. The Americans again were extremely fortunate.

Major Kyle, on the other hand, was particularly vulnerable in his enclave along Black Beach; a thousand Japanese defended to the east, with hundreds more in small pockets all around the enclave. His composite force had sustained at least sixty casualties during the day's sharp fighting.

Years later, Gen. Julian Smith looked back on the pivotal day and night of 21 November 1943 at Betio and admitted, "We were losing until we won." Many things had gone wrong, and the Japanese had inflicted severe casualties on the attackers, but from this point on the issue was no longer in doubt at Tarawa.[53]

CHAPTER NINE

Fight to the Finish

*It looks as though the Marines are winning
on this blood-soaked, bomb-hammered,
stinking little abattoir of an island.*
—Keith Wheeler, dispatch from Tarawa, D+2.

COLONEL EDSON HAD HIS HANDS FULL AS MID-
night passed and the third day began on Betio. Repeatedly, he
pressed Colonel Shoup and Major Culhane for tactical details
concerning the strengths and positions of the division's scattered landing teams and the Japanese defenders. No one knew
more about the situation ashore than Shoup and Culhane, but
neither officer could provide the chief of staff with anything
but the sketchiest of assumptions. The struggle for Betio
simply did not lend itself to neat lines and symbols on a map.
Exhaustion weighed heavily on both men. Shoup's wounds,
minor but untreated, were galling. Culhane, "the screamer,"
was losing his voice.

Edson finally issued his attack orders at 0400. Reduced to
the nub for radio transmission, the chief of staff's plan for D+2
was this: "1/6 attacks at 0800 to the east along south beach to
establish contact with 1/2 and 2/2. 1/8 attached to 2dMar
attacks at daylight to the west along north beach to eliminate
Jap pockets of resistance between Beaches Red 1 and 2.
8thMar (–LT 1/8) continues attack to east." (McLeod's
LT 3/6, still embarked at the line of departure, would land at
Shoup's call on Green Beach.)[1]

Edson's plan was aggressive but complex. Execution would
require careful choreography between disparate units—
hampered by uncertain communications—along the narrow
axis of the fire-swept island. The danger of fratricide, "friendly

fire," would be rampant. The key to the entire plan would be the eastward attack by the fresh troops of Major Jones's landing team 1/6.

At this point Edson received another rude introduction to operating conditions on Betio. Communications between the CP and Jones's position on Green Beach failed. Hour after hour, Edson's radio operators could reach neither Jones nor Ryan. Green Beach lay barely nine hundred yards to the west, but Commander Sugai's strong positions along the pocket still blocked the overland and beach routes.

The battle of Tarawa produced a number of enterprising individuals on both sides who stepped forward at critical points to lend their services. Here was such an occasion. Seeing Edson's frustration, Major Tompkins quietly volunteered to deliver the attack order to Jones. Edson eyed him appraisingly, then accepted the offer. Tompkins's harrowing odyssey to Green Beach took nearly three hours, a process of evading scores of nervous sentries, Japanese and American alike. By quirk, the radio nets started working again just before Tompkins reached LT 1/6. Jones had the good grace not to admit to Tompkins that he already had the attack order when the exhausted messenger arrived.[2]

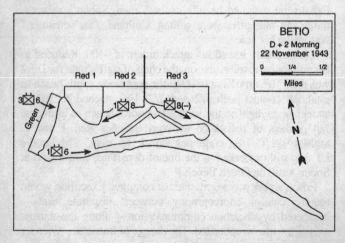

Meanwhile, at the highest levels of the American command for Operation Galvanic, the policy toward the Southern Attack Force at Tarawa continued to be one of "hands off." To their great credit, and despite the continuing grim and garbled reports, neither Spruance, Turner, nor Holland Smith pestered Harry Hill or Julian Smith for details or resorted to long-distance tactical suggestions. While Turner and Holland Smith worried about the bloody struggle obviously still under way at Tarawa, they remained preoccupied by the threat of a Japanese counterattack from the Marshalls and the 27th Infantry Division's own problems in overcoming Makin's outnumbered but stoutly resisting defenders. Admiral Spruance set the tone from the top. The man was a tower of silent strength. His principal subordinates knew they had his unquestioning support.

Off Tarawa, Julian Smith remained philosophical about the slow progress. "The Japs were well dug in," he said, "and they had to be well dug out." But Smith grew eager to move ashore. He gave orders for his command group to prepare to land at noon. In the interim, Smith kept close to his radio operators on the *Maryland*, waiting for news of the morning's attacks.[3]

With Edson now commanding all forces ashore, his principal subordinates became Colonels Hall and Shoup. Hall was content to retain command of the two battalions of the 8th Marines—Crowe's 2/8 and Ruud's 3/8—operating east of the pier. Shoup still held significant command responsibilities: the three battalions of his own 2d Marines, plus Hays's 1/8 and (temporarily, until Colonel Holmes could land) Jones's 1/6.

Major Hays figured that now was the time to even the score with the rikusentai in the Pocket who had shot up his troops so viciously the previous morning. During the night, close to two hundred of his men had straggled in from points of refuge taken during the earlier fire storm. Shoup linked Major Schoettel's small force of LT 3/2 (less Ryan's composite force on Green Beach) to Hays's 1/8 for the assault on the Pocket.

The 1st Battalion, 8th Marines, was a veteran outfit. Many of Hays's staff noncommissioned officers had field experience beyond Guadalcanal, including combat in China and "the

Banana Wars" in Central America and the Caribbean. One first sergeant had even fought the Germans in France during World War I. These veterans spent the night reorganizing the shattered battalion into a smaller, yet effective, fighting force. But LT 1/8 would not recover this day from the loss of its entire stock of flamethrowers and other assault weapons the previous morning.[4]

Starting from the vicinity of the division CP on Red Beach Two, Major Hays launched his attack promptly at 0700, advancing westward on a three-company front. Engineers with satchel charges and bangalore torpedoes helped neutralize several inland Japanese positions, but the strong points along the Pocket remained impervious. Marine light tanks made brave frontal attacks against the fortifications, even driving directly against the positions to fire their 37-mm guns point-blank into the embrasures, but they were inadequate for the task. When enemy fire blew up one tank, Hays withdrew the other two.

Hays then asked Shoup for a section of 75-mm half-tracks. Shoup promptly complied. More bad luck. Japanese gunners immediately knocked out the first half-track with a direct shot in its radiator, but the other survived, using its heavier 75-mm gun to advantage. The center and left flank companies managed to curve around behind the main complexes, effectively cutting the Japanese off from the rest of the island. Along the beach, however, Hays had to measure his progress in yards.[5]

The bright spot of the day for 1/8 came late in the afternoon, when a small party of rikusentai tried to sortie from their strong points against the Marine lines. Until then Hays's men had seen the enemy as only a series of wicked muzzle flashes appearing between slits in coconut logs. Finally given real targets in the open, the Marines cut down the attackers with a will.[6]

On Green Beach Major Jones made final preparations for the assault of 1/6 to the east. Willie K. and Mike Ryan had been good friends since their mutual deployment to Iceland with the 6th Marines in 1941; Jones prevailed on their friendship to "borrow" Ryan's two battle-scarred Shermans for the assault.

This took some doing. Ryan had his own plans for continuing the assault eastward, unaware for the moment of Edson's grander scheme of maneuver.

Jones, a twenty-seven-year-old Missouri native, would spend the entire war with the 1st Battalion, 6th Marines. He would become renowned in World War II for his valor in withstanding two savage Japanese night counterattacks. One would occur the following year at Saipan. The first would happen this night to come.[7]

Unlike Hays's lightly armed attack now under way to the east, Major Jones's LT 1/6 had assault weapons in the order of an embarrassment of riches. And Jones was more proficient in employing combined arms than any other battalion commander on the island (with the exception of the recently earned experience of Major Ryan). Jones ordered his borrowed Shermans to range no farther than fifty yards ahead of his lead company, and he personally maintained radio contact with the tank commander (the stern-mounted tank-infantry phone had yet to be perfected for Marine Corps Shermans). Jones also assigned a platoon of water-cooled .30-caliber machine guns to each rifle company and attached his combat engineers with their flamethrowers and demolition squads to the lead company.[8]

The nature of the terrain and the necessity for giving Hays's battalion wide berth made Jones constrain his attack to a platoon front in a zone of action only one hundred yards wide. "It was the most unusual tactics that I ever heard of," recalled Jones. "As I moved to the east on one side of the airfield, Larry Hays moved to the west, exactly opposite. . . . I was attacking towards Wood Kyle who had 1st Battalion, 2d Marines."[9]

Jones's preparations showed no adverse effects from the short fuse between late receipt of Edson's attack order and the early kickoff time. The landing team would execute Edson's difficult choreography to perfection. This manifested the obvious advantage of having in place a fresh tactical unit with integrated supporting arms. Jones's 1/6 made rapid progress along the south coast, killing about 250 Japanese defenders and reaching the thin lines held by 2/2 and 1/2 within three hours. American casualties to this point were light. Croaked

Major Culhane at the division CP, "We got 'em by the eyeballs now!"[10]

Nothing came that easy on Betio, though. Lieutenant Lake commanded the second platoon of Charlie Company, 1/6, initially leading the entire landing team. The "column of platoons" proved inadequate to the task. "Thirty-odd men in a line could not cover a hundred-yard front with all those pillboxes and still maintain momentum." Capt. Joe Golding, commanding Charlie Company, moved Lake's platoon to the left, guiding on the southern edge of the airstrip, and brought the first platoon up on the right, guiding along Black Beach. While the Shermans performed yeoman service—"They saved a lot of Marine lives," stated one noncommissioned officer—the tank-infantry communications net performed erratically.[11]

As 1/6 approached the aircraft revetments, Lieutenant Lake and Sgt. Clifton E. Fomby, a Guadalcanal veteran, tried to gain the attention of one of the Shermans operating aimlessly ahead of the advance troops. "Few things are as blind as a buttoned-up tank," said Lake. "They may have thought we were Japs." A burst of machine-gun fire, perhaps from the tank, perhaps from a Japanese position nearby, hit Sergeant Fomby in the stomach. He died in Lake's arms. The two men had grown up near each other, across the Louisiana-Arkansas border. "The first combat loss is special." The entire island was a shooting gallery.[12]

Major Jones relieved Charlie Company with Capt. George Krueger's Baker Company as the advance unit passed the western apex of the airstrip and taxiway. The battalion paused to catch its breath once they linked up with Woody Kyle's exhausted remnants of the 2d Marines, wearily clinging to the trenches and craters of their enclave along Black Beach.

Back at Green Beach Ryan's "orphans" looked for new worlds to conquer. Having heard nothing from Shoup during the night, Major Ryan radioed at 0800, "We shall attack east on Beach Red One." Ten minutes later came Shoup's reply: "Stay in position. Eighth Marines [1/8] will attack towards you."[13]

Now it was Ryan's turn to sit and wait. That morning Major Cortelyou, commanding Mike Company, the weapons outfit for 3/2, showed up on Green Beach. Cortelyou had grown impatient with Major Shoettel's hesitations on D-Day, hitched a ride ashore on PFC Richard D. Sommerville's short-lived LVT-1, and spent the ensuing forty hours working his way west to rejoin his men and Ryan on the west coast. Cortelyou, senior to Ryan, assumed command of the composite force. Said Ryan, "I became a Battalion Commander Emeritus!"[14]

At 1100 Shoup called Major Jones to his CP to receive the afternoon plan of action. Jones's acting executive officer, Maj. Francis X. Beamer, took the occasion to rotate the lead rifle company once again. Landing Team 1/6 now faced stiffer resistance. A Japanese sharpshooter hit Captain Krueger in the neck, paralyzing him. His exec, 1st Lt. Norman K. Thomas, took command of Baker Company. The oppressive heat began to take a toll. Beamer made superhuman efforts to get more water and salt tablets for his men, but he lost several troops to heat prostration. According to Sergeant Michelony of 1/6, the Marines faced two enemies on Tarawa: "the Japanese and the heat." Tarawa's sands, he added, were "as white as snow and as hot as red-white ashes from a heated furnace."[15]

Back on Green Beach, now eight hundred yards behind LT 1/6, McLeod's LT 3/6 began streaming ashore. The Japanese could not oppose this landing, but the process nevertheless took hours to execute. Edson's earlier estimate of the situation had been right on the money. The reef on Green Beach extended too far to seaward and suffered too frequently from a pounding surf. McLeod's troops had spent nineteen forgettable hours languishing in small boats off shore. Now it was 1100, the same time that Jones's leading elements linked up with the 2d Marines, and 3/6 hurriedly reorganized itself ashore.

The attack order for the 8th Marines remained the same as the previous day: assault the strong points to the east. The obstacles were just as daunting on D+2. Three fortifications proved especially formidable: a steel pillbox near the contested Burns-Philp pier, a coconut-log emplacement with multiple machine guns, and the large "bombproof" shelter farther inland. All three had been designed by Admiral Shibasaki's various engineering experts to be mutually supported by fire and observation. And notwithstanding Major Crowe's fighting spirit, these strong points had effectively contained the combined forces of 2/8 and 3/8 since the morning of D-Day.

On the third day, Crowe reorganized his tired forces for yet another assault. First, the former marksmanship coach obtained cans of lubricating oil and made his troops field strip and clean their Garands—by relays—before the attack. Crowe placed his executive officer, Major Chamberlin, in the center of the three attacking companies. Though nursing a painful wound in his shoulder from D-Day, Chamberlin became a driving force in the assaults against the three strong points.

At 0930, a 60-mm mortar crew from King Company, 3/8, lobbed a direct hit on top of the coconut-log emplacement. The round penetrated the bunker and detonated the ammunition stocks. The Marines greeted the huge column of fire and smoke with wild cheers. Within minutes came another stroke of good fortune. Chamberlin's men directed a rain of covering fire while the fire-scorched medium tank "Colorado" maneuvered close enough to the steel pillbox to penetrate it with direct 75-mm fire. Abruptly, the attackers had silenced two of the three emplacements.

The massive bombproof shelter, however, remained dominant, still lethal. Japanese machine gunners in heavily shielded bunkers on top of the mound, augmented by other gunners firing through narrow emplacements, repeatedly shot Crowe's improvised flanking attacks to pieces before they could gather momentum. Somehow, the Marines had to suppress the Japanese fire long enough to get combat engineers on top of the mound to smother the machine gunners with flame and drop thermite grenades down the air vents to force the internal defenders out in the open.

The task proved exceedingly risky. For all its obvious advantages, American firepower could not help much in this situation. The fortification's soft-sand covering and angled slope rendered it impervious to direct fire weapons such as tanks, pack howitzers, or naval rifles. Navy dive-bombers could do the trick, perhaps, but no one on the ground had much faith in the pinpoint accuracy of that delivery system—especially when the target blended so artfully with its surroundings. An airburst 5-inch/38 shell from one of the supporting destroyers in the lagoon (similar to the fortuitous shot on D-Day that caught Admiral Shibasaki and his staff in the open not far from this site) would certainly take care of the topside machine gunners, but by now the area was too crowded with friendly forces to risk even the slightest inaccuracy in range or deflection. Crowe, Chamberlin, and Ruud continued to lob mortar shells at the complex, hoping for another lucky hit.

The standoff on Red Beach Three attracted a number of unassigned Marines to the sound of guns. One of these was Private First Class Fratt, the survivor from McBride's Easy, 2/8 outpost on D-Day, still armed with his Springfield and looking for new adventures. Another man who showed up to lend a hand as early as the second day was a shore party lieutenant from the 2d Battalion, 18th Marines, with an engaging grin and deep southern accent, Sandy Bonnyman.

Seizing the fortified shelter required individual heroism on the part of many Marines, plus well-coordinated teamwork. Of all these brave men, Lieutenant Bonnyman's light shines the brightest. The intriguing aspect about Bonnyman is that he didn't have to be there. He didn't have to be on Red Reach Three on D+2; he didn't even have to be in the war.

Sandy Bonnyman was thirty-three, far older than most of his contemporaries on Betio. Born in Atlanta and raised in Knoxville, he had studied engineering at Princeton and played guard for the 1928 Tigers football team. Leaving school early, Bonnyman worked at first for his father, president of the Blue Diamond Coal Company. But young Bonnyman was an avid outdoorsman who loved hunting and camping, and he yearned for more adventure in his life. In 1932 he joined the Army Air Corps to begin flight school at Kelly Field in San Antonio. This did not take. He was too free a spirit: he "buzzed too many control towers." Dismissed from the flight program, he at least left San Antonio with a bride, socialite Josephine Bell. The couple had three daughters.

When war broke out, Bonnyman owned one copper mine and part of another in New Mexico. These represented essential defense industries, which exempted Bonnyman from the draft, but the fact bothered him. In an outburst of unabashed patriotism, Bonnyman enlisted in the Marines in July 1942, asking for overseas service. Col. Gilder Jackson, commanding the 6th Marines, liked what he saw of Bonnyman's unselfish competence and nominated him for a field commission. Lieutenant Bonnyman served with distinction at Guadalcanal, at one point using his engineering skills to build a bridge across the flooded Poha River.[16]

Like many other shore party officers at Tarawa, Bonnyman was essentially out of a job for the first fifty hours or so. Typically, he offered his services to Major Crowe, and despite the highly visible shore party markings on his helmet and trousers, he made several forays into no-man's-land to retrieve wounded Marines to safety. Crowe then asked him to give Chamberlin a hand in attacking the Japanese stronghold on the eastern flank.

Bonnyman spent the equivalent of a full day hunkered down on the eastern edge of the complex, studying the layout, getting Chamberlin's guidance, and quietly assembling and training a makeshift squad of assorted engineers. One of these men, Cpl. Harry Niehoff of Able, 1/18, led a demolition and flame-thrower squad attached to Crowe's 1/8. Niehoff and Cpl. John Borich, one of his experienced flamethrower operators, had two fully charged weapons, plenty of explosives, and some practical combat experience to share with Bonnyman. Neither Niehoff nor Borich knew the lieutenant. "He just showed up," said Niehoff, "but until that time we were being held down to no gain." Bonnyman listened to the men, studied the approaches to the bunker, pointed out the large air vents and machine-gun nests, then devised his attack plan. He had twenty-one men in his "Forlorn Hope," the equivalent of an eighteenth-century storming party.

One of the men accompanying this party was Cpl. Obie Newcomb, a Marine photographer. Newcomb had experienced enough combat to realize he was in the presence of a most unusual Marine in Bonnyman. Fortunately for posterity, he followed the lieutenant's actions during the assault with his camera. The photographs belie the common myth of Bonnyman himself strapping on a flamethrower or single-handedly repelling the swarming Japanese counterattack. Bonnyman's valor this day was not melodramatic but intelligent, sensible, unselfish—and absolutely fearless.

When Bonnyman sensed each member of his makeshift team had been instructed, equipped, and motivated sufficiently for the assault, he signaled Major Chamberlin to lay down a base of fire. The surrounding Marines cut loose with rifles, automatic weapons, mortars, and 37-mm guns. Bonnyman rolled over the seawall, darted for the shelter of a wooden fence perpendicular to the mound, and snaked his way to the edge. The others followed at disciplined intervals. Another signal to Chamberlin. The Marines shifted their base of fire higher.

What happened next, though witnessed by hundreds, remains kaleidoscopic. Bonnyman and his men scrambled up the sandy slope, drawing immediate fire, taking losses. Corporal Borich made it up the left side, released a short blast to roast the near machine gunner, then a longer blast to cover Niehoff's approach right behind the flames to throw a short-fused TNT charge at the middle of the crest. The explosion and smoke provided enough distraction for other engineers to tackle the air vents.[17]

In the midst of this came Chamberlin's booming voice, "Go!" The infantry needed no urging. Thirty or forty Marines came flying across the once-deadly vale and up the slope. Borich emptied his flamethrower against the remaining machine gunner while Bonnyman and Niehoff took up prone firing positions on the eastern edge of the crest to deliver covering fire for the infantry. Corporal Niehoff tells what happened next. "As Bonnyman and I were almost elbow to elbow, we heard a cry from the men on the south rim. Suddenly Japanese were running all over and our men were yelling they had breached a log and sand tunnel below them, which explained the appearance and disappearance of Japanese in the area the last few days."[18]

At once, a hundred or more Japanese seemed to be boiling out of the sanctuary. The Marines scrambled for clear shots.

Private First Class Fratt cursed the slow speed of his bolt-action Springfield. The tank crew of the "Colorado" fired a single "dream shot" canister round which cut down several dozen fleeing Japanese. Other rikusentai stopped and raised their muzzles. A vicious, close-range shoot-out erupted. Bonnyman yelled for more demo charges to toss down the south slope. In Niehoff's words: "Lieutenant Bonnyman raised himself up on one elbow, looked back to tell someone behind us to get more charges, when I heard the bullet hit him. He never moved and I knew he was dead. I felt I was next because we were lined up on the top rim like ducks in a shooting gallery."[19]

Corporal Newcomb was perhaps the only other Marine at the scene who knew Bonnyman and tracked him throughout the melee. As he wrote the family after the battle: "He didn't have to go up to take that blockhouse, [but] there was no stopping him. It was a perfect hell hole and the boys needed a little urging when things started to break. I can still see him waving the boys up over that blockhouse and [hear] his southern voice urging them on. . . . He was one of the most courageous and bravest men we had with us."[20]

Brave Sandy Bonnyman was dead, but the 8th Marines hardly knew him, and the battle raged on to the east. Corporal Niehoff returned for one last look after the shooting died down, but he was bitter. "His body was still in the same position on the edge of the shelter, next to the Japanese machine-gunner, as when I left him," Niehoff stated. "Who knew him until they read his dog tag? He was already unrecognizable." Merely thirteen of the original twenty-one members of Bonnyman's scratch Forlorn Hope survived the assault. Major Chamberlin, Niehoff, and Borich provided enough corroboration for Gen. Julian Smith to recommended Bonnyman for the Congressional Medal of Honor. Somewhere up the line, an intermediate agency downgraded the award to the Navy Cross. To its credit, the 2d Marine Division remained persistent; the Navy Department at length reversed the earlier decision and awarded Bonnyman the posthumous Medal of Honor three years after the battle.[21]

It is more than coincidence that two of the four highest

awards at Tarawa went to combat engineers. The performances of Sergeant Bordelon on D-Day and Lieutenant Bonnyman on D+2 were representative of hundreds of other engineers on just a slightly less spectacular basis. As one example, nearly a third of the engineers who landed in support of LT 2/8 became casualties. According to Lt. B.W. Rental of Charlie Company, 1/18, the survivors used two fifty-four-pound blocks of TNT and an entire case of gelatin dynamite on the large bombproof shelter alone. Engineers applied each of these charges by hand, literally hugging the deadly fortification in the process.[22]

THE SEVERITY OF THE FIGHTING CAUSED Marine casualties to soar. Betio still offered few secure places. Wounded men remained at grave risk until they could be evacuated from the island. Admiral Hill ordered the troopship *Doyen* into the lagoon to serve as primary receiving ship for critical cases. This was a gamble: four destroyers had already gone aground in those shallow waters, plus the Japanese still managed to launch an occasional large-caliber shell downrange. The *Doyen* did fine. Lt. Comdr. James Oliver, Medical Corps, USN, led a five-man surgical team with recent experience in the Aleutians. The team treated 390 severely wounded Marines; only nine died.[23]

Later that afternoon Julian Smith ordered "B-Med"—Baker Company, 2d Medical Battalion—to establish a field hospital ashore on Bairiki Island. The unit served hundreds more of the wounded.[24]

Too often we consider the battle's cost in terms of single-dimensional numbers. Betio was an unmitigated bloodbath. Combat artist Kerr Eby was dead right in describing Tarawa as a time of "utmost savagery." Most of the fighting occurred at terribly close range, and despite the profusion of Japanese field guns, many American casualties came from rifles, machine guns, and grenades. The following dozen samples, taken at random from one battalion's roster (and disregarding the coldly cryptic format) provide a sense of the nature of this savage fighting:

- Gunshot wound chest, compound fracture left arm
- Burns, third degree, face, both hands, and forearms
- Gunshot wound, multiple, face and right shoulder
- Shrapnel wound, left arm, chest, face
- Gunshot wound, left arm, chest, shoulder, right foot
- Gunshot wound, right side of upper lip to left side of neck
- War neurosis
- Shrapnel wound, left arm and leg, burns both arms and face
- Bayonet puncture, right knee
- Gunshot wound, scrotum and right foot, concussion left eye
- Gunshot wound, multiple, right shoulder and arm, left knee, right thigh, left posterior chest, right anterior chest
- Shrapnel wound, multiple, left leg; amputation traumatic left leg at thigh.[25]

At this point in the battle, some surviving Japanese radio operator evidently managed to restore power for one final transmission from the garrison. "Our weapons have been destroyed and from now on everyone is attempting a final charge. . . . May Japan exist for 10,000 years!" Interestingly, the *Katori Maru* in Kwajalein never received such a message, although a "slightly sensitive signal" (without intelligible words) from Tarawa appeared intermittently between 0725 and 1325 on the third day of the battle. Edward Van Der Rhoer, a member of the special OP-20-G-2 section in the Office of Naval Intelligence, mentions a MAGIC intercept of this nature on 22 November. The wording in his account differs slightly in the last sentence: "May his Majesty the Emperor live ten thousand years." The message was hardly a swan song. The garrison still numbered at least a thousand men; each had plenty of fight left.[26]

Gen. Julian Smith embarked in a Higgins boat with his forward CP, tired of the "fog of war" rampant on the flagship. Smith left his disgruntled ADC, General Hermle on the *Maryland*, to deal with Admiral Hill, but he took two other senior officers with him, General Bourke, commanding the 10th Marines, and Brig. Gen. James L. Underhill, the senior observer from the 4th Marine Division. This high-powered group landed on Green Beach shortly before noon. Smith observed the deployment of McLeod's LT 3/6 inland and conferred with Major Ryan (trying to ignore the latter's blood-stained jacket).

But Smith soon realized the main fighting now took place in the center of the island. He led his group back across the reef to their landing craft and ordered the coxswain to make for the pier. As the craft hurried along parallel to the north shore, the commanding general received his own rude welcome to the facts of life on Betio. Although Hays's and Schoettel's Marines were grinding away at the Japanese strongholds at the Pocket, the defenders still held mastery over the approaches to Red Beaches One and Two. Well-aimed machine-gun fire disabled the boat and killed the coxswain; the distinguished occupants had to leap over the far gunwale into the water. Major Tompkins, ever the right man in the right place, then waded through occasional fire for half a mile to find an LVT for the generals.

Even this was not an altogether safe exchange. The approaching LVT drew the attention of a lone sniper, whose accurate fire wounded the driver and scattered the riders. General Smith did not reach Edson and Shoup's combined CP until nearly 1400. The experience sobered the commander. As the former guerrilla fighter would soon write his wife, "I would have liked to have had time to take a rifle and stalk that bastard, but he's dead now and I'm not so what's the difference."[27]

Red Mike Edson in the meantime had assembled his subordinate commanders and issued orders for continuing the attack to the east that afternoon. Major Jones's 1/6 would continue along the narrowing south coast, supported by the pack howitzers of 1/10 and all available tanks. Colonel Hall's two battalions of the 8th Marines would continue their advance along the north coast. Jump-off time was 1330. Naval gunfire and air support would blast both areas for an hour in advance.

Colonel Hall spoke up on behalf of his exhausted, decimated landing teams ashore who had been in direct contact since D-Day morning. The two reinforced battalions had enough strength for one more assault, he told Edson, but then they must get relief. Edson promised to exchange the remnants of 2/8 and 3/8 with Ray Murray's fresh LT 2/6 on Bairiki at the first opportunity after the assault.

Jones returned to his troops in his borrowed tank and issued the necessary orders. Landing Team 1/6 continued the attack at 1330, passing through Kyle's lines in the process. The Marines immediately ran into heavy opposition. The deadliest fire came from heavy weapons mounted in a turret-type emplacement near the south beach. This took ninety minutes to overcome. The light tanks, once again, moved up bravely but could not contribute. Neutralization took sustained 75-mm fire—nearly a hundred rounds—from one of the Shermans. Japanese resistance increased markedly throughout Jones's zone, and his casualties began to mount. The team had conquered eight hundred yards of enemy territory fairly easily in the morning, but they could attain barely half that distance in the long afternoon.

The 8th Marines sought to capitalize on fresh momentum caused by their breakout from the three-bunker nemesis and seized the concrete blockhouse, Shibasaki's former headquarters. But Hall's thin formations soon encountered stiff resistance and ran out of steam past the eastern end of the airfield. Shoup had been right the night before: the Japanese defenders may have been abandoned by the Imperial Navy, but they still had an abundance of bullets and esprit left. Major Crowe pulled his leading elements back into defensive positions for the night. Jones halted too and ordered Charlie Company north of the airfield for a direct link with Crowe. Jones had no intention of leaving men exposed after dark on the airstrip; he gave orders for the companies along both sides to interlock their flank machine guns across that obvious avenue of approach.

On nearby Bairiki, Colonel Shell now had all of 2/10 in position and firing artillery missions in support of Crowe and Jones. With the 2d Medical Battalion's field hospital now functional, the *Doyen* suspended her emergency medical duties and eased out of the lagoon to begin preparations for the eventual landing of the 4th Battalion, 10th Marines, over Green Beach. The fleet tug USS *Arapaho* (AT 68) came in close to pull a dangerously vulnerable destroyer clear of the coral head that had grounded her. Ray Murray's LT 2/6, eager to enter the fray, waited in vain for boats to arrive to move them to Green Beach. Scant landing craft were available; most seemed crammed with miscellaneous supplies as the transports and cargo ships continued general unloading, regardless of the needs of the troops ashore.[28]

On Betio, Navy Seabees worked diligently to repair the airstrip, using bulldozers and graders despite enemy fire. From time to time the Marines would call for help in sealing a bothersome bunker, and a bulldozer operator would swing into action, blade high, engine roaring, to do the job. "Thanks, Grandpa!" the Marines good-naturedly jibed. "Anytime, Junior," the Seabee would reply.

Navy beachmasters and shore party Marines on the pier continued to keep the supplies coming in, the wounded going out. The first order of business this day had been the stacking of

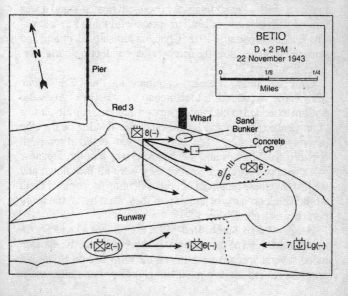

crates to buttress the top of the pier for protection against incessant sniper fire. Japanese infiltrators still popped up in the nearby hulks to pepper the working parties. Colonel Salazar set up a pair of .50-caliber machine guns alongside the pierhead. These did the job. At 1550 Edson requested a working party "to clear bodies around pier . . . hindering shore party operations."[29]

The strain of the prolonged battle began to take its toll. Colonel Hall reported that one of his Navajo Indian codetalkers had been mistaken for a Japanese and had been shot. A derelict, blackened LVT drifted ashore, filled with dead Marines. At the bottom of the pile was one who was still breathing, somehow, after two and a half days of unrelenting hell. "Water," he gasped. "Pour some water on my face, will you?"[30]

The surging tides scattered derelict craft and lifeless bodies throughout the lagoon and beyond, into the open ocean. Lieutenant Schneidmiller came across one shattered Higgins boat drifting in the partial moonlight. "The boat was nearly split in two by a shell—I can't imagine how it still floated—and it was littered with burned bodies. The most awful thing I ever saw." The *LaSalle* reported: "1015: Chaplain left ship, identified and sank three bodies floating nearby after conducting burial services from boat."[31]

Capt. C. Julian Wheeler, commanding the USS *Mobile* (CL #36), expressed astonishment that Betio's gruesome flotsam extended to his gunfire support station, six miles at sea. "I remember Marine and Japanese corpses floating by the ship in great numbers. . . . The only way you could distinguish between the Marines and the Japanese was that the Japanese wore wrapped leggings. . . . But they were all face down and we just saw these hundreds of bodies floating by, some of them would catch on parts of the ship as they went by, in the scuppers. It was a ghastly sight."[32]

Neither Julian Smith, Red Mike Edson, nor David Shoup could see the end of the struggle. In relative terms, the division made several spectacular gains on the third day on Betio, but progress overall seemed maddeningly slow, extremely costly.

At 1600 General Smith sent this pessimistic report to General Hermle on the flagship:

> Situation not favorable for rapid clean-up of Betio. Heavy casualties among officers make leadership problems difficult. Still strong resistance. . . . Many emplacements intact on eastern end of the island. . . . In addition, many Japanese strong points to westward of our front lines within our position that have not been reduced. Progress slow and extremely costly. Complete occupation will take at least 5 days more. Naval and air bombardment a great help but does not take out emplacements.[33]

General Smith assumed full command of operations ashore on Betio and Bairiki at 1930. By that time he could count about seven thousand Marines ashore, struggling against perhaps a thousand Japanese defenders. Updated aerial photographs revealed many defensive positions still intact throughout much of Betio's eastern tail. Smith and Edson believed they would need the entire 6th Marines to complete the job.

Col. Maurice Holmes, the last of the regimental commanders to land on Betio, came ashore with his headquarters group late on D+2. Smith told Holmes to take command of his three landing teams by 2100. Smith then called a meeting of his commanders to assign orders for the following morning.

The division commander directed Holmes to have McLeod's 3/6 pass through the lines of Jones's 1/6 in order to have a fresh battalion lead the assault eastward. Murray's 2/6 would land on Green Beach and proceed east in support of McLeod. All available tanks would be assigned to McLeod. Shoup's 2d Marines, with 1/8 still attached, would continue to reduce the Pocket. The balance of the 8th Marines would be shuttled to Bairiki. And the 4th Battalion, 10th Marines, would land their heavy 105-mm guns on Green Beach to augment the fires of the two pack-howitzer battalions already in action. Many of these plans, however, would be overcome by events of the evening.

The long-expected Japanese counterattack materialized in

the form of a series of vicious firefights throughout the night. As Edson put it, the Japanese obligingly "gave us very able assistance by trying to counterattack." Western historians tend to dismiss all such tactics as banzai attacks: typically a suicidal, headlong charge by poorly armed, sake-soused fanatics seeking a quick and honorable death. Such attacks did occur—notably at Saipan—but the attacks on Betio were intelligently planned and professionally executed.

The surviving Japanese operated under several imperatives. One was surely the doctrinal edict for island defenders to counterattack any invader's penetration. A second motivation would have come from the belief persistent in the imperial ranks that Japanese forces were superior night fighters, that darkness evened the tactical odds. Other factors held influence: the chronic Japanese emphasis on the offensive; the infantry's traditional affinity for hand-to-hand fighting; the natural preference of any fighting man to die moving forward rather than wait passively for the inevitable flamethrowers.

Yes, they screamed "Banzai!" Likewise, Stonewall Jackson's Confederates screamed something known as the rebel yell as they launched their night attack at Chancellorsville. The U.S. Marines had their own battle cries. By whatever name, the 2d Marine Division was about to be hit by a large-scale, well-conceived, well-executed Japanese counterattack.[34]

Major Jones sensed his exposed forces would be the likely target for any night attack and judged his greatest threat would come from the east, the island's yet untouched tail. Gathering his artillery forward observers and naval fire control spotters, Jones registered field artillery support starting seventy-five yards from his frontlines to a point five hundred yards beyond, where naval gunfire would take over. He placed Able Company on the left, next to the airstrip, and Baker Company on the right, next to the south shore. Jones used a tank to bring a stockpile of grenades, small arms ammunition, and water to be positioned fifty yards behind the lines.

The Japanese officers who had thus far escaped death divided Petty Officer Onuki's dismounted tank unit into two forces: one to help with the initial probe, the other—including

Onuki—to join the major thrust later in the night. Onuki never got the chance. A late patrol, probably from the 8th Marines near the blockhouse, found Onuki's bunker, dynamited the entrance, then seared it with a flamethrower. Onuki somehow lived, buried by the burned bodies of his friends, but his war had ended.[35]

Warrant Officer Ota recalled his own preparations for the counterattack.

> An orderly managed to find me and told me, in a low voice, that we all had to meet at headquarters. In spite of my damaged knee I went to the headquarters, clinging to my sword. A senior officer said, "We will make a night attack. At 10 o'clock tonight we will attack the enemy group which occupies the center of the island, drive them back on the sea and destroy them." . . . I called my men together to make arrangements . . . saddened to find that of the original 30 men in my squad who faced the Americans on the lagoon beach, only six were left. We prepared ourselves for the attack and waited. Each man was so loaded down with hand grenades that he could scarcely walk.[36]

The Americans seemed to sense something coming. As radio operator Gus Hall of Headquarters Company, 1/10, dug his foxhole at twilight, he was startled by a strong hand gripping his shoulder. "I looked up to see General Julian Smith. He didn't say anything, just smiled as if to say, 'I believe we've got things under control.'"[37]

The first counterattack came at 1930. A force of fifty Japanese infiltrated past Jones's outposts in the thick vegetation and penetrated the boundary between the two companies south of the airstrip. Jones's reserve force, composed of "my mortar platoon and my headquarters cooks and bakers and admin people," contained the penetration and killed the enemy in two hours of close-in fighting under the leadership of Capt. Lyle "Spook" Specht, commanding the Weapons Company. "The lines became badly misshapen," Specht reminisced. "I crawled all night getting them back in order."[38]

Specht also helped call and adjust star shells from the two destroyers just offshore, the USS *Sigsbee* (DD 502) and the USS *Shroeder* (DD 501). Steady fire from the pack howitzers of 1/10 and 2/10 prevented the Japanese from reinforcing the penetration. By 2130 firing died down. Seeking to reconstitute a reserve force, Jones sent a request back to Major Kyle for a company from LT 1/2 to be positioned one hundred yards to the rear of his lines. Kyle, strapped and exhausted, could at best provide a composite force of platoon strength from the 2d Marines.

The Japanese struck Jones's lines again at 2300. One force made a noisy demonstration across from Able Company's lines—taunting, clinking canteens against their helmets, yelling insults in fair English ("Japanese drink Marines' blood!")—while a second force attacked Baker Company with a silent rush. The Marines repulsed this attack too, but they were forced to use their machine guns, thereby revealing their positions. Jones, more worried now, asked McLeod for a full company from 3/6 to reinforce the 2d Marines to the rear of the fighting.

Other Japanese took advantage of the distraction caused by the sharp fighting under way in the center of the island to attack the long pier, scene of frenzied unloading by American "bucket brigades." Salazar's shore party guards intercepted several rikusentai in the water under the pier. They did so just in time. Each infiltrator carried a large can of gasoline.[39]

Major Jones's LT 1/6 experienced a third attack at 0300 when the Japanese moved several 7.7-mm machine guns into nearby wrecked trucks and opened fire on the previously exposed Marine automatic-weapons positions. Marine non-commissioned officers volunteered to crawl forward against this oncoming fire and lob grenades into the improvised machine-gun nests. This did the job, and the battlefield grew silent again. Specht called for more star shell illumination from the destroyers in the lagoon.

At 0400 a force of some three- to four-hundred Japanese launched a frenzied attack against the same two companies. The Marines met them with every available weapon. Artillery

fire from the 10th Marines' howitzers on Red Beach Two and
Bairiki Island rained a murderous cross fire. The *Shroeder* and
the *Sigsbee* opened up on the flank. The wave of screaming
attackers took hideous casualties but kept coming. Pockets of
men locked together in bloody hand-to-hand fighting. Pvt. Jack
Stambaugh of Baker Company killed three swarming Japanese
with his bayonet; an officer impaled him with his samurai
sword; another Marine brained the officer with a rifle butt. First
Lieutenant Thomas, serving his first night as Baker Company
commander, reached Major Jones on the field phone. "We're
killing them as fast as they come at us, but we can't hold out
much longer; we need reinforcements!"[40]

Jones's reply was tough. "We haven't got them; you've *got*
to hold!"[41]

Warrant Officer Ota's version of the counterattack indicates
that he participated in the final assault at 0400 rather than the
preliminary probes, as perhaps originally planned. " 'Ready!'
We disabled the safeties on our hand grenades. 'ATTACK!'
We rushed all together, here and there. I completely forgot my
wounded knee. The dark night was lighted as bright as day.
There were heavy sounds of grenade explosions, the disor-
dered fire of rifles, the shrieks, yells, and roars. It was just like
Hell. The night battle was over in half an hour. Altogether,
about 750 of us had entered the night attack. Almost all were
killed, but I was somehow still alive."[42]

Jones's Marines lost forty dead and a hundred wounded in
the wild fighting, but hold they did. By morning nautical twilight it was all over. The supporting arms never stopped
shooting down the Japanese, attacking or retreating. Both
destroyers emptied their magazines of 5-inch shells. The near
constant blast of the *Shroeder*'s guns popped rivets in the after
deckhouse and caused the accidental launch of a depth charge
from the port Y-gun. Her gun crews experienced nine breech
jams in the hasty loading but cleared each one coolly, quickly.
"Those destroyers saved our lives," said Sergeant Michelony.
"There was absolutely no break between the flash and the
bang—they were that close!"[43]

The overworked 75-mm pack howitzers of 1/10 fired

thirteen hundred rounds that long night, many shells being unloaded over the pier while the fire missions were under way. At first light the Marines counted two hundred dead Japanese within fifty yards of their lines. An additional 125 bodies lay beyond that range, badly mangled by artillery or naval gunfire. Other bodies were scattered throughout the Marine lines. Major Jones had to blink back tears of pride and grief as he walked his lines at dawn. Several of his Marines grabbed his arm and muttered, "They told us we had to hold, and by God, we held."[44]

"THIS WAS NOT ONLY WORSE THAN GUADAL-canal," admitted Colonel Carlson, "it was the damnedest fight I've seen in 30 years of this business." Nor was it over as the sun rose on the fourth day, 23 November. But now the Marines could see the end of the road.

General Smith surveyed the death and destruction all around him on Betio and recalled the occasions on the *Maryland* the past few days when Admiral Hill had asked him—bluntly but politely—why the Marines were taking so long to secure the small island. Sensing an opportunity to educate the amphibious task force commander, Smith sent Hill this message: "Decisive defeat of enemy counterattack last night destroyed bulk of hostile resistance. Expect complete annihilation of enemy on Betio this date. Strongly recommend that you and your chief of staff come ashore this date to get information about the type of hostile resistance which will be encountered in future operations."[45]

Meanwhile, following a systematic preliminary bombardment, the fresh troops of McLeod's LT 3/6 passed through Jones's decimated lines and commenced their attack to the east. Marine assault tactics on D+3 bore little resemblance to the disjointed efforts on the first day. Led by tanks and combat engineers with flamethrowers and high explosives, the troops of 3/6 made rapid progress. One solitary bunker, a well-armed complex along the north shore, provided effective opposition. McLeod took advantage of thick underbrush along the south shore to bypass the obstacle, leaving one rifle company to encircle and eventually overrun it.

While plenty of Japanese remained in their bunkers, their fierce fighting spirit seemed to flag, as if the losses sustained in the early morning counterattacks had ripped the hearts out of the survivors. The attacking Marines experienced little difficulty maintaining their momentum. McLeod reached the eastern tip of Betio by 1300, having inflicted more than 450 Japanese casualties at the loss of thirty-four of his Marines.

McLeod's report summarized the general collapse of the Japanese defensive system in the eastern zone following the counterattacks: "At no time was there any determined defense. We used flamethrowers and could have used more. Medium tanks were excellent. My light tanks didn't fire a shot."[46]

Over time, all supporting arms improved in proficiency of execution at Betio. Of these, however, the close air support had the most to learn. No one could ever question the valor of the pilots of Task Group 53.6, who flew 650 support sorties off the escort carriers *Sangamon* (CVE 26), *Suwanee* (CVE 27), *Chenango* (CVE 28), *Barnes* (CVE 20), and *Nassau* (CVE 16). Close air support is a tremendously complex operational process. At Tarawa, bad communications, inexperience, enemy fire, and the small size of the island combined to limit its effectiveness. Lt. Comdr. Bernard M. Strean, USN, commanded a fighter squadron whose forty-five planes were divided between the *Nassau* and *Barnes* ("Each jeep carrier could only carry 24 planes").[47]

Preflight mission briefings were short on details. "They would tell us to destroy an enemy position or an enemy revetment of some sort and they would give us a grid mark of it as to where to hit. . . . There wasn't much opposition. The Japanese had nothing in the air. It was only the ground fire, which was pretty severe."[48]

On some occasions all the problems with air support took place on the ground. Witness this D-Day radio exchange between the commanding officer of LT 3/2 in his boat off the reef and the company commander of King Company inland and fully engaged along Red Two.

CO, 3/2 (1050): "Do you want air support?"

K Co (1100): "Do not call for air support until I have given you the word where our line is."

CO, 3/2 (1115): "Can we give you air support now?"

K Co (1120): "Do not want air support."

CO 3/2 (1130): "We have called for air support."

K Co (1140): "Stop air strafing! Hitting own men!"[49]

The final measure of effectiveness of the close air support at Betio should come from those who were among its targets. In this regard, Warrant Officer Ota told his captors that he had "a much greater fear of aerial bombardment and strafing" than he did naval gunfire, adding that the constant attack of the carrier planes had a "marked effect on the morale of his men."[50]

Warrant Officer Ota was the lone survivor of a Japanese bunker that received the full American "corkscrew and blow-torch" treatment on D+3. Automatic-weapons fire poured through the embrasures, followed by hand grenades, brief silence, and finally "a brilliant orange-red flare"—the flamethrower. Ota escaped suffocation and burning by the clot of other bodies in the bunker. The Americans pulled him out, semiconscious, but relatively unhurt. He would be the senior ranking rikusentai captured alive in the Gilberts.[51]

Betio remained a deadly island for both sides until the bitter end. Capt. Thomas B. Royster, USMC, commanding Baker Company, 2d Amphibian Tractor Battalion, had one of the few remaining operational LVTs. Learning that both 1/6 and 3/6 were short of ammunition along the south coast, Royster offered to make the delivery. Cpl. Lambert Lane, a radio operator from Forest, Mississippi, volunteered to drive. Other volunteers manned the machine guns. For some reason, Royster decided not to cross the island and follow the trace of the two landing teams. Presumably, all amtrackers by then knew of the mines along Green Beach from the explosion that destroyed one of 1/6's two LVTs the evening of D+1. Royster took the water route, regardless, and traversed the shallows off Green Beach without incident.

As the LVT rounded the southwest point and proceeded along Black Beach, however, it struck one of the horned anti-boat mines. The tremendous explosion killed both Lane and Royster and wounded the others severely. Lieutenant Ward, who had already witnessed the violent deaths of fellow amtrac officers Major Drewes, Captain Little, and Warrant Officer Bernard Shealy, saw the fireball that killed Royster and Lane. Ward and his men buried Royster in a solitary grave near the junction of Black and Green Beaches. Ironically, the Marine Corps had just notified Royster's family of his promotion to major. He was the brother of Vermont Royster, editor of the *Wall Street Journal* for two decades.[52]

Klatt (the Seabee with architectural training) came ashore from the USS *Thuban* (AKA 19) the third morning. He found Betio hot, noisy, and pungent. Klatt soon emptied his canteen, worried about it, then found a water barrel with a spigot. "I set my carbine down, knelt on one knee, and filled my canteen. As I screwed on the top I felt a hot breeze by my left ear and heard the 'snap!' of a Japanese rifle. The shot came from *behind* me, 25 yards away, and the back of my head had just been in his sights." Five Marines quickly swarmed over the supposedly neutralized pillbox. For the rest of his life Klatt would wonder, "Who moved my head, the other guy's forearm?"[53]

Japanese riflemen rarely missed, even this late in the battle. When a radio operator from the 8th Marines regimental head-quarters ventured forth into the "neutralized" center of the island to look for souvenirs on the fourth day, Japanese sailors hit him three times; another shot him in the nose as he staggered back to the aid station.[54]

The toughest fight of the fourth day occurred on the Red Beach One/Two border where Shoup directed the combined forces of Hays's 1/8 and Schoettel's 3/2 against the Pocket. The Japanese defenders manning this position were clearly the most disciplined, and the deadliest, on the island. From the Pocket, Japanese gunners had thoroughly disrupted the land-ings of four different battalions, and they had very nearly killed General Smith the day before. Wrecked LVTs and bloated bodies littered the lagoon approaches to these positions. While Commander Sugai and his staff may have all been dead by now, the Sasebo sailors within their coconut-log-and-coral bunkers still exacted a high price on the attackers.

Major Hays finally got some flamethrowers (from Crowe's engineers when Edson ordered LT 2/8 to stand down), and the attack of 1/8 from the east made steady, if painstaking, progress. Major Schoettel, finally back in command of all elements of his battalion and eager to atone for his D-Day performance, pressed the assault of 3/2 from the west and south. To complete the circle, Shoup ordered an infantry platoon and a pair of 75-mm half-tracks out to the reef, thus keeping the defenders pinned down from the lagoon.

Some of the Japanese committed hara-kiri; the remainder, exhausted, fought to the end. Hays's Marines had been attacking this complex ever since their bloody landing on the morning of D+1. In those forty-eight hours, 1/8 fired 54,450 rounds of .30-caliber rifle ammunition. But the special weapons of the engineers and the direct fire of the half-tracks did the real damage. Appropriately, Lieutenant Leslie (the engineer who had teamed with Deane Hawkins to initiate the battle for Betio), led his reequipped assault platoon against

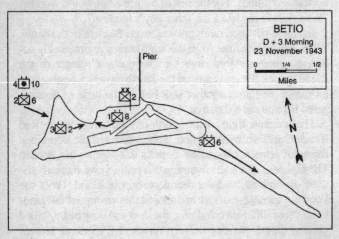

the final thirty-five bunkers in the Pocket. Capture of the largest position, a concrete pillbox near the beach, enabled easier approaches to the remaining pillboxes. By 1300 it was all over.[55]

At high noon, while the fighting in both sectors still raged, a Navy fighter plane landed on Betio's airstrip, weaving around the Seabee trucks and graders. Nearby Marines swarmed over the plane to shake the pilot's hand. A PB2Y also landed to take out initial press reports and the haggard observers, including Evans Carlson and Walter Jordan.

Admiral Hill and his staff came ashore at 1245. The naval officers marveled at the strength and complexity of the Japanese bunker system. Hill would command amphibious forces in many of the greater invasions to come in the Pacific, but this was a sobering moment for him. He compared Betio to Gibraltar and complimented the Marines on their valor under fire.

Hill's well-chosen words meant something to the Marines in his vicinity, but the normally self-effacing Julian Smith began to show signs of a slow burn. Hill had already begun claiming credit for selecting the northwest beach, Betio's sole remaining unmined approach. Smith, Edson, and Shoup had picked those landing beaches in early September, before Hill assumed command of the Southern Attack Force, and fully six weeks before Hill even arrived in New Zealand.

Smith also still smoldered about Hill's impetuous decision to cease fire support twenty minutes before the LVTs touched down on D-Day. Although the general suppressed his anger, he confided to correspondent Sherrod: "The Navy supported us well—gave us everything we asked for, but Goddammit, they didn't let us run the show as promised. They didn't know what we were up against. Hill came ashore today and measured the cement fortifications—then went back. He still doesn't know."[56]

When Smith received the nearly simultaneous reports from Colonels Shoup and Holmes that both final objectives had been seized, he shared the good news with Hill. Despite Smith's rising irritation, he maintained the appearance of "seamless" unity between the two commanders. Compared to the acrimony of other amphibious operations in the war, the two had worked together in relative harmony to achieve this victory. Between them, they drafted a message to Admiral Turner and Gen. Holland Smith announcing the end of organized resistance on Betio. It was 1305, about seventy-six hours after Private First Class Moore first rammed the LVT "My Deloris" onto the seawall on Red Beach One to begin the direct assault.

The stench of death and decay overwhelmed the island. "Betio would be more habitable," reported Sherrod, "if the Marines could leave for a few days and send a million buzzards in." Working parties, many of the men wearing gas masks, sought doggedly to identify the dead. Often the bodies were so badly shattered or burned as to eliminate distinction between friend and foe. Chaplains worked alongside burial teams equipped with bulldozers. The island suddenly seemed too small to accommodate the thousands of corpses. Pharmacist's Mate Bowen recalled the horror. "You could not dig a grave for a body without exposing another body." Seabee Klatt and his crew had the gruesome task of burying a hundred Japanese in a swale near Black Beach One. "Where possible, we dragged these guys by their heels into this swale. Many of these were so badly hit that by taking them by their heels, it was doubtful that the shoulders would follow."[57]

No one had any appetite that night. But Commander Tull took the best possible care of his 18th Seabees, casting a weather eye about the island to determine the direction of the prevailing winds, then selecting a bivouac site clearly upwind of the carnage.[58]

The grimy Marines on Betio took a deep breath and sank to the ground. Many had been awake since the night before the landing. As Captain Hoffman recollected: "There was just no way to rest; there was virtually no way to eat. Mostly it was close, hand-to-hand fighting and survival for three and a half days. It seemed like the longest period of my life." Lieutenant Lillibridge had no nourishment at all until the afternoon of D+3. "One of my men mixed up a canteen cup full of hot water, chocolate, coffee, and sugar, and gave it to me, saying he thought I needed something. It was the best meal I ever had."[59]

PFC Robert L. Kinley, a demolitions man with Dog, 2/18, had reached the point of total debility when the firing finally died. Finding dubious shade in the bottom of a huge shell crater, he collapsed into a deep sleep. He awoke, disoriented, terrified, to rough handling: the burial team had taken him for dead and were dragging him toward a common grave.[60]

Colonel Shoup remarked to one emaciated Marine after the shooting stopped, "This business kinda takes a fellow's appetite, doesn't it?" The survivor stared at Shoup and replied, "Colonel, every minute I have fed on what I feared would be the last memories of my wife and baby boy."[61]

CHAPTER TEN

The Gilberts Aflame

*In the waters of the lagoon, drifting gently now to seaward
with the tide, still floated face down the dead who tried to
land across the fatal reef. I always expected them to lift their
heads for air, but they never did. . . .*
—Tarawa survivor interviewed by Hanson W. Baldwin

MARINES IN THE RANKS TOOK THEIR COM-
mander's proclamations that "enemy resistance has ended"
with a grain of salt. Indeed, some of the bloodier counterattacks at Tinian and Iwo Jima came *after* such victory decla-
rations. While tiny Betio did not lend itself to similar surprises
of that scale, the troops nevertheless spent a decidedly uncomfortable night following the joint pronouncement of General
Smith and Admiral Hill. A thermite grenade intended for a
pillbox detonated a Japanese 140-mm ammunition magazine;
the first night of peace thus became the noisiest night of all.
Taking advantage of the distraction, Japanese survivors crept
from their burned-out bunkers and fell upon the exhausted 6th
Marines, bayonetting three to death.

The tenacity of the die-hard survivors astonished the
Marines for weeks to come. Unlike most other island battle-
grounds in the Pacific, Betio offered neither jungles nor caves
as a sanctuary for stragglers, yet time and again another emaciated rikusentai would appear for one last shot. Commander
Strean, commanding the first fighter squadron to utilize the
captured airstrip at Betio, recalled: "You'd hear a ping which
you'd recognize as a Japanese rifle, and one of our Marines
would drop over. . . . We pilots would lie behind a coconut log
and watch them dig out that sniper. . . . They always got him
but he never gave up. . . . He was going to kill as many people
as he could."[1]

The most lethal Japanese weapon faced by the Central Pacific Force during Operation Galvanic proved to be the fleet submarines, the only segment of the *Hei* counterattack plan that materialized in strength. Six of the nine submarines reached the Gilberts by D+2. Admirals Spruance, Turner, and Hill took this threat seriously. Reports of periscope sightings caused frequent disruptions to amphibious support operations conducted by Hill's Southern Attack Force throughout the Tarawa operation. Often these so-called periscopes turned out to be discarded swab handles or, more likely, empty shell cases jettisoned by the fire support ships.[2]

On other occasions, the submarine threat was real. The destroyers *Frazier* (DD 607) and *Meade* (DD 602) of the Southern Attack Force discovered and sank the sub *I-35* within Tarawa's amphibious objective area on D+3. Two days later the *Radford* (DD 446) sank the *I-40* in the northern Gilberts. But the Japanese did achieve one spectacular hit. The submarine *I-175* torpedoed the merchant-hulled escort carrier *Liscome Bay* (CVE 56) just before sunrise on 24 November off Makin. The torpedo struck the ship's thinly shielded bomb magazines, causing such a terrific explosion that Admiral Hill saw the flash at Tarawa, ninety-three miles away. The ship sank quickly, taking 644 souls to the bottom, including Rear Adm. Henry M. Mullinnix, commander Air Support Group (CTG 52.3).[3]

These losses, combined with casualties sustained when Japanese torpedo planes damaged the light carrier *Independence* (CVL 1) and the appalling fatalities caused by a turret explosion on the battleship *Mississippi* (BB 41), nearly equaled the number of deaths suffered by the landing force at Tarawa. This provided more fuel to the Navy's argument in favor of speed in execution of amphibious assaults to free the covering forces from their vulnerable orbits around the target islands.[4]

Shortly before Gen. Julian Smith's announcement of victory at Betio, his Army counterpart, Gen. Ralph Smith, signaled, "Makin taken!" In three days of sharp fighting on Butaritari Island, the 165th Regimental Combat Team destroyed the

Japanese garrison at a cost of two hundred American casualties. Gen. Holland Smith, commanding the V Amphibious Corps, found the prosecution of the assault by the green soldiers "excruciatingly slow," prompting bad blood with Gen. Ralph Smith that would erupt again with serious consequences the following year during the Saipan invasion.

The troops on Betio conducted a joint flag-raising ceremony, although they were hard put to find two surviving palm trees side-by-side and a Union Jack to accompany the Stars and Stripes. Major Holland, the New Zealander whose home had been on neighboring Bairiki and whose dire predictions about low tides on D-Day had proven so prophetic, produced the British flag. A field musician sounded colors on his bugle. Marines all over the island stood and saluted. Each could reckon the cost. Gen. Julian Smith noticed that some of his troops had exchanged their reeking, overheated, camouflaged utilities for the fresh white uniforms of the Imperial Japanese Navy. "Take those off!" he thundered. Other Marines, eyeing Adm. "Handsome Harry" Hill at a distance in his starched khakis and sunglasses, assumed he was Gen. Douglas MacArthur, flown in secretly for the occasion.[5]

The Marines stared dazedly at the desolation that surrounded them. Julian Smith sent a hasty note to Happy: "I am well, a little tired, and very dirty. I can't talk about it yet." Chaplain Willard walked along Red Beach One, the stretch so long dominated by the Japanese gunners in the Pocket. "Along the shore," he wrote, "I counted the bodies of 76 Marines staring up at me, half in, half out of the water." The carnage sobered veteran correspondent Sherrod during his exploration of the island after the fighting. "What I saw on Betio was, I am certain, one of the greatest works of devastation wrought by man."[6]

The proliferation of heavy machine guns and what he called 77-mm guns (actually Type 88 dual-purpose 75-mm weapons) along the northwest shore further astounded Sherrod. As he described one scene: "Another 77mm gun has not been touched by shellfire, but the eight Japs in the pit were killed by rifle fire. Amtrack Number 4-8 is jammed against the seawall barricade. Three waterlogged Marines lie beneath it. Four others are scattered nearby, and there is one hanging on a two-foot-high strand of barbed wire who does not touch the coral flat at all. Back of the 77mm gun are many hundreds of rounds of 77mm ammunition."[7]

Julian Smith kept his promise to the assault troops. Immediately after the ceremony, scores of landing craft appeared in the lagoon to evacuate the 2d and 8th Marines and their attached units to the transports, waiting to take them immediately to Hawaii. To Lieutenant Lillibridge, going back on board ship seemed like going to heaven. "The Navy personnel were unbelievably generous and kind," he recalled. His troops were still in shock, so dehydrated and exhausted they could not pull themselves all the way up the cargo nets. Without an order being given, sailors swarmed down the nets to help the Marines on board. The sailors helped care for the troops as gently as they would infants, guiding them to showers, providing clean dungarees, leading them down to the mess decks where the captain and his officers served "a full-scale turkey dinner."[8]

But Lillibridge, like many other surviving troop leaders, suffered from post-combat trauma. The lieutenant had lost half his platoon in the battle; guilt consumed him.[9]

Some Marines held up their embarkation to tend to a heartbreaking order of business. Sherrod encountered a band of engineers sifting through bodies near a wrecked LVT #1-5 ("Worried Mind") about two hundred yards east of the Bird's Beak along Red Beach One. The men were survivors of Dog Company, 2/18, attached to Schoettel's 3/2. Thirty-one of these engineers died in the effort to carve out a toehold against the face of the deadly reentrant that became known as the Pocket.

Sherrod described the trail of dead engineers leading from the disabled landing craft, across the barbed wire, and inland toward the first ring of pillboxes. He watched as the volunteers, organized by Cpl. Joseph F. Sobolewski, recovered fifteen bodies, including that of Private First Class Jarrett (the Illinois farmboy-turned-metal worker), and two classmates from

Central Catholic High School in San Antonio, PFCs Gene G. Seng and Charles Montague, who had joined the Marine Corps together, survived the sharp fighting on Gavutu, and—on D-Day—died together at Tarawa. "The bodies," Sherrod noted, "are tenderly gathered up and taken fifteen or twenty yards inland, where other Marines are digging graves for them."[10]

Cpl. Emory B. Ashurst, another Gavutu veteran and one of the Dog Company survivors, read a brief memorial service over the fresh graves. When Sherrod returned by the spot later, the engineers had gone, catching the last boat to the departing transports, but each grave supported a clearly marked cross, and a larger wooden cross guarded the site, inscribed simply "D-2-18."[11]

Other units suffered severe losses in the battle: the 2d Amphibian Tractor Battalion, LT 3/2, and LT 2/2 in particular. Easy Company of 2/2 made the landing over Red Beach Two on D-Day with 166 officers and men; two out of three—112 Marines—became casualties. While Red Spencer of Easy Company came through without a scratch, the difference represented less than an inch. "I've got two bullet holes in my jacket—evidence that if I'd been running a little faster I would have got it in the heart." The entire experience seared and mystified him. "I'll never understand or stop being grateful why my life was spared while other boys all around me were being taken."[12]

Sherrod stopped abruptly as he approached the seawall near the Bird's Beak on the fifth day: the tide had come in. "The full tide is now washing against the seawall to a depth of three feet," he observed, "and the Marines who were lying on the beach this morning are now washing against the seawall." He vividly recalled how welcome the seawall had seemed to him at the end of his agonizing wade ashore on D-Day. Now he realized that, "The tide during those first two critical days was exceptionally low," otherwise, the Marines, "would have had no beachhead at all! This was truly an Act of Providence."[13]

Accounting for casualties proved nightmarish for the surviving first sergeants and personnel chiefs. In many cases boat

crews evacuated clusters of wounded Marines to one ship,
where they were hastily screened and transferred without
record to yet another ship. Many of the more seriously injured
Marines—like Lieutenants Nygren and Edmonds, Sergeant
McBride, and Corporal Moise—rode a transport all the way to
Apamama for transfer to the hospital ship *Solace* and eventual
delivery to the Navy hospital in Aeia, Hawaii. The ships conducted burials at sea almost daily ("This is a grim war," swore
Julian Smith, witnessing one ceremony).[14]

Only slowly did the stragglers coalesce within their original
units. Major Ryan expressed delight to find that the losses in
Love Company, 3/2, "were only thirty-five percent." He had
feared twice that. Eddie Albert found his last duty at Tarawa
especially repugnant: retrieving and identifying swollen
corpses from the lagoon. The grisly work served to reduce the
long, sad list of Marines originally reported missing in action.
The final number of missing came to eighty-eight, but as late as
1 January 1944 the division could still not account for 206
men.[15]

Gen. Holland Smith became the first "Brass Hat" external to
the Southern Attack Force to inspect the island. Sherrod
accompanied Julian Smith and Holland Smith on their tour.
The normally outspoken senior Smith, a veteran of the fighting
in France during World War I, seemed overwhelmed by the
sights and smells of the battlefield. "These Japanese were mas-
ters of defensive construction. . . . The Germans never built
anything like this in France." One poignant scene brought tears
to the corps commander's eyes. As recorded by Sherrod, "The
most stirring sight is the Marine who is leaning in death against
the seawall, one arm still supported upright by the weight of his
body. On top of the seawall, just beyond his upraised hand, lies
a blue and white flag, a beach marker to tell succeeding waves
where to land. Says Holland Smith, 'How can men like that
ever be defeated?' "[16]

Admiral Spruance came ashore next, soon joined by
Admiral Nimitz, who flew from Pearl to Funafuti to Betio,
although his Marine Corps cargo plane had to circle the island

for an hour while Seabees frantically cleared the ends of the runway to make room. "The stench," Nimitz admitted, "was terrific," adding, "It was the first time I've ever smelled death." But Nimitz manfully endured the horrors, examining each blasted Japanese fortification with professional interest and concern. Obviously, the great naval bombardment had failed to do the job. What could be done to improve the performance for the next operation in the Marshalls—and beyond?[17]

Before leaving reeking Betio, Nimitz ordered the preparation of engineering drawings of the Japanese fortifications on a priority basis. Several agencies responded, including a pair of stay-behind members of the 8th Marines intelligence staff, the Division D-2 intelligence section, and the Seabees. The most useful drawings came from an 18th Naval Construction Battalion team centered on the former architect student, Larry Klatt, and two others "with drafting board experience," Benson Moore and Henry Dumont. The team borrowed measuring tapes, T-squares, scales, and drawing paper from the newly arrived and generously equipped 74th Naval Construction Battalion. Klatt did most of the finished work, and his distinctive logo appeared on drawings that later surfaced in the headquarters of CinCPac, the chief of naval operations, and the Office of Naval Intelligence.[18]

The most beneficial dividend from this prompt and detailed calibration of the ruined battlements became evident only a few weeks later on the Hawaiian island of Kahoolawe, the bombardment target island for the Pacific Fleet. Here the CinCPac staff used the Seabee drawings to construct exact replicas of many Betio emplacements to test improved fuses, warheads, and trajectories to benefit the assaults to come in the Central Pacific.

BETIO AND MAKIN MAY HAVE BEEN "SECURED," but the rest of the Gilberts still eluded capture. Julian Smith worried about the force of two hundred Japanese Special Naval Infantrymen on the loose in the outer islands of Tarawa atoll, which the division scouts had reported earlier and shadowed since. By now, the Marines knew what damage an organized force of even such a few rikusentai could inflict. Colonel Murray had angrily expressed his disappointment in missing the bulk of the fighting on Betio; this seemed to Smith to be a good mission for LT 2/6. On 23 November, Lt. Col. Manley Curry's 3d Battalion, 10th Marines, landed on Eita Island under the protective cover of the scouts. The battalion's pack howitzers at first aimed toward Betio, but the defeat of the Japanese counterattack there the night before reduced the number of meaningful targets. Curry then prepared to support Murray's chase of the rikusentai force through the outer islands.

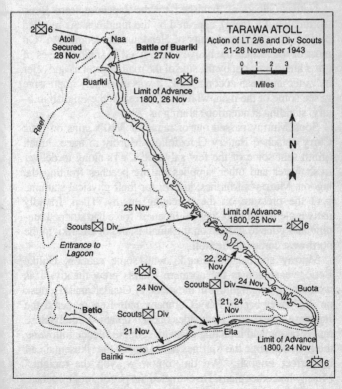

At 0500 on 24 November Murray led LT 2/6 aboard landing craft at Betio, crossed the lower sector of the lagoon, and landed on Eita Island. Captain Nelson, commanding the scouts, briefed him on the enemy strength, weapons, and location. Murray wasted no time. Accompanied by the scouts and covered by the guns of 3/10, LT 2/6 set a blistering pace "around the elbow" and north, executing, in effect, a thirty-five-mile "forced-march movement to contact." Murray tried to time it so his column could cross between the islets at low tide, but this did not always work. PFC Bob Groves of George Company remembered "wading in water up to our necks."[19]

Native Gilbertese, banished by the Japanese from Betio (fortunately for them), appeared by the hundreds. As recalled by PFC Ray M. Lamoreaux of Headquarters Company: "On most of the islands the natives, who lived in small villages of grass huts, came out by the side of the road to greet us and offer us water and fresh coconut milk. It was especially impressive to see some of the men, who [had] served in the English military, standing at attention saluting us."[20]

Soon Murray passed out of range of 3/10's guns on Eita. Curry detached Battery G to follow Murray in trace. Julian Smith sent some of the few salvaged LVTs along to deliver fresh water and other supplies on the beaches fronting the lagoon. Murray's Marines, known for their physical stamina, kept the pressure on the retreating enemy. Then, friendly natives alerted Murray that the Japanese force had stopped running and gone to ground on the small island of Buariki, in the northwest corner of the atoll.

Murray approached Buariki with some caution. Unlike Betio, vegetation in the northern islands grew thickly. This would be jungle fighting in the mode of Guadalcanal. At dusk on 26 November an Easy Company patrol encountered the Japanese main body. Both sides opened up at extremely close range, taking and inflicting casualties. In the silence following the first exchange the Marines heard one of the rikusentai call in perfect English: "We die tomorrow, you die tonight." Murray had other plans. He extracted the patrol, broke contact, and issued orders for an all-out attack on the morrow. He further called for a destroyer to patrol the island throughout the night to prevent any "reverse leap-frogging." The Japanese, however, decided to dig in and fight.

The battle of Buariki on 27 November became the last engagement with organized Japanese forces in the Gilberts. Murray attacked at first light with two companies abreast, getting one salvo from Battery G before the lines intermingled. An artillery officer accompanying the assault companies reported, "Ran into main body of Japs at very close range (20 yards); knee mortars active and men picked off behind coconut logs. Casualties began to appear." As Murray recounted: "It was a real sharp fight. It was very dense underbrush and as our leading units came upon them, they just opened up and killed and wounded quite a few. . . . you just had to work your way through it very carefully."[21]

The battle featured savage hand-to-hand brawling in the tangled brush. Some Japanese fighters, camouflaged till the end, popped up in the middle of the American advance to shoot Marines in the back before being shot, stabbed, or clubbed down by the nearest survivors. Private First Class Lamoreaux went down with a bullet through the shoulder. The fighting reminded Private First Class Groves vividly of Guadalcanal. "Very intense firing, hot, no drinking water, Marine wounded everywhere."[22]

The rikusentai fought to the last man. The fight hardly lasted an hour, as vicious a sixty-minute period for its scale as any in the Pacific War. The end of the shooting revealed 175 dead Japanese. Murray's victory came dearly bought: thirty-two killed, fifty-nine wounded.

In another theater, at an earlier time, the fighting at Buariki would have earned headlines. Eclipsed by Betio, however, the battle rarely rates a footnote in postwar histories. Samuel Eliot Morison, in fact, dismissed the event as a squad-sized affair, an injustice to a dangerous mission speedily executed by one of the best-conditioned infantry battalions in the Marine Corps at that time.[23]

The following day, 28 November, Murray sent a force to

Naa, the last islet. The Marines found no more Japanese. Given this news, Julian Smith proclaimed by radio, "remaining enemy forces on Tarawa wiped out." To his wife Smith wrote: "The battle finally ended this morning when the last Jap was exterminated on the northern tip of the atoll. . . . [at Betio] they fought for every inch of ground until they were killed one by one. . . . I'm not going into the terrible details of the fighting. I can't. . . . My heart bleeds for the mothers of these boys."[24]

Julian Smith pulled the scouts out of Tarawa atoll after Murray's force ran the Japanese to the ground. He needed their talents elsewhere in the Gilberts. On 29 November, Captain Nelson embarked 130 scouts, plus a mortar squad from 1/6, on board the minesweeper *Pursuit*, now free from her duties as primary control ship on Betio's line of departure. This small force had the mission of searching the atolls of Abaiang, Marakei, and Maiana for residual pockets of Japanese.

The *Pursuit* landed scout units sequentially on the three atolls during 30 November to 1 December. They found no Japanese on either Marakei or Maiana; the natives welcomed the Americans warmly. Only on Abaiang did the scouts run into trouble. A small party of five Japanese, likely a coast watching/radio team, escaped by paddling a small boat madly across the lagoon and out of range. A vicious surf then capsized the Marines' rubber boats as they approached the beach, drowning one man and destroying the unit's radio equipment. Extraction through the surf simply took time, which for once in the operation became available. The scouts eventually escaped the surf zone to reach the *Pursuit* and returned to Tarawa the next day.[25]

THE 2D MARINE DIVISION AND THE SOUTHERN attack force had Operation Boxcloth as a second mission in the Gilberts; namely, the capture of Apamama atoll, seventy-six miles from Tarawa. Compared to Betio's slaughterhouse, Boxcloth was a cakewalk for Task Force 53. A small joint force under Gen. Holland Smith's cognizance did the dirty work in advance.

Apamama became the only atoll in the war to be captured by

a landing party and a submarine. The transport submarine *Nautilus*, under Comdr. William D. Irwin, USN, and the VAC Reconnaissance Company under Capt. James L. Jones, USMC, achieved this distinction.

Jones's VAC Recon Company comprised the heart of the landing force. The unit had originated at the very start of the war in Quantico, Virginia, as a joint Army-Marine Corps "Observer Group," part of the G-2 section, Amphibious Corps Atlantic Fleet, under the overall command of Holland Smith. Jones headed the unit from its inception. In 1942 the Marines formed their own unit and moved to Camp Pendleton, California, for rubber boat launching and landing, plus tactical reconnaissance training. In 1943 the unit moved to Pearl Harbor and assumed its new designation.[26]

Gen. Holland Smith assigned the recon company the mission of reconnoitering the atoll to determine the presence of Japanese. Should he find the enemy there in force, Jones had orders not to seek a major engagement, merely to mark the best landing beaches and boat channels for the follow-on forces from the 2d Marine Division who would be along once the business at Betio ended.

The landing party for Boxcloth included three platoons of the VAC Recon Company (Holland Smith assigned one platoon to assist the Army at Makin), a squad of ten soldiers from the 102d Combat Engineers, liaison officers from the 8th Defense Battalion and the 95th Naval Construction Battalion (units that would garrison the island and build the airfield), and Lt. George Hand, retired from the Ocean Island Defense Force, along as an interpreter. The unit carried standard infantry weapons, including Browning automatic rifles and air-cooled .30-caliber machine guns.[27]

As events developed, the process of reaching Apamama proved more hazardous than the subsequent mini-invasion. The *Nautilus* stopped at Tarawa en route on 19–20 November to collect last-minute intelligence and to provide a plane guard for any aviators shot down during the final raids. That job done, the big submarine turned for Apamama, but she encountered a heavy westerly current and could make only 1.5 knots

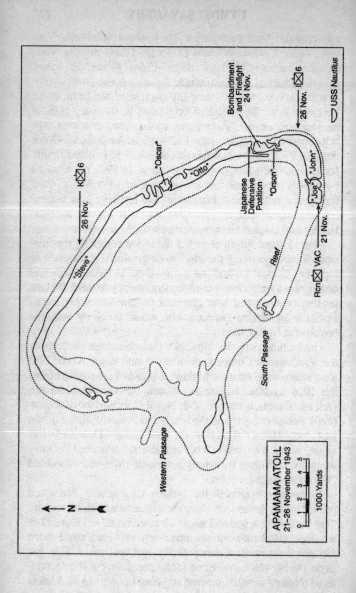

APAMAMA ATOLL
21–26 November 1943

0 1 2 3 4 5

1000 Yards

N

Western Passage

South Passage

Reef

Rcn ⊠ VAC

21 Nov.

"Joe"
"John"

"Orson"

Japanese Defensive
Position

Bombardment
and Firefight
24 Nov.

"Steve"

26 Nov.

K ⊠ 6

"Oscar"

"Otto"

26 Nov.

⊠ 6

26 Nov.

◁ USS Nautilus

submerged. Running on the surface in those waters would be risky, but Commander Irwin had no choice, given his mission of landing his small force at Apamama the next day.

Unfortunately, the *Nautilus* ran directly into the vanguard of the Southern Attack Force, led by the intrepid *Ringgold*. While Turner's staff fully knew the submarine's mission and schedule, Admiral Hill evidently did not. He authorized the *Ringgold* to take the unidentified sub under fire. The destroyer expended sixty-nine rounds of 5-inch/38 at the intruder, but only the first struck home, nailing the submarine in the conning tower as she frantically dove. Ironically, this shot did not detonate; it was a dud, just as the Japanese shells awaiting the *Ringgold* in the lagoon would prove to be a few hours later.[28]

Captain Irwin took the stricken boat down to three hundred feet and started emergency repairs. This took much of the night. Later, when the captain dared bring her to the surface, the sub almost capsized. Eventually, the crew restored buoyancy and a modicum of surface speed. Water continued to pour down the conning tower, straining the pumps to their full capacity. Irwin asked one Marine if he was scared and was comforted to hear, "No, sir, not in the least—but this is a hell of a place to have to dig a foxhole." Lt. Leo B. Shinn, UMSC, tried to keep calm by playing cribbage in the wardroom, from which "we could watch the water pouring right down into the control room."[29]

The *Nautilus* survived and eventually reached Apamama, albeit a day late. Irwin and Jones began planning the launch, trying to orient themselves through the periscope. The major land portions of Apamama atoll resemble a curving banana, fractured into closely adjoining islets. The Marines gave up on the native tongue-twisting names and assigned code names instead. The islets of tactical importance became, from left to right, extending from the south passage around the horn to the east: Joe, John, Orson, Otto, Oscar, and Steve. The Marines wanted to land on John and expected to find the Japanese, if any, holed up on Orson. In execution, they were off by one islet in each direction.

Commander Irwin brought the *Nautilus* to the surface three

thousand yards south of John islet at 0300 on 21 November. The crew inflated eight LCPRs and positioned them on the fantail. Jones, meanwhile, assembled his Marines and Army engineers forward. At a signal, the troops filed into their assigned boats, Irwin submerged the fantail, the boats floated off, and the submarine settled down to periscope depth. The *Nautilus* would keep a careful watch for a red rocket, the prearranged signal for a "Bear Trap" ambush.

But Jones's problems, which arose immediately, had nothing to do with the Japanese, everything to do with Mother Nature and Murphy's Law. Most of the outboard motors failed to start; a rainsquall threatened to scatter the small force; strong currents pushed the paddlers dangerously close to the barrier reef with its high surf. Getting ashore took four strenuous hours. They landed on Joe, not John, glad to be on firm ground, back in their element.

In short order, Jones's men captured and disabled a Japanese landing craft, enlisted several natives as guides, and learned that a force of about twenty-five Japanese occupied the island—and knew of their landing. The Marines got the best of the first shooting encounter. Thereafter, the Japanese withdrew to the south side of Otto islet, which featured prepared defenses and several machine guns. Jones probed the position, considered a waterborne flanking attack using his rubber boats, but discarded the idea when he saw the Japanese had several motor vehicles that would enable them to reach any landing point in force, quicker.

Technically, Jones had already achieved his mission. He could have simply waited for the 2d Marine Division elements and let them steamroller the Japanese. Instead, he paddled back out to the *Nautilus* and made attack plans with Commander Irwin.

What ensued would have been familiar to the eighteenth-century Navy-Marine team of Issac Hull and Presley O'Bannon in Tripoli: close fire support from a "gunboat" parallel to the advance of the ship's expeditionary force. Initial communications smacked of the same milieu: white bedsheets strung from palm trees to mark the Marines' position along the northern edge of Orson. The plan required the *Nautilus* to pound the Japanese positions on Otto with both her 6-inch deck guns, enabling the Marines to rush the defenses.[30]

The *Nautilus* was a wonderful submarine—she had delivered and extracted Carlson's raiders at Makin the year before and landed 7th Division scouts before H-Hour at Attu—but precise naval bombardment was perhaps a mission too far. Irwin used super-quick fuses in hopes of hitting the tops of the palm trees over the Japanese positions, thus spraying the area below. But the elevating mechanism went awry on one gun, which launched several rounds into the ether. The other crew did their best, firing seventy rounds while Irwin and Jones maintained a running dialogue on their radio channel. Occasionally, military courtesy gave way to stark necessity. As Irwin recalled, "A couple of times he shouted, 'You stupid jackass, I said to the right! You shot to the left and almost hit me!'"[31]

"The submarine fire," reported Lieutenant Shinn, "though generally accurate, had little or no effect toward decreasing the enemy's fire." In fact, as Jones moved forward to determine if a charge across the reef passage would now be feasible, the Japanese unleashed a fierce fusillade of machine-gun and rifle fire. Grazing fire seemed particularly heavy to Lt. Russel Corey, whose third platoon occupied the immediate bank across from Otto's main defenses. Corey described the action: "PFC Miller, BAR man, was hit by two machine-gun bullets. Private Zumberge while attempting to render first aid to Miller was also hit twice in the upper left arm, between shoulder and elbow, one bullet fractured arm. He continued to render first aid and tried to shield Miller with his own body . . . but Miller was hit twice more."[32]

Jones realized he had bitten off more than he could chew. He broke contact and pulled back to a perimeter, bringing Corey's casualties with him. Miller died, Zumberge would live. Surprisingly, these would be the only combat casualties sustained by Jones's force. Two other Marines fell victim to the usual first-night jitters of any green troops: an accidental discharge in one case; a sentry shot by other sentries in another. Jones evacuated these to the submarine, then, still looking for alternate ways of skinning the cat, sent his executive officer, 1st Lt. Merwin H. Silverthorn, Jr., in a rubber boat out to enlist the aid of a passing destroyer. That evening the USS *Gansevoort* (DD 608) obliged by firing a few rounds in the vicinity of the Japanese positions.

Captain Jones thought then that he had no remaining offensive options, but soon the Japanese *Bushido* code broke the stalemate. The surviving rikusentai, having fought bravely and lacking the means to escape, donned ceremonial headbands and killed themselves. The natives, seeing this, hurried to tell Jones. On 25 November, their fifth day ashore, Jones's men cautiously approached the silent enemy position and found that it was so. Each Japanese sailor lay dead. Jones and Irwin together had captured an atoll. Later that day, as Admiral Hill and General Hermle—and the 3rd Battalion, 6th Marines—approached Boxcloth expecting to find a fight on their hands, the lookouts spotted a lone oarsman in a small craft, waving at the task group. It was Captain Jones. "It's over," he said. "It's ours!"

Gen. Holland Smith said this of the Apamama operation: "It was a brilliant side-show on a small scale." The Americans attained a strategic windfall of immediate value. The 8th Defense Battalion and 95th Naval Construction Battalion hit the ground running. The Japanese survey team that visited Apamama six months earlier had been absolutely correct in its findings: the atoll had the potential of providing the best airfield in the Gilberts. Within one month the Seventh Air Force deployed heavy bombers to Apamama's newly constructed airfield. By January these aircraft were hitting Japanese targets in the Marshalls.[33]

The Seabees infested the captured islands like carpenter ants. Three airfields became operational in short order, including two—O'Hare Field on Apamama and Mullinnix Field on Buota—that were created out of whole cloth. At Gen. Julian Smith's personal request, the Navy named Betio's captured airstrip Hawkins Field in memory of the gallant Lt. Deane Hawkins, the first nonaviator to be so recognized.

One atoll in the Gilberts remained to be reconquered: Nonuti, 150 miles southeast of Tarawa, which the Japanese had seized and swept on 25 September 1942. While the V Amphibious Corps had earlier considered Nonuti a potential subsidiary objective of Galvanic, the actual task went to the unlikeliest of small naval units: the *PC 599*, a 163-foot-long patrol craft manned by five officers and sixty-three sailors.[34]

The *PC 599* reached Apamama on 20 December. There the senior naval officer directed the craft to proceed to Nonuti, one hundred miles away, and eliminate Japanese resistance, rescue the exiled king of Apamama, and return him to his rightful "throne." There was a catch. No Marine or soldiers were available to constitute a landing force. The advanced base commander could provide just a single Higgins boat, which the crew of the *PC 599* towed astern as they steamed, rather nervously, to the island.

As gunnery officer, Ens. Landon H. Roberts took charge of the landing party. He equipped twenty sailors and himself with "a hodgepodge of weapons, including rifles, shotguns, and pistols." Arriving off the main island, Roberts and his men boarded the Higgins boat for the run to the beach. Almost immediately they received the same rude shock that awaited all landing parties in the Gilberts: the fringing coral reef, several hundred yards offshore. With growing uneasiness Roberts led his men over the side and began to wade through chest-deep water toward the beach. At this most vulnerable moment, a flotilla of outrigger canoes "appeared out of nowhere," bearing down on the startled sailors. Ensign Roberts prepared for the worst. Suddenly, he could see the canoes were filled with grinning Gilbertese, not Japanese Special Naval Landing Forces. The natives yelled, "All Jappie dead!" This was wonderful news. The Americans clambered aboard the canoes, rode in style to the beach, and promptly raised the Stars and Stripes.

The next day the exiled ("and absolutely toothless") king of Apamama and the lord high commissioner of the Gilbert Islands led a triumphant procession along a path strewn with palm branches and lined by thousands of natives on Nonuti.

Noticing the American flag, a protocol-sensitive U.S. officer ordered Roberts to "strike that ensign!"[35]

"No, sir!" replied Roberts. A compromise followed: both the British and American flags soon flew side by side, as they did on Betio.[36]

On Christmas Eve 1943, the *PC 599* somehow embarked the king and a hundred other natives aboard their small craft for a memorable return to Apamama for even greater pageantry. For the first time since 8 December 1941, the Gilbert Islands were free of Japanese invaders.[37]

THE JAPANESE HIGH COMMAND HAD A TOUGH time coming to grips with the rapid loss of the Gilberts and their seemingly impregnable citadel at Betio. As early as 22 November, when Adm. Osami Nagano, chief of the Naval General Staff, attempted to convey the emperor's words commending and encouraging the Tarawa garrison, there was no response from the island. Two days later a search plane from Roi found "no evidence of Japanese forces left on Tarawa" but reported "great activity by enemy on building of airstrips."[38]

Vice Admiral Kobayashi continued to lash at the U.S. Central Pacific Force with his land-based aircraft. Temporarily reinforced by the 24th Air Squadron, the inner South Seas commander launched sizeable forays against Turner and Spruance on 25, 26, and 28 November. While the first of these took the life of Comdr. E. H. "Butch" O'Hare, one of the Navy's finest fighter pilots, the attackers did little other damage.

Japanese aviators, however, exuberantly reported the sinking of two American carriers in each of the three engagements. The news briefly lit up the gloomy headquarters buildings in Kwajalein. Six carriers! As we have seen, though, the only U.S. ship of the one hundred vessels in the Fifth Fleet to be damaged by enemy air attack during Galvanic was the *Independence*, hit by an aerial torpedo the night of 20 November.

Kobayashi's elation did not last long. When the level of American carrier air strikes against the Marshalls increased sharply instead of diminishing, Kobayashi knew his defeat in the Gilberts had been total. On 4 December Admiral Koga, the

Combined Fleet commander, ordered the termination of *Hei* Operation #3 and reassigned the frustrated Ko Detachment counterlanding force to Mili Island in the Marshalls.[39]

Imperial General Headquarters waited until 20 December 1943 to announce the setback.

> The Imperial Navy Landing Force defending Tarawa and Makin Islands fought with 50,000 or more enemy landing force with a small force of 3,000 after 21 November. They fought under persistent enemy aerial strafing and bombing and naval bombardment. They gave great damages to the enemy several times larger than they gave us. . . . On 25 November they performed their last attack and were all killed in action. The commander of the defending force was Rear Admiral Keiji Shibasaki. Also, the civilian employees of the Navy in these two islands, numbering 1,500, cooperated with the defending forces to the end and were also killed in action.[40]

Emperor Hirohito made an unusual appearance before the Japanese Diet the month after the battle of Tarawa to announce, "The war situation is most serious." Meanwhile, after the fall of the Gilberts, the Japanese government began its first active measures to help the civilian population cope with enemy raids, now a certain consequence ahead.[41]

Significantly, none of the Japanese reports and records that have surfaced since the war mention whether any evacuation plans existed for Tarawa, whether to extract Admiral Shibasaki, in the mode of General MacArthur's removal from Corregidor, or to remove the entire garrison, as the Imperial Japanese Navy had so masterfully done with much larger forces at Guadalcanal and Kiska that same year. By November 1943, we may conclude that IGHQ fully expected the admiral and his men to die defending the island. The great counterattack by the Combined Fleet envisioned in the *Yogeki sakusen* grew more problematical as the year waned.

In retrospect, the Tarawa garrison lost its last legitimate chance for relief on 5 and 11 November when Admiral

Sherman's Task Force 38 struck Rabaul, destroying so many of Admiral Koga's priceless, carrier-qualified aviators. That took the Combined Fleet out of the equation in the battle for the Gilberts. The ragtag force of light cruisers and destroyers that Admiral Kobayashi finally assembled in the Marshalls would have been sunk in an hour had it made a serious move toward the Gilberts.

In the end, Shibasaki's solitary hope would have been to conduct a "Wake Island defense," as the Americans had done in 1941, in this case stinging the Southern Attack Force so painfully as to cause reconsideration of the Central Pacific campaign. As we have seen, the garrison's tenacity, marksmanship, and fortification skills came close to making that happen in the first thirty hours. The defenders' great opportunity came and went the first night when Crowe and Shoup seemed so dangerously vulnerable on the eastern flank. The death of Shibasaki that afternoon evened the odds. The Americans could thank their fates that of all the many duds and richochets that plagued naval gunfire on D-Day, one fortuitous shell detonated fully on target—dead center.

CHAPTER ELEVEN

Pyrrhic Victory

Tarawa Costly Conquest for Marine Corps
—Dallas Times-Herald, 2 December 1943

INITIAL NEWS REPORTS OF TARAWA'S HIGH casualties shocked America. Few people had ever heard of the place. On a typical household map the atoll seemed a mere speck in the huge bowl of the Pacific Ocean, so many thousands of miles east of Tokyo. Many Americans questioned whether the capture of such a small, desolate place had been worth such frightful losses.

In Washington, Marine Corps headquarters came under intense pressure from the Navy Department, the Roosevelt administration, and the media to release Tarawa's casualty lists. The headquarters staff spent ten unpleasant days holding these agencies at arms' length while waiting for the 2d Marine Division to count its scattered flock and report its losses. The chaotic nature of the battle followed by the immediate reembarkation of the survivors made this delay inevitable, but Washington became increasingly impatient. Many newspapers during this period filled the factual void with speculation of enormous losses squandered in some Central Pacific Balaklava during an ill-fated amphibious attack. Lurid headlines proclaimed the blood, blunders, and wreckage of the beachhead.

Part of this early notoriety about Tarawa stemmed from the Marines' own decision to provide combat correspondents an unrestricted and generally uncensored view of the proceedings. Many of these journalists and photographers shared the worst of the hell of Betio the first thirty-six hours and simply reported what they observed. Their accounts were responsible and accurate. Their stateside editors, however, selected sensational headlines that were disproportionate to the stories.

This happened to Marine Corps Master Technical Sgt. James C. Lucas, whose graphic report of his observations received front-page coverage in the 4 December 1943 *New York Times* under the appended headline: "Grim Tarawa Defense a Surprise, Eyewitnesses of Battle Reveals; Marines Went in Chuckling, To Find Swift Death Instead of Easy Conquest." This infuriated Edson and Shoup, whose detailed Estimate of the Situation before the assault demonstrated convincingly that few Marines would go "chuckling" across that line of departure.

As the controversy intensified, some senior Marines added fuel to the fire with ill-chosen or lukewarm remarks to reporters. Gen. Holland Smith likened the D-Day assault to Pickett's charge at Gettysburg. The soon-to-retire commandant, General Holcomb, provided little clarification or endorsement with the terse comment: "This was our first atoll attack and I'm afraid our casualties will be very heavy."[1]

The 2d Marine Division also contributed to the illusion that Tarawa was an ill-conceived blunder by trying at first to suppress any reports of the successful use of LVTs in leading the assault ashore. The idea made sense. Japanese defenders in the Marshalls and Marianas might still believe their coral reefs protected them from conventional landing boats. But Shibasaki's flash message on D-Day reported "more than one hundred amphibious tanks" led the American assault, and Imperial General Headquarters quickly shared this intelligence with other island commanders.

The Marines would have been much better off allowing full media disclosure. Positive publicity about their LVT gamble would have provided a valuable offset to the initial dire reports. Restricted from mentioning LVTs, the correspondents naturally concentrated on the ordeal of the men wading ashore, a vivid experience many of them shared. Unleavened by any reports of LVTs penetrating the reef, the landing sounded more and more like botched planning and bad intelligence. Not until two weeks after the battle did military journalist Hanson Baldwin (not at Tarawa) break the story about the role of LVTs in a *New York Times* essay in which he favorably described a "new amphibian vehicle" unveiled at Tarawa that can "swim through deep water, crawl over the coral projections and waddle directly on the beach, bringing its men dry-shod to shore."[2]

The "Bloody Tarawa" controversy raged throughout much of December. General MacArthur offered his unsolicited opinion directly to the secretary of war—bypassing the Joint Chiefs of Staff—declaring, "These frontal assaults by the Navy, as at Tarawa, are a tragic and unnecessary massacre of human lives." Later, he took pains to lecture both President Roosevelt and Admiral Nimitz on the folly of forcible amphibious assault. "Frontal assault is only for mediocre commanders," he said, adding, "Good commanders do not turn in heavy losses."[3]

Meanwhile, a woman wrote Admiral Nimitz, accusing him of "murdering my son." Some members of Congress demanded a special investigation.[4]

At the heart of the problem lay the fact that to this point the administration had chosen to shield the American public from most of the harsh realities of war reporting. Indeed, *Life* magazine only two months prior to Tarawa had shocked the nation by publishing a photograph by George Strock of three slain soldiers on a beach at Buna, the first general distribution of any pictures of dead American servicemen. The photographs from Tarawa were even more graphic. These images, professionally captured under great stress, conveyed a real sense of the desperate fighting. One wide-angle, black-and-white photograph of Betio's devastation by Frank Filan of the Associated Press would win the Pulitzer Prize.[5]

The motion-picture coverage of the assault on Tarawa proved just as riveting. The composite, color-tinted movie footage of the fighting taken by Sergeant Hatch and other combat photographers would win an Academy Award. In the meantime, however, President Roosevelt struggled with the decision about releasing the documentary to the movie theaters of America. On one hand, a public glimpse of the horrors of the war currently being waged in the Pacific might boost the sale of war bonds, then lagging. On the other hand, the combat footage represented an order-of-magnitude change from the usual sugarcoated war news.

Roosevelt saw Robert Sherrod in a crowd of White House reporters, knew the *Time-Life* journalist had just returned from the battlefield, and asked him privately for his advice about releasing the documentary. Sherrod believed the public knew little about the real nature of the war with Japan and recommended the film be shown without restriction. FDR did so. Almost overnight the film "With the Marines at Tarawa" became a national sensation. The documentary's most poignant segment, a cluster of Marine bodies floating in the shallows off Red Beach Two, both horrified and sobered the public. War bond sales increased markedly. Marine Corps recruitment, however, dropped 35 percent during the same period.[6]

The Marine Corps brought Colonel Edson home at the height of the post-battle controversy to defuse some of the lingering adverse criticism. Edson found this ironic, having to publicly defend a tactical plan more or less imposed by Navy restrictions that he had initially opposed, but the Corps made it up to him with a deep selection to brigadier general. Edson proved to be the right choice to explain Tarawa to the Washington press corps. He was well known, articulate, and widely respected. Speaking before a Betio map in the commandant's office in Washington, Edson held the reporters in thrall.

He emphasized the two points that were the crux of the criticism. First, he established that there had been no mistake about the tide; planners had known that their information was sketchy at best, and they had decided to use the amphibious tractors precisely to deal with the possible lack of water over the reef. He further pointed out that the perception of heavy casualties due to the tide was simply wrong: More than 80 percent of the losses had been sustained ashore. . . . [Edson continued] "I think the

American people should realize the psychology of the
people we are fighting—to make the campaigns as costly
as possible because they don't believe we can take it."[7]

Edson's blunt assessments carried weight. Newspaper edi-
torials began to pick up on his last point: the need for the nation
to steel itself for the longer, bloodier battles to come in the
Pacific. Admiral Nimitz stuck to his guns, speaking of the
value of Tarawa as "an unsinkable carrier" in the forthcoming
campaign in the Marshalls, then pausing to praise the courage
of the Marines, saying, "Never before was such a tough job
done so completely in such a short time."[8]

Tarawa's high casualties had saddened but not shocked
Edson. As the senior amphibious veteran in the division before
the battle, Edson had studied Betio thoroughly and predicted
stiff losses. In a letter to headquarters shortly before D-Day,
Edson requested that the division be assigned two full replacement battalions, about two thousand men, by D+15.[9]

Colonel Shoup, although new to amphibious assaults,
seemed to realize the magnitude of the division's losses soon
after the shooting stopped. His field notebook contains this
entry: "2MARDIV Tarawa: Dead 784, Wounded 2,094,
Missing 205." The division's total casualties, according to
Shoup at that point, would equal 3,083 men. Troop officers
mustered their weary men again and again. The ensuing flurry
of priority messages between ships and hospitals caused the
figures to change every day. The "errata" sheets to the unit rosters for November eventually reached half the number of pages
in the original reports.[10]

The final casualty figures ("final" being a moving target
itself for some time) exceeded Edson's grim predictions and
Shoup's initial estimates. The 2d Marine Division would
require the equivalent of *four* replacement battalions to restore
its pre-Tarawa strength. The official, "final" statistics, compiled in August 1952, reveal that the division sustained these
casualties during Operation Galvanic, principally within
Tarawa atoll.

Dead: 997 Marines and 30 Navy (organic medical)
Missing and presumed dead: 88 Marines
Wounded: 2,233 Marines and 59 Navy
    Total: *3,407* casualties.[11]

By itself, the total body count fails to tell the story. After all, the Marines suffered a similar number of casualties during the previous campaign in Guadalcanal. Yet Marine participation in combat in Guadalcanal lasted six months. Most of Tarawa's losses occurred within seventy-six hours. Moreover, the ratio of killed to wounded at Tarawa was significantly high: one Marine died for every three hit, a reflection of the savage, close-quarters fighting on Betio. The 2d Marine Division's casualties represented 19 percent of its total strength embarked for Galvanic, a steep but overall acceptable loss factor. But these figures are skewed by the fact that probably one full third of the division did not (in fact, *could* not) land until the assault units secured Betio. We can safely estimate that Gen. Julian Smith had about twelve thousand troops ashore by 1300 on D+3, the moment he and Hill declared the island "secure."

This provides a more realistic appraisal of the American combat losses at Tarawa. Close to 30 percent of those twelve thousand men directly involved in the fighting ashore died or sustained wounds in the battle.

The division reported moderate losses among its tanks and half-tracks, and damned heavy losses in LVTs: 90 of the 125 vehicles either wrecked, sank, or were otherwise knocked out of action.[12]

Julian Smith visited his wounded men in the Navy hospital at Aiea, Hawaii, and mingled with his unwounded survivors in their new training camp on the big island of Hawaii. He reported to the commandant (General Vandegrift relieved General Holcomb on 1 January 1944) that morale was never better, and such may well have been the case. The division had seized a formidable citadel in a matter of days, prevailing over a tough foe and knocking down the front door to the Central Pacific.

Nevertheless, each Marine wrestled with a sustained sense

of personal shock and guilt produced by the heavy losses and savage fighting. Some would be haunted by it all their lives. "I'm proud I served my country," said one survivor at the fiftieth anniversary ceremony, "but I'm not proud of what I had *to do* to serve my country." Others—particularly in the shot-up assault battalions—mourned the loss of so many close companions, tentmates, shipmates.

For historians, some of the most revealing and useful accounts of the battle of Tarawa are those that appeared within the first several weeks, both in official and unofficial channels. Surprisingly (because he never went to Tarawa), Admiral Turner's report of the entire Galvanic campaign remains the most forthright and comprehensive of the early accounts by senior commanders. Turner was a driven man, a perfectionist. The Fifth Amphibious Force commander appears to have written much of the report himself while en route to Pearl Harbor from the Gilberts in early December. Reflecting on the Americans' first taste of atoll warfare, Turner observed: "Attack on an atoll resembles in many respects the assault on a fort . . . with the added complication of having to initiate the assault with the ship-to-shore movement."[13]

Turning to the general disappointment experienced by most Galvanic commanders in "the war's greatest preliminary bombardment," Turner bluntly stated:

> Air and naval gunfire preparations for two or three hours is not adequate. This preparation should begin several days prior to D-Day and should be designed both for destruction and for unrelenting harassing effect. This preparation may be at times augmented by secondary landings on adjacent islands either on or prior to D-Day, for the purpose of placing artillery in position. Maximum use of beach barrage rockets and boat guns should be made in direct support of the assault waves.[14]

Interestingly, Turner and Holland Smith continued to spar about the value of LVTs in the assault. Where Smith declared in the VAC report, "Without the amphibian tractor, it is believed that the landing at Tarawa would have failed," Turner merely stated, "The capture of Tarawa would have been far more difficult had these vehicles not been employed."[15]

The best appraisal of LVT employment during Galvanic came from Gen. Ralph Smith, who commanded the 27th Infantry Division at Makin. "All of the LVTs reached the beach, and from prisoners it was learned that they caused consternation to the Japanese. It is believed that these vehicles are of utmost importance to successful amphibious operations against organized defensive positions."[16]

Colonel Edson's personal letter to his friend Col. Gerald C. Thomas on 13 December 1943 represents the most comprehensive account in narrative form of the landing force perspective at Tarawa. Edson knew that Thomas would share the letter with General Vandegrift, the commandant-designate, and pulled no punches in reporting his observations of the battle, the amphibious operation, naval gunfire, air support, weapons, and the performance of the senior officers involved. Julian Smith knew of this letter and, in fact, kept his "Dear Archer" letter to Vandegrift purposefully short because Edson had covered the subject so thoroughly.

Edson criticized the Navy's initial overreliance on preliminary bombardment, the aviators' lack of training in close air support, the ungainly amount of heavy vehicles and equipment in the division, and the Corps' tendency to retain overaged regimental commanders at their combat posts. He also praised Shoup's performance, stated that, "Without LVTs I doubt if we could even have reached the beach," and expressed his great concern about the vulnerability of the Marines ashore to a Japanese counterattack the first night of the battle.[17]

The subject of employing LVTs as assault craft moved front and center immediately. Shoup spent much of the week before Christmas being grilled by representatives from Admiral King's office and Marine Corps headquarters. The consensus of each commander—Nimitz, Spruance, Turner, Hill, and both Smiths—provided a strong endorsement. The Central Pacific Force, indeed the amphibious ships and landing forces throughout the Pacific, would need many more LVTs, up to three hundred per division. Nor would jury-rigged armor plating for field-converted logistics vehicles suffice in the future. The Galvanic veterans demanded factory-installed armor plating, greater firepower (including separate but accompanying armored LVT(A)s with turret-mounted weapons), more safety features, better communications, and a rear ramp to eliminate the vulnerable leap over the topside gunwales.[18]

Resource planners in Washington listened intently, got the green light from the Department of the Navy, and commenced a high priority development and construction program. The aging LVT-1 Alligators had led their first assault; the landing at Cape Gloucester on 26 December 1943 would be their last. Field-modified LVT-2s would suffice for the Marshalls; brand-new LVT-4s and LVT(A)-4s would be on hand in spades for Operation Forager in the Marianas seven months later.[19]

An equally urgent subject for the Tarawa leaders to assess concerned the Japanese mines encountered at Tarawa. "Some solution has got to be found to eliminate underwater mines," wrote Edson to Thomas, "which I think is the most dangerous thing we have to combat at the moment." While the division staff knew of Japanese mines in the waters in advance, it was not until ten days after D-Day that they received aerial photographs of sufficient detail (1:2,000 scale) to reveal the total distribution of enemy mines still lying along Betio's southern, western, and northeastern coasts. Lt. Col. A. Vincent Wilson, an Army staff engineer for Gen. Holland Smith, prepared a detailed report of mines and obstacles found on his immediate post-battle analysis of the island.[20]

Wilson's report was a sobering, ex post facto primer regarding the extent of the mine threat. Julian Smith and his staff would whistle at their luck in capturing Betio when they did, with the Japanese garrison having more than three thousand additional mines on the island awaiting tactical distribution. Learning this, and knowing of the large stockpiles of steel rails and barbed wire awaiting the resupply of cement, Smith, Edson, and Shoup never second-guessed the choice of landing dates, regardless of the fickle tides. Edson pointed out to Thomas, "Every beach except the one we landed on was heavily mined." As Shoup explained later: "Division planners could plainly see the seaward beaches were mined, but the lagoon side was a different matter. The enemy troops there were in the business of working on their defenses.... The question was what you would do if you were on the island. Chances are you would mine everything but the place you use daily—that would be the last place to be sewed up. This conclusion was a very definite factor in our decision to land where we did."[21]

Commanders at all levels within the Southern Attack Force came forth quickly after the battle with their analyses of what worked and what failed at Tarawa. These reports were remarkably free of self-serving rhetoric. Most commanders admitted mistakes, scrutinized plans and doctrine, and suggested practical improvements. All participants could sense the critical value of these lessons learned of Tarawa. The Marshalls campaign loomed on a fast track. Beyond lay other fortified islands in the Central Pacific.

As Admiral Hill saw it, "We knew that our report of this operation was going to be a textbook for future operations, so we tried to spell out everything—any mistakes that we made or faults that we found."[22]

Within roughly two weeks the 2d Marine Division compiled and forwarded fourteen specific recommendations, ranging from amphibian tractors to signal communications. Most of them centered on the execution of amphibious doctrine: naval gunfire and aviation support, ship-to-shore assault, command and control, shore party operations, the works. Other recommendations provided a critical analysis of the way the Fleet Marine Force organized, armed, trained, and equipped itself for amphibious assault.

The battle of Tarawa had a tremendous effect on the Marine Corps and the emerging amphibious Navy. Virtually every other Marine and "gator" sailor in the Pacific knew their turn would soon come against another Betio down the line. Tarawa's lessons attracted close scrutiny for months to come.

The topic of naval gunfire support of amphibious operations received the most intense review after Tarawa. In this case, neither sea service could truly blame the other for Tarawa's shortcomings since by doctrine the attack force and the landing force shared responsibilities for planning naval fire support. All hands could agree that the hasty "saturation" fires at Betio, which planners deemed sufficient in view of the competing requirement for speed of execution, proved essentially useless against fortified positions. Most of all, amphibious assaults against defended atolls would need sustained, deliberate, aimed fire.

Nevertheless, Admiral Hill could state with some accuracy that Tarawa provided the essential watershed between Gallipoli and the great amphibious landings of 1944–45. Naval gunfire at Gallipoli had failed miserably. At Tarawa the preliminary bombardment failed to do its job and was lifted too soon, but the subsequent fire support proved superb, providing a major tactical advantage to the fighting ashore.

Close air support needed much improvement, but even here the battle presented several breakthroughs. Until Tarawa, planners assumed that naval gunfire and air support had to be sequential, not concurrent: the "little sky, big bullet" approach. Tarawa proved that support aircraft could operate effectively above the trajectory of ships' guns. Tarawa also gave a huge boost to the effectiveness of escort carriers (the CVEs) in direct support of amphibious operations. This in turn would help free the new fleet carriers for their greater operational mission of controlling the sea and air throughout the theater of advance.

Tactical communications during the Betio assault were awful. The Marines needed waterproof radios. The Navy needed a dedicated amphibious command ship, not a major combatant whose big guns would knock out the radio nets with each salvo. Such command ships, designated AGCs, began to appear during the Marshalls campaign. Better radios, the SCR series, soon made their way into the Fleet Marine Force.

Betio showed the critical need for underwater swimmers who, before the landing, could stealthily assess and report reef, beach, and surf conditions to the task force. This concept, first envisioned by amphibious warfare prophet Maj. Pete Ellis in the 1920s, came quickly to fruition. Admiral Turner thus had a fledgling underwater demolition team on hand for the Marshalls.

The Marines liked the new Sherman medium tanks and saw no further requirement for the light tanks. While Betio proved to be an unholy baptism by fire for the Shermans, most of their losses came from operating independently, buttoned up, essentially blind and unsupported. In this fashion Japanese sappers disabled two tanks by slapping a magnetic mine on the steel hulls, a single Japanese 75-mm mountain gun knocked out three Shermans in a row, and several more tumbled into unseen shell holes. These losses mandated closer coordination with the infantry, and the Shermans thereafter functioned with effectiveness and virtual impunity inshore from the seawall during the remainder of the battle.

Future tank training would emphasize integrated tank, infantry, engineers, and artillery operations. As a critical corollary, tank-infantry communications needed immediate improvement. All casualties among Sherman tank commanders at Betio resulted from the individuals having to dismount from their vehicles to talk with the infantry in the open.

The backpack flamethrower won universal acclaim from the Marines on Betio. Each battalion commander recommended increases in quantity, range, and mobility for these assault weapons. Some suggested that larger versions be mounted on tanks and LVTs, presaging the appearance of "Zippo Tanks" in later campaigns in the Pacific.[23]

THE JAPANESE COULD READILY SEE THAT THE American seizure of the Gilberts rendered their island outposts in the Marshalls extremely vulnerable. Imperial General Headquarters accorded top priority to the delivery of critical fortification materials to the Mandates. The 6th Special Base Defense Commander received explicit instructions about the lessons learned from Tarawa, specifically, the need to reorient atoll defenses to cover landing approaches from within the lagoons.[24]

None of these precautions would suffice. The Pacific War had changed. American submarines increasingly interdicted cargo ships bound for the outer islands. The new fast-carrier task forces ranged widely through the Central Pacific, packing enough firepower to fight their way clear of any concentration of Japanese forces they might encounter. Seventh Air Force medium and heavy bombers, fully escorted by fighters, began pounding Japanese installations throughout the Marshalls from airfields at Tarawa and Apamama. Soon, the beleaguered Japanese garrisons at Roi, Kwajalein, and Eniwetok came to realize their terrible isolation in the face of the "storm landings" to come.

Only a handful of Tarawa's vaunted Japanese defenders remained alive after the battle. The 2d Marine Division captured 146 prisoners at Tarawa atoll, but conscripted Korean laborers comprised the overwhelming majority. The division identified nineteen prisoners as Japanese (or "probably Japanese"). Two of these died on board ship; a third became a mental case. Two were crewmen from the sunken submarine *I-35*. Six were members of the 111th Construction Battalion, including a carpenter, a stone mason, and a barber, a "pick and shovel man." Only eight men—a leading seaman, six petty officers, and a warrant officer—could be classified as rikusentai of either the Sasebo 7th Special Naval Landing Force or the 3d Special Base Defense Force. Before the battle these two units reported 2,571 men on their rolls. Thus, their fatality rate at Tarawa was *99.7 percent*.[25]

On 10 February 1944 the Imperial Japanese Navy promoted Keiji Shibasaki posthumously to vice admiral. His superior officers at the time of the American landing fared less well. Vice Admiral Kobayashi, abashed by the loss of the Gilberts and weakened by poor health, asked Admiral Koga on 17 February to relieve him as commander of the 4th Fleet/Inner South Seas Unit, and he returned to Japan in disfavor. Koga died in a plane crash in the Philippines the last day of March. Koga's replacements would continue to seek to execute the "Z Plan's" climactic battle against the American Fleet, leading to spectacular defeats in 1944 at the Battle of the Philippine Sea and the Battle of Leyte Gulf.[26]

WHEN IT CAME TO COMBAT AWARDS FOR THE Battle of Tarawa, one veteran suggested that either the entire 2d Marine Division receive awards, or no one. The heroism and valor seemed evenly divided among all those who tried to cross the fringing reef. Gen. Julian Smith wanted most of all for the division to receive the Presidential Unit Citation, which in its original context signified that all hands had fought at the aggregate level of valor as high as that which merited the Navy Cross. Few who had read the reports or seen the combat films would question whether the division qualified. The coveted award was forthcoming.

Nominations for individual combat awards stirred some of the usual grumbling: too many awards for one outfit, not enough for another; too many officers, not enough troops; and so forth. Examining the division's consolidated award nomination list, however, reveals a fairly even distribution that would appear distinctly austere under modern standards. Keeping in mind that the Bronze Star and Navy Commendation Medals had not yet materialized at the time of Tarawa, the division had this range of personal medals from which to chose: Medal of Honor, Navy Cross, Distinguished Service Medal, Silver Star, or Legion of Merit. In addition, the commanding general could request CinCPac letters of commendation from Admiral Nimitz or issue his own (recipients later converted many of these to the Navy Commendation Medal). Gen. Julian Smith finally agreed on this distribution for valorous service at Tarawa:

Medal of Honor	4	(3 posthumous)
Navy Cross	46	(22 posthumous)
Distinguished Service Medal	4	
Silver Star	248	
Legion of Merit	21	
Total medals	(323)	

CinCPac Letter of	
Commendation	80
CG Letter of Commendation	96
Total commendations	(176)
Total Awards	499[27]

The total number of 2d Marine Division members nominated represented less than 5 percent of those who participated
in the fighting, a healthy restraint. Gen. Julian Smith nominated fifty Navy personnel for awards. Nineteen corpsmen or
field surgeons received nominations for either the Navy Cross
or the Silver Star. Nine civilian combat correspondents,
including Robert Sherrod, Keith Wheeler, Richard Johnston,
and Frank Filan, received CinCPac commendations. Two of
the nominations for Distinguished Service Medal went to
Shoup's forward command group: Maj. Thomas Culhane and
Capt. John Bradshaw. Maj. Mike Ryan received the Navy
Cross. So did Maj. Jim Crowe, his exec Maj. Bill Chamberlin,
and Cpl. John Spillane, the former baseball prospect who
lost his hand tossing Japanese grenades out of his still-loaded
LVT. Among the posthumous Navy Cross nominations were:
Sgt. James Atkins, Lt. Col. Herbert Amey, and fallen am-
trackers Maj. Henry Drewes and Capt. Bonnie Little.[28]

Julian Smith nominated Deane Hawkins, Alexander Bonnyman, and William Bordelon for the posthumous Congressional
Medal of Honor. Then, with Holland Smith's consent, he nominated Col. David Shoup to be the only living recipient of that
high honor. This irked Edson. Although he supported such
recognition for Shoup, Edson also believed his own role in
planning and executing the battle, including command ashore
in relief of Shoup, should make him equally qualified.

Smith did not see it that way. He valued Edson highly, even
nominating him for deep selection to brigadier general, but in
terms of combat awards for Tarawa, Smith recommended just
a Distinguished Service Medal for his chief of staff. When
this nomination saw further downgrading to a Legion of
Merit, Edson experienced some understandable bitterness. The

choice could not have been an easy one for Smith, but Edson already had a Medal of Honor, Shoup had next to nothing, and it had been on Shoup's broad shoulders that the battle of Tarawa balanced so precariously those first thirty-six hours.[29]

Post-battle award nominations are, of course, the domain of the survivors, the living. The remains of the fallen at Tarawa, on the other hand, would know little peace. Many of the graves had to be moved up to four different times, partly to accommodate wartime expansion of the airstrip, partly because of subsequent resettlement by natives. With this disruption, and the fact that the ships had to bury so many men at sea, barely one-fourth of the dead made it home to America, identified, for burial. Of the most honored dead, the bodies of Bill Bordelon, Deane Hawkins, and Sandy Bonnyman now lie in Oahu's Punchbowl, the National Cemetery of the Pacific.[30]

Epilogue

*I have always had the feeling that the margin between
success and failure in an amphibious operation conducted
against strongly defended positions was a narrow one.*
—Adm. Raymond A. Spruance, USN

Tarawa's Enduring Legacy

SPRUANCE MADE THIS REMARK IN AN ADDRESS
to the Amphibious Warfare School, Marine Corps Schools,
Quantico, Virginia, in 1948. During that same lecture to
company-grade Marine and Navy officers five years after the
battle, Spruance declared that the principal lesson he had learned
at Tarawa was the necessity for using "violent, overwhelming
force, swiftly applied." He would do so in the Marianas, at Iwo
Jima, and Okinawa; he had done so convincingly at Tarawa. For
all of Betio's graphic horrors, Spruance had led his Central
Pacific Force to swift, violent success in Operation Galvanic.[1]

In many respects, American forces won the short, savage
battle of Tarawa elsewhere, earlier, at different echelons, well
before the reinforced 2d Marines began crossing the line of
departure on D-Day. Tarawa, for one thing, reflected invaluable combat lessons learned at Guadalcanal by the many veterans in the ranks of the 2d Marine Division. Guadalcanal may
have given them malaria, but it also equipped the survivors
with discipline, teamwork, endurance, adaptability, and mental
toughness. Similarly, the daring strike against the Japanese
Mobile Fleet in Simpson Harbor, Rabaul, by Admiral
Sherman's Task Force 38 on 5 November (and again, with
Admiral Montgomery on 11 November) knocked the wheels
off the great *Hei* Plan #3.

As awful as Betio proved to be, at least the Marines clinging
to those beachheads would never have to experience the

"eighty minutes of hell" inflicted at leisure against the defenders of Guadalcanal by two Japanese battleships on 13–14 October the previous year. There would be no counterattack by Japanese carriers and battleships at Tarawa.

Likewise, the outpouring of war material from America's shipyards and ordnance plants influenced strategic decisions rendered by the Joint Chiefs of Staff to use these resources in a truly global war, which in turn contributed to victory at Tarawa. By late 1943 America had the strategic direction and the material to conduct a major war in Europe *and* maintain a limited offensive in the Pacific. For the Marines and sailors of the Southern Attack Force, this meant America finally had the resources—and the moxie—to whipsaw the Japanese with powerful landings at Bougainville and the Gilberts within a three-week period. The ships, planes, and troops Spruance commanded for Galvanic were easily twice those available to Adm. Robert Ghormley for Operation Watchtower (soon renamed "Shoestring") at Guadalcanal.

The force ratio buildup continued at a geometric progression. Spruance would have four times the Guadalcanal numbers at Saipan; eight times as many at Iwo Jima. Unlike Guadalcanal, the troops fighting for Tarawa enjoyed the benefit of near total "battlespace dominance" established by the fast-carrier task forces, built around the *Essex*-class fleet carriers.

The subsequent campaigns of 1944–45 in the Pacific came so rapidly that Tarawa became eclipsed by the larger, costlier battles of Saipan, Peleliu, Iwo Jima, and Okinawa. Although Tarawa may have seemed primitive by 1945 standards, the battle continued to be considered pivotal. Few fighting men in the Central Pacific really forgot Tarawa or its significance to the Pacific War. Even while the war itself continued to rage, the 1943 seizure of Betio assumed the permanence of a landmark event, a turning point. This prominence took two different levels. In the context of naval campaign planning, Tarawa proved significant as a test bed, a bloody but beneficial validation of the doctrine of amphibious assault. The direct application of fresh knowledge gained in the crucible of Tarawa to the quick seizure of the Marshalls had been obvious to all.

Tarawa's other landmark contribution during the war was psychological. Once the American public came to deal with the shock of the bodies floating in the shallows along Red Beach, the national mood became one of grim determination. Kiska, we came to realize, had been an aberration. Henceforth we could expect the Japanese to defend each island to the death. So be it, the public seemed to say. The Pacific War would become a war of virtual extermination. Tarawa revealed that the road to Tokyo would take time and blood and treasure. Tarawa also provided confidence that Americans could prevail.

One postwar blemish in the Tarawa legacy occurred in 1948 with the publication of Gen. Holland Smith's memoirs in *Coral and Brass*, which was serialized in the *Saturday Evening Post*. Smith startled his former amphibious counterparts by declaring that Tarawa had been a mistake from the beginning, a "futile sacrifice," strategically useless, "a terrible waste of life and effort." None of Smith's Galvanic shipmates shared his view. Indeed, Nimitz, Spruance, Hill, Julian Smith, Edson, and Shoup all spoke out against the assertation, insisting that Tarawa had been very much worth the cost. "I certainly do not believe Tarawa was a mistake," countered Julian Smith. "Moreover," he added, "I do not recall that General H. M. Smith at the time offered any objection to moving against Tarawa." At another point, Julian Smith argued, "There have been many larger and better battles than Tarawa, but few with greater influence on the future course of the war."[2]

Admiral Spruance reviewed the strategic considerations at the time and dispassionately commented: "I do not agree with General Holland Smith's thesis that Tarawa was a mistake and that we should have gone directly to Kwajalein. I feel sure he would have been most unwilling to attempt the capture of any defended island without adequate aerial photographs. . . . those of Kwajalein became available only after we had taken the Gilberts and built airfields on them."[3]

Tarawa's only justification, Holland Smith declared, was its value as an educational process that would improve efficiency and thereby save future lives. "We were entering a new, uncharted land," wrote Smith, "a field of military enterprises in which we were guided only by theory and peace-time maneuvers."[4]

That lukewarm qualifying statement seems curiously out of character coming from the outspoken, widely acknowledged "Father of Amphibious Assault." By the time of Tarawa, Holland Smith surely knew that the balance of the Pacific War would require complex amphibious assaults against heavily fortified islands. More than any other senior officer in the naval service, Smith knew what these critical campaigns would demand in terms of training, special technology, and coordination, and how abysmally below that level of readiness the amphibious forces in 1943 really were.

Before Tarawa, for example, how fiercely did officials at Marine Corps headquarters or the Navy Department seek to solve the problems of waterproof radios or fording kits for Sherman tanks or armored, reef-crossing, ship-to-shore vehicles? Why was it left for Julian Smith, a division commander in far-off New Zealand, to field-modify his overaged LVT-1s and stridently demand a few new LVT-2s to provide reef-crossing assault capabilities for an upcoming naval campaign that had been envisioned and war-gamed for twenty years? Why did an Army National Guard division land at Makin equipped with ship-to-shore barrage rockets and bunker-busting bazooka launchers while the nearby "amphibiously-trained, atoll-specialists" of the 2d Marine Division had none? Tarawa changed all that.

One wonders if Holland Smith really wanted to postpone giving his new doctrine of offensive amphibious warfare a real trial by fire until later in the war. Suppose there had been no Tarawa. Imagine trying to iron out the basic wrinkles of a new operational doctrine while under the Japanese guns at Saipan or Iwo Jima. Imagine what would have happened to a landing force at Saipan or Iwo attempting the time-consuming choreography of Shoup's ship-to-boat-to-LVT-to-shore plan; or allowing Hill's twenty-three-minute gap in final prep fires; or conducting helter-skelter general unloading of combat cargo with total disregard for the man on the beach. The results, in my opinion, would have been catastrophic. The assault from the sea would have failed with great loss of life, and Smith would have been swiftly sacked.

"There had to be a Tarawa," testified Gen. Julian Smith again and again. Men died because of mistakes made, but the doctrine worked. The Gilberts fell. Amphibious warfare proved to be a complex operational art to master. Flawless amphibious assaults belonged in the realm of myth. The learning process had to recycle continuously. Deficiencies, once identified, debated, and corrected, became dividends. Tarawa provided American planners and commanders the essential confidence to wage offensive amphibious operations of increasing complexity throughout the duration of the war.

Tarawa was indeed an amphibious benchmark, but did Spruance, Turner, and Holland Smith possess alternate means to skin the cat at Betio in November 1943? With hindsight, the alternatives to a direct, frontal assault on Betio's northwestern shoreline the morning of 20 November were these: bypass Betio; use poison gas or other special weapons to neutralize the garrison; seize neighboring Bairiki Island first as an artillery base, then land at a different point along Betio's perimeter; land at night; or delay the landing several weeks.

Holland Smith's postwar preference called for bypassing Tarawa. Precedents for leapfrogging already existed in the Pacific War. As one example, Admiral Halsey opted to bypass heavily defended Kolombangara in the Central Solomons to seize Vela Lavella instead, leaving the former bastion to die on the vine. MacArthur also used this strategy effectively in his New Guinea campaign. But Spruance, Turner, and Smith had already convinced Nimitz and the JCS to bypass Nauru, one of the original Galvanic objectives. Seizing the Gilberts without erasing either the airfields at Nauru or Tarawa would have been inconceivable. The Central Pacific Force critically needed the Gilberts airfields to take the Marshalls. New fields in captured Makin and Apamama atolls would have been offset by residual enemy fields at both ends of the Gilberts.

The American top command expressed little interest in resorting to poison gas that early in the war. Nor did the Roosevelt administration welcome any first-use policy suggestions from the military. Roosevelt proclaimed his policy on 8 June 1943: "We shall under no circumstances resort to the use of such weapons." At best, the United States possessed a limited capability for retaliatory use of poison gas, should the Japanese have initiated its use. Shallow, windswept Betio was hardly a lucrative target for employing gas warfare of any kind. Nevertheless, both sides had gas masks available during the battle for Betio, neither quite trusting the other.[5]

Other special weapons were in limited supply at the time of Betio. The often "cussed and discussed" two-thousand-pound daisy-cutter bombs would have certainly made a difference if accurately delivered on both flanks of Red Beach before the troops fought their way ashore. Shoup, as we have seen, believed the failure of that air mission to materialize to have been the worst deficiency of the battle.

Napalm bombs might have proven effective during the preliminary bombardment and, with caution, on the eastern tail of the island throughout much of the battle. But these weapons would not appear in the Central Pacific until Tinian, eight months after Tarawa. "How much easier it might have been had we had napalm," mused one of Shoup's staff officers after the battle. Shoup took it upon himself to write Admiral Nimitz after the battle of Tarawa suggesting the development of a "soft bomb," essentially a special bag of "molten TNT" that would detonate "with great shock and no fragments" as the landing troops neared the beach. Adm. Frederick C. Ashworth, Kelly Turner's aviation officer at the time, recalled that some of the antisubmarine planes dropped depth charges on Tarawa. Good ideas all. But no real special weapons existed at that point, in that theater.[6]

An award-winning examination of tactical options at Betio appeared at the time of the fiftieth anniversary commemoration in "The Legacy and Lessons of Tarawa" by Maj. Jon T. Hoffman, USMCR. Hoffman suggested that Colonel Edson's original plan of seizing Bairiki, establishing an artillery fire support base, and pounding Betio in advance represented the most sensible approach. Hoffman believed these preliminaries could have best been followed up by a shore-to-shore landing from Bairiki against Betio's eastern tail.[7]

Whether the division could have landed effectively in a column of companies against the minefields, obstacles, and gun positions that protected the narrow tail is moot. Hoffman (and Edson's) approach may well have represented a safer landing than the frontal assault that ensued, but the facts of the time ruled out the entire option in advance. Nimitz and Spruance listened to the Marines' proposal and rejected it on the basis of what they perceived to be the greater imperatives: "Get the hell in, get the hell out." The Navy fully expected a coordinated counterattack by the Imperial Japanese Navy. More Marines could be lost by the sinking of a transport, they argued, than would ever fall in a frontal assault.

Americans and their allies had conducted nighttime amphibious assaults in the Mediterranean in 1943, although not satisfactorily. Admiral Turner experimented with this technique at Rendova earlier. Would a night landing have been possible at Betio? Possible, yes; practical, no. Again, the time factor comes to bear. With only three hours allotted for the "greatest preliminary bombardment of the war," Admiral Hill and his captains needed daylight to observe and adjust their fires. The Marines, similarly, desired many hours of daylight to get established ashore before the expected counterattack. That complex a ship-to-shore plan would have been difficult to control at night. More LVTs would have blundered into Shibasaki's offshore obstacles. Yet, it is difficult to imagine the landing being more disorganized than it became once the boats tried to land. Anything that could have diminished the unerring sight picture enjoyed by Japanese gunners that first bright morning would have saved lives. Given 20-20 hindsight, I personally would have chosen to land in the dark.

Delaying the operation by several weeks would have offered a better tide (certainly not the apogean neap tide of 20 November), more time for training and rehearsing, a chance to coordinate carrier air and naval gunfire properly, and an opportunity to work with the new Shermans and Water Buffaloes. But Spruance was absolutely correct; sometimes it is better to attack before you're fully ready. Six weeks of grace would likely have given Shibasaki his resupply of cement and other construction materials; he certainly would have used the time to sow those remaining three thousand mines along the north coast, perhaps even to block the lagoon entrance with antiship mines. Imperial General Headquarters had already given the go-ahead for construction of an airfield on Apamama, which would have brought many more troops to that atoll. In my opinion, within the context of what planners thought they knew at the time, 20 November was an acceptable D-Day, regardless of the uncertainties.

We come back to the inescapable. The Central Pacific Force, although by no means fully prepared for the horrors at hand, assembled an overwhelming force in the Gilberts from various ports throughout the Pacific, attained strategic surprise, isolated the objective, then proceeded—methodically, stubbornly, mercilessly—to seize the islands from the Japanese in short order with stiff but acceptable overall losses.

Realizing that any battle is greater than the sum of its parts, allow me to state the essence of Tarawa in five memorable components.

Grave Risk. Both sides took risks in the battle. The Japanese bet heavily that their fortified atoll could withstand American landing attempts even without air cover or the fleet. General Akiyama, the visiting chief of fortifications, knew the Japanese lines were overextended. They would have fared better pulling back, probably to the Marianas. For the Americans, the landing was still a near-run thing. Failure at Betio would have terminated Operation Galvanic. The Central Pacific drive would have stalled indefinitely. The concept of offensive amphibious assaults against fortified positions would have been discredited, with obvious consequences in both theaters of war.

Utmost Savagery. Consider the conditions: small space, little cover, short range, high-velocity weapons, flamethrowers, no sanctuaries. The ratio of killed to wounded tells the story. So does the notion of six thousand men killed in three days within a radius of three hundred acres. The slaughter was Tarawa's distinguishing characteristic. The only redeeming blessing: no natives lost their lives in the fighting; no native villages or temples were flattened. Betio was a boxing ring for the antagonists only.

Lady Luck. The Americans were unlucky with the apogean neap tide. They were lucky that no Japanese submarines or land-based bombers broke through Admiral Hill's defensive cordon to sink a loaded transport, say the *Feland*, loaded with Major Jones's rubber-boat-trained Corps reserves waiting to land at Green Beach. Luck could also be measured in airburst munitions. The time-fused shells the Japanese lobbed over the open tops of the LVTs approaching the beach did no damage. An American airburst from one of the destroyers in the lagoon killed Admiral Shibasaki and his entire staff the first afternoon.

Tactical Surprises. The Americans surprised the Japanese by forcing their way into the lagoon to land on the north shore, using tracked amphibians to cross the reef with assault troops, plastering the island with unrelenting naval gunfire and aerial bombardment, and demonstrating their apparent willingness to face hell on earth to reach the objective. The Japanese surprised the Americans by *surviving* the great bombardment and fighting thereafter with such ferocity till the end. Clearly, the rikusentai of the Sasebo 7th Special Naval Landing Force and the 3d Special Base Defense Force comprised some of the best light infantry the U.S. Marines ever faced in close combat.

Shoup vs. Shibasaki. We still know little about Admiral Shibasaki, but the evidence gathered herein indicates he was brave, savvy, energetic, effective. And doomed. Shoup came out of obscurity into the national limelight. His performance in command of the forces ashore at Betio the first thirty-six hours of the battle quite likely provided the margin of safety needed for the landing to succeed. Shoup's leadership was not the dramatic, upfront, "Follow me!" style of Majors Chamberlin or Ryan. Indeed, some troops who wandered back across the airfield from Kyle's position along the south shore stared with disdain at the colonel and his entourage still huddled behind the blockhouse. (With good reason: Japanese still occupied the blockhouse; others nearby shot down more than a dozen messengers coming or going from the command post.)

Shoup contributed more to the battle simply by being there,

ashore, available, in command. He was a rock to Jordan, Kyle, Crowe, Ruud, and Rixey. Even as an occasional voice, filled with static, on the other end of a bad radio connection, he was likewise a rock to the more distant Ryan, Jones, Hermle, and Julian Smith. Either Crowe, Ryan, or Chamberlin could just as well have qualified for the Medal of Honor, but if Tarawa was to have a single surviving honoree at that stratosphere, Shoup was the right choice. He was the lead architect and chief executioner of the assault plan. In spite of hell on earth, it worked, and he prevailed.

IN ONE OF HIS FINAL PUBLIC APPEARANCES THE late Robert Sherrod told a gathering of veterans and historians at the Admiral Nimitz Foundation Seminar in San Antonio that there would never be another battle like Tarawa again, that those on both sides who fought there "achieved a haunting immortality that will never again be seen."

I believe the battle of Tarawa will continue to hold a special fascination for us. It was a classic fight to the finish between two tough, seasoned, well-armed forces on a tiny island from which there was virtually no escape. Once engaged, both forces were locked together—like two scorpions in a bottle—in a duel to the death. The Americans had superior firepower and learned to use it well, but even after days of pounding, hundreds of Japanese rikusentai survived in their emplacements, still armed and lethal. Then it came down to small groups of Marines, using basic leadership and raw courage, working together to overrun the last pillboxes, one by one, till the end.

Tarawa was the 2d Marine Division's finest hour. Tarawa was one of America's finest hours. The Japanese people have every reason to honor their valiant garrison. Both sides surpassed themselves.

Ten years after the battle Julian Smith expressed his reflections with these words from the heart. "For the officers and men, Marines and sailors, who crossed that reef, either as assault troops, or carrying supplies, or evacuating wounded I can only say that I shall forever think of them with a feeling of reverence and the greatest respect."[8]

Notes on Sources

THE ORIGINAL COMBAT REPORTS SUBMITTED by participating units shortly after the battle constitute an unusually rich vein for Tarawa. The single best document, in my view, is the 2d Marine Division's "Recommendations Based on Tarawa Operations." Merritt Edson's long letter to Gerald Thomas on 13 December 1943 (Box 5, Edson Papers) is the best informal summary of the campaign. Likewise, Edson's "Estimate of the Situation—Gilberts" (5 October 1943) should be required reading for all who have claimed that the campaign was poorly planned. Higher-echelon commanders provided cogent reports as well. The best of these are Harry Hill (CTF 53/Southern Attack Force), Holland Smith (CG, VAC), and Kelly Turner (COM5thPhibFor). At the opposite end, the report of the VAC Recon Company's capture of Apamama is a gem. All of these (less Edson's letter) are available through the Marine Corps Historical Center.

From the Japanese side, the *Senshi Sosho* War History Series, once translated, provides a welcome new dimension for Western historians. These accounts contribute records of planning conferences, strategic and logistic decisions, major fleet and force deployments, unit histories, biographies, messages, diaries, and postwar recollections—each to be assessed on its own merits. Overall, these accounts are valuable but not necessarily the final authority. I've tried to balance this new information against the extensive JICPOA translations, other intelligence reports, and declassified ULTRA message intercepts now available through the National Archives.

After all these years I still find Shaw, Nalty, and Turnbladh's *Central Pacific Drive* to be the best single historical account. Crowl and Love's *Seizing the Gilberts and Marshalls* is a respectable second choice. No one will ever improve the narrative flavor presented in Bob Sherrod's *Tarawa*. Hammel and Lane's *76 Hours* is the best anecdotal account.

The Shoup Papers contain several invaluable items related to Tarawa, including his handwritten journal (a remarkable find, although it ends at noon on D-Day), his cryptic dispatch log, the revealing essay "Some of My Thoughts," and the engrossing account of Warrant Officer Kiyoshi Ota, the senior surviving rikusentai in the Gilberts, as translated by Keith Williams.

I used Ota's account frequently because I could validate much of it against his other statements in the interrogation records and *Senshi Sosho*. On the other hand, I used Petty Officer Onuki's words sparingly, and then quoted only from the translation of his 1970 essay in Japan. Over the years Onuki's role in the battle has taken on a life of its own in the hands of some of our undocumented journalistic accounts. Sufficient evidence does exist, however, to confirm Onuki's claim that he set out to accompany Admiral Shibasaki's transfer of command posts. The "sudden huge shells" that killed his tank crewmen would likely have been the same salvo from the lagoon destroyers on D-Day afternoon.

Likewise, I made the effort to corroborate the various U.S. veterans' accounts cited in the book. "There are more damned stories about Tarawa," said Shoup to a reporter in 1973; "Every man has a different one." That's true, of course, of all battles, but many strange things occurred during the battle for Betio. Not many Americans—not even Shoup—saw more than a finite sector of the battlefield. Only a handful saw the action in several hot corners: mainly messengers (Major Tompkins comes to mind), or the demo men and corpsmen in such heavy demand everywhere. The story of Tarawa is still being told. . . .

Finally, this book has been graced by the superb drawings and paintings of two Tarawa veterans, Larry E. Klatt and Richard M. Gibney. Both artists have recently donated their works to the Marine Corps Combat Art Collection. I'm privileged to be the first to publish some of their work, as presented here in *Utmost Savagery*.

Notes

GENERAL NOTES

Kerr Eby's "utmost savagery" comment comes from Robert Sherrod, "Kerr Eby: Combat Artist," *Leatherneck*, November 1992, 67. The original quote appeared in "What's New," published by the Abbott Laboratories in May 1944.

The following abbreviations are used in the Notes:

Follow Me	Newsletter of the 2d Marine Division Association
MCG:	Marine Corps *Gazette*
MCHC:	Marine Corps Historical Center, Washington, DC
MCOHC:	Marine Corps Oral History Collection
NHC:	Naval Historical Center, Washington, DC
NIOHP:	Naval Institute Oral History Program
SS #:	*Sensi Sosho* (War History Series, #)
USNIP:	U.S. Naval Institute *Proceedings*

PROLOGUE

1. Shoup Journal, August–November 1943, Box 3, David M. Shoup Papers, Hoover Institute Archives, Stanford, California [hereafter: Shoup Journal]; and biographic material from Shoup files, Reference Section, MCHC.

2. 2d Amphibian Tractor Battalion, "Special Action Report," 23 December 1943, Archives Section, MCHC [hereafter: 2dAmtracBn Report].

3. Stockton, *Tarawa*, 17. Intelligence Section, 2d Marine Division and Joint Intelligence Center, Pacific Ocean Areas, "Study of Japanese Defenses of Betio Island (Tarawa Atoll), Part I, Fortifications and Weapons," 20 December 1943, 58–59, Archives Section, MCHC [hereafter: D-2/JICPOA Report]; Shoup memo for G-3, VAC, 19 December 1943, regarding tanks at Betio, 1, Archives Section, MCHC; and 2d Tank Battalion "Special Action Report," 14 December 1943, 6, Archives Section, MCHC.

4. 2d Marine Division, D-3 Journal, 20 November 1943, Archives Section, MCHC, [hereafter: D-3 Journal].

5. Ibid.

6. Hata, ed., *Nihon Rikukaigun Sogo Jiten* [Japanese Army-Navy Comprehensive Dictionary—hereafter: *Dictionary*] provides biography of Keiji Shibasaki; and *SS #62: Chubu Taiheyo homen rikugen sakusen (2)*, [Navy Operations in the Central Pacific, vol. I, 1973], 471 [hereafter: *SS #62: Navy CentPac (2)*]; and Akira Shibasaki, to author, 16 May 1995.

7. Kiyoshi Ota, "Tarawa, My Last Battle," translated by Keith S. Williams, n.d. ca. June 1964, 3, Shoup Papers, Box 18, Hoover Institute Archives [hereafter: Ota/Williams Account]. Ota became the senior surviving rikusentai captured in the Gilberts.

8. JICPOA translation item #3776, "Captured Notebook of Petty Officer Chuma," Operational Archives, NHC [hereafter: Chuma Account]; and Lt. Col. A. Vincent Wilson, USA, report to CG, VAC, "Helen, Study and Report of Conditions At," 23 December 1943, 2, Archives Section, MCHC [hereafter: Wilson Report].

9. Third Battalion, 2d Marines, "Narrative Account of Tarawa Operation," 14 December 1943, 1–2, Archives Section, MCHC [hereafter: 3/2 Account]; and D-3 Journal, 20 November 1943.

10. 2d Marine Division, "Recommendations Based on Tarawa Operation," Enclosure (12), Scout-Sniper Platoon, 12 January 1944, Archives Section, MCHC; and Darling, *William Deane Hawkins: Nonpareil Texan*.

11. First Battalion, 2d Marines, "Report of Operations on Betio Island," 12 December 1943, Archives Section, MCHC. USS *Harry Lee* (APA 10) "Operation Report, GALVANIC," 6 December 1943, 1–2, Archives Section, MCHC; D-3 Journal, 20 November 1943; and interview, Col. Maxie R. Williams, USMC (Ret.), 10 November 1993.

12. Shaw, Nalty, Turnbladh, *Central Pacific Drive*, 55; and Johnston, *Follow Me! 118*.

13. *SS #6: Chubu Taiheyo homen rikugen sakusen (1)* [Army Operations in the Central Pacific, vol. I], 184, 187 [hereafter: *SS #6: Army CentPac (1)*].

14. *SS #62: Navy CentPac (2)*, 468–69, 471. This account cites the "War-Time Diary" of *Katori Maru* (communications ship stationed in Kwajalein during the Tarawa campaign) as one source.

15. D-3 Journal, 20 November 1943.

16. USS *Dashiell* (DD 659) "Action Report," 5 December 1943, Box 180, Operational Archives, NHC [hereafter: *Dashiell* Report]; and Col Elwin B. ("Al") Hart, USMC (Ret.) to author, 29 June 1994 [hereafter: Hart Account].

17. Shoup Journal, 5–7; and Shaw, Nalty, Turnbladh, *Central Pacific Drive*, 67.

CHAPTER ONE

1. Col. Rathvon McC. Tompkins, "After Ten Years," in Sherrod, *Tarawa: The Story of a Battle* (50th anniversary edition), 199; Sherrod, *On to West-*

ward, 78; and Sherrod, remarks on Tarawa, Nimitz Foundation Seminar on 1943 in the Pacific, San Antonio, 3 May 1993.

2. Wilkes, *Narrative of the United States Exploring Expedition During the Years 1838–1842,* vol. 5 (1842), 68–70.

3. *SS #6, Army CentPac (1),* 145–46.

4. Joint Chiefs of Staff 311, "Mobility and Utilization of Amphibious Assault Craft" (Report by the Joint War Plans Committee), 15 May 1943, Record Group 165, ABC 561.1, National Archives. This report reveals the scarcity in mid-1943 of amphibiously trained troops, as well as attack transports, cargo ships, and landing craft, especially in the Pacific.

5. Nimitz to King, 1 July 1943, cited in Hayes, *The History of the Joint Chiefs of Staff in World War II: The War Against Japan,* 423–24 and 840n [hereafter: Hayes, *JCS History*]. Nimitz rejected the concept of attacking the Marshalls first "primarily because of the difficulties of obtaining adequate photographic reconnaissance." The Pacific Fleet commander recommended attacking Tarawa first. The subsequent aerial photography of Tarawa provided by the Seventh Air Force from bases in the Ellice Islands proved to be invaluable to Navy and Marine Corps planners (see chapter 4).

6. Hayes, *JCS History,* 424. Vice Adm. Raymond A. Spruance to Professor Jeter A. Isely, 14 January 1949, "The Princeton Papers," Personal Papers Section, MCHC [hereafter: Spruance to Isely]; and Admiral Spruance address to the Royal United Service Institution in London, October 1946, quoted in Karig, et al, *Battle Report: The End of an Empire,* 77–78.

7. Appendix B (Enemy Search Chart) to Enclosure A (Detailed Analysis of Operations) to Joint Planning Staff 205, "Operations Against the Marshall Islands," 10 June 1943, Record Group 165, ABC 384, National Archives [hereafter: JPS #205].

8. United States Navy, Fleet Training Publication #167, *Landing Operations Doctrine,* 1938 (with Change 3, dated 1Aug43), Chapter II. This policy received top-level support from Admiral Nimitz in a 28 October 1943 modification to the CinCPac Operation Plan. See Dyer, *The Amphibians Came to Conquer,* vol. II, 636 [hereafter: Dyer, *Amphibians* II].

9. Hayashi and Coox, *Kogun: The Japanese Army in the Pacific War,* 57. The fact that the Imperial Japanese Navy did not pay much attention to defensive measures in the occupied islands of the Pacific until after Midway is discussed in *SS #6: Army CentPac (1),* 104, section entitled, "The Change in the Isolated Islands Defense Strategy Concept."

10. Summarized from the diary of Col. Joichiro Sanada, IJA, for 29 May 1943, *SS #6: Army CentPac (1),* 110.

11. Ibid.

12. Crowl and Love, *Seizure of the Gilberts and Marshalls,* 65; and *SS #6: Army CentPac (1),* 131–32.

13. Lt. Gen. Tokusaburo Akiyama, IJA, *SS #6: Army CentPac (1),* 83.

14. *SS #6: Army CentPac (1),* 109.

CHAPTER TWO

1. Sherrod, *Tarawa*, 26; and Frank, *Guadalcanal*, 78.

2. Hata, *Dictionary*, 737. Rikusentai means, in general, "special naval landing forces." *Tokubetsu rikusentai* was such a force deployed to foreign shores to protect the lives and properties of Japanese citizens there.

3. Col. Allan R. Millett, USMCR, "Assault from the Sea: The Development of Amphibious Warfare Between the World Wars," unpub. ms. prepared for the Director of Net Assessment, Office of the Secretary of Defense, 1993, 6 (copy in possession of the author).

4. Ibid., 30; War Department Technical Manual TM-E30-480, *Handbook on Japanese Military Forces*, 56 [hereafter: *Handbook*]; and Stewart, "The Japanese Assault on Timor, 1942," and Von Lehman, "Japanese Landing Operations in World War Two," both in Bartlett, ed., *Assault from the Sea*, 204–9 and 195–201, respectively.

5. Strength figures of the Imperial Japanese Navy at the time of Midway from *SS #6: Army CentPac (1)*, 85; and Ota/ Williams Account: "Biographical Data." Contrary to recently published accounts, the Sasebo 7th Special Naval Landing Force was not a veteran of fighting in the Solomons; it was formed in Japan in February 1943 and deployed to Tarawa six weeks later. See *SS #62: Navy CentPac (2)*, 368–69; Chuma Account; Petty Officer First Class Tadao Onuki, "The End of the Tarawa Garrison," Ito, Tomaika, Inada, eds., *Jitsuroku Taiheyo sense (3)* [Real Accounts of the Pacific War, vol. III], 31 [hereafter: Onuki Account]; and Japanese Naval Register, 1940, Box 160, Operational Archives, NHC.

6. *Handbook*, 56–59.

7. Ibid., 6; and Manchester, *American Caesar*, 323, 388.

8. Dyer, *Amphibians* II, 761; and Interrogation of Rear Adm. Shunsaku Nabeshima, Interrogation of Japanese Officials, vol. II of *United States Strategic Bombing Survey: Campaigns in the Pacific*, 411 [hereafter: Nabeshima Account].

9. Hata, *Dictionary*, 190; and *SS #62: Navy CentPac (2)*, 627.

10. Nabeshima Account, 411.

11. Layton, Pineau, and Costello, *"And I Was There,"* 363.

12. Goldstein and Dillon, *Fading Victory: The Diary of Admiral Matome Ugaki, 1941–45* (translated by Masataka Chinaya), 185.

13. Ibid., 194.

14. Crowl and Love, *Seizure of the Gilberts and Marshalls*, 63–64.

15. "Keeping an Eye on Japanese Warships," *The Kapito* [Auckland, New Zealand], January–February 1986, 15–16 (copy provided by Col. Edward J. Driscoll, USMC [Ret.]); Michael Field, untitled essay from New Zealand source, reprinted in *Follow Me*, January–February 1993, 9–11; and Barclay, *The Gospel of John*, 224. "Matzu Shosa" is identified in the first reference as the alleged slayer of the twenty-two prisoners on Betio. Comdr. Keisuke Matsuo was the senior Japanese officer in the Gilberts at the time. "Shosa" is the Japanese word for the rank of major or lieutenant commander. After the battle, the New Zealand government erected a cross on Betio which lists the

names of the victims. Robert Sherrod's original notebook for the battle (#17: "Tarawa, November 1943," 113) mentions this atrocity in an entry still legible through the censor's red scratches. Sherrod listed five names, including "Reverend Sadd, London, missionary." The entry continues: "Postmaster Frank [a Gilbertese?] says all tied up and killed after stringing them up—with swords cut heads off—brought natives in to see execution."

16. Hayashi and Coox, *Kogun*, 65.

17. *SS #6: Army CentPac (1)*, 85–86.

18. Ibid., 85, 105–7.

19. Ibid., 82.

20. Ibid., 82–83.

21. *SS #62: Navy CentPac (2)*, 263. The 101st Construction Unit and elements of the Fourth Construction Force built the airstrip.

22. Ibid., 278. The task organization of the 111th Construction Battalion is contained in Figure 2, JICPOA Bulletin #8-44, "Japanese Forces in the Gilbert Islands," Operational Archives, NHC. See also Lt. Isao Murakami, "An Account of the Construction of Fortifications at Tarawa, Nauru, and Ocean Islands," n.d. [ca. June 1943], JICPOA translation item #5085, document captured on Tarawa 24Nov43, Operational Archives, NHC [hereafter: Murakami Account].

23. Ibid.

24. Murakami Account, 3–5.

25. Ibid., 5; and *SS #62: Navy CentPac (2)*, 266.

26. Murakami Account, 3.

27. Tomonari's biography from "List of Flag Officers, Japanese Navy, Active Service, 1Jun45," a compilation of CINCPAC/CINCPOA #43-45 and #91-45, Box 159, Operational Archives, NHC. Creation of the 3d Special Base Force is described in *SS #62: Navy CentPac (2)*, 281–82. Tomonari's forces are identified in JICPOA Bulletin #8-44, "Japanese Forces in the Gilbert Islands," 1–2, Operational Archives, NHC.

28. Yokosuka 6th Special Landing Force, TARAWA Headquarters, "Battle Dispositions," October 1942, JICPOA translation item #3764 [emphasis added]; and 3d Special Base Unit Secret Order #3, "Combat Policies and Gist of Combat," n.d. [ca. May 1943], JICPOA translation item #3678, both items from Box 145, Operational Archives, NHC. The author is also indebted to insights on Japanese defensive philosophies provided by historian Theodore L. Gatchel, whose forthcoming book on the problems of defending against amphibious assaults should be most valuable.

29. *SS #62: Navy CentPac (2)*, 368–69; and "Translation of Station List, Sasebo 7th Special Navy Landing Force," Intelligence Section, 2d Marine Division, "Preliminary Intelligence Report of Tarawa Operation," 7Dec43, contained in Box 9, Gilberts Campaign, VAC Preliminary Intelligence Report of 22Dec43, Archives Branch, MCHC. A useful wiring diagram of this unit can be found in JICPOA Bulletin #8-44, "Japanese Forces in the Gilbert Islands," previously referenced.

30. JICPOA Bulletin #8-44, "Japanese Forces in the Gilbert Islands," 4.

31. Ibid. The Japanese Naval Register for 1940 identifies Watura Ezaka as "Gunnery Officer and Instructor, Seaman Guard and Receiving Station, Sasebo."

32. Tomonari's report of the air raid is contained in *SS #62: Navy CentPac (2)*, 321.

33. Chuma Account, entry for 27 April [Tokyo time] 1943.

34. *SS #6: Army CentPac (1)*, 105–7; Holmes, *Double-Edged Secrets*, 143; and Winton, *ULTRA in the Pacific*, 148.

35. *SS #39: Daihon'el Kaigunbu Rengo Kantai (4)* [Navy Division Imperial Headquarters and the Combined Fleet, vol. IV], 1970, 170–73 [hereafter: Navy Division/Combined Fleet (4)]. The account of Kuroshima's tearful toast to the remote garrisons is from Comdr. Koichi Hiyashi, IJN, 6th Base Force, who attended the events. See also *SS #6: Army CentPac (1)*, 111.

36. *SS #6: Army CentPac (1)*, 131–32; *SS #62: Navy CentPac (2)*, 345; and *SS #39: Navy Div/ Combined Fleet (4)*, 174–75.

37. Hata, *Dictionary*, 199.

38. *SS #62: Navy CentPac (2)*, 454–55; and Akira Shibasaki, to author, 2 April and 16 May 1995. Akira was ten years old when his father left Kure to command the "Number Three Special Strategic Point Unit" in the Gilberts in July 1943. His father's final letter urged him and his sister to take care of their mother, study hard in school, and nurture the admiral's "three rare red canaries."

CHAPTER THREE

1. JPS #205, 2. The report noted that the 7th Infantry Division, U.S. Army, veterans of the Aleutians landings, also qualified for consideration, but the planners concluded the Marine Corps divisions were better trained and equipped for the atoll war ahead (15).

2. Shoup Journal, 1. Entry reads: "Conf. with Spruance. [Negative?] on plastic boats. Beginning of training and tests with amphtracs."

3. James R. Stockman, "Notes on Interview with Col. David M. Shoup," 26 May 1947, 1–2, "Monograph Comments File," Archives Section, MCHC [hereafter: Stockman/ Shoup Interview].

4. Ibid.

5. Details concerning the division's history and service in Guadalcanal from Johnston, *Follow Me! passim*.

6. Details on Julian Smith are available in his biographical file, Reference Section, MCHC, and the Julian C. Smith Collection, Personal Papers Section, MCHC. See also Harriotte Byrd Smith, *But, That's Another Story*; and Maj. Gen. Raymond L. Murray, USMC (Ret.), oral memoir, 1988, 147, MCOHC, MCHC. Smith's comment on the tides is taken from Lt. Gen. Julian C. Smith, USMC (Ret.) oral memoir, 1973, 284, MCOHC, MCHC. See also Smith obituary, The *Washington Post*, 14 November 1975, B-16.

7. Edson's biographical details are available in the Reference Section, MCHC, but the definitive source is the welcome biography of Merritt Edson by Jon T. Hoffman, *Once a Legend*.

8. Johnston, *Follow Me!* 90.

9. Biographical details on Shoup from Reference Section, MCHC; the Shoup Papers, Hoover Institute Archives; Sherrod, *Tarawa*, 29; and Barrow, "The Stick Wavers," *Naval History* 4 (Summer 1990); *passim*. Shoup's field notebook is held in the Personal Papers Section, MCHC. I am indebted to General Shoup's biographer, Dr. Howard Jablon, who graciously shared the advance chapter he wrote for Allan R. Millett, ed., *The Commandants of the Marine Corps* (Naval Institute, forthcoming).

10. Isely, "Notes on Conferences with H. W. Hill, J. C. Smith, and Jeter A. Isely," 28–29 October 1948, 13, "The Princeton Papers," Personal Papers Section, MCHC [hereafter: Isely/Hill/Smith Conferences].

11. Julian Smith to Holcomb, 1Sep43, Julian C. Smith Collection, Personal Papers Section, MCHC.

12. Hawkins background from Darling, *Deane Hawkins: Nonpareil Texan*. Bonnyman background provided by Mrs. Alexandra Bonnyman Prejean. Bordelon background provided by his brother, Mr. Tom Bordelon.

13. Details of arms and equipment issued assault troops for the initial landing at Guadalcanal from interview with Col. Robert J. Putnam, USMC (Ret.), 8 June 1990. Putnam commanded King/3/1 in that campaign.

14. Table of Organization E-100 Marine Division [including "Major Weapons and Transportation"] is contained as Appendix F to Shaw and Kane, *Isolation of Rabaul*, 571–73.

15. Shoup Dispatch Log, entry for 23Oct43, Box 3, Shoup Papers, Hoover Institute Archives [hereafter: Shoup Dispatch Log].

16. Details concerning vehicles embarked by the 2d Marine Division from Shaw, Nalty, and Turnbladh, *Central Pacific Drive*, 45. Edson estimated that the division used only 30 percent of its organic equipment at Tarawa. See Hoffman, *Once a Legend*, 276.

17. Moran, *U.S. Marine Corps Uniforms and Equipment in World War II*, 58–61. Combat photographs taken during the battle of Tarawa reflect a wide range of field uniforms. The classic snapshot of the division command post on D+2 shows Shoup in plain utilities without a helmet cover talking to one of his assistants in full camouflage rig, while Lt. Col. Evans Carlson sits at their feet wearing the "Snipers version" of the helmet cover with its green elastic band, favored by the Raiders.

18. Darling, *Deane Hawkins, Nonpareil Texan*, 7, 12–13; and Hawkins to Clara Jane Hawkins 25 April 1943, copy provided by Lt. Col. Clay Darling. Details on training and equipping the division's scout-sniper platoons contained in CG, 2d Marine Division to CG, V Amphibious Corps, "Recommendations Based on Tarawa Operation—Scout Sniper Platoons," 12 January 1944, Archives Section, MCHC.

19. Interview with Col. Edward J. Driscoll, Jr., USMC (Ret.), who served as communications chief for the scout company at Tarawa, 13 Dec 1993 [hereafter: Driscoll Account]; and Edson to Cliff [Cates], commanding Marine Corps Schools, 21 September 1943, Box 5, Edson Papers, Manuscript Division, Library of Congress (copy provided by Maj. Jon T. Hoffman, USMCR).

20. H. T. Vance, code AO-775, HQMC, memorandum for Col. D. M. Shoup, "Development of Special Equipment for Amphibious Warfare," 11 December 1944, Shoup Papers, Box 19, Hoover Institute Archives; and Driscoll Account.

21. Lt. Gen. William K. Jones, USMC (Ret.), to author, 11 July, 22 July, 30 July, and 11 August 1992.

22. Bevan, *United States Forces in New Zealand*, 210; William D. Bethard to author, 17 June 1994; and Larry E. Klatt to author, 12 August 1994.

23. Shaw, Nalty, Turnbladh, *Central Pacific Drive*, 16. Sherrod, *History of Marine Corps Aviation in World War II*, 224–26.

24. Smith to Maj. Gen. Commandant Thomas Holcomb, 1 September 1943, Julian C. Smith Collection, Personal Papers Section, MCHC; and Johnston, *Follow Me!* 90.

25. Information on the 2d Amphibian Tractor Battalion and the employment of LVTs at Tarawa from Croizat, *Across the Reef*, chapter 3; interviews with fourteen veterans of the battalion during 1993–94; and the author's professional service as an assault amphibian officer in the Marine Corps for nearly three decades, for which the study of Tarawa's ship-to-shore assault was both a prerequisite and a joy.

26. Dyer, *Amphibians* II, 622; Holland Smith and Finch, *Coral and Brass*, 120; Shoup Dispatch Log, entry for 2 October 1943; and Capt. Harry B. Stark, USN (Ret.), former flag secretary to Rear Adm. Richmond Kelly Turner on board the flagship *Pennsylvania* during Operation GALVANIC, to author 5 December 1993. According to Captain Stark, the tide factor at Betio bothered Turner intensely. "It plagued him, tortured him to the Nth degree."

27. Bevan, *United States Forces in New Zealand*, 219; unpublished diary of former petty officer William J. Morgan, USN, a member of the 18th Marines (Engr) (copy provided by his son, William J. Morgan, Jr., 22 February 1994); and Bob Hanger, former member of F/2/10, "New Caledonia to Tarawa via New Zealand," *Follow Me*, September–October 1993, 21–22.

28. Bevan, *United States Forces in New Zealand*, chapter 14; Driscoll Account; Jones to author, 11 July–11 August 1992; and Shoup Dispatch Log, 10 October 1943: "Another ship pulled out for urgent boiler repairs."

29. Smith to Vandegrift, 22 July 1943, and Smith to Commandant Holcomb, 1 September 1943, both contained in Julian C. Smith Collection, Personal Papers Section, MCHC.

30. Hoffman, *Once a Legend*, 159, 242.

31. Bevan, *United States Forces in New Zealand*, 218; Col. Henry P. Crowe oral memoir, 1979, 159, MCOHC, MCHC; and former chief pharmacist's mate Robert E. Costello, USN, to author, 19 February 1994 [hereafter: Costello Account].

32. Sgt. Maj. Lewis J. Michelony, Jr., USMC (Ret.), to author, 28 July 1992 [hereafter: Michelony Account].

33. Interview with Col. Maxie R. Williams, USMC (Ret.), 10 November 1993 [hereafter: Williams Account].

34. Col. Thomas A. Culhane, Jr., USMC, "After Ten Years," in Sherrod, *Tarawa* (50th anniversary edition), 201.

35. Bevan, *United States Forces in New Zealand*, 228; and Michelony Account. Casualties, by rank, from Sherrod, *Tarawa*, 163 ff.

36. Sherrod, *History of Marine Corps Aviation in World War II*, 118. The Joint Planning Staff rationale for nominating the two Marine divisions for the Central Pacific drive included these comments: "[T]he Marine divisions are considered the best trained and equipped. This is due to their long and specialized preparation (with particular emphasis on the assault of atolls)." JPS #205, 15.

CHAPTER FOUR

1. Sherrod, *History of Marine Corps Aviation in World War II*, 264–65.

2. *SS #62: Navy CentPac (2)*, 177.

3. 3d Special Base Force Gungokuhi [military—very secret], "Results of the Conference Held by the Defense Planning Section," 16 August 1943, JICPOA translation item #4002, Box 145, Operational Archives, NHC [hereafter: Defense Planning Section Conference]. U.S. Marines captured the document on Tarawa on 24 November 1943, after the fighting. The document reveals the Japanese officers debated whether to retain the mobility of their light tanks or bury them up to their revolving turrets in sand. They deplored the growing shortage of cement, which was so sorely needed to harden defensive positions. Commander Ezaka acknowledged the conflicting requirements on the troops: trying to achieve full combat readiness while simultaneously having to work on the fortifications.

4. War History Office, Defense Agency of Japan, to Historical Branch, G-3 Division, USMC, 19 November 1962, which provided comments on draft vol. 3, *History of the U.S. Marine Corps Operations in World War II*. Copy available in "Comments" File, Archives Section, MCHC. Source: retrospective account of Comdr. Koichi Hayashi, staff officer of 6th Base Force. See also Wilson Report; Maj. Norman E. Ward, USMC (Ret.), to author, 8 April 1994 [hereafter: Ward Account]; and Carl J. H. Doyle, USN, to Rear Adm. Delaney, "LVT Conference at Pearl Harbor," 25 December 1943, 5, Julian C. Smith Collection, Personal Papers Section, MCHC.

5. *SS #62: Navy CentPac (2)*, 335. Imperial General Headquarters approved the construction of an airbase on Apamama in directive #184 dated 11 October 1943. The American invasion the following month ended this project.

6. Brief mention of the Tateyama Gunnery School is contained in Hata, *Dictionary*, 431; and Chuma Account. The Imperial Navy established the school on 1 June 1941. Many of the naval reserve officers killed in the battles of Tarawa and Iwo Jima received advanced land combat training at Tateyama.

7. Defense Planning Section Conference, *passim*.

8. Lewin, *American MAGIC: Codes, Ciphers, and the Defeat of Japan*, 194. See also Layton, Pineau, and Costello, *"And I Was There"*; Holmes, *Double-Edged Secrets*; and Winton, *ULTRA in the Pacific*.

9. Colley, "The Aerial Photo in Amphibious Intelligence," MCG 32 (October 1948): 32, 34–35; and Stockman/Shoup Interview, 3.

10. Stockman, *Tarawa*, Appendix I, 85; Bartsch, "Tarawa and Operation GALVANIC," *After the Battle* vol. 15 (February 1977): 24. The distinguished naval historian Samuel Eliot Morison may have been the first to establish the myth of "the Singapore guns" in his history series written in the late 1940s. The claim reappeared in books published as late as 1993.

11. D-2/JICPOA Report.

12. Enfield, "The Victory at Tarawa Came at a Terrible Price," *Philadelphia Inquirer*, 20 November 1993, A-1.

13. "Knox Upholds Plan of Tarawa Action: Attack So Costly to Marines in Part Because Wind's Shift Stranded Landing Craft," *New York Times*, Wednesday, 1 December 1943, 4; J. Smith to Vandegrift, 13 December 1943, 1, Box 5, Edson Papers; H. Smith and Finch, *Coral and Brass*, 135; and Mc-Kiernan, "The Tide That Failed," USNIP 46 (February 1962): 41–43.

14. "The Tide at Tarawa," *Sky and Telescope*, November 1987, 528. The author is indebted to the editors of *Sky and Telescope* for permission to reproduce Dr. Olson's harmonic analysis chart of the tidal ranges at Tarawa during the battle. The author also benefited from two telephonic interviews with Dr. Olson in November 1993, plus the use of Dr. Olson's initial manuscript, "Tarawa, November 1943: A Historically Significant Apogean Neap Tide."

15. King to Nimitz, 4 November 1943, in Hayes, *JCS History*, 479n.

16. Spruance to Isely, 14 January 1949, "The Princeton Papers," Personal Papers Section, MCHC.

17. Potter, *Nimitz*, 257; and Adm. Harry W. Hill, USN (Ret.), oral memoir, 1969, 313, MCOHC, MCHC.

18. Biographic data on Spruance, Turner, Hill, and Knowles from Operational Archives, NHC; and information on Julian Smith and Edson from Reference Section, MCHC.

19. J. Smith to Vandegrift, 13 December 43, Box 5, Edson Papers.

20. 2d Marine Division Estimate of the Situation—Gilberts, 5 October 1943, Archives Section, MCHC.

21. Ibid.

22. Ibid. Julian Smith's staff also anticipated a problem with the tides on 20 November, noting in the estimate (4) that "the reef dries completely at low tide." Lt. Col. Colley, the D-2, knew this from aerial photograph interpretations. For tidal range determinations, Colley asked the aviators to use vertical kodachrome transparencies. "In these," he later wrote, "the relative depths of water can be readily told by the variation in color of the water as reproduced in the film. Live submerged coral can be differentiated by its greenish color from the coral which dies and is turned brown by strong sunlight when receding tides leave it awash or dry." See Colley, "The Aerial Photo in Amphibious Intelligence," MCG 32 (October 1948): 32.

23. Norman V. Cooper, "The Military Career of General Holland M. Smith," USMC, dissertation, University of Alabama Graduate School, 1974, 215–16 (copy available in Reference Library, MCHC).

24. Mrs. Harriotte B. Smith to author, 20 October 1993. General Smith's 1973 oral memoir does not shed very much light on the subject. One passage relates to the Honolulu conference: "Frankly, I never quite got that sense of urgency as to time, but I did know that they ordered me to take Betio first and wouldn't give me any opportunity to land artillery on the other islands of the atoll because of the time element. They couldn't spare the time." Lt. Gen. Julian C. Smith, USMC (Ret.), oral memoir, 1973, 193, MCOHC, MCHC. The oral memoirs of then-Brig. Gen. Graves B. Erskine, Holland Smith's chief of staff at the time, do not mention the incident. The recollection of Maj. Mac Asbill, USMC, who was Holland Smith's aide at the time, may shed further light, but his "Notes on H.M. Smith" is no longer held by the MCHC. Julian Smith later stated that Holland Smith had confided to him: "Hell, if the 6th Marines were not in Corps Reserve there would be no excuse for me being in the Gilberts." See Isely/Hill/Smith Conferences, 15.

25. HQ, VAC OPPLAN #1-43, 13 October 1943, 2, para. 3A(1), Archives Section, MCHC (emphasis added).

26. Former lieutenant John A. Speed to author, 7 March 1994; and Croizat, *Across the Reef*, 87–88.

27. Fiji Detachment message 160645, October 1943, contained in Shoup Papers, Box 18, Hoover Institute Archives.

28. FTP-167, Landing Operations Doctrine, with Change 2, dated 1 August 1942, para. 401d(3).

29. Krulak, *First to Fight*, 105–7; and Lt. Gen. Victor H. Krulak, USMC (Ret.), to author, 16 March 1993 and 13 March 1995. IMAC forwarded Krulak's report to the commandant on 5 May 1943. CMC readdressed it "for information" to the CG, Amphibious Corps, Pacific Fleet, on 9 June.

30. JPS #205, 10–11; and Colonel Nimmer's oral memoir (MCOHC, MCHC), which is—unfortunately—incomplete for this portion of his service.

31. Shoup's Dispatch Log for 3 October 1943 mentions trying to locate "the IMAC LVT test report." Note that this was two months after Spruance's visit to Wellington, which prompted the search for a means of crossing the reef at Tarawa. Julian Smith's oral memoir (285) credits Shoup with the idea of using LVTs as assault craft at Tarawa.

32. Former Marine Mirle W. Yancey to author, 1 February 1994 [hereafter: Yancey Account]; former captain Wallace E. Nygren, USMC, to author, 19 and 20 March 1994 [hereafter: Nygren Account]; and Croizat, *Across the Reef*, 87–88.

33. Nygren Account; and former lieutenant Manuel Schneidmiller, USMC, to author, 2 April 1994 [hereafter: Schneidmiller Account].

34. Former captain Sidney S. Key, USMC, to author, 30 May 1993; and Yancey Account.

35. The author's personal experience operating with World War II–vintage LSTs and LVTP-5s, notably in heavy seas off Barking Sands, Kauai, in 1961–1963—glory days. You could drive an LVT on board, bow first, only in an emergency because neutral steer on the tank deck tore up the dunnage

(postwar LSTs would feature a handy turntable). This meant the vehicles had to back aboard, always hairy without frequent practice in the open seas.

36. 2d Marine Division OpOrder #14, dated 25 October 1943, Archives Section, MCHC; and Edson to Gerald C. Thomas, 13 December 1943: "No 2,000-pound bombs were dropped, although a total of 54 had been previously scheduled," Box 5, Edson Papers.

37. Lt. Col. Peter Lake, USMCR (Ret.), to author, 22 January 1994; and Bevan, *United States Forces in New Zealand*, 224, 314.

38. Diary of former petty officer William J. Morgan, provided by his son, William J. Morgan, Jr. [hereafter: Morgan Diary].

39. Interview with Mr. Eddie Albert, 8 July 1993 [hereafter: Albert Account]; Shoup Journal, 31 October–2 November 1943; and Smith, *But That's Another Story*, 244.

40. JICPOA translation item #3872, "Diary of an Artilleryman in Yokosuka 6th Special Naval Landing Force," a document no longer held in the Operational Archives, NHC. This account from Crowl and Love, *Seizure of the Gilberts and Marshalls*, 67n; and JICPOA #4051, "Report on Present Conditions at Tarawa Air Base on 29 September 1943," Box 145, Operational Archives, NHC.

41. Crowl and Love, *Seizure of the Gilberts and Marshalls*, 68–69.

42. JICPOA #42-43, "Enemy Positions in the Gilbert Islands," 1 October 1943, 72–73, Operational Archives, NHC.

43. JICPOA translation item #5086: "Secret Gilberts Area Defense Force OPORDER #19," 20 October 1943, Operational Archives, NHC. Shibasaki figured he needed 1,500 tons of cement, 4,500 pieces of steel rail, and 31.5 tons of steel reinforcing wire just to complete the 4,500 obstacles desired (23–24).

44. Preliminary Interrogation, Ensign [I list him as warrant officer] Kiyoshi Ota, Intelligence Section, 2d Marine Division, "Preliminary Intelligence Report of Tarawa Operations," 7 December 1943, Archives Section, MCHC. The Wilson Report mentions the absence of concrete on the island. "Sketches of the Japanese Installations Found on Tarawa," by PFC J. Rotkowski, Intelligence Section, 2d Battalion, 8th Marines, Archives Section, MCHC, is one source about the use of chain in concrete fortifications. Larry E. Klatt to author, 21 August 1994. CINCPAC Message 180553Nov43 reported an ULTRA intercept of a Japanese message to the Tarawa 3d Base Force announcing the scheduled arrival in Tarawa of the merchant ship *Mikage Maru* on the morning of 19 November [D-Day!]; and SMRN 038, Record Group 457, National Archives [hereafter: ULTRA File].

45. Vice Adm. Shigeru Fukudome, IJN, USSBS, Interrogations of Japanese Officials, vol. II, 516. Admiral Koga met with Admiral Ito, vice chief of staff, Navy Division, IGHQ, at the end of October to discuss his decision to commit forces to Rabaul, despite the risks. Koga told Ito, "If only half of 1st Air Flotilla comes back after this operation we will still use it in Z Operation [counterattack in the Central Pacific]. By all means don't tell about this to anyone outside, because this will have a serious effect on the morale of those defending the Marshalls and Gilberts. . . . Those men on the Gilberts and Marshalls are

prepared to sacrifice themselves for the victory of the Combined Fleet." Source: *SS #71: Daihon'ei Kaigunbu Rengo Kantai (5)* [Navy Division Imperial Headquarters and the Combined Fleet, vol. 5], 118–19.

46. Lt. Gen. William K. Jones to author, 11 July–11 August 1992; and Dyer, *Amphibians*, II, 702–3.

47. Edson to Thomas, 13 December 1943, 11, and J. Smith to Vandegrift, 13 December 1943, 2, both Box 5, Edson Papers.

48. Col. Maxie R. Williams, USMC (Ret.), to author 3 February 1994; Barrow, "The Stick Wavers," *Naval History* 4 (Summer 1990): 32; and Muster Report, H&S Company and Weapons Company, 2d Marines, November 1943, Reference Library, MCHC.

49. Morgan Diary, 12–13 November 1943.

50. Smith, *But That's Another Story*, 244.

51. Sherrod, *Tarawa*, 42–43.

52. Crowl and Love, *Seizure of the Gilberts and Marshalls*, 56.

53. Ibid.

54. *SS #62: Navy CentPac (2)*, 454. The post-battle JICPOA count was slightly higher, at 4,836. The difference may be in how the Korean laborers were counted. The military significance of these figures: Shibasaki had plenty of shooters, a very healthy tooth-to-tail ratio despite his administrative and logistical responsibilities as a regional commander.

55. Crowl and Love, *Seizure of the Gilberts and Marshalls*, 74.

56. Morgan Diary, 14 November 1943.

57. Smith, *But, That's Another Story*, 245.

58. Ibid.

CHAPTER FIVE

1. Nygren Account. Note: portions of the D-Day material provided by Wallace and Violet Nygren previously appeared in William Banning, ed., *Heritage Years: 2d Marine Division Commemorative Anthology* (Paducah: Turner Publishing Co., 1988).

2. USS *LST 243* Report of Action, 29 November 1943, Archives Section, MCHC. The ship delivered seventeen LVT-2s, plus four officers and sixty-eight enlisted men of Company "A-1," 2d Amphibian Tractor Battalion, from Samoa, via Funafuti, to the amphibious objective area at Tarawa. An uncommonly strong bond developed between the ship's crew and the amtrackers during the voyage. The crew particularly mourned the death of Major Drewes, who debarked just behind Lieutenant Nygren earlier that morning. Details of the landing plan are contained in 2d Marine Division Operation Order #14, dated 15 October 1943, especially Annexes F and I, Archives Section, MCHC. Shoup and Edson had few choices to reduce the complicated pre-H-Hour choreography. An earlier rendezvous with the LST convoy may have afforded the opportunity to cross-deck the assault troops of the second and third waves of the LSTs, thereby permitting a direct launch on D-Day, but it is doubtful that Admiral Hill would have stopped the task force for the several hours this

would have entailed, a dangerous risk and a detriment to achieving strategic surprise.

3. *SS #62: Navy CentPac (2)*, 469–70. The bomber detachment under the command of Lt. Comdr. Kaoru Ishihara, IJN, left thirty members of the ground crew behind at Betio in their hasty departure on the morning of the nineteenth. These men joined forces with the garrison and died on the island.

4. Nygren Account, 1.

5. Ibid.

6. Ibid., 1–2.

7. In comparison to Tarawa's overly long ship-to-shore assault, the Fifth Fleet at Saipan, seven months later, had sufficient LVTs and LSTs to preload all assault troops and conduct a direct launch just seaward of the line of departure on D-Day, six thousand yards from the beach.

8. USS *Pursuit* (AM 108), "Report of Action Against Gilberts Islands," 6 December 1943; USS *Requisite* (AM 109), "Action and Operational Report," 5 December 1943, both from Operational Archives, NHC; and letter submitted by Murray Dear, "In Contact," *Naval History* 8 (March/April 1994): 4. All three New Zealanders received the Bronze Star for bravery in piloting the ships into the lagoon under intense fire.

9. USS *Ringgold* (DD 500), "Action Report," 1 December 1943 [hereafter: *Ringgold* Report], in Operational Archives, NHC. According to the *Ringgold* report, the second Japanese round penetrated several sections of the ship until the unexploded shell finally stopped at the main deck, port side, spinning crazily. Gunner's Mate First Class Frank O. Begor, Jr., USNR, calmly picked it up and threw it overboard.

10. *Dashiell* Report in Operational Archives, NHC.

11. Sherrod, *Tarawa*, 62; Master Sgt. Roger M. Emmons, USMC, "Battle of Tarawa," unpublished ms., n.d., Box 2, page 4, Personal Papers Section, MCHC; and Johnston, *Follow Me!* 112.

12. USS *Anderson* (DD 411), "Gilbert Islands Action Report," 1 December 1943, 2, Archives Section, MCHC [hereafter: Anderson Report].

13. Commanding Officer, USS *Salt Lake City* (CA 25) comment and CTF 53 [Admiral Hill] comment both from Office of Naval Intelligence Information Bulletin #15-11, "Battle Experiences: Supporting Operations Before and During the Occupation of the Gilbert Islands, November 1943," n.d., 67:126–27 and 67:130, respectively, Command File-WW II, Operational Archives, NHC.

14. Office of Naval Intelligence Combat Narrative: The Capture of the Gilberts, n.d., 21, Command File-WW II, Operational Archives, NHC; interview with former lieutenant Raymond F. Myers, USNR, 31 December 1990; Bob Hanger (F/2/10), "New Caledonia to New Zealand to Tarawa," *Follow Me*, September–October 1993, 22–23 [hereafter: Hanger Account]; Anderson Report, 3–4; and Rear Adm. F. S. Withington, USN (Ret.), who served on board the *Indiana* during Galvanic, recalled in his oral memoir for the Naval Institute oral history program, "The bombardment of this tiny island was thought to be quite sufficient, but most of the shells ricocheted off" (vol. I, 64).

15. Ota/Williams Account, 4–5.

16. Annex C to Commander Fifth Amphibious Force Operation Plan A2-43, 23 October 1943, Operational Archives, NHC.

17. Vice Adm. Frederick L. Ashworth, USN (Ret.), to author, 18 October 1993. See also Admiral Ashworth's oral memoir, recorded in an interview with Paul Stillwell on 9 June 1990 and maintained on NIOHP.

18. Rear Adm. Henry L. Miller, USN (Ret.), interview with John T. Mason, Jr., 24 March 1971, NIOHP, vol. I, 65. The action reports of Commander Carrier Group Nine and Commander Fighting Squadron One are contained in Dyer, *Amphibians* II, 712.

19. Shoup Field Notebook, 1, Personal Papers Section, MCHC; and Shoup Journal, "D-Day."

20. Shoup Field Notebook, 1, Personal Papers Section, MCHC; and Stockman/Shoup Interview, 4. A subsequent interview with Shoup, then a general and commandant, 14 August 1962: "Daisy-cutters never got to Tarawa. Check 7th Air Force" (Shoup files, Reference Section, MCHC); Edson lecture to staff of Marine Corps Schools, Quantico, 6 January 1944, the Julian C. Smith Collection, Personal Papers Section, MCHC [hereafter: Edson Lecture]; Shaw, Nalty, Turnbladh, *Central Pacific Drive*, 39; and Bernard C. Nalty to author, 8 June 1993. The comment about the Seventh Air Force flying the longest distances to attack the smallest targets came from Air Force historian Gary D. Null at the Nimitz Foundation Seminar on World War II in the Pacific, 4 May 1993, San Antonio.

21. 2dAmtracBn Report, 3.

22. *SS #62: Navy CentPac (2)*, 471. This passage cites the War Diary of the *Katori Maru*, the communications ship for 6th Base Force in Kwajalein, the recipient of both of Shibasaki's messages.

23. *Ringgold* and *Dashiell* Reports. Admiral Dyer is one of the few historians who discovered the fact that the lagoon destroyers honored the cease-fire. See *The Amphibians Came to Conquer*, vol. II, 708. Commander Fire Support Section Four, in his endorsement to the *Dashiell* report, blames the lack of visible targets rather than the cease-fire restrictions, stating he had "full authority to fire on any damned Jap who sticks his head up" from Hill's chief of staff. Yet the *Dashiell* clearly saw some of the field pieces firing on the assault waves and felt constrained by the cease-fire to await a green light. For an opposing view, see Hill oral memoir, 326–27, MCOHC, MCHC.

24. Ibid.

25. Ota/ Williams Account, 5.

26. Ibid.

27. Technical information on the Type 88 gun provided from the extensive technical library of Jim Alley, ISDA Books, formerly a foreign weapons specialist at Aberdeen Proving Ground.

28. Ota/Williams Account, 6.

29. Onuki Account, 31.

30. 2dAmtracBn Report, 3–4; and USS *Harry Lee* (APA 10), "Operation

Report (GALVANIC)," 6 December 1943, report of Ensign Farrell, Boat Officer.

31. Fenlon A. Durand, quoted in Stevenson, Norfolk *Virginian-Pilot*, 20 November 1978; and Ward Account, 4.

32. Master Sgt. Edward J. Moore, USMC (Ret.), to author, 14 March 1993 [hereafter: Moore Account].

33. Ota/Williams Account, 6; and Yancey Account.

34. Nygren Account, 3.

35. Former Marine James A. Thompson to author, 7 April 1994 [hereafter: Thompson Account].

36. Interview with former lieutenant Sidney S. Key, USMC, San Antonio, 4 May 1993 [hereafter: Key Account]; former Sgt. James C. Walker, USMC, to author 15 March 1994; Schneidmiller Account; and former sergeant Floyd M. North, USMC, to author, 11 April 1994 and 25 May 1994.

37. Nygren Account, 4.

38. Thompson Account, 2. All three crewmen, though burned and wounded, survived the ordeal.

39. 2dAmtracBn Report, 4–8.

40. Norman S. Moise, "Unconquerable Ground Reclaimed," first-person narrative, *World War II*, November–December 1993, 45–46, and interviews with author, 19 July 1994.

41. Key Account. Of the many poignant photographs taken at the battle's end, one of the most evocative is entitled "Quiet Lagoon," which shows Key's stricken vehicle near the seawall at high tide, two of her crewmen still floating face down in the water by their LVT.

42. Letters Section, *Time*, 10 April 1944 (copy provided by former lieutenant John A. Speed, August 1994).

43. Walter J. Buczak to author 29 January 1994; and Ward Account. The author also benefited from research on this incident performed by Tarawa veteran and former U.S. Representative J. T. Rutherford of the 2d Amphibian Tractor Battalion Association. According to the action report of LST 243, that ship tied up alongside the *Sheridan* the next morning and the news of Major Drewes's death shocked the LST crew. The *Sheridan*'s chaplain performed the funeral service; the honor guard committed Drewes's body to the deep, a good man gone.

44. Interview with Maj. Norman T. Hatch, USMC (Ret.), 4 May 1993, 8 August 1993; Hart Account; and Simmons, "Remembering the Legendary 'Jim' Crowe," Part I, *Fortitudine*, Winter 1991–92, 3–7.

45. Muster Roll, 3d Battalion, 2d Marines, November 1943, which lists the casualties and reports the type of wounds incurred (copy at the Reference Library, MCHC).

46. Interview with Maj. Gen. Michael P. Ryan, USMC (Ret.), San Antonio, 4 May 1993 [hereafter: Ryan Account].

47. Ibid.

48. 3/2 Account, para. 4.

49. We can only speculate about the source. It may have come from the sur-

vivors of the assault platoons just inland from Red One or Two. Nor can we rule out a bogus transmission. Many of the rikusentai on Betio spoke English. The division intelligence officer reported one spurious radio message from the Japanese garrison but did not provide the specifics.

50. Shoup Journal, 5.

CHAPTER SIX

1. Interview with former captain Aubrey Edmonds, USMC, 24 November and 20 December 1993, 13 January 1994 [hereafter: Edmonds Account].

2. Interview with former Marine William Fratt (E/2/8), 30 January 1994 [hereafter: Fratt Account]; and interview with former sergeant Melvin McBride (E/2/8), Camp Lejeune, NC, 19 November and 7 December 1993, 13 January 1994 [hereafter: McBride Account].

3. McBride and Fratt Accounts.

4. Fratt Account.

5. Edmonds, Fratt, McBride Accounts.

6. Onuki Account, 31.

7. Edmonds Account.

8. Edmonds, McBride, Fratt Accounts.

9. Col. Carroll D. Strider (C/1/18), "Tarawa Remembered," *Follow Me*, November–December 1993, 17–18; and Strider to author 5 August 1993, 17 August 1994.

10. Hart and Driscoll Accounts.

11. Former Marine M. F. Swango, "Assault on Tarawa," *Follow Me*, November–December 1993, 8–10; and Alexander, "Baptism by Fire: Sherman Tanks at Tarawa," *Leatherneck*, November 1993, *passim*.

12. Alexander, op. cit.

13. Ota/ Williams Account, 6–7.

14. The author in indebted to Mr. Tom Bordelon for personal and official information concerning his late brother. This account reflects Staff Sgt. Bordelon's biography (from the Reference Section, MCHC), the Congressional Medal of Honor Citation, a letter from Bordelon to his parents dated 18 April 1942, and an undated (ca. 1944) newspaper clipping "Pal Says San Antonio Marine Killed on Tarawa Belongs in Hall of Fame," which includes the statements by Sgt. Eldon Beers, USMC [herafter: Beers Account]. The author is further indebted to Maj. Gen. J. J. McMonagle, USMC (Ret.), for temporary loan of copies of Bordelon's service records.

15. Ibid.

16. Beers Account; PFC Jack Ashworth, USMC, to Mr. and Mrs. W. J. Bordelon, 26 January 1944; and Maj. Paul R. Zidek to wife, 1 February 1944 (copy given to the Bordelon family that year).

17. The author is indebted to the extensive research performed by William D. Bethard concerning the death of his uncle, PFC Russell L. Jarrett, USMC, and the other combat engineers of D/2/18 who died on Red One in direct support of LT 3/2 on D-Day. See also Sherrod, *Tarawa*, 127–28.

18. Information on David Spencer's experiences with E/2/2 at Betio pro-

vided from taped interview with his son in 1992 (transcript given to author 28 November 1993 by John Spencer).

19. Former Marine [and editor of the 2d Marine Division Association newsletter] Howard Frost (I/3/2), quoted by Marlowe Churchill, "Memories of a Marine Triumph," *The Press Enterprise*, 21 November 1993, reprinted in *Follow Me*, January–February 1994, 11–12.

20. Interview with former Marine Perry F. Grisdale (L/3/2), 20 October 1993.

21. Former Coast Guardsman Karl Albrecht, "Tarawa Remembered," *Follow Me*, November–December 1993, 28–31.

22. Lt. George D. Lillibridge, USMC, Memoirs, Personal Papers Section, MCHC [hereafter: Lillibridge Account].

23. Sherrod, *Tarawa*, 68. The last sentence comes from Sherrod's account of the battle, "One Square Mile of Hell," *Time*, 6 December 1943.

24. D-3 Journal, 20 November 1943.

25. Maj. Norman T. Hatch, USMC (Ret.), oral memoir, 1983, 98, MCOHC, MCHC; and Sherrod, *Tarawa*, 72.

26. Shoup Journal, 5–6.

27. Maj. Gen. Carl W. Hoffman, USMC (Ret.), oral memoir, 1988, 19, MCOHC, MCHC.

28. D-3 Journal, 20 November 1943; and Col. Robert H. Ruud, USMC, "Comments on Draft Volume III," 10 August 1962, Archives Section, MCHC.

29. Maj. Gen. Raymond L. Murray, USMC (Ret.), oral memoir, 1988, 141–42, MCOHC, MCHC.

30. Ibid.

31. Maj. William C. Chamberlin, USMC, quoted in Karig, *Battle Report: The End of an Empire*, 88; Ota/Williams Account, 5; and *Ringgold* and *Dashiell* Accounts.

32. Shoup Journal, 7.

33. Ibid., 7–8.

34. Ibid., 8; D-3 Journal, 20 November 1943; and 2d Marine Division "Special Action Report—Narrative Account," 6 January 1944, Archives Section, MCHC [hereafter: 2dMarDiv Narrative Account].

35. Ibid.

36. Norfolk *Virginian-Pilot*, 16 October 1947, 1, and 17 October 1947, 6, both clippings provided courtesy of Col. Richard T. Poore, USMC (Ret.). Jordan previously served as executive officer of the Marine detachment assigned to the 1939 New York World's Fair.

37. Action reports, previously cited, from the *Ringgold, Dashiell, Pursuit, Requisite*. The two small minesweepers treated sixty wounded Marines each while marking the line of departure.

38. Former corpsman Stanley Bowen (F/2/8), "Tarawa," *Follow Me*, March–April 1994, 14–16 [hereafter: Bowen Account]; and Muster Roll, Headquarters, 2d Marine Division, November 1943. Two of the bandsmen died while serving as stretcher bearers; ten others suffered wounds.

39. Costello Account; and Zurlinden, "Pillbox Is Used as Hospital for Tarawa Wounded," *Honolulu Advertiser*, 4 December 1943, 1.

40. D-3 Journal, 20 November 1943.

41. Ibid.

42. D-3 Journal, 20 November 1943; and 2dMarDiv Narrative Account.

43. 3/2 Account. Although Major Schoettel's combat performance improved considerably after D-Day, he had lost the confidence of Gen. Julian Smith, who subsequent to the battle relieved him of command and transferred him to the 4th Marine Division. Historians should not rush to judgment in Schoettel's case. D-Day at Tarawa was a shattering experience. Schoettel soon redeemed himself, commanding a shore party outfit at Eniwetok, then assuming command of the 2d Battalion, 22d Marines during the battle of Guam. Japanese diehards killed Schoettel on Guam on 17 August 1944, well after the island was declared secure. The late Robert Sherrod, incidently, shared these sentiments in a letter to the Peacock Press dated 14 February 1983 (copy provided the author by Mr. Bill Bethard).

44. For an early description of the Model 1923-E pack howitzer, see Pierce, "The New 75mm Pack Howitzer," MCG 14 (March 1930): 31–32.

45. Edson Lecture, 26; and Isely/Hill/Smith Conferences, 12.

46. Ryan Account.

47. Tompkins quoted in Shaw, *Tarawa: A Legend Is Born,* 75.

48. Robert Sherrod aptly described Jim Crowe as "cool as icehouse lettuce" in *Tarawa*, 98; and Hoffman oral memoir, 20–21, MCOHC.

49. USS *Arthur Middleton* (APA 25), "Report of landing phase of operations at Tarawa Atoll, Gilbert Islands," 7 December 1943, Archives Section, MCHC.

50. As often as I've heard this "Flying Dutchman account," I cannot authenticate it. *Zeilin*'s action reports are detailed yet do not mention the incident. Suffice it to say that several LVTs became disabled and drifted with the current on D-Day, some fire-seared and filled with dead Marines. According to Lieutenant Ward's account, "One of our tractors was [later] spotted 125 miles at sea with twelve dead Marines" (Ward to author, 4 April 1994).

51. Navy Cross citation, Lt. (jg) Robert J. Kiechlin, USNR. Unit history provided by Comdr. Robert Green, USN (Ret.), USS *Zeilin* Association, 5 April 1994.

52. USS *Biddle* (APA 8), "Report After Battle—Operation GALVANIC," 28 November 1943; USS *Harry Lee* (APA 10), "Operation Report (GALVANIC)," 6 December 1943; and USS *LaSalle* (AP 102), "Report on Landing Phase of Operations at Tarawa," n.d. (each document obtained through Archives Section, MCHC).

53. Interview with Mr. Eddie Albert, 8 July 1993 [hereafter: Albert Account].

54. Darling, *Deane Hawkins: Nonpareil Texan*, 14–17. I cannot explain why Hawkins did not simply jump into the water from the pier and wade ashore hours earlier. He may well have been ordered to remain in place on the

pier. Surely the frustration he experienced in the long period of inactivity on D-Day afternoon contributed to his extraordinary initiatives on D+1.

55. "Report of the 1st (Assault) Platoon, Company 'A,' 1st Bn, 18th Mar (Engr)," in "Combat Reports" of 18th Marines (Engineers), 23 December 1943, Archives Section, MCHC.

56. Lillibridge Account, 2.

57. Sherrod, *Tarawa*, 79, 92.

58. D-3 Journal, 20–21 November 1943; Isely/Hill/Smith Conferences, 13; and Lt. Gen. Leo D. Hermle, USMC (Ret.), oral memoir, 1973, 77–79, MCOHC, MCHC. As Hermle recalled, "They [Shoup and Crowe] told me there was no place to come ashore," [78].

CHAPTER SEVEN

1. *SS #62: Navy CentPac (2)*, 474. A somewhat different version is contained in *SS #6: Army CentPac (1)*, 184.

2. *SS #6: Army CentPac (1)*, 182; and *SS #62: Navy CentPac (2)*, 474. Japanese times used in their accounts of the battle were three hours earlier than "Yoke" time used by the Americans. The Army account reports Shibasaki died "around noon" [1500 Yoke]; the Navy account: 1400 [1700 Yoke]. After the war, another surviving rikusentai told Shibasaki's son that the admiral willingly gave up his concrete blockhouse in order to provide a sheltered site for his casualties (Akira Shibasaki to author, 2 April 1995).

3. *Dashiell* Report 4; and *Ringgold* Report, 12.

4. FTP 167, Landing Operations Doctrine (with Change 3), "Standard Naval Gunfire Support Batteries," 119; and Weller, "The Development of Naval Gunfire Support in World War Two," in Bartlett, ed., *Assault from the Sea*, 264. The Marines had few other weapons ashore on D-Day capable of delivering an explosion of such force described in the accounts. No artillery pieces were operational by that time, only a few tanks and a handful of 81-mm mortars. While deducing "who killed Cock Robin" may approximate efforts to define Davy Crockett's death at the Alamo, I am convinced—both as a combat veteran and a military historian—that one of the two lagoon destroyers fired the fatal salvo which killed Admiral Shibasaki.

5. Onuki account, 32. Post-battle photographs show two Japanese tanks knocked out on either side of Shibasaki's original blockhouse CP.

6. Sherrod, *Tarawa*, 82–83.

7. Smith, "Tarawa," USNIP 79 (November 1953): 1173; Hill, oral memoir, 328–29: "We were really deeply concerned [that night]," MCOHC, MCHC; and Edson to Thomas, 13 December 1943, Box 5, Edson Papers. Considerably more than "500–600 Japanese" were to the east of Crowe's positions that first night.

8. Col. Henry P. Crowe, USMC (Ret.), oral memoir, 1979, 154, MCOHC, MCHC.

9. Pratt, *The Marines' War*, 155; Spruance to Isely, 14 January 1949 and 3 July 1949, "The Princeton Papers," Personal Papers Section, MCHC; Buell, *The Quiet Warrior*, 198–99; and Rear Adm. Carl J. Moore, USN (Ret.),

"Assault on Tarawa and Apamama," in Mason, ed., *The Pacific War Remembered*, 175–76.

10. Shoup Journal, 3 [Day before D-Day: "Plan of withdrawal with exec and 3"].

11. Potter, *Nimitz*, 257.

12. Shaw, Nalty, Turnbladh, *Central Pacific Drive*, 66; Willard, *The Leathernecks Come Through*, 214; USS *Pursuit*, "Report of Action Against Gilbert Islands," 1 December 1943, 5; and Hanger, "New Caledonia to Tarawa via New Zealand," *Follow Me*, September–October 1993, 23.

13. Albert Account [note: subsequently published by the author in *World War II*, January–February 1995].

14. Ibid; Wyeth, *The Leathernecks Come Through*, 210; and former lieutenant Frank Plant, USMC, account, Personal Papers Section, MCHC.

15. Stockman/Shoup Interview, 6; and *Ringgold* Report, 12.

16. D-3 Journal, 21 November 1943.

17. Ibid.

18. Ibid.

19. Ibid. There is no evidence that either Shoup ashore or Hermle at the end of the pier received any of these messages. Note that the amphibious task force had dispersed into nighttime steaming formations, thereby extending the *Maryland*'s range to the beach.

20. Ibid., 9. Differences exist in terms of date-time-groups and specific wording of the messages sent by General Hermle from the *Ringgold* as recorded in the Division D-3 Journal and the ADC Journal for D+1 (both documents available through Archives Branch, MCHC). Since the division journal recorded events more or less as they occurred, and the ADC Journal appeared seven weeks later (7 January 1944), I have chosen to follow the former. See also Julian Smith's comments about his ADC to Professor Isely in Isely/Hill/Smith Conferences, 13.

21. *SS #6: Army CentPac (1)*, 184–87.

22. Ibid. The author benefited greatly from reading Allan R. Millett's unpublished ms. "Assault from the Sea," n.d., 1993, especially 62–63 concerning Japan's vitiated counterlanding capabilities in 1943.

23. Information provided by Staff Sgt. A.H. McNeil, I/3/8, Camp Lejeune, 2 January 1994. According to McNeil, unit tradition ever since Tarawa requires the junior lieutenant in the outfit to keep the chalice tied to his body during operational deployments. The chalice has survived the ensuing half century.

CHAPTER EIGHT

1. Lillibridge Account, 4; and Shaw, *Tarawa: A Legend Is Born*, 80.

2. D-3 Journal, 21 November 1943.

3. Olson, "The Tide at Tarawa," water level chart for D+1.

4. Edson Lecture.

5. Hatch oral memoir, 98, MCOHC, MCHC.

6. Sherrod, *Tarawa*, 88–89.

7. D-3 Journal, 21 November 1943.

8. Former lieutenant Dean Ladd (B/1/8), account published in *Follow Me*, November–December 1993, 32–34, which was excerpted from his earlier book *Faithful Warriors*. See also Ladd, "Reliving the Battle: A Return to Tarawa," MCG 67 (November 1983): 93–96.

9. Plant Account; and D-3 Journal, 21 November 1943.

10. Bill Crumpacker, "Memoirs of Beastly Tarawa," *Follow Me*, November–December 1993, 12; Lt. Albert Tidwell, USMC, quoted by Curran, "Indelible Tarawa," *The American Legion*, November 1983, 56; and Willard, *The Leathernecks Come Through*, 214–15.

11. Interviews with former sergeant John H. White, USMC (C/1/8), 19 November and 4 December 1993.

12. Ibid.

13. Interview with former private first class William Murphy (C/1/8), 4 May and 23 November 1993.

14. Costello Account.

15. D-3 Journal, 21 November 1943. The two messages are recorded for 1130 and 1131. Shoup at the time had no encouraging word of Ryan's progress on the west. Major Schoettel radioed about this time to report one boat, probably one of Hays's strays, "attempted to land on Beach Red One. Encountered heavy MG fire and were driven back to their boats in retreat." Shoup had few options left, but a rubber boat landing over the same shooting gallery just traversed at such cost by Hays's LT 1/8 would have been a slaughter pen for Jones's LT 1/6. Nevertheless, Col. Maurice Holmes, commanding the 6th Marines, requested the rubber boats of 1/2 and 1/8 be provided his command from the host ships.

16. USS *Sheridan* (APA 51), "Action Report Tarawa," 29 November 1943, Archives Branch, MCHC; Albert Account; and former boatswain's mate Larry Wade, USN, to author, 20 August 1994.

17. Ibid.

18. Ibid.

19. Commanding Officer, H&S Company, 2d Marines, "Operations Report of Scout Snipers Platoon," 15 December 1943, 2; and Darling, *Deane Hawkins: Nonpareil Texan*, 17–18.

20. Ibid.

21. Ibid., and Costello Account, 10, 13.

22. Ibid.

23. Generally attributed to Shoup; see Sherrod, *Tarawa*, 108.

24. Williams Account.

25. Williams Account; Curran, "Indelible Tarawa," 56; and Fratt Account.

26. Lillibridge Account.

27. Crowe oral memoir, 157–58, MCOHC, MCHC.

28. Anderson Account.

29. Seventh Special Naval Landing Force "Station List," n.d. [ca. July 1943], captured on Tarawa, reproduced in Division D-2 report. Lieutenant (junior grade) Minami evidently lost his lead platoon commander, Reserve

Ensign Mikio Hirayami, per reassignment back to Japan just before the battle. Both Hirayami and Lt. Hideo Takiura, the original commander of the First Company and another early transferee, contributed to the naval history of the buildup of Tarawa's defenses as reported in *Senshi Sosho*.

30. Ryan Account.

31. Biographic details on Major General Ryan from Reference Section, MCHC; Ryan Account; and Ryan commentary, "Death Tide at Tarawa," video produced by Lou Reda Productions for Arts and Entertainment Network's "Our Century," 16 November 1993.

32. Ibid.

33. Ibid.

34. D-3 Journal, 21 November 1943; USS *Anderson* (DD 411), "Gilbert Islands Action Report," 1 December 1943, 6; and Ryan Account.

35. D-2/JICPOA Report.

36. D-3 Journal, 21 November 1943.

37. Ibid.

38. *Requisite* Report, 6–7.

39. Drury, *The History of the Chaplain Corps*, vol. II, 186–87; and Willard, *The Leathernecks Come Through*, 217–24.

40. Sherrod, *Tarawa*, 101.

41. Rixey quoted by Sherrod, *Tarawa*, 101.

42. Sherrod field notebook #17, 103, November 1943, Tarawa.

43. D-3 Journal, 21 November 1943.

44. Sherrod, *Tarawa*, 101.

45. The account of LT 1/6's landing on Green Beach is derived from USS *Feland* (APA 11) "Report of Landing Operations," 7 December 1943, 1–3, Archives Section, MCHC; interviews with Lt. Gen. William K. Jones, USMC (Ret.), during 11 July–11 August 1992; and Jones, "Tarawa: That Stinking Little Island," MCG 71 (November 1987): 30–41. Former lieutenant Baine Kerr's quote from Bob Tutt, "Everything Seemed To Be on Fire in Fight for Tarawa," *Houston Chronicle*, 14 November 1993, 26a. Choppy seas complicated the debarkation of 1/6 from *Feland* into the eighty-four rubber boats; the process took ninety-three minutes.

46. Ota/Williams Account, 8. Ota had been sorely wounded: "One side of my face and head, where I had been hit by a grenade splinter, was terribly swollen and it felt as if my eye would burst."

47. Rixey and Best, "Artillery at Tarawa," MCG 28 (November 1944): 34, 37.

48. Ibid.

49. VAC G-3 Report, 2 December 1943, Enclosure B to VAC "Report of GALVANIC Operations," Archives Branch, MCHC; and D-3 Journal, 21 November 1943 [serial #196], serial #196].

50. Commanding Officer, Company D (Scouts), 2d Tank Battalion, "Special Action Report," 20 December 1943, Archives Section, MCHC; Haley, "Reconnaissance at Tarawa Atoll," MCG 66 (November 1980): 51–55; and Driscoll Account.

51. Hermle oral memoir, 78–79, MCOHC, MCHC.

52. Hall's quote appears in Shaw, Nalty, Turnbladh, *Central Pacific Drive*, 73.

53. Julian Smith quoted in Barrow, "The Stick Wavers," *Naval History* 4 (Summer 1990), 32.

CHAPTER NINE

1. 2dMarDiv Narrative Account, 9.

2. Shaw, *Tarawa: A Legend is Born*, 106, 110; and Jones interviews, 11 July–11 August 1992.

3. Smith, *But, That's Another Story*, xv.

4. Former Marine Robert L. Roberts (B/1/8), [currently vice president, 2d Marine Division Association], to author, 21 November 1993.

5. Shaw, Nalty, Turnbladh, *Central Pacific Drive*, 81–83.

6. Ibid.

7. Maj. William K. Jones, USMC, biography from Reference Section, MCHC; other details from Jones interviews, previously cited.

8. Lt. Gen. William K. Jones, USMC (Ret.), oral memoir, 1976, 26, MCOHC, MCHC; and Jones interview.

9. Ibid.

10. Sherrod, *Tarawa*, 108.

11. Lt. Col. Peter Lake, USMCR (Ret.), to author 22 January 1994 and 23 March 1994 [hereafter: Lake Account].

12. Ibid.

13. Ryan Account.

14. 3/2 Account; Ryan Account; Muster Roll of Officers and Enlisted Men, 3d Battalion, 2d Marines, 1–3 November 1943, 4728; and former Marine Richard D. Sommerville to author, 12 February and 19 March 1994.

15. Lake Account. Sgt. Maj. Lewis J. Michelony, USMC (Ret.), presentation during Nimitz Foundation Symposium, 3 May 1993, San Antonio, and subsequent interview with author, 3–5 May 1993 [hereafter: Michelony Account].

16. Bonnyman biographical and personal information comes from these sources: Bonnyman File, Reference Section, MCHC; "Alexander Bonnyman, Jr., '32, in Line of Duty," *Princeton Alumni Weekly*, 10 March 1944; and Col. Gilder D. Jackson, USMC, to Mrs. Alexander Bonnyman, Jr., 4 January 1944, and to Mr. Alexander Bonnyman, Sr., 30 May 1944. These documents and other material provided courtesy of Mrs. Alexandra Bonnyman Prejean, June 1994.

17. Former Marine Harry Niehoff to author 27 February and 4 March 1994 [hereafter: Niehoff Account]. See also Hammel and Lane, "Third Day on Red Beach," MCG 54 (November 1970): 22–25.

18. Ibid.

19. Ibid. This account of Lieutenant Bonnyman's death differs distinctly from that presented in most previous histories, including Stockman, Shaw, and Alexander.

20. Sgt. Obie Newcomb, Jr., USMC, to Bonnyman family, 23 March and 7 May 1944 (copies provided courtesy of Mrs. Alexandra Bonnyman Prejean).

21. Niehoff Account; and 2d Marine Division Awards Nominations, Gilberts Campaign, March 1944. The Navy Department replaced Bonnyman's Navy Cross with the Medal of Honor on 28 October 1946 (presented to his family 22 January 1947).

22. Report of 2d Platoon, "C" Company, 1st Battalion, 18th Engineers, n.d., 2d Lt. B. W. Rentel, USMC, Archives Branch, MCHC.

23. USS *Doyen* (APA 1) "Galvanic Report," 3 December 1943, 6.

24. 2dMarDiv Narrative Account.

25. Samples taken at random from Muster Roll of Officers and Enlisted Men, 3d Battalion, 2d Marines, 1–30 November 1943.

26. *SS #62: Navy CentPac (2)*, 477; and Van der Rhoer, *Deadly Magic: A Personal Account of Communications Intelligence in World War II in the Pacific*, 167. Cryptanalysts for commander in chief, Pacific Fleet, monitored more than fifty outgoing urgent messages from the Tarawa garrison during the battle. Only a handful seem to have survived. See CINCPAC Messages 192120, 202053, 212122, 212133, and 220634Nov43 in ULTRA File.

27. Smith, *But, That's Another Story*, 246.

28. Chief Quartermaster Dominick Bruni, USN (Ret.), to author 29 March 1994.

29. D-3 Journal, 22 November 1943.

30. Commanding Officer, 8th Marines, "Combat Report," 1 December 1943; and Sherrod, *Tarawa*, 116–17. Combat artist Gil Bundy had a similar nightmarish experience on a derelict craft full of dead men. See Sherrod, *Tarawa*, 119.

31. USS *LaSalle* (AP 102), "Report on Landing Phase of Operations at Tarawa," n.d., 5; and Schneidmiller Account.

32. Rear Adm. C. Julian Wheeler, USN (Ret.), interview with Etta-Belle Kitchen, 16 August 1969, 272, NIOHP.

33. 2dMarDiv Narrative Account, 6.

34. Col. Saburo Hayashi wrote of "the principle of hand-to-hand fighting, a tradition of the Japanese infantry," Hayashi and Coox, *Kogun*, 16. See also Thompson, "Behind the Fog of War," in *How the Japanese Army Fights*, 36.

35. Onuki Account, 32.

36. Ota/Williams Account, 8–9.

37. Account of former Marine Gus Hall (H&S/1/10), *Follow Me*, March–April 1994, 20.

38. Col. Lyle Specht, USMC (Ret.), to author 24 September, 23 October, and 27 November 1993.

39. HQ, 2d Battalion, 18th Marines, "Report of LTSPCC 2d Marines," 22 December 1943, 4.

40. Jones Account.

41. Ibid.

42. Ota/Williams Account, 9. In this account, Ota also says that his commanding officer and staff officers committed suicide before the assault out of

concern about being taken prisoner in the melee. Since Ota served in the Sasebo 7th Special Naval Landing Force, he must have been talking about Comdr. Takeo Sugai and Lt. Masashi Okada, adjutant, and possibly Comdr. Goshiro Miura, gunnery officer. Since Ota did not witness this event, and since he did not address it in his account in the *Senshi Sosho* series, I can only offer the information as unsubstantiated—but likely. The whole series of attacks that night reflects a masterful hand. It could have been coordinated by Lt. (jg) Goichi Minami, but I have always suspected the experienced leadership of Commander Sugai.

43. Commanding Officer, USS *Schroeder* (DD 502) report summarized in ONI Information Bulletin #15-11: "Battle Experiences: Supporting Operations Before and During the Occupation of the Gilbert Islands, November 1943," n.d., 67: 225, Operational Archives, Command File, WWII, NHC; and Michelony Account. The errant depth charge did not explode; its safeties had been set.

44. Jones, oral memoir, 27–28, MCOHC, MCHC.

45. 2dMarDiv Narrative Account, 10.

46. McLeod's combat report is quoted in Shaw, Nalty, Turnbladh, *Central Pacific Drive*, 90.

47. Vice Adm. Bernard M. Strean, USN (Ret.), interview with John T. Mason, Jr., 8 May 1974, 86–88, NIOHP.

48. Ibid.

49. 3/2 Account, 1–2.

50. Forward Echelon Intelligence Section, 2d Marine Division, 7 December 1943, P.O.W. Interrogation Report, Kiyoshi Ota, 19–20.

51. Ibid.; and Ota/Williams Account, 10–11.

52. Information on the death of Captain Royster and Corporal Lane provided from research conducted by the Honorable J. T. Rutherford, a veteran of the 2dAmtracBn at Tarawa, 17 July 1993. The Marines were extremely lucky to lose only two LVTs to Betio's many mines.

53. Larry E. Klatt to author 15 January and 2 February 1994.

54. 2d Marine Division Newspaper, 20 January 1944, copy provided by former Marine Hank Mast of the 2d Marine Division Association.

55. Commanding Officer, 8th Marines, "Combat Report," 1 December 1943; Enclosure (1): Report of LT 1/8; 3/2 Account, 3, plus Unit Journal for D+3; and 1st Battalion, 18th Marines, "Combat Reports, Tarawa Atoll," 22 December 1943, 5. (All documents are from Archives Section, MCHC.)

56. Julian Smith remarks to Robert Sherrod as recorded in Sherrod's Field Notebook #17, "Tarawa: November 1943," 114–15 (copies provided author courtesy of William Bethard). Sherrod prudently did not reproduce these comments in *Tarawa*. The correspondent simply used Smith's lead sentence ("We made mistakes, but you can't know it all the first time") on page 148 of his book.

57. Sherrod, *Tarawa*, 142; Bowen Account, 17; and Klatt Account.

58. Klatt Account.

59. Hoffman oral memoir, 24, MCOHC, MCHC; and Lillibridge Account, 6.

60. Former Marine Robert L. Kinley (D/2/18) to author 19 and 27 November 1993.

61. David M. Shoup, "Some of My Thoughts," 2, Shoup Papers, Box 3, Hoover Institution Archives.

CHAPTER TEN

1. Strean oral memoir, 104, NIOHP. Strean commanded Fighter One at Hawkins Field, Tarawa, immediately after the battle.

2. The destroyer *Anderson* (DD 411) responded to two of these false alarms, one at 0720 on D-Day, finding nothing, but noting, "Many empty [shell] cartridges in the vicinity of all those periscope sightings," and again at 0300 the next morning, responding to a radar contact that turned out to be a lost landing craft ("The boat was directed to the lagoon entrance and cautioned against impersonating a submarine."), USS *Anderson* (DD 411) "Gilbert Islands Action Report," 1 December 1943, 4–5.

3. Hill oral memoir, 332, MCOHC, MCHC.

4. Dyer, *Amphibians* II, 730–31.

5. Interview with former Marine Billy Spratt White, 24 December 1993.

6. Julian Smith to wife, 24 November 1943, Smith, *But, That's Another Story*, 245; Willard, *The Leathernecks Come Through*, 221; and Sherrod, *Tarawa*, 123.

7. Sherrod, *Tarawa*, 130.

8. Lillibridge Account, 6. See also Alexander, "Red Sky in the Morning," USNIP 119 (November 1993), 45.

9. Ibid.

10. Sherrod, *Tarawa*, 127–28.

11. Supporting research provided courtesy William D. Bethard, nephew of the late PFC Russell L. Jarrett, and included: Muster Rolls for "D" Company, 2d Battalion, 18th Marines for November 1943; a copy of the front page of *The Montague Press*, Bandera, Texas, 21 January 1944, which reported the deaths of Privates First Class Seng and Montague; and interviews with survivors of that distinguished outfit, including former Marines Emory B. Ashurst and Joseph F. Sobol [post-war name]. On 14 February 1995, Emory Ashurst received a belated Purple Heart Medal for wounds sustained at Tarawa a half-century earlier.

12. PFC David S. Spencer to family, 28 December 1943, and other accounts provided courtesy of his son Mr. John Spencer, 30 November 1993. Easy/2/2 casualties compiled by former Marine Gene Johnson, a survivor.

13. Sherrod, *Tarawa*, 138.

14. Julian Smith to wife, 2 December 1943, Smith, *But That's Another Story*, 246.

15. Ryan Account. The 2d Marine Division D-1 Memo dated 1 January 1944 reported the following MIAs: 1 officer, 202 Marine enlisted, 3 Navy enlisted (copy provided courtesy of Lt. Col. R. C. Darling, USMC); and Albert Account.

16. Sherrod, *Tarawa*, 139.

17. Potter, *Nimitz*, 260–61.

18. L. E. Klatt, "Letters," *Smithsonian*, January 1994; Klatt to author 16 January 1994; and D-2/JICPOA Report. The Wilson Report, cited previously, contains many of Klatt's drawings, which were forwarded through the chain to Pearl Harbor and Washington.

19. Account by former Marine Bob Groves (G/2/6), *Follow Me*, November–December 1993, 16 [hereafter: Groves Account].

20. Account by Ray M. Lamoreaux (HQ/2/6), *Follow Me*, November–December 1993, 19 [hereafter: Lamoreaux Account].

21. Murray oral memoir, 145–46, MCOHC, MCHC; and Capt. Colby D. Howe, USMC, "Record of Events of G Battery [3/12] During Tarawa Campaign," 7, Personal Papers Section, MCHC.

22. Groves and Lamoreaux Accounts; and former Marine Gene Ratner (E/2/6) account, *Follow Me*, January–February 1994, 12–13.

23. Morison, *The Two-Ocean War*, 305. Murray's 2/6 would find redemption the following year at Saipan.

24. Julian Smith to wife, 28 November 1943, contained in Smith, *But, That's Another Story*, 245. By this time the Japanese high command had identified Smith. An ULTRA-intercepted message of 24 November advised, "The landing force at Tarawa is the Second Division of Marines under Major General Julian Smith" (CINCPAC Message 280754Nov43 in ULTRA File).

25. USS *Pursuit* (AM 108), "Report of Scouting Mission to Abaiang, Marakei, and Maiana Atolls, Gilbert Islands, 29 November–1 December 1943," 6 December 1943; and Driscoll Account. The scouts made a point of calling their LCPRs "rubber *boats*," never "rubber rafts."

26. Col. Leo B. Shinn, USMC (Ret.), to author, 24 August 1993 [hereafter: Shinn Account].

27. Commanding Officer, Reconnaissance Company, VAC, "War Diary, Reconnaissance, and Operations on Boxcloth Atoll," 12 December 1943, Archives Section, MCHC [hereafter: ReconCo Report].

28. Rear Adm. William D. Irwin, USN, "Trials of the *Nautilus*" in Mason, ed., *The Pacific War Remembered: An Oral History Collection*, 182–84, [hereafter: Irwin Account]; and USS *Ringgold* (DD 500) "Action Report," 1 December 1943. Admiral Hill's lack of advance knowledge of the *Nautilus*'s presence along his approach route to Tarawa is reflected in these two messages from CTF 53 to the *Ringgold*: 2142—"All restrictions on use of your offensive weapons are removed"; and 0315—"Well done." The "friendly fire" very nearly became a double tragedy. The destroyer first fired two torpedoes, one of which circled back and chased the ship, requiring emergency flank speed. In the engagement, the *Ringgold* fired sixty-nine rounds of 5-inch/38 AA common; the cruiser *Santa Fe* (CL 60) fired seventy-seven rounds from her 6-inch turrets. The whole affair was scary. Hill, to his credit, later visited the submarine to apologize once he learned the facts.

29. Irwin Account, 184; and Shinn Account.

30. ReconCo Account; and Irwin Account, 187.

31. Ibid.

32. War Diary of 1st Lt. Leo B. Shinn, USMC; War Diary of 1st Lt. Russel Corey, USMC; and all enclosures to ReconCo Account.

33. In addition to the primary documents cited above, see also Alexander, "Capture of Apamama," *Leatherneck* 76 (November 1993): 30–31.

34. Annex How (Intelligence) to VAC Operations Order 1-43 of 13 October 1943 included this item among the list of "Essential Elements of Information": "Where can landings be made by assault forces with landing boats or amphibian vehicles on . . . Nonuti?" JICPOA Report #42-43, "Enemy Positions in the Gilberts," 1 October 1943, Operational Archives, NHC.

35. Interview with Mr. Landon Roberts, 25 February 1992. Deck Log for *PC 599* contained in the National Archives, Washington, researched as a courtesy to the author by Mrs. Mickie Booth and Ms. Catherine Booth, friends and historians.

36. Ibid.

37. Ibid.

38. *SS #6: Army CentPac (1)*, 184. Source was the 6th Base Force communications ship *Katori Maru* at Kwajalein. Karig, *Battle Report: The End of an Empire*, 91.

39. *SS #2: Navy CentPac (2)*, 488–89.

40. Ibid., 503. The same message appears in *SS #6: Army CentPac (1)*, 191. Dates are Tokyo time zone.

41. *Newsweek*, 3 January 1944, 22; and Havens, *Valley of Sorrow: The Japanese People in World War II*, 135–36.

CHAPTER ELEVEN

1. "Tarawa's Captor Reviews Victory," *New York Times*, 30 November 1943, 4.

2. Efforts to restrict media reports of LVT employment appear in Shoup's field notebook, page 1; Edson to Julian Smith, 6 May 1944, 3, Box 5, Edson Papers; Robert R. McCormick, "The Tarawa Campaign," as broadcast over WGN and the Mutual Broadcasting System, 13 April 1946, which principally quotes from a letter from Julian Smith; and Hanson W. Baldwin, "Reefs Menace Troops," *New York Times*, 3 December 1943, 4.

3. Potter, *Nimitz*, 264, 280; and Potter, *Bull Halsey*, 259. MacArthur's remarks to President Roosevelt and Admiral Nimitz, Pearl Harbor Conference, 1944, quoted in Manchester, *American Caesar*, 426.

4. Potter, op. cit.

5. Public reaction to Strock's photograph of the three dead infantrymen at Buna can be assessed by this subsequent letter to *Life* (11 October 1943) from a woman in New York: "The War Department has made a terrible mistake. . . . *Life* has erred even more seriously in editorially masking morbid sensationalism with talk about the necessity of arousing people to the meaning of the war." Frank Filan's award-winning photograph, "Tarawa Island," appeared on pages 30–31 of the 13 December 1943 issue of *Life*. The photograph won Filan the 1944 Pulitzer Prize for best "Spot News Photograph" (*New York Times*, 2 May 1944, 16–17). One recent book on Tarawa (1993) erroneously attrib-

uted the Pulitzer Prize to Cpl. Obie Newcomb, USMC, for Tarawa photography. Newcomb's photographs were superb, in my opinion, but Filan won the honors for Tarawa.

6. "With the Marines at Tarawa" won the 1944 Academy of Awards "Oscar" for best documentary of the previous year. Robert Sherrod provided me his account of advising FDR to release the Tarawa documentary to the public when we worked together taping "Death Tide at Tarawa" for Lou Reda Productions in September 1993.

7. Hoffman, *Once a Legend*, 262.

8. Both quotes from Nimitz are contained in the 50th anniversary edition of Sherrod, *Tarawa*, 194.

9. Hoffman, *Once a Legend*, 246.

10. Shoup Field Notebook, 7, Personal Papers Section, MCHC. For "*errata samples*" in casualty accounting, see November 1943 rosters for Headquarters, 2d Marines and the 3d Battalion, 2d Marines, both held in Reference Library, MCHC.

11. Shaw, Nalty, Turnbladh, *Central Pacific Drive*, Appendix H, 636–37.

12. Morison, *Gilberts and Marshalls* (vol. VII of his series on U.S. Naval Operations in World War II), page 186, reports that Gen. Julian Smith advised him that his LVTs were lost in this fashion:

Sunk in deep water by gunfire:	35
Sunk in reef by gunfire:	26
Burned up by gas tanks igniting from gunfire:	9
Wrecked by underwater mines:	2
Wrecked on the beaches:	10
Wrecked by mechanical failures:	8
Total Losses	90

Note that the 2d Marine Division reported losing only eight LVTs during the initial assault. The subsequent loss of the remaining eighty-two vehicles reflects the persistence and accuracy of the Japanese heavy machine guns and light antiboat weapons virtually until the end of the battle. The 2d Amphibian Tractor Battalion reported the same total, but in somewhat different categories. Obviously, some of the LVTs caught fire and eventually sank or were shot to pieces by machine-gun fire on the beach, only to sink in deep water. The battalion also salvaged a number of these vehicles. Others—reduced to rusting track links—are still there.

13. Commander, Fifth Amphibious Force, "Report of Amphibious Operations for the Capture of the Gilbert Islands," 4 December 1943, Enclosure G, "General Notes on Atoll Attack," 6–7, Archives Section, MCHC.

14. Ibid.

15. Ibid., 10; and Commanding General, VAC, "Report of GALVANIC Operation," 11 January 1944, 12, from Archives Section, MCHC.

16. Commanding General, 27th Infantry Division, "Participation of 27th

Division in GALVANIC (Makin) Operation," 11 December 1943, 7, from Archives Section, MCHC.

17. Edson to Thomas, 13 December 1943, Box 5, Edson Papers. See also Julian Smith to Vandegrift, same date, same collection. Another contemporary account of the battle from the perspective of the division commander is found in Julian Smith to George Lockwood, 28 December 1943, Julian C. Smith Collection, Personal Papers Section, MCHC.

18. HQ, CINCUS, "Memo for Rear Admiral Delaney, subject; LVT conference at Pearl Harbor," 25 December 1943, Enclosure A: "Interview with Colonel Shoup, USMC"; and HQ, CINCPAC/VINVPOS, "Memorandum Report of Conference Held in the Office of the CINCPOA, Subj: Amtrac and DUKW program," 18 December 1943 (both documents from Archives Branch, MCHC).

19. Croizat, *Across the Reef*, Appendix 2, 243.

20. Edson to Thomas, 13 December 1943, previously cited.

21. Ibid.; 2d Marine Division, Intelligence Annex to Special Action Report, 4 January 1944, 2; and Wilson Report. Shoup's comments were written on 14 August 1962 and appear as footnote 17 on page 31 of Shaw, Nalty, and Turnbladh, *Central Pacific Drive*; and Julian Smith oral memoir, 290, MCOHC, MCHC.

22. Hill oral memoir, 350, MCOHC, MCHC.

23. The CG, 2d Marine Division, submitted fourteen specialty reports, "Recommendations Based on Tarawa Operation," beginning with "Amphibious Tractors" on 27 December 1943 and concluding with "Weapons" and "Signal Communications," both on 13 January 1944. The specific mention of the vulnerability of tank crewmen to enemy fire when forced to dismount to communicate "face-to-face" with the infantry is found on page 7 of "Recommendations based on Tarawa Operation Number 4—Tanks," submitted to CG, VAC, 2 January 1944. Each of these reports, lumped under the file "Tarawa Recommendations," is available through Archives Section, MCHC. For more discussion of the employment of Sherman tanks at Betio, see Alexander, "Baptism by Fire," *Leatherneck* 76 (November 1993): 34–37. Also useful is Burns, "The Origin and Development of USMC Tank Units, 1923–1945," Marine Corps Command and Staff College, 2 May 1977, 56–60.

24. *SS #6: Army CentPac (1)*, 214, 230. Based on Admiral Shibasaki's alarming reports of the U.S. invasion, on 21 November the commander, 6th Base Force, in Kwajalein ordered all forces in the Marshalls to "be alert for enemy landing from within the reef" (CINCPAC Message 212100Nov43, ULTRA File). See also CINCPAC Message 230127Nov43: "as result recent Uncle Sugar landings in Gilbert atolls from lagoon side of islands, other enemy atoll bases alerted to this technique" in SRMN-013, Part III, Record Group 457, National Archives.

25. CG, 2d Marine Division to CMC, "Prisoners of War Captured," 17 December 1943. Initial strength figures for the two main combatant units at Tarawa from *SS #62: Navy CentPac (2)*, 455. To the best of my knowledge, these were the surviving rikusentai:

PO 2/C T. Goto
PO 2/C H. Kawashima
Leading Seaman T. Kigawa
PO 2/C K. Kikuchi
PO 1/C T. Onuki
Ensign* K. Ota
PO 1/C H. Sato
PO 2/C K. Suzuki

*The Division listed Ota as a special duty ensign; *SS #2: Navy CentPac (2)* identifies him (185) as a senior chief petty officer (*joto seibi heiso*); he identified himself in the Williams translation as a warrant officer, which I have chosen to use.

26. CINCPAC/CINCPOA #43-45: "Register of Japanese Naval Officers, 20 February 1945, Part I, 29, Operational Archives, NHC. The final entry for Shibasaki: "10Feb44: Promoted to Vice Admiral to date from 25Nov43; killed at Tarawa."

27. 2d Marine Division Award Recommendations, n.d. [ca. March 1944], copy contained in Julian C. Smith Collection, Personal Papers Section, MCHC.

28. Ibid.

29. Ibid. See also Clay Barrow, "The Stick Wavers," *Naval History* 4 (Summer 1990): 32. Holland Smith nominated Julian Smith for a gold star in lieu of a second Navy Cross for his performance in command of the 2d Marine Division at Tarawa. Higher echelons, perhaps due to the uproar about Tarawa's casualties, reduced the award to the Distinguished Service Medal.

30. Sherrod, *Tarawa* (50th anniversary edition), 155. Official burial records from Bordelon, Bonnyman, and Hawkins provided by Mr. William Bethard, whose uncle, PFC Russell L. Jarrett, was reburied in Punchbowl Cemetery.

EPILOGUE

1. Buell, *The Quiet Warrior*, 214–15.

2. H. Smith and Finch, *Coral and Brass*, 111–13, 134; "Marine General Defends Attack on Tarawa, Contradicting Chief," *Washington Star*, 28 November 1948, 1; and Julian Smith, "Tarawa," USNIP 79 (November 1953): 1163.

3. Spruance to Isely, 14 January 1944, 10, "The Princeton Papers," Personal Papers Section, MCHC.

4. H. Smith and Finch, *Coral and Brass*, 132.

5. Brophy and Fisher, *The Chemical Warfare Service: Organizing for War*, 86–88.

6. Lt. Col. John T. Bradshaw, USMC, quoted in Sherrod, *Tarawa* (50th anniversary edition), 204; Shoup to Commander-in-Chief Pacific, 24 January 1944, Shoup Papers, Hoover Institution Archives; and Vice Adm. Frederick L. Ashworth, USN (Ret.), oral memoir, 265, NIOHP.

7. Hoffman, "The Legacy and Lessons of Tarawa," MCG 77: November 1993, 63–72.

8. J. Smith, "Tarawa," USNIP 79 (November 1953): 1175.

Bibliography

This is a simplified bibliography. I have not included the "collections." Shoup's papers are found in the Hoover Institute Archives, Edson's in the Library of Congress. The Marine Corps Historical Center, Washington, retains the Julian C. Smith Collection, the "Princeton Papers" of Professor Jeter A. Isely, and the "Comments" files on the draft Tarawa monograph and the third volume of *History of United States Marine Corps Operations in World War II*. Nor have I listed here the various unit and ship reports for Tarawa, available through both the Marine Corps Historical Center and the Naval Historical Center. Included in this category are muster rolls, biographies, ship histories, Joint Intelligence Center, Pacific Ocean Area translations and reports, Japanese naval registers, Office of Naval Intelligence battle assessments, and the like (as cited in the notes). What follows is mainly a listing of books, essays, oral histories, and interviews; I conducted the latter either in person, by phone, or by letter—frequently all three.

ABBREVIATIONS USED

Follow Me   Newsletter of the 2d Marine Division Association
HQMC: Headquarters Marine Corps
MCG: Marine Corps *Gazette*
MCOHC: Marine Corps Oral History Collection
NIOHP: Naval Institute Oral History Program
USNIP: U.S. Naval Institute *Proceedings*

Albrecht, Karl (USS *Middleton* [APA 25]). "Tarawa," *Follow Me*, November–December 1993: 28–31.
Albert, Eddie (USS *Sheridan* [APA 51]). Interview, 1993.
Alexander, Joseph H. "Red Sky in the Morning," USNIP 119 (November 1993): 39–45.

———. "Bloody Tarawa," *Naval History* 4 (November–December 1993): 10–16.

———. "Baptism by Fire: Sherman Tanks at Tarawa," *Leatherneck* 76 (November 1993): 34–37.

———. "Capture of Apamama: Tarawa's 'Brilliant Little Sideshow,'" *Leatherneck* 76 (November 1993): 50–51.

———. *Across the Reef: The Marine Assault of Tarawa* [50th anniversary monograph]. Washington: History and Museums Division, HQMC, 1993.

Ashworth, Frederick L. Oral memoir, 1990, NIOHP.

Baldwin, Hanson W. "The Bloody Epic That Was Tarawa," *New York Times Magazine*, 14 November 1958: 19–21, 68–73.

———. "Reefs Menace Troops," *New York Times*, 3 December 1943: 4.

Barclay, William. *The Gospel of John*, vol. II. Philadelphia: Westminster Press, 1975.

Barrow, Clay. "The Stick Wavers," *Naval History* 4 (Summer 1990): 28–32.

Bartlett, Merrill L. *Assault from the Sea: Essays on the History of Amphibious Warfare*. Annapolis: Naval Institute Press, 1983, 1985.

Bartsch, William J. "Tarawa and Operation GALVANIC," *After the Battle* 15 (February 1977): 1–33.

Bethard, William D. Interviews, 1993, 1994.

Bevan, Denys. *United States Forces in New Zealand, 1942–1945*. Alexandra, New Zealand: Macpherson, 1992.

Boardman, Eugene P. Oral memoir, 1982, MCOHC.

Bordelon, Charles D. Interview, 1994.

Bowen, Stanley (8th Marines). "Tarawa," *Follow Me*, March–April 1994, 14–16.

Brophy, Leo D., and George J. B. Fisher. *The Chemical Warfare Service: Organizing for War*. Washington: Department of the Army, 1959.

Brugioni, Dino. "Tarawa: A New Perspective," *Leatherneck* 66 (November 1983): 32–39.

Bruni, Dominick (USS *Arapaho*). Interview, 1994.

Buczak, Walter J. (2dAmtracBn). Interview, 1994.

Buell, Thomas B. *The Quiet Warrior: A Biography of Adm. Raymond A. Spruance*. Boston: Little, Brown, 1974.

———. *Master of Sea Power: A Biography of Fleet Admiral Ernest J. King*. Boston: Little, Brown, 1980.

Burns, Arthur E. III. "The Origin and Development of U.S. Marine Corps Tank Units, 1923–1945," Marine Corps Command and Staff College, Quantico, 2 May 1977.

Colley, Thomas J. "The Aerial Photo in Amphibious Intelligence," MCG 32 (October 1945): 32, 34–35.

Cooper, Norman V. *The Military Career of Gen. Holland M. Smith, USMC*, dissertation, University of Alabama, 1974.

Costello, Robert E. (2d Marines). Interview, 1994.

Croizat, Victor J. *Across the Reef: The Amphibious Tracked Vehicle at War.* Quantico: Marine Corps Association, 1992.

Crowe, Henry P. Oral memoir, 1979, MCOHC.

Crowl, Philip A., and Edmund G. Love. *The War in the Pacific: Seizure of the Gilberts and Marshalls.* Washington, Department of the Army, 1955.

Crumpacker, Bill (8th Marines). "Memoirs of Beastly Tarawa," *Follow Me*, November–December 1993, 12.

Curran, William. "Indelible Tarawa," *The American Legion*, November 1983, 20–21, 54–56.

Darling, R. Clay. *Deane Hawkins: Nonpareil Texan*, Marine Corps Command and Staff College, Quantico, 1991.

Dear, Murray. "In Contact," *Naval History* 8 (March–April 1994): 4.

Driscoll, Edward J., Jr. (Division Scouts). Interviews, 1993, 1994.

Drury, Clifford M. *The History of the Chaplain Corps, U.S. Navy*, vol. II. Washington: Department of the Navy, 1961.

Dull, Paul S. *A Battle History of the Imperial Japanese Navy 1941–1945.* Annapolis: Naval Institute Press, 1978.

Dyer, George C. *The Amphibians Came to Conquer*, vol. II. Washington: GPO, 1969.

Edmonds, Aubrey (8th Marines). Interviews, 1993, 1994.

Emmons, Roger M. "Battle of Tarawa," unpublished ms. Marine Corps Historical Center.

Frank, Richard B. *Guadalcanal.* New York: Random House, 1990.

Fratt, William (8th Marines). Interview, 1994.

Frost, Howard (2d Marines). "Memories of a Marine Triumph," *Follow Me*, January–February 1994, 11–12.

Goldstein, Donald M., and Katherine V. Dillon. *Fading Victory: The Diary of Adm. Matome Ugaki, 1941–1945.* Pittsburgh: The University of Pittsburgh Press, 1991.

Green, Robert (USS *Zeilin* [APA 3]). Interview, 1994.

Grisdale, Perry F. (2d Marines). Interview 1993.

Groves, Bob (6th Marines). "Tarawa," *Follow Me*, November–December 1993, 16.

Haley, J. Frederick. "Reconnaissance at Tarawa Atoll," MCG 66 (November 1980): 51–55.

Hall, Gus (10th Marines). "Tarawa," *Follow Me*, March–April 1994, 20.

Hammel, Eric, and John E. Lane. *76 Hours: The Invasion of Tarawa.* Pacifica: Pacifica Press, 1985.

———. "Third Day on Red Beach," MCG 54 (November 1970): 22–26.

Hanger, Bob (10th Marines). "New Caledonia to Tarawa via New Zealand," *Follow Me*, September–October 1993, 1, 20–24.

Hart, Elwin B. (8th Marines). Interview, 1994.

Hata, Ikuhiko. *Nihon Riku-Kaigun Sogo Jiten* [Japanese Army and Navy Comprehensive Dictionary]. Tokyo: Tokyo Daigaku Shuppankai, 1991.

Hatch, Norman T. Oral memoir, 1983, MCOHC. Interviews, 1993–94.

Havens, Thomas R. H. *Valley of Darkness: The Japanese People in World War II.* New York: Norton, 1978.

Hayashi, Saburo, and Alvin D. Coox. *Kogun: The Japanese Army in the Pacific War.* Quantico: Marine Corps Association, 1959.

Hayes, Grace P. *The History of the Joint Chiefs of Staff in World War II: The War Against Japan.* Annapolis: Naval Institute Press, 1982.

Hermle, Leo D. Oral memoir, 1973, MCOHC.

Hill, Harry W. Oral memoir, 1969, MCOHC.

Hoffman, Carl W. Oral memoir, 1988, MCOHC.

Hoffman, Jon T. *Once a Legend: "Red Mike" Edson of the Raiders.* Novato: Presidio, 1994.

———. "The Legacy and Lessons of Tarawa," MCG 77 (November 1993): 63–67.

Holmes, W. J. *Double-Edged Secrets.* Annapolis: Naval Institute Press, 1979.

Howe, Colby D. "Record of Events of G Battery [3/12] During Tarawa Campaign," unpublished ms. Marine Corps Historical Center.

Infield, Tom. "The Victory at Tarawa Came at a Terrible Price," *Philadelphia Inquirer,* 20 November 1993, A-1, A-6, 7.

Isely, Jeter A., and Philip A. Crowl. *The U.S. Marines and Amphibious War.* Princeton: Princeton University Press, 1951.

Johnston, Richard W. *Follow Me! The Story of the 2d Marine Division in World War II.* Nashville: The Battery Press, 1948.

Joint Chiefs of Staff 311. "Mobility and Utilization of Amphibious Assault Craft," 15 May 1943.

Joint Planning Staff 205. "Operations Against the Marshall Islands," 10 June 1943.

Jones, William K. Oral memoir, 1976, MCOHC. Interviews, 1992–93.

———. "Tarawa: That Stinking Little Island," MCG 71 (November 1987): 30–41.

Karig, Walter, Russell L. Harris, and Frank A. Manson. *Battle Report: The End of an Empire.* New York: Rinehart, 1948.

Key, Sidney S. (2dAmtracBn). Interview, 1993.

Kinley, Robert L. (18th Marines). Interview, 1993.

Klatt, Larry E. (18th Marines), "Letters," *Smithsonian,* January 1994, 11.

———. Interview, 1994.

Krulak, Victor H. *First to Fight.* Annapolis: Naval Institute Press, 1984.

———. "Tests of Amphibian Tractor under Surf and Coral Conditions," 3 May 1943, special report.

Ladd, Dean. "Reliving the Battle: A Return to Tarawa," MCG 67 (November 1983): 93–96.

———. "Tarawa," *Follow Me,* November–December 1993, 32–34.

Lake, Peter (6th Marines). Interviews, 1993, 1994.

Lamoreaux, Ray M. (6th Marines). "Tarawa," *Follow Me,* November–December 1993, 19.

Layton, Edwin T., Roger Pineau, and John Costello. *"And I Was There":*

Pearl Harbor and Midway, Breaking the Secrets. New York: William Morrow, 1985.

Lewin, Ronald. *The American MAGIC.* New York: Farrar, Straus, Giroux: 1982.

Lillibridge, George D. "Not Forgetting May Be the Only Heroism of the Survivor," *American Heritage* 34 (October–November 1983): 26–35.

———. (2d Marines). "Tarawa Memoir," unpub. ms. Marine Corps Historical Center.

Manchester, William. *Goodbye, Darkness: A Memoir of the Pacific War.* New York: Bell, 1982.

———. *American Caesar.* Boston: Little, Brown, 1978.

Mason, John T., Jr., ed. *The Pacific War Remembered.* Annapolis: Naval Institute Press, 1986.

Mast, Henry (18th Marines). Interviews, 1993, 1994.

McBride, Melvin (8th Marines). Interviews, 1993, 1994.

McCormick, Robert R. "The Tarawa Campaign," transcript of radio broadcast on WGN and the Mutual Broadcasting System, 13 April 1946.

McKiernan, Patrick. "The Tide That Failed," USNIP 46 (February 1962): 38–49.

McNeil, A. H. (8th Marines). Interview, 1994.

Michelony, Lewis J., Jr. (6th Marines). Interviews, 1992, 1993.

Miller, Edward S. *War Plan Orange.* Annapolis: Naval Institute Press, 1991.

Miller, Henry L. Oral memoir, 1971, NIOHP.

Millett, Allan R., ed. *The Commandants of the Marine Corps.* Annapolis: Naval Institute Press, pending.

———. "Assault from the Sea: The Development of Amphibious Warfare Between the World Wars." Unpub. ms. prepared for the director of Net Assessment, Office of the Secretary of Defense, 1993.

Moise, Norman S. "Unconquerable Ground Reclaimed," *World War II,* November–December 1993, 43–47.

———. Interview, 1994.

Moore, Edward J. (2dAmtracBn). Interviews, 1992, 1993.

Moran, Jim. *U.S. Marine Corps Uniforms and Equipment in World War II.* London: Windrow and Green, 1992.

Morgan, William J. (18th Marines). 1943 diary provided by William J. Morgan, Jr.

Morison, Samuel E. *Aleutians, Gilberts, and Marshalls, June 1942–April 1944.* Boston: Little, Brown, 1951.

———. *The Two-Ocean War.* Boston: Little, Brown, 1963.

Murphy, William (8th Marines). Interview, 1993.

Murray, Raymond L. Oral memoir, 1988, MCOHC.

Myers, Raymond F. (USS *Bunker Hill* [CV 17]). Interview, 1993.

Niehoff, Harry (18th Marines). Interview, 1994.

North, Floyd M. (2dAmtracBn). Interview, 1994.

Nygren, Wallace E. (2dAmtracBn). Interview, 1994.

Olson, Donald W. "The Tide at Tarawa," *Sky and Telescope*, November 1987, 526–29.

———. "Tarawa, November 1943: A Historically Significant Apogean Neap Tide," original research ms., 1987.

Onuki, Tadao. "The End of the Tarawa Garrison," in Masanori Ito, Sadatoshi Tomiaka, and Masazumi Inada, eds., *Jitsuroku Taiheyo sense* (3) [Real Accounts of the Pacific War, vol. III]. Tokyo: Chuo Koron Sha, 1970.

Ota, Kiyoshi. "Tarawa, My Last Battle," translated by Keith S. Williams, unpub. ms., n.d. [ca. 1964], Shoup Papers, Box 18, Hoover Institute Archives.

Owen, Eddie (18th Marines). Interview, 1993.

Pierce, H. C. "The New 75mm Pack Howitzer," MCG 14 (March 1930): 31–32.

Plant, Frank (8th Marines). Tarawa Account, Marine Corps Historical Center.

Potter, E. B. *Nimitz*. Annapolis: Naval Institute Press, 1976.

———. *Bull Halsey*. Annapolis: Naval Institute Press, 1985.

Prejean, Alexandra Bonnyman. Interview, 1994.

Putnam, Robert J. Oral memoir, 1990, MCOHC.

Ratner, Gene (6th Marines). Tarawa account, *Follow Me*, January–February, 1994, 12–13.

Reynolds, Clark G. "The U.S. Fleet-in-Being Strategy of 1942," *The Journal of Military History* 58 (January 1994): 103–18.

Rixey, Presley M., and Wendell H. Best. "Artillery at Tarawa," MCG 28 (November 1944): 32–37.

Roberts, Robert L. (8th Marines). Interview, 1993.

Roberts, Landon (*PC 599*). Interview, 1992.

Ronck, Wil A. (2dAmtracBn). Interview, 1994.

Russ, Martin. *Line of Departure: Tarawa*. New York: Doubleday, 1975.

Rutherford, J. T. (2dAmtracBn). Interviews, 1993, 1994.

Ryan, Michael P. (2d Marines). Interview, 1993.

Schneidmiller, Manuel (2dAmtracBn). Interview, 1994.

Senshi Sosho [Japanese War History series]:

———. #6: *Chuba Taiheyo homen rikugen sakusen (1)* [Army Operations in the Central Pacific, vol. I].

———. #39: *Daihon'ei Kaigunbu Rengo Kantai (4)* [Navy Division, Imperial Headquarters, and the Combined Fleet, vol. IV], 1970.

———. #71: *Daihon'ei Kaigunbu Rengo Kantai (5)* [Navy Division, Imperial Headquarters, and the Combined Fleet, vol. V.]

———. #62. *Chuba Taiheyo homen kaigun sakusen (2)* [Navy Operations in the Central Pacific, vol. II], 1973.

———. #102: *Riku kaigun nenpyo: fu heigo yogo no kaisetsu* [Army-Navy Chronology with a Glossary of Military Terms], 1980.

Shaw, Henry I., Jr., and Douglas T. Kane. *Isolation of Rabaul: History of U.S. Marine Corps Operations in World War II*, vol. II. Washington: HQMC, 1963.

———, Bernard C. Nalty, and Edwin T. Turnbladh. *Central Pacific Drive:*

History of U.S. Marine Corps Operations in World War II, vol. III. Washington: HQMC, 1966.

———. *Tarawa: A Legend is Born*. New York: Ballantine, 1968.

Sherrod, Robert. *Tarawa: The Story of a Battle*. Fiftieth anniversary edition: Fredricksburg, TX: Nimitz Foundation, 1993.

———. *On to Westward*. New York: Duell, Sloan, and Pierce, 1945.

———. *History of Marine Corps Aviation in World War II*. Washington: The Association of the United States Army, 1952.

———. "Kerr Eby: Combat Artist," *Leatherneck* 75 (November 1992): 62–67.

———. Interview, 1993.

Shibasaki, Akira. Interview, 1995.

Shinn, Leo B. (VAC Recon). Interview, 1993.

Simmons, Edwin J. "Remembering the Legendary 'Jim' Crowe, Part I," *Fortitudine* 16 (Winter 1991–92): 3–7.

Smith, Harriotte Byrd. *But, That's Another Story*. New York: Vantage, 1992.

———. Interviews, 1993, 1994.

Smith, Holland M., and Percy Finch. *Coral and Brass*. New York: Scribner's, 1948.

Smith, Julian C. "Tarawa," *USNIP* 79 (November 1953): 1163–75.

———. Oral Memoir, 1973, MCOHC.

Sommerville, Richard D. (2dAmtracBn). Interview, 1994.

Specht, Lyle (6th Marines). Interview, 1993.

Spector, Ronald H. *Eagle Against the Sun*. New York: Free Press, 1985.

Speed, John A. (2dAmtracBn). Interview, 1994.

Spencer, David (2d Marines). Interviewed by his son, John Spencer, 1992; transcript provided to author 1994.

Stark, Harry B. (5thPhibFor). Interview, 1993.

Stevenson, John. "Tarawa Veteran Tells of Heroisms" [interview with Henry P. Crowe and Fenlon A. Durand], *Virginia Pilot*, 20 November 1978.

Stockton, *The Battle for Tarawa*. Washington: HQMC, 1947.

Strean, Bernard M. Oral memoir, 1974, NIOHP.

Strider, Carroll D. (18th Marines). Interviews, 1993, 1994.

Swango, M. F. (2dTankBn). "Assault on Tarawa," *Follow Me*, November–December 1993, 8–10.

Thompson, James A. (2dAmtracBn). Interview, 1994.

Thompson, Paul W. "Behind the Fog of War," *How the Japanese Army Fights*. Washington: Infantry Journal Press, 1942.

Toland, John. *The Rising Sun*. New York: Random House, 1970.

Tutt, Bob. "Everything Seemed To Be on Fire in Fight for Tarawa," *Houston Chronicle*, 14 November 1993, 26-A.

U.S. Department of War. *Handbook on Japanese Military Forces*, Technical Manual TM-E30-480, 1944.

U.S. Navy. Fleet Training Publication #167, *Landing Operations Doctrine*, 1938, with Change Three, 1 August 1943.

Van der Rhoer, Edward. *Deadly MAGIC*. New York: Scribner's, 1978.

Wade, Larry (USS *Heywood* [APA 6]). Interview, 1994.

Walker, James C. (2dAmtracBn). Interview, 1994.

Ward, Norman E. (2dAmtracBn). Interview, 1994.

Wheeler, C. Julian. Oral memoir, 1969, NIOHP.

White, Billy S. (2d Marines). Interview, 1993.

White, John H. (8th Marines). Interview, 1993.

Wilkes, Charles. *Narrative of the U.S. Exploring Expedition During the Years 1838–1842*, vol. V [1842]. Philadelphia: 1849.

Willard, W. Wyeth, *The Leathernecks Come Through*, 2d. ed. New York: Revell, 1944.

Williams, Maxie R. (2d Marines). Interviews, 1993, 1994.

Winton, John. *ULTRA in the Pacific*. London: Cooper, 1993.

Withington, F.S. Oral memoir, 1969, NIOHP.

Yancey, Mirle W. (2dAmtracBn). Interview, 1994.

Zurlinden, Peter. "Pillbox Is Used as Hospital for Tarawa Wounded," *Honolulu Advertiser*, 4 December 1943, 1.

Index